FOR MY MOTHER AND FATHER

THE PROCLAMATIONS
OF THE
TUDOR QUEENS

FREDERIC A. YOUNGS, JR

ASSOCIATE PROFESSOR OF HISTORY
LOUISIANA STATE UNIVERSITY

CAMBRIDGE UNIVERSITY PRESS
CAMBRIDGE
LONDON · NEW YORK · MELBOURNE

CAMBRIDGE UNIVERSITY PRESS
Cambridge, New York, Melbourne, Madrid, Cape Town, Singapore, São Paulo, Delhi

Cambridge University Press
The Edinburgh Building, Cambridge CB2 8RU, UK

Published in the United States of America by Cambridge University Press, New York

www.cambridge.org
Information on this title: www.cambridge.org/9780521210447

First published 1976
This digitally printed version 2008

A catalogue record for this publication is available from the British Library

Library of Congress Cataloguing in Publication data
Youngs, Frederic A. 1936–
The proclamations of the Tudor queens.
Based on the author's thesis, Cambridge.

Includes index.

1. Great Britain – Proclamations. 2. Great Britain – History – Mary I, 1553–1558.
3. Great Britain – History – Elizabeth, 1558–1603.
4. Great Britain – Politics and government – 1553–1558.
5. Great Britain – Politics and government – 1558–1603. I. Title.
KD4435.Y6   320.9′42′054   75–30442

ISBN 978-0-521-21044-7 hardback
ISBN 978-0-521-08880-0 paperback

CONTENTS

vii

PREFACE

The role of royal proclamations in Tudor society has been touched on in many historical studies. The greatest attention has been given to their constitutional importance, usually within the narrow focus of the meaning of the Statute of Proclamations of 1539. The debate over whether that act was intended to equate proclamations and statutes, and thus to provide the means for a would-be absolute monarch to subvert Parliament's place in the constitution, continues to this day. Other scholars have considered individual proclamations in so far as they played a part in their studies of special aspects of Tudor history. The possibility of a systematic study of the proclamations as such was considerably enhanced in the last decade by an edition of the texts by Paul L. Hughes and James F. Larkin.

This study attempts to consider not only the constitutional importance of the later Tudor proclamations, but also their impact in the areas with which their contents dealt. It concentrates particularly on their enforcement, because proclamations provide a valuable and manageable opportunity to test whether the policies of the central government were translated into effective action locally.

My investigation began as a doctoral dissertation at the University of Cambridge on aspects of the Elizabethan proclamations. It has been expanded by considerable additional research in libraries and archives, particularly in local record offices. It has also been broadened to include the proclamations of Mary I, so that it would complement the study by Dr Rudolph W. Heinze of the proclamations of 1485–1553. We have taken some poetic license with the titles of the respective studies: his *The Proclamations of the Tudor Kings* is strictly correct, but my title slights the kingship of Philip. It is an omission which Mary would not have liked, but which many of her subjects would have appreciated.

Dr Heinze and I have tried to integrate our approaches, but it became apparent that a parallel presentation was not possible. His chronological treatment was dictated by the greater number of monarchs and the prevalence of individual advisers; his constitutional focus was naturally on the Statute of Proclamations. The Council was more fixed in composition in the latter half of the century, and Elizabeth's use of proclamations as temporary legislation differed from the earlier period, so that this became the constitutional focus for my study.

Two difficulties have arisen in the course of this work. To evaluate the impact of the proclamations required a presentation of the contexts in which they were issued. No one can be a master of the complexities of the economy, or of the religious situations, or of the politics of the moment, but I have considered it worth the risk to present my understanding of the particular settings in order to evaluate the proclamations' impact, even if in some cases my appreciation of the situation might be found incomplete. The second problem was in the manner of presentation, because the 446 proclamations vary so greatly in content. Part I attempts to consider them as a whole, as a prelude to and a summation of the individual studies in Parts II, III, and IV.

It is particularly pleasant to acknowledge those who have been so involved in my graduate training. Professor Paul L. Hughes directed my master's work and kindly made the typescripts of the Elizabethan proclamations available at an early stage. Professor George Abernathy painstakingly guided my first work in the proclamations. Above all, I am appreciative of Professor G. R. Elton who directed my doctoral work at Cambridge, sharing so generously his learning and many, many personal kindnesses. Professors Joel Hurstfield and J. J. Scarisbrick examined the dissertation, offering useful suggestions and encouragement.

Professors Rudolph W. Heinze and James F. Larkin have been unstinting in sharing their learning and friendship, and my understanding of proclamations owes much to long discussions with them. A period of additional work in local archives in England was supported by a grant from the California State University, Long Beach Foundation, and by a travel grant from the American Philosophical Society. Professors Elton, Hurstfield, Larkin, and Wallace MacCaffrey served as referees. Parts or all of the manuscript were read by Professors Elton, Heinze, and Larkin, and I appreciate their useful suggestions.

One is fortunate to have worked with many librarians and archivists who share learning as well as facilities, and while all are deserving of thanks I would in particular express my appreciation to the staff of the Henry E. Huntington Library in San Marino. Among the friends who have been so helpful are Professors Eugene L. Asher, Walter C. Richardson, Leland H. Carlson, and James I. Miklovich. Of course above all else my greatest appreciation is to my wife.

FREDERIC A. YOUNGS, JR

ABBREVIATIONS

Proclamations are cited by the number assigned by Hughes &
Larkin, followed by an oblique, followed by the number assigned by
Steele. Items not in one or the other are indicated by —.

Add. MSS	Additional Manuscripts, British Library
Add. Procs.	Frederic A. Youngs, Jr, 'Additional Marian and Elizabethan Royal Proclamations', *BIHR*, XLVIII (1974), 234–44
Agrarian Hist.	*The Agrarian History of England and Wales*, Vol. IV: *1500–1640* (ed. Joan Thirsk; London, 1967)
Annals Ref.	John Strype, *Annals of the Reformation*... (new ed.; 4 vols.; Oxford, 1824)
APC	*Acts of the Privy Council of England* (ed. John Roche Dasent; 32 vols.; London, 1890–1907)
App.	Appendix
BIHR	*Bulletin of the Institute of Historical Research*
Bk	Book
BL	British Library
Bristol AO	Bristol Archives Office
Camden	William Camden, *The History of the Most Renowned and Victorious Princess Elizabeth* (4th ed.; London, 1688)
Cardwell	Edward Cardwell (ed.), *Documentary Annals of the Reformed Church of England* (new ed.; 2 vols.; Oxford, 1844)
Chamb. Accts	Chamberlains' Accounts
Chester CRO	Chester City Record Office
CJ	*Journals of the House of Commons* (1803ff.)
Corp.	Corporation

Corp. London RO	Corporation of London Record Office
CSP Foreign	*Calendar of State Papers Foreign*
CSP Spanish	*Calendar of State Papers Spanish*
CSP Venice	*Calendar of State Papers Venice*
Ct	Court
Devon RO	Devon Record Office
Eccl. Mem.	John Strype, *Ecclesiastical Memorials, Relating Chiefly to Religion*... (rev. ed.; 3 vols.; Oxford, 1822)
EcHR	*Economic History Review*
ed(s).	editor(s)
EHR	*English Historical Review*
Essex RO	Essex Record Office
E. Sussex RO	East Sussex Record Office
Flenley	Ralph Flenley (ed.), *A Calendar of the Register of the Queen's Majesty's Council in...Wales...* (London, 1916)
fo(s).	folio(s)
GLC (Middx) RO	Greater London Council (Middlesex Records) Record Office
Harl. MSS	Harleian Manuscripts, British Library
Heinze	Rudolph W. Heinze, *The Proclamations of the Tudor Kings* (Cambridge, 1976)
Hil.	Hilary (law term)
Hist. J.	*Historical Journal*
HLRO	House of Lords Record Office
HMC	*Historical Manuscripts Commission* (report)
Hughes & Larkin	Paul F. Hughes and James F. Larkin (eds.), *Tudor Royal Proclamations* (3 vols.; New Haven, 1964, 1969)
Kent AO	Kent Archives Office
Lansd. MSS	Lansdowne Manuscripts, British Library
Libr.	Library
LJ	*Journal of the House of Lords* (London, 1846ff.)
m(m).	membrane(s)
Machyn	Henry Machyn, *The Diary of Henry Machyn*... (ed. John Gough Nichols; Camden Society, XLII; London, 1848)

Mich.	Michaelmas (law term)
no(s).	number(s)
Norf. & Norw. RO	Norfolk and Norwich Record Office
PRO	Public Record Office
Proc(s).	Proclamation(s)
pt	part
r	*recto*
Raine	Angelo Raine (ed.), *York Civic Records*, Vols. v–viii (Yorkshire Archaeological Society, cx, cxii, cxv, cxix; York, 1946, 1948, 1950, 1953)
Rcvrs Accts	Receivers' Accounts
Read, *Burghley*	Conyers Read, *Lord Burghley and Queen Elizabeth* (London, 1960)
Read, *Cecil*	Conyers Read, *Mr. Secretary Cecil and Queen Elizabeth* (London, 1955)
Rpt	Report
Southampton CRO	Southampton Civic Record Office
STC	*A Short-Title Catalogue of Books Printed in England...1475–1640* (ed. A. W. Pollard and G. R. Redgrave; London, 1926)
Steele	Robert Steele (ed.), *A Bibliography of Royal Proclamations of the Tudor and Stuart Sovereigns and of others published under authority 1485–1714* (2 vols.; vols. v and vi of *Bibliotheca Lindesiana*; Oxford, 1910)
Stiffkey Papers	*The Official Papers of Sir Nathaniel Bacon of Stiffkey, Norfolk, as Justice of the Peace 1580–1620* (ed. H. W. Saunders; Camden Society, 3rd series, xxvi; London, 1915)
Stow	John Stow, *The Annales of England* (London, 1605)
TRHS	*Transactions of the Royal Historical Society*
Trin.	Trinity (law term)
v	*verso*
VCH	*Victoria Histories of the Counties of England*
Wriothesley	Charles Wriothesley, *A Chronicle of England During the Reigns of the Tudors, from A.D. 1485 to 1559* (ed. W. D. Hamilton; 2 vols.; Camden Society, new series, xi, xx; London, 1875, 1877)
York CA Dept	York City Archives Department

PART ONE

THE THEORY: THE NATURE AND ROLES OF ROYAL PROCLAMATIONS

I

INTRODUCTION

The Sheriffs and other officials of London, mounted on horseback and dazzling in their robes and insignia of office, waited with their retinues just within the City, watching the procession move toward them from the west. When it had arrived, the heralds detached themselves from the entourage with which they had moved throughout Middlesex from the palace at Westminster, and joined the Londoners waiting just within Temple Bar. The new procession wound its way through the city streets, stopping now at the end of Chancery Lane near Fleet Street, again at the great cross in Cheapside, moving on to Leadenhall and then finally to St Magnus's corner. At each place, after the sounds of the trumpets' blast and the criers' oyez had died away, the heralds with great solemnity proclaimed the words of the Queen's proclamation. Soon the same words would be repeated at market crosses, in front of guildhalls, and at other customary places throughout the realm, solemnized in the traditional way by the officials in the respective areas.

The Tudor subjects who witnessed such spectacles heard proclamations not infrequently. They were an integral part of the procedure of the law, since by orders of the Justices of the Peace the Sheriffs proclaimed the sessions, defendants who were acquitted were freed by proclamation, and fugitives were hunted in the same fashion. The Justice at the sessions who had a copy of Rastell's Collection of all the statutes could find in it an impressive five main entries and fifty-seven cross references under the heading 'Proclamation'.[1] A man who attended on the Queen's Court might hear a herald proclaim war, announce the style of a newly created peer, or proclaim that lord's titles one final time at his funeral. The Queen's accession day was marked by proclamations, and when she moved throughout the realm on progress, her marshals proclaimed her coming. Parliament's statutes and the orders for its prorogation were often pro-

---

[1] William Rastell (ed.), *A Collection of all the statutes, from the beginning of Magna charta, vnto this present yere of our Lorde God 1572* (London, 1573 [new style]), pp. 409–11.

3

claimed, and notices of its subsidies invariably were. The simpler pleasures and pains were similarly proclaimed by local officers – the fairs, mirths, and the ordinances which regulated men's lives.[2]

But of all those innumerable types of proclamations, none interested the subjects of those days more – or us now – than the proclamations which were issued by the monarch's authority. They did what few other documents could do, speaking to the hearers in the very words, in the exact context, and with the specifically chosen rationalization which the leaders of the realm wanted. A fortunate few might hear the Queen speak; a larger number present at the Court might hear a councillor speak for her; a still larger crowd might hear her thoughts spoken at Paul's Cross by an officially sanctioned preacher. But the royal proclamation, which was dispersed throughout the realm with a text short enough to be printed on a few broadside sheets, had the potential of exciting an illiterate hearer's attention and then later, by its posted presence, of reminding him of its contents.

The importance of the royal proclamations was not limited to their use as propaganda. Often they commanded procedures which were the fruit of long years of conciliar experimentation intended to find a satisfactory way of handling a vexing problem. They exemplified the power of the prerogative when they framed temporary legislation in areas not already defined in the law. And because so many of the proclamations were occasioned by extraordinary problems – crises of a military, religious, economic, or diplomatic type, or even some natural disaster – they provide an opportunity to measure the degree to which the government was willing to innovate. Since the procedures often rested on no other sanction than the royal authority, the proclamations offer the means to test, in one sphere, what we today call the constitutionality of the reigns of the Tudor Queens.

It is the intent of this study to move beyond the words of the Marian and Elizabethan royal proclamations, to find out why they were issued, what they intended to do, what means they used, how they were enforced or ignored, and what impact they had on the different aspects of life. When this is done we should be in a position to evaluate their place in Tudor society.

[2] See Appendix 2 for a survey of non-royal proclamations.

NATURE AND NUMBER

The point of departure for a study of royal proclamations must be to understand what they were and how many there were, but it is no simple matter to establish these points. There is, first of all, the problem arising from how the evidence survived, since one can find not only proclamations in print or manuscript, but also references to others which have not survived. To ignore the latter would artificially limit the corpus of proclamations and mislead us about the extent of their use. A second complication arises from the differing intentions and procedures of the many collectors, cataloguers, and editors who have been concerned with them, since each included many items which are not truly royal proclamations. One must therefore begin with a survey of earlier works, to arrive at a total potential canon of royal proclamations.

There was no official collection of Marian or Elizabethan royal proclamations. The originals, which were written on parchment, survive only in a small number of instances; the copies which might have been made and then retained in conciliar records or in what are now called the state papers are few in number; the printed copies were dispersed widely, and although each local authority to which they were directed was a potential source for a collection, the elements would have taken their toll when the proclamations were posted as the writ required.[3] No list of proclamations remains, but there are partial lists in books of precedents, other lists made after the reigns, and books in special offices such as the Mint into which proclamations which were relevant to the work of that office were copied.[4]

[3] The best local collections are those of Rye (E. Sussex RO, Rye MSS 47 and 48), Sandwich (Kent AO, Sandwich MS Sa/ZP 3), New Romney (Kent AO, New Romney MS NR/ZPr 3), and Exeter (Exeter CRO, Royal Proclamations, 16th and 17th centuries, Box 1), none of which contains as many as forty. Rye MS 47 is calendared in *HMC 31: 13th Rpt, App. IV (Rye MSS)*, pp. 66–121. Most proclamations were copied into London's records which therefore form the single most useful source of information about their reception, and often provide the unique survival of a text. The pioneer work in those archives was Ada Haesler Lewis, 'Elizabethan Proclamations in the Records of the Corporation of London (1558–1603)', *BIHR*, III (1925), pp. 102–9.

[4] A partial list, fuller for earlier reigns and including Elizabethan proclamations adjourning law terms, is in the Chancery's precedent book PRO, PRO 30/26/116. Lists made after 1603 are in All Souls College MSS 222, 226 (in the papers of Owen Wynne, a clerk to Charles II), and 259. Seventeen Marian and Elizabethan proclamations on the coinage are copied in a book of memoranda for the Mint, now Society of Antiquaries MS 116; a request for a copy of a proclamation on the coinage, directed to the Master of the Mint, is in BL, Harl. MS 660, fo. 73. A special Admiralty collection which includes proclamations is in All Souls College MS 208. A list of proclamations on Scottish affairs is copied in BL, Cotton MS Caligula B V, no. 15.

Fortunately a collection of Elizabethan proclamations was made in 1618 by a London notary, Humphrey Dyson, and was formed into several sets, none identical, of which seven are known. His own set is now in the Folger Shakespeare Library, Washington; other very full sets are in the British Library, the Bodleian Library, and at Queen's College, Oxford; slightly less complete sets are at the Privy Council Office, Whitehall, and in the Houghton Library of Harvard University.[5] The set which came into the possession of the Society of Antiquaries in London was disassembled to serve as the nucleus for a magnificently expanded collection of proclamations which spans many reigns.[6] The only collection of Elizabethan proclamations seemingly independent of Dyson is to be found at Queen's College, Oxford.[7] There was no Marian collection, but the expanded collection of the Society of Antiquaries is now the most extensive source for that reign. Many of them have been reproduced in facsimile by the Society.[8]

Obviously Dyson could not always find the seven or more issues which he needed of the Elizabethan proclamations, so he searched governmental offices, visited the office of the King's printer where stocks of proclamations had probably existed for sale to individuals, and cajoled the printers who were entitled to copies of the work which they produced.[9] When in spite of all that effort he could not find enough copies, Dyson had duplicates printed with no distinguishing marks, a practice which has complicated the work of later cataloguers who, unaware of his procedures, have listed the

[5] Catalogued as follows: Folger Shakesp. Libr., STC 7758a; BL, G 6463; Bodleian Libr., Arch. G.c.6 (formerly Arch. F.c.11 as listed in Steele); Queen's College, Sel[ect].b[ook].230; Privy Council, unnumbered; Harvard, fSTC 7758.5. On Dyson, see R. L. Steele, 'Humphrey Dyson', *Library*, 3rd series, I (1910), 144–51. Details of the descent of the copies are in William A. Jackson, 'Humphrey Dyson and his Collections of Elizabethan Proclamations', *Harvard Libr. Bulletin*, I (1947), 76–89, and in Steele, p. v. Dyson's title page reads *A Booke Containing All Svch Proclamations, As Were Published Dvring the Raigne of the late Queen Elizabeth, Collected Together By the industry of Humfrey Dyson, of the City of London Publique Notary. 1618.*

[6] See Rupert Bruce-Mitford, *The Society of Antiquaries of London. Notes on its History and Possessions* (Oxford, 1951).

[7] Queen's College Sel. b. 228 (formerly 79 A.1 as in Steele), from which BL, Lansd. MS 198 was seemingly copied.

[8] *Tudor Proclamations. Facsimiles of Proclamations of Henry VII, Henry VIII, Edward VI, and Philip & Mary. Now in the Library of the Society of Antiquaries of London* (Oxford, 1897).

[9] Many of the broadsides were proof copies; see Jackson, 'Humphrey Dyson and his Collections of Elizabethan Proclamations', pp. 79–80. Workmen were entitled to copies of everything printed in their shop; see Francis R. Johnson, 'Printers' "Copy Books" and the Black Market in the Elizabethan Book Trade', *Library*, 5th series, I (1946), 97–105. Examples of purchases by individuals, *HMC 2: 3rd Rpt*, App., p. 44; by a corporation, Exeter CRO, Rcvrs. Accts 29 & 30 Eliz.

reprints as separate 'editions'.[10] Dyson also included a rather large number of items which were not truly royal proclamations, in which practice unfortunately he was followed later by others.

Although there is evidence of initial work on an analytical index at an earlier date,[11] it was not until late in the nineteenth century that a complete catalogue was begun. An interest in his own family's collection stirred James Ludovic Lindsay, Earl of Crawford, to make an initial hand list of about seven hundred items, and then to expand the list to include as many other proclamations as he could find.[12] Having brought the list to over 5,500 entries, he engaged the services of Robert Steele to assist in the work.

Steele's work is a bibliographic masterpiece. He accepted nearly all of Dyson's compilations and referenced each of the five sets of which he knew, included the proclamations in the expanded set at the Society of Antiquaries, searched private collections in the then British Museum and elsewhere, and found references to many proclamations for which the texts did not survive.[13] Although he numbered the Dyson reprints as 'editions', he did not place the later reissues of earlier proclamations in the proper chronological order. So influential was Steele's catalogue that it was accepted without question as the basis for almost the entire listing of proclamations in the *Short-Title Catalogue*, and for Edward Arber's list of printed works in the reign of Elizabeth.[14] Steele's list of Marian proclamations was the first systematic work for that reign. But in spite of his useful introduction and of the work's great accuracy, an analytical study of the proclamations still required consulting the originals, because the length of the catalogue allowed him space only to summarize the contents of each proclamation. And since he included 'others pub-

[10] Jackson, 'Humphrey Dyson and his Collections of Elizabethan Proclamations', pp. 79–80.

[11] Society of Antiquaries MS 799. A more recent analysis is Gloria J. Tysl, 'An Analytical Survey of the Elizabethan Royal Proclamations' (unpublished M.A. thesis, DePaul University, Chicago, 1967).

[12] *Hand List of a Collection of Broadside Publications Issued by Authority of the Kings and Queens of Great Britain and Ireland* (London, 1886); *First Revision Hand-List of Proclamations*, Vol. 1: *Henry VIII – Anne, 1509–1714* (Aberdeen, 1893); *First Revision Hand-List of Proclamations. Supplement 1521–1765* (Aberdeen, 1901).

[13] Steele. Vol. II covered Ireland and Scotland, and was published in 1910 as well. Steele transferred three items in Dyson to his second volume, left out the two royal prayers in print which Dyson had included, and also omitted a personal printed ordinance made by Lord Burghley.

[14] *STC*. Edward Arber (ed.), *A Transcript of the Registers of the Company of Stationers of London; 1554–1640 A.D.* (5 vols.; vols. 1–4, London, 1875–7; vol. 5, Birmingham, 1894), v, *passim*. Hereafter, *Stationers' Register*.

lished under authority' as well, he perpetuated Dyson's inclusion of many extraneous documents.

Paul L. Hughes and James F. Larkin, C.S.V., undertook the task not only of making the texts readily available, but also of providing a thorough scholarly apparatus with which one could begin to investigate the role and impact of the proclamations.[15] By a painstaking search in a large number of local archives and in other places, they were able to add the texts of five Marian and sixty-four Elizabethan proclamations to the corpus catalogued in Steele.[16] Not only is their edition a model of its type, but they also began the work of assessing critically the items in Dyson and Steele, and to eliminate documents which were not truly royal proclamations, most notably those issued by persons other than the monarch. Given the accuracy of their work and the far-flung dispersion of the originals, scholars owe the two editors a great deal of gratitude.

A good number of proclamations for which no text survives are vouched for by references to their issue. These are found frequently in the financial records of the local chamberlains, among the payments to messengers for the delivery of the proclamations. The very large number of references shows that proclamations were used more extensively in certain areas of government than had been realized. Since many of them were issued as a part of the rating of wages according to the Statute of Artificers of 1563, it appears that the law was complied with, and that it had not become a dead letter as has often been supposed.[17]

Combining all the items which were included by Dyson and later scholars, we arrive at a total potential corpus of eighty-one Marian and 484 Elizabethan proclamations. To exclude completely the extraneous items, however, requires a norm for testing, a definition of a true royal proclamation. Steele defined them by characteristics:

'They have been proclaimed, they have passed (potentially or actually) under the Great Seal, and they have been made by the advice and consent of the Council. Of these characteristics the first two are invariable while as to the third we can only affirm it to be true in every case of which we know the facts...the essential characteristic is a schedule to a Chancery Writ validated by the Sign Manual as a superscription.'[18]

Hughes and Larkin defined the early Tudor proclamation as 'a public ordinance issued by the King, in virtue of his royal preroga-

[15] Hughes & Larkin.   [16] Half came from local archives.
[17] *Add. Procs.*   [18] Steele, pp. ix, xx.

tive, with the advice of his council, under the Great Seal, and by a royal writ'.[19] There is a good deal of agreement between the two definitions, but the element of conciliar advice does not seem to add any distinguishing characteristic. One can presume the advice (not the consent, however, since that implies a limitation on the monarch which none claimed), infer it from the routine formula of the writ, and suppose it from other sources, but it cannot be demonstrated very often and is only mentioned in a third of the proclamations in the later period. Furthermore, the advice would not be different from that which the Council offered in most other governmental matters, and nothing of its deliberations would have been known by a clerk in the Chancery who routinely copied the formula of the writ.

Something more is needed if the definition is to be truly descriptive: there was a distinctive format which was used for proclamations, whether they were printed or not. When they were engrossed on parchment, the text could be included within the opening and closing parts of the writ of proclamation, as was often the case when a proclamation was intended for only one locality.[20] But in later years printing was the regular practice and simple engrossment on parchment the rarity, so that while a third of the proclamations of the first half of the century were in print, nearly all of Elizabeth's were.[21] A distinctive format can be discerned in the proclamations printed as broadsides. They were headed 'By the Queen' and occasionally had a title, and they concluded with the place of issue preceded by the phrase 'Given at...', with the invocation 'God save the Queen', and with the identification of the royal printer. Even though none of those points was unique to proclamations, the combination was.[22] Printing had become so regular by late in Elizabeth's reign that one local official expressed uncertainty about receiving one which was not in print.[23] Half of Mary's were printed, and doubtless the number would have been larger had there not been a pressing urgency in so many cases, as for example with the nearly one-fifth which were issued while a rebellion was in progress.

A comprehensive definition seems to be that a royal proclamation was a royal command, normally cast in a distinctive format, which was validated by the royal sign manual, issued under a special

---

[19] Hughes & Larkin, I, xxiii.

[20] E.g., as printed on proc. 457/507.   [21] Heinze, p. 23 n. 74.

[22] Normal letters began with a salutation concomitant with the addressee's rank, 'trusty and well beloved', 'right trusty', etc. Letters patent began with the royal style and concluded 'In witness whereof...Teste me ipsa...'.

[23] PRO, SP 12/106/2.

Table 1. *Establishing the canon of royal proclamations*

Potential (by source)	Marian		Elizabethan	
Dyson Collections				
Texts: printed			315	
Texts: manuscript			4[a]	
			—	319
Added by Steele				
Texts: printed	38		30	
Texts: manuscript	27		16	
References	7		5	
	—	72	—	51
Added by Hughes & Larkin				
Texts: printed	1		12	
Texts: manuscript	4		52	
References			2	
	—	5	—	66
Additional				
Texts: printed			1	
Texts: manuscript			3[b]	
References	4		44	
	—	4	—	48
Total potential		81		484
Excluded (by categories)				
Not Royal Commands				
Made by others	6		45	
Statutes	5		4	
	—	11	—	49
Royal Commands, not under Writ of Proclamation		6		41
Not proclaimed				6
Miscellaneous				
Irish proclamations			3	
Renumbering			3[c]	
			—	6
Total excluded		17		102
Royal proclamations		64		382

[a] Includes two printed proclamations altered by pen to represent separate issues.

[b] Includes one copy in manuscript copied from a printed proclamation which is no longer extant.

[c] Steele and Hughes & Larkin separated parts of two proclamations and counted the parts individually.

Chancery writ sealed with the Great Seal, and publicly proclaimed. Applying this definition to the whole potential corpus excludes seventeen Marian and 102 Elizabethan items which are not royal proclamations. Full particulars of the deletions are to be found in

Appendix 2; what follows here is a brief survey of the categories which have been excluded, lest the non-royal proclamations become a disproportionate concern.

Many items not issued by the Crown were in the collections, including orders by military commanders, officials of the Admiralty, ecclesiastical commissioners, heralds, local authorities, and even by the rebel Wyatt and a Spanish general in 1599. The large number of Elizabethan deletions is accounted for partly by the fact that the Council began to issue its own proclamations.[24] The royal printer was used for these, and he naturally cast them in a similar format. Also to be rejected are the statutes printed as broadsides. Before the advent of printing, copies of the statutes had been sent under special writs to be proclaimed throughout the realm, and even as late as the 1540s statutes 'printed in proclamations' were prepared for every act.[25] Only a few were printed in that manner in Mary's reign, and none beyond the acts of Elizabeth's first Parliament, after which books of the acts of later sessions appear.[26]

Nearly fifty items were royal commands not issued under the special writs. The largest group within the category consisted of articles framed by the Council which did not fall within the sanction of the proclamation. Such were the form of the oath issued after the rebellion in 1569 for those who wished to benefit from the pardon which had just been proclaimed, or the orders for the exchange published a week after a proclamation on the subject, or the 'Articles annexed to the Commission' intended for the use of commissioners for dealing with seminary priests and Jesuits, printed not long after the proclamation announced that the commissions would be issued.[27] Also to be excluded are the 'exemplifications' of royal grants which officers and patentees had printed to enhance their use of the privileges. Such were the Marian letters patent which ordered that Cardinal Pole's legatine authority be obeyed, and which appointed

[24] Steele, p. lxxvi. None ever began 'By the Queen', but one used 'By the Queen's Commandment' and another 'By the Privy Council' (procs. 712/874 and —/870, respectively). The ending 'Given at...' was never used, but rather 'From the Court', 'At', or 'Dated'. In four cases the signatures of councillors were printed.

[25] BL, Add. MS 28196, printed in *Stationers' Register*, II, 50–6, and in W. H. Black and F. H. Davis (eds.), 'Thomas Berthelet's Bill, as King's Printer, for Books Sold and Bound, and for Statutes and Proclamations Furnished to the Government in 1541–43', *Journal of the British Archaeological Association*, VIII (1853), 44–52.

[26] *Statutes of the Realm* (ed. Alexander Luders *et al.*; 11 vols., London, 1810–28), I, xlv, and Appendix B, lvii.

[27] Many 'articles', however, were in fact comprised within the sanction of proclamations, such as the breviates of statutes and added instructions which formed part of so many proclamations on apparel.

the Marquis of Winchester Lieutenant of the Realm during the wars with France. In Elizabeth's reign, patentees often had their grants printed, especially the 'church briefs' which authorized individuals or corporations to ask for contributions in churches so that the damages from a natural disaster or from the decay of a harbor might be repaired.

Because the third element of the definition of a proclamation requires deleting items which were not publicly proclaimed, the drafts which never received final approval can be rejected. Of the more notable of this type were the proposals to bring the English calendar into line with the Gregorian reforms, and to introduce a copper coinage in small denominations.

Obviously a general definition will not fit all cases, and there are areas open to disagreement or for which there is only limited evidence. The special problems in those cases are clearly identified in the introduction to Appendix 2 which includes the rejected items. A full list of the sixty-four Marian and 382 Elizabethan proclamations accepted as the canon for this study is in Appendix 1.

SUBJECT MATTER

The most obvious means of classifying the proclamations is by subject matter. No system can be entirely free of overlapping categories, but it seems that six major areas can be distinguished: the monarch, in which are grouped the proclamations concerning the royal person and the Crown's rights; domestic security; foreign affairs; economic matters; social matters; and religion. Table 2 presents such a classification, with actual and percentage figures for each major category, and for sub-categories when ten or more proclamations were issued on the same topic. Occasionally a proclamation dealt with more than one matter, and so has been counted in all relevant categories.

Under 'Monarch' have been included the traditional proclamation made at each Queen's accession, others which were issued to protect her from the plague, and a few on financial matters such as commandments for prompt payments of debts due the Queen and announcements that her own would be paid. Elizabeth issued four proclamations to insure that she received her share of the spoils taken by privateering ships which she had helped outfit. The Marian number is large because many were issued in connection with her marriage with Philip.

Table 2. *Analysis of proclamations by subject matter*

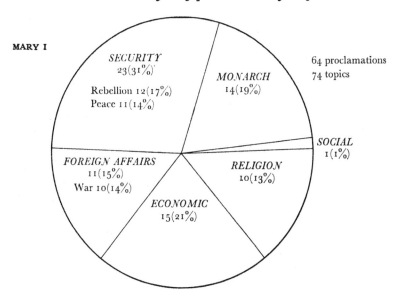

MARY I

SECURITY
23(31%)

Rebellion 12(17%)
Peace 11(14%)

MONARCH
14(19%)

64 proclamations
74 topics

SOCIAL
1(1%)

FOREIGN AFFAIRS
11(15%)
War 10(14%)

RELIGION
10(13%)

ECONOMIC
15(21%)

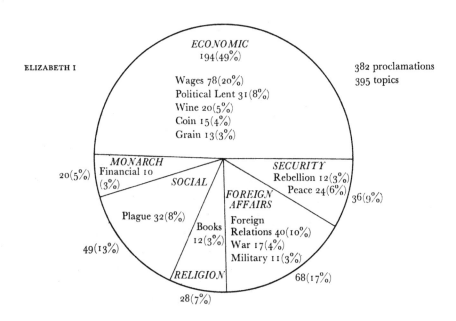

ELIZABETH I

ECONOMIC
194(49%)

Wages 78(20%)
Political Lent 31(8%)
Wine 20(5%)
Coin 15(4%)
Grain 13(3%)

382 proclamations
395 topics

MONARCH
20(5%) Financial 10
(3%)

SOCIAL

SECURITY
Rebellion 12(3%)
Peace 24(6%)
36(9%)

Plague 32(8%)

FOREIGN
AFFAIRS

49(13%)

Books
12(3%)

Foreign
Relations 40(10%)
War 17(4%)
Military 11(3%)

RELIGION

68(17%)

28(7%)

The Marian proclamations on 'Domestic security' were over three times as large on a percentage basis, because she had more rebellions to meet and because keeping the peace was so proportionately great a concern. Many of Elizabeth's peace-keeping proclamations were issued in the early 1590s when many of the soldiers and mariners returning from military service refused to return home and increased the number of vagabonds.

The 'Social' proclamations in Elizabeth's reign dealt with many problems in addition to protection from the plague, most of which concerned maintaining social ranks. There were proclamations against retaining for the higher echelons of society and against the wearing of apparel of too fine a quality for the lesser sort. Efforts were made late in Elizabeth's reign to prevent the increase of buildings in London because of the stresses on the city from an increased population.

The number of proclamations on 'Religion' and their percentages appear small in the totals, but they represented a vigorous use of the royal prerogative. Both Queens issued royal proclamations to make an interim settlement of religion until the more permanent settlement was made by their first Parliaments. Both used proclamations to suppress the dissident books which challenged the official religious policy, and the number is greater in Elizabeth's reign because the challenges came from both catholics and protestants.

Nearly half of Elizabeth's and a fifth of Mary's proclamations were in the category 'Economic'. Both Queens regulated the coinage by royal proclamations. The years of inclement weather and bad harvests which produced severe dearths in the latter years of Elizabeth's reign occasioned a good number of proclamations. Yet even though a variety of economic concerns was reflected in the Elizabethan proclamations, the number is so large because of the many proclamations which rated servants' wages and which enforced the political lent, the days of abstinence from meat designed to bolster the economic position of the fishing industry. The initiative for the former was taken by the local Justices of the Peace when they certified the rates upon which they had agreed into the Chancery as required by the Statute of Artificers, after which they were published in a royal proclamation. Many of the almost annual proclamations for lent must have been made by local officials who exercised the right given to them in the proclamation of 1561 to reproclaim its text yearly.[28] The use of royal proclamations to publish the authorized

[28] Proc. 477/538. Verbatim reissues were not common before Elizabeth's reign.

Table 3. *Separately devised proclamations*

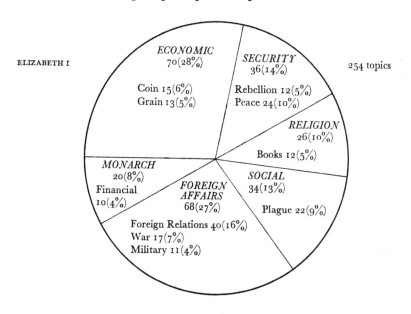

ELIZABETH I

254 topics

ECONOMIC
70(28%)

Coin 15(6%)
Grain 13(5%)

SECURITY
36(14%)

Rebellion 12(5%)
Peace 24(10%)

RELIGION
26(10%)

Books 12(5%)

MONARCH
20(8%)
Financial
10(4%)

FOREIGN
AFFAIRS
68(27%)

SOCIAL
34(13%)

Plague 22(9%)

Foreign Relations 40(16%)
War 17(7%)
Military 11(4%)

Table 4. *Authority or activity for issue of proclamations*[a]

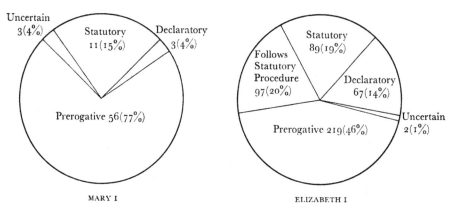

Uncertain
3(4%)

Statutory
11(15%)

Declaratory
3(4%)

Prerogative 56(77%)

MARY I

Statutory
89(19%)

Follows
Statutory
Procedure
97(20%)

Declaratory
67(14%)

Prerogative 219(46%)

Uncertain
2(1%)

ELIZABETH I

[a] See pages 16 and 42.

prices for wines for the following year became routine in Elizabeth's reign, the format different only because of the variation in price from year to year.

Because so many of the Elizabethan proclamations were either possibly the product of local initiative (such as those on wages and the political lent), and because the use of others (such as those pricing wine) became routine and were essentially reissues, these have been deleted from the new totals in Table 3 which reflect exclusively the 'separately devised proclamations'. The name is a bit awkward, but it does allow one to appreciate better the royal proclamations which unquestionably had their origin in an action of the central government, and which represented a fresh attempt to meet some current problem. The fuller totals in Table 2 help one to appreciate the extent to which proclamations had become a 'traditional' way of meeting some problems, so that the differing totals allow one to see two dimensions of the use of proclamations.[29]

Another scheme of classification was made by Professor G. R. Elton when reviewing the first volume of the edition by Hughes and Larkin. He distinguished declaratory proclamations which merely announced some fact, statutory, which were based on some existing law, and prerogative, which rested on the Crown's inherent powers.[30] Table 4 classifies the Marian and Elizabethan proclamations on that basis. It should be noted that the Elizabethan proclamations in particular are not so amenable to such a division. In general they average a length half as great again as the earlier proclamations, often deal with more than one topic, and sometimes are based on the authority of both statute and the prerogative. This is illustrated well by the proclamations on apparel which both enforce some points of the earlier laws and also make new regulations in areas not covered in them; by those for the political lent which set new offenses for those who sold meat whereas the law – ordered to be enforced as well – dealt only with its consumption; and by many proclamations which announced a forthcoming commission and thus could be considered declaratory, while also threatening additional penalties for men who did not reform before the commissioners began

---

[29] The proclamations deleted to form the reduced canon: seventy-eight rating wages, twenty-seven on the political lent, thirteen pricing wines, five reissues on caps, five reissues on vagabonds, two reissues on keeping the peace in churchyards, ten adjournments of part of a term because of plague, one reissue suspending the use of commissions to dig saltpeter.

[30] G. R. Elton, 'Government by Edict?', review article, *Hist. J.*, VIII (1965), 266–71.

their work. Fully 15 percent of the Marian and 20 percent of the Elizabethan proclamations rested on such 'dual' authorities. The percentages in Table 4 do show a vigorous exercise of the prerogative.[31]

The methods of classification considered to this point have been based on a complete canon of proclamations, but it is worth noting that two attempts were made early in the seventeenth century to define the categories of proclamations, without making an effort to divide the actual proclamations among them.

Sir Thomas Egerton, the noted Elizabethan and Jacobean jurist, formed four categories: mandatory, prohibitory, declaratory and explanatory, and dispensatory. The precedents he cited were from pre-Tudor proclamations, so that under mandatory he included orders for the assize of bread and for buying and selling victual; under prohibitory, commands against sending wool or coin out of the realm, or against using false coin; under declaratory and explanatory, numerous instances when Kings explained the true meaning of statutes; and under dispensatory, revoking part of a statute for alnagers of cloth and granting rights to aliens which contravened the charters of the towns in which they resided. Only in connection with the sections on mandatory and prohibitory proclamations did he consider any actual Tudor and Stuart proclamations, but rather than give exact precedents he merely listed subject headings. For the mandatory proclamations he mentioned ordering corn to the markets in time of dearth, commanding Lieutenants and Justices to leave London and return to their homes, two provisions to protect the King and his subjects from the plague, the limiting of attorneys' fees, and an unexplained heading 'armour'; for the prohibitory, the receiving of pirates' goods, the access of recusants to court, prohibiting plays and bearbaitings, cancelling fairs, printing and dispersing of books, and wearing excessive apparel.[32]

Thomas Ashe published a treatise on the common law in 1614, and although he did not classify the proclamations he did list forty-

[31] Elton's concern in the review article was to evaluate the differences in use under Henry VII, Wolsey, Cromwell, Henry VIII (1540–6), Somerset, and Northumberland, and to determine the relation of statutes and proclamations. There are difficulties in comparing the figures with Table 4, such as the fact that many Elizabethan proclamations were part of the procedures specified in a statute; see below, p. 42.

[32] Huntington Libr., Ellesmere MSS 438, 439.

six instances in which proclamations had a role at law.[33] Many
abridgments which had been published in the sixteenth and early
seventeenth centuries had references to statutes which dealt with
proclamations, but Ashe's list was different and more important for
our purposes in that he provided citations to legal opinions and
reports, many of which are noted in the following chapter.

PROMULGATION

Each of the 446 proclamations had a separate, unique history. The
situations which occasioned them differed, as did the deliberations
about the relative usefulness of issuing a proclamation, about the
proper measures to include, and about how to supervise their
enforcement afterwards. Those matters form the subject of most of
the ensuing chapters. But the steps through which each went from
the time the decision was made to use a proclamation until it reached
the local authorities were essentially the same – printing, sealing,
distribution, and proclamation.

It would seem that in Mary's reign the proclamation which had
been engrossed on parchment and signed by the Queen went to the
Chancery first and only afterwards to the royal printer, that early in
Elizabeth's reign the authenticated original went directly to the
printer and was returned to the Chancery with the printed copies,
and that later there was a return to the Marian procedures. The
change in procedure is evident from a study of the original texts
which for Mary's reign and the last decade of Elizabeth's are primarily in the Public Record Office, and which for 1559-76 are in
the Hunter collection at the University of Glasgow.[34] The former
have the ornate personal monograms of lesser clerks in the Chancery
in the left margin, often the signature of the signet clerk who had
written out the original, and occasionally the signature of the
Attorney General who had examined it.[35] On the latter there are

---

[33] Thomas Ashe, *Le Second Volvme Del Promptuarie, ou Repertory Generall de les Annales, et
Plvsors Avters Livres del Common Ley Dengleterre* (London, 1614), pp. 247v-249.

[34] PRO, C 82; Glasgow, Hunterian MSS S.1.3, V.1.17. The four originals in the
Folger Shakesp. Libr. are contemporary with the early Elizabethan items in the PRO,
and like them have no flourishes or notations (MSS X.d.84-7).

[35] By Sir Thomas Egerton on procs. 752/856 and 760/886, both dispensingcompletely
with previously adjourned law terms; by Sir Edward Coke, on 812/922 which terminated
the monopolies in certain areas in 1601 when Parliament pressured Elizabeth, and
807/912 which dispensed from certain statutes on cloth. PRO, C 82/1548, 1561, 1668,
and 1567 respectively.

several notations to the printer, and the use of the word 'warrant' as the authority to the printer occurs from time to time.[36]

Neither the original proclamation nor the printed copies were normally sealed, but rather the Great Seal was applied to the special writ of proclamation directed to the local officials. The two exceptions were both in Elizabeth's reign, one when the sentence against Mary Queen of Scots was published, the other in 1588 against anyone who possessed books intended to prepare for the arrival of the Armada.[37]

There was no reason why the original proclamation should pass under the signet or the privy seal, since the course of the seals had become mainly a formality which benefited the clerks. No copies and only a few docquet entries touching proclamations survive in the records of those offices.[38] Yet twelve Elizabethan proclamations have a closing phrase 'Given under our Signet...', and another has a title which indicates that the signet was used. In his study of royal proclamations in the first half of the century, Professor R. W. Heinze has found that the proclamations with references to the signet correlated with the issue of separate letters of instruction from the Council,[39] but there is no evidence at all to suggest why the signet was used in those few Elizabethan proclamations. The best conjecture possible has to do with the subject matter: four dealt with foreign affairs and could have used the signet for solemnity's sake; two others temporarily dispensed from a statute; another dealt with pensions for former monks and nuns and thus was a revenue matter; a former Crown grant to a patentee was cancelled; and another

[36] On procs. 492/560, 533/610, and 577/656, in University of Glasgow, Hunterian MS S.1.3, fos. 9v, 25v, 62v; notations of 'warrants' on 499/573, 556/632, and 614/704, in *ibid.* fos. 12v, 68v, and 36v respectively.

[37] Procs. 685/790, 699/802. The Great Seal was also used in 1559 to validate an Irish proclamation offering a pardon to rebels, Steele, p. xx.

[38] Signet Office records: PRO, SP 40/1, for sign manual warrants and Queen's bills; PSO 2/11–20 (entire reign) for signet bills; C 82 (entire reign), many volumes of privy seal writs. Docquet books for Elizabeth's reign for the Signet Office, SP 38/1–6, and Index 6800 (1585–97) classification replaces former SO 3; docquet for the Privy Seal Office, W. P. W. Phillimore (ed.), *An Index to Bills of Privy Signet Commonly Called Signet Bills, 1584 to 1596 and 1603 to 1624, with a calendar of Writs of Privy Seal, 1601 to 1603* (The Index Library, VII; London, 1908), which replaces the former index SO 4; docquet books for the office of the Clerk of the Crown (July 1597–17 March 1603) in Index 4208. Copies of proclamations are found only for 780/840 (SP 38/2, fo. 47) and 714/816 (Index 6800/1, under date 24 July 1589). The docquet book for the Crown Office has only procs. 812/922, 815/927 and 817/930, in Index 4208, fos. 243, 266, and 282 respectively, but over forty were issued in the period which it covers. I have found no indication that proclamations passed under the privy seal; the slits earlier in the century which Hughes & Larkin noted (I, xxiv) do not appear in the second half.

[39] Heinze, p. 25.

dispensed certain courtiers from both statutory and prerogative regulations on apparel.[40] Another possible explanation might be suggested by the coincidence of nearly half the proclamations under the signet with the first year of Sir Robert Cecil's Secretaryship.[41]

The Queen's printer held his office by a patent which included the exclusive right to print the royal proclamations.[42] In the time of Elizabeth printers charged ½d per sheet for proclamations; probably they hoped to sell copies to individuals at higher prices, and one of them claimed that he lost money because of the suddenness with which proclamations were brought for quick printing.[43] According to an early printing bill, the largest number printed was 700 copies, but in the reign of James I over 1,000 and even up to 1,300 were normally printed.[44] Just what quantity a printer could run from a single type setting is uncertain, but multiple 'editions' or printings from more than one type setting were not infrequent. Leaving aside the reprints Dyson had made in 1618 to complete his sets, there were twenty-eight cases in which two settings were run on Elizabethan proclamations and one for a Marian issue, and eight of the Elizabethan ones had more than two settings. Reissues at a later date which were undated probably account for some of the double runs; perhaps the royal printer even shared his work with other printers.[45]

For the clerks of the office of the Clerk of the Crown in Chancery, the important thing was that they had a warrant for drawing the writs 'de proclamatione facienda' which would command the local officers to proclaim the text. Normally their warrant was the receipt of the parchment original of the proclamation with the sign manual superscribed, but the rates of wages had no separate endorsement or warrant, but were authorized directly by the Council.[46] The clerks

[40] Procs. 465/520, 732/832 (in title only), 782/885, 788/892; 720/823, 807/912; 485/551; 714/816; 787/891. The remainder dealt with various matters: 534/611 announcing commissions to enforce the statutes for furnishing horses and geldings; 781/884 dealing with a dearth of corn; 786/890 for reforming disorders in apparel; 804/910 enforcing regulations on guns.

[41] Just why they appeared at that time is unexplained, however. Procs. 781/884, 782/885, 786/890, 787/891, 788/892. Neither the proclamation on rates of wages nor 784/888 which was an order on grain was, however, sealed with the signet.

[42] The names of successive printers are in Steele, pp. xxiv–xxv.

[43] The charge for statutes printed as broadsides was higher, 1d per sheet, as per the bill in BL, Add. MS 5756, fo. 138, printed in *Stationers' Register*, I, 576.

[44] BL, Add. MS 5756, fos. 138–40, printed in *Stationers' Register*, II, 23.

[45] PRO, SP 12/161/11.

[46] '...this day the Lord Keeper of the Great Seal showed unto their Lordships such certificates as he had received in this matter, which his Lordship was by their Lordships desired to cause to be printed and sent abroad according to the tenor of the said act'; *APC*, VII, 230; similar cases, *ibid.* X, 287; XIII, 132; XIV, 187; XVI, 168; XVII, 411.

did not normally endorse the originals with the date on which they were received, as was required by statute, the few exceptions occurring because a legal officer had been involved in drafting the proclamation.[47] The variants were few: only one warrant from Elizabeth to her Lord Keeper can be found which ordered the issue of a proclamation, only once was there a warrant which altered the text and the date intended for its publishing, and only twice can one find a proclamation issued at an earlier date signed directly by Elizabeth, presumably as the warrant for its reissue in the later year.[48] The clerks received no fees, but a recommendation late in Elizabeth's reign suggested a fee of 8d per writ.[49]

The few surviving writs are on parchment, some twelve inches long and one and one half inches wide; the text was rather standard, varied only to fit the addressee.[50] Steele found no lists of localities earlier than Charles II, nor indications of how many writs were prepared, but a copy of the writ for London and a list of jurisdictions to which writs were sent are found in the common-place book of an Elizabethan Clerk of the Crown, Stephen Powle. The writ and a translation of the jurisdictions are reproduced in Table 5. The only record of the number of writs actually used for an Elizabethan proclamation, against which Powle's list can be compared, is for 100 writs in 1602 when a proclamation was issued against Jesuits and seminary priests. That number slightly exceeds the total of the individual English shires and the forty-four towns on Powle's list, but perhaps the difference is represented by the unspecified number for undersheriffs.[51] When a proclamation was of special interest in a locality, the list of jurisdictions could be enlarged, as was the case when proclamations about East Anglian cloth and about ships were received in Dunwich, Suffolk, and when a proclamation to force unwelcome pirate ships out of southern ports was received at Ports-

[47] 18 Henry VI, c. 1. Steele, p. xx, cited two instances from the Hunterian collection (procs. 497/570, 594/681), and there are two among the Chancery warrants in PRO, C 82/1561 (760/866) and C 82/1678 (816/929).

[48] Proc. 636/733; PRO, PRO 30/26/116, fos. 212v–214, a precedent book which may indicate that the case was unusual; University of Glasgow, Hunterian MS V.1.17, fo. 37 and fo. 35, both concerned with proc. 471/530 which was the first announcement of the recoinage; 469/527 and 477/534.

[49] Bodleian Libr., Tanner MS 168, fo. 163, but the outcome is not noted.

[50] The practice does not seem to have been so standard earlier in the century, Heinze, p. 26. Occasional Elizabethan variants: Clarencieux King-at-Arms mentioned in the writ for proc. 467/522, copied in Corp. London RO, Journal xvii, fo. 220v; the date and time for the proclamation of the sentence on Mary Queen of Scots was specified, and the Council sent additional instructions, APC, xiv, 261–2 (685/790). The writ was printed along with the text on proc. 498/572.   [51] PRO, Index 4208, fo. 282 (proc. 817/930).

Table 5. *Writ of proclamation*[a]

Elizabeth dei gratia Anglie Francie et Hibernie Regina fidei defensor &c. Maiori et vicecomitibus London' salutem. Vobis precipimus quod statim visis presentibus in singulis locis infra Civitatem predictam, tam infra libertates quam extra, ubi magis expedire videritis ex parte nostra publice & solempniter proclamari facietis quandam proclamacionem per nos de avisamento Consilij nostri conceptam et factam quam in scedulis huic brevi nostro annexatam vobis mittimus mandantes preterea quod immediate post proclamacionem sic ut premittitur per vos factam, omnes & singulas huiusmodi scedulas in seperatis distinctis & publicis locis ut subditis et ligeis nostris plenius apparere poterit in tabulis et postibus affigi & poni similiter facietis. Et hoc sub periculo incumbentis nulla tenus omittitatis. Teste me ipsa apud Westmonasterium. / Powle

Maiori et vicecomitibus London'
de proclamacione fienda   Powle.

LIST OF JURISDICTIONS TO RECEIVE PROCLAMATIONS[b]

To the mayor and sheriffs of the cities of

London
Bristol
Norwich
Lincoln
Canterbury
Exeter
Chester
Gloucester
York
Coventry
Lichfield

To the mayor and baliffs of the towns of

Cambridge
Northampton
Leicester
Bedford
King's Lynn

To the mayor of the towns of

Orford
St Albans
Lyme Regis
Grimsby
Portsmouth
Abingdon

To the mayor and sheriffs of the towns of

Nottingham
Southampton
Kingston-upon-Hull
Newcastle upon Tyne
Poole

To the baliffs of the towns of

Colchester
Albury
Ipswich
Warwick
Yarmouth
Shrewsbury
Stafford

To the baliff of the city of Worcester
To the mayor of the city of Hereford
To the sheriffs, undersheriffs

To the Cinque Ports – the direction in the commission of peace

[a] Bodleian Libr. Tanner MS 168, fo. 104v.   [b] *Ibid.* translated.

mouth.[52] Several special jurisdictions seemingly received the proclamations and retransmitted them under separate writs: those

[52] *HMC 55: Var. Coll. (Corp. of Dunwich MSS)*, p. 88; *HMC 13: 10th Rpt, App. IV (Corp. of Plymouth MSS)*, p. 537. A retransmittal from New Romney, one of the Cinque Ports, to that port's members is in Kent AO, New Romney MS NR/ZPr 3, 40A.

received at Ludlow were sent to the Welsh shires within the jurisdiction of the Council in the Marches of Wales; at Dover Castle, by the Lord Warden to the member ports of the Cinque Ports; at York, to towns under the Council in the North; and for the marches against Scotland, but usually without separate writs.[53] On occasion writs were not used at all, either because of the need for urgency or because the proclamations were enclosed with a letter to some nobleman or officer,[54] and writs could also be used to transmit more than one proclamation at a time.[55]

In the slightly over 150 instances for which the dates of writs can be determined, most often because they were copied in the records of London, it would appear that there was a normal delay between the date on the printed proclamation and the date of the writ. Only about 15 percent were issued on the same day, half within three days, nearly 90 percent within a week, and only 6 percent over ten days later. Most of the longer delays were accounted for by proclamations fixing the prices for wines and those which adjourned part of a law term because of plague. One proclamation which announced that Elizabeth would repay her debts was issued eleven days later – no need to rush that.

The writs having been prepared, the Lord Keeper or Chancellor issued a warrant to the Clerk of the Hanaper to carry the proclamations out. The towns which received them usually referred to the messengers as 'pursuivants', but in the records of the Chancery for the fifth regnal year of Elizabeth they were called Messengers of the Receipt of the Exchequer, and a list of officers of state drawn up in

[53] Flenley, pp. 93, 96, 104, 119, 158, 165, 194; there were no transmittals to the four English shires within its jurisdiction or to Monmouth. From the Lord Warden, Kent AO, Sandwich MS ZB 3 68, fo. 55, and New Romney MS NR/CPw84 (writs for the reign of Henry VIII are in New Romney MSS NR/ZPr 2, ZPr 3, and ZPr 6). Marches, proc. 782/885 received with a letter from Sir Robert Cecil to the Warden of the Eastern Marches, noted in Joseph Bain (ed.), *Calendar of Letters and Papers Relating to the Affairs of England and Scotland Preserved in Her Majesty's Public Record Office London* (Edinburgh, 1896), II, 180, with a similar instance in 1549 noted in *HMC 39: 15th Rpt, App. II (Hodgkin MSS)*, p. 23. The practice for York is cited in R. R. Reid, *The King's Council in the North* (London, 1921), p. 158, but the latest example cited was Elizabeth's accession; a retransmittal in her reign is in York CA Dept, YC/A 25, fos. 2–2v. Writs of proclamation ran in the County Palatine of Chester, as noted in *HMC 77: De L'Isle I*, p. 345, and in Joseph Brooks Yates (ed.), 'The Rights and Jurisdiction of the County Palatine of Chester...', *Chetham Miscellanies*, II (Chetham Society, XXXVII; Manchester, 1856), 32–4.
[54] No writ, Norf. & Norw. RO, Norwich MS Mayor's Ct Bk 10, fo. 469; enclosed with letters, *APC*, II, 24, 31, 80–1, and Exeter CRO, AB 4, fo. 71.
[55] Corp. London RO, Letter Bk V, fo. 222v (procs. 560/637 and 561/638); *ibid.* Journal XXII, fo. 136, and Norf. & Norw. RO, Norwich MS Mayor's Ct Bk 11, fo. 509 (procs. 677/770 and 678/782).

1592 called them Messengers of the Chancery.[56] The choice probably varied, depending on the urgency and the availability of men. Early in Elizabeth's reign four men were used and paid £4 each to deliver proclamations 'into every part of the realm'. Five years later the rate had been raised to £6 each, a rate still in effect at the beginning of James I's reign.[57] The rate seems to have been calculated on a per diem basis, assuming thirty days for the task.[58] The messengers also regularly received a payment from the towns to which deliveries were made. Exeter, for example, paid 3s 4d for each proclamation early in Elizabeth's reign, and raised it to 5s by the early 1570s; York, Canterbury, Bristol and Oxford paid 3s 4d; Nottingham, 2s, and Rye merely 8d, probably because the messenger came from the Lord Warden and not directly from Westminster.[59]

The length of time for the deliveries depended on the number of men used and the routes which they took.[60] Some towns recorded the dates of receipt: the fullest evidence is for York (19 days average, 9 days fastest and 35 slowest), Norwich (17 average, 5–31), Exeter (14 average, 5–24), and Rye (13 average, 5–26), the last of which was probably slower because of the retransmittal via Dover.[61] The more fragmentary evidence for other localities shows an average of 13 days to Leicester and Nottingham, 8–11 days to the Council in Wales, 11 to Oxford, 12–13 to Shrewsbury, 14 to New Romney via Dover, and 23 to Ipswich.[62] An idea of how quickly the task could be

[56] BL, Add. MS 5756, fo. 79; R. L. Rickard (ed.), 'A Briefe Collection of the Queenes Majesties Most High and Most Honourable Courtes of Record, by Richard Robinson', *Camden Miscellany*, xx (Camden Society, 3rd series, LXXXIII; London, 1953), 14.

[57] BL, Add. MS 5756, fos. 79, 83.

[58] *Ibid.* fo. 79.

[59] Exeter CRO, Rcvrs Accts, *passim*; York CA Dept, Chamb. Accts, *passim*; Canterbury, in headnotes in Hughes & Larkin, *passim*; Bristol, in Wm Livock (ed.), *City Chamberlains' Accounts* (Bristol Record Society, XXIV; Bristol, 1953), pp. 121–7; Oxford, in William H. Turner (ed.), *Selections from the Records of the City of Oxford...* (Oxford, 1880), *passim*; W. H. Stevenson (ed.), *Records of the Borough of Nottingham* (6 vols.; London and Nottingham, 1889), I, *passim*; E. Sussex RO, Rye MS Chamb. Accts 60/7, *passim*. A recommendation that the fees be disallowed because of the abuses is in PRO, SP 12/125/61.

[60] The division of the work and the routes taken almost never followed the same pattern.

[61] York CA Dept, YC/A 21, fos. 37, 98v; A 24, fo. 41; A 25, fo. 2; A 27, fo. 177v. Chamb. Accts 5, fo. 141. Norf. & Norw. RO, Norwich MS Mayor's Ct Bk 7, fos. 303, 342, 613; 8, fo. 678; 9, fo. 469; 10, fos. 429, 492, 620; 12, fos. 541, 597; 13, fo. 251. Exeter CRO, AB 4, fo. 118; Rcvrs Accts 21–2 Eliz., 42–3 Eliz., 43–4 Eliz.; HMC 73: *Exeter*, p. 314; E. Sussex RO, Rye MSS Chamb. Accts 60/7, fos. 101v, 221, 221v, 249, 250, 256, 275v; 47/20/14; 48, fo. 71; 1/4, fo. 305.

[62] Mary Bateson (ed.), *Records of the Borough of Leicester* (rev. ed. by W. H. Stevenson and J. E. Stocks; 3 vols.; Cambridge, 1905), III, 189, 207; Stevenson (ed.), *Records of the Borough of Nottingham*, I, 147, 163, 183, 197; Flenley, pp. 93, 97; Turner (ed.), *Selections*

accomplished can be got from the fact that the proclamation which announced the accession of James I reached Bristol and Nottingham in two days, and Exeter in five.[63] To all the normal times must be added an allowance for the travelling of the Sheriffs to the usual places in their shires where proclamations were made.

How and when the proclamations were announced varied with the needs of the moment and with local tradition. Although the Statute of Proclamations of 1539 had been long since repealed, its requirement that a Sheriff should publish proclamations within fourteen days after their receipt very probably described the existing practice. The Statute had also commanded that the proclamations be made at four market towns if there were that many, or at six other towns and villages.[64] Some proclamations were made in the presence of the monarch to add solemnity, as happened in 1564 when the peace between England and France was proclaimed at Windsor before Elizabeth and the French Ambassador, and again in 1569 when the earls in rebellion were proclaimed traitors.[65] Several locations were used in London: the great cross 'at Cheepe', now Cheapside at Wood Street, St Magnus in Fish Street, Leadenhall, the conduit in Fleet Street, and Lombard Street.[66] Some towns had traditional places, such as the pavement before the Minster in York, and the church porch known as 'the proclamation house' in Southampton.[67]

The manner of proclamation could vary from the simple to the ornate. When done solemnly in London, as was noted at the beginning of this chapter, the expense was heavy. The City paid the principal King of Arms 20s, the other Kings of Arms present 13s 4d,

from the Records of the City of Oxford, pp. 33, 332; W. A. Leighton (ed.), *Early Chronicles of Shrewsbury, 1372–1603*, reprinted from *Trans. Shropshire Archaeological and Natural History Society* (n.p., 1880), pp. 71, 74, 75; Kent AO, New Romney MS NR/ZPr 3/51; *HMC 8: 9th Rpt, Part I (Corp. of Ipswich MSS)*, p. 249.

[63] John Fox (ed.), *Adam's Chronicle of Bristol* (Bristol, 1910), p. 178; T. M. Blagg and K. S. S. Trains (eds.), 'Extracts from the Paper Book of Robert Leband, Vicar of Rolleston, 1583–1625', *A Second Miscellany of Nottinghamshire Records* (Thoroton Society Record Series, XIV; Nottingham, 1951), pp. 16–17; Richard Izacke, *Remarkable Antiquities of the City of Exeter* (2nd ed.; London, 1724), p. 143.

[64] 31 Henry VIII, c. 8.

[65] *VCH Berks.*, III, 15; PRO, SP 12/59/40.

[66] Wriothesley, p. 163.

[67] A plaque on the façade of Marks and Spencer on the site notes *inter alia* that proclamations were made there; F. J. C. Hearnshaw and D. M. Hearnshaw (eds.), *Court Leets Records* (Southampton Record Society, 1; Southampton, 1905), I, part 2, 90. At market crosses: *HMC 8: 9th Rpt, Part I (Corp. of Plymouth MSS)*, p. 278; *HMC 31: 13th Rpt, App. IV (Corp. of Hereford MSS)*, p. 328; *HMC 13: 10th Rpt, App. IV (Corp. of Kendal MSS)*, p. 306, noting proclamation at the market crosses of Carlisle, Penrith and Appleby in the west marches.

every herald present and the City's Common Crier 6s 8d, and every pursuivant and trumpeter 3s 4d.[68] On less solemn occasions the Common Crier would make the proclamation.[69] Nobles could be pressed into service, either simply to attend or even to make the proclamation.[70] In Exeter the Mayor made the proclamation, preceded by the Sword Bearer and by four serjeants.[71] Concomitant festivities added majesty, as when the peace was proclaimed in Mary's reign. Then there was a high mass, Te Deum and sermon, a procession of crosses and parish banners, with the Bishop of London carrying the Sacrament of the Altar, attended by the Lord Mayor and the Aldermen in their robes and by citizens in livery. In the evening there were bonfires, banqueting, and free wine for all.[72] In the meanwhile, the proclamations would have been posted throughout the locality, to serve as a reminder.[73]

[68] Queen's College MS 153, fo. 99; PRO, SP 12/261/100.

[69] P. E. Jones, 'Common Crier and Serjeant-at-Arms', *Trans. of the G.H.A. [Guildhall Historical Association]*, III (1961), 80–7.

[70] Camden, p. 610.

[71] Iohn Vowell alias Hoker [John Hooker], *The Description of the Citie of Excester* (ed. Walter J. Harte, J. W. Schopp, and H. Tapley-Soper; Devon and Cornwall Record Society, XI; Exeter, 1947), III, 804.

[72] Wriothesley, p. 163.

[73] Special details on posting: mounted on tables and posts, Norf. & Norw. RO, Norwich MS Mayor's Ct Bk 9, fo. 469, and 12, fo. 541; Charles Henry Cooper (ed.), *Annals of Cambridge* (5 vols.; Cambridge, 1842–1908), II, 171. Frame for the proclamation for weights and measures: Richard Savage (ed.), *Minutes and Accounts of the Corporation of Stratford-upon-Avon*, Vol. IV: *1586–1592* (Dugdale Society, X; London, 1929), 56.

2

THE ROLES OF PROCLAMATIONS

Parts II–IV of this study will consider the individual proclamations and attempt to evaluate their impact. But first we need to look at them in general, to understand their roles and the limits on their use, to see how they reflected the aims and influences of the Queens and their advisers, and to consider their provisions at face value. There is no contemporary treatise which explains why and how royal proclamations were used, so that we must piece together the evidence to form the frames of reference in which individual proclamations can be evaluated.

POWERS AND PREPARATION

Limitations: theory and the law

The question of the proper relationship between royal proclamations and the law seems not to have been considered before the 1530s, but between 1531 and 1553 there were a number of attempts to come to grips with the problem.[1] In the former year Thomas Cromwell referred the matter to the chief legal officers who suggested that a search should be made 'to see whether there were any statute or law able to serve for the purpose', and if so that a proclamation should be based on it 'adding thereunto politickly certain things for the putting of the King's subjects and other in more terror and fear'. The search was successful, but Cromwell posed a further question about the proper course had there been no statute. The judges answered that the King might make proclamations or use other policies 'as well in this case as in any other like for the avoiding of any such dangers and that the said proclamations and policies so devised

------

[1] The pioneer work of Heinze (pp. 34–7) on this subject is extremely thorough, and on it rest my remarks on the earlier years. For the reader's convenience I have repeated his citations for the important opinions.

by the King and his Council for any such purpose should be of as good effect as any law made by Parliament...'.[2]

The judges had prefaced their opinion with the comment that there had been 'diverse opinions', and the opposing interpretations surfaced once again when several judges met informally in the Easter term in 1556 to consider the question. Their conclusion was that 'no proclamation in itself can make a law which was not made before', and that the proper role for proclamations was 'to confirm and ratify a law or statute, and not to change a law or to make a new law...'. But once again the opinion was qualified since 'diverse precedents were found and drawn out of the Exchequer to the contrary'.[3]

The alternatives were rather clear: recognize a discretionary power inherent in the prerogative which could legislate independently in the face of a compelling danger, or restrict their scope to a subordinate position vis-à-vis the statutes. Proponents for both sides seem to have been able to call on precedents, and while the balance was tilted toward the broader interpretation in the meeting in 1531, it went the other way in 1556. The only other explicit reference to proclamations in the earlier legal writings was in Fitzherbert's *La Novel Natura Brevium*, and it dealt with the use of proclamations in one particular case rather than with the general question.[4]

The uncertainty had been reflected in the parliamentary forum as well. In the session of 1539 a government bill was introduced, debated at length and amended, and finally enacted as 'An Act that Proclamations Made by the King Shall Be Obeyed'.[5] Even though it was repealed in 1547, its provisions and the stages leading up to its enactment shed considerable light on the role of proclamations, and provide an additional context for our eventual understanding of the Marian and Elizabethan proclamations.

Much scholarly effort has been spent in this century[6] in an attempt to reconstruct the provisions of the original bill (now lost) and the

---

[2] R. B. Merriman, *The Life and Letters of Thomas Cromwell* (2 vols.; Oxford, 1902), I, 410 (spelling modernized). The correct date of the letter as 1531 is shown in G. R. Elton, 'The Rule of Law in Sixteenth-Century England', in *Tudor Men and Institutions. Studies in English Law and Government* (ed. Arthur J. Slavin; Baton Rouge, 1972), p. 282, note 34.

[3] BL, Harl. MS 5141, fo. 31, printed with variants in Gulieme Dalison, *Les Reportes Des Divers Special Cases...* (London, 1689), p. 241. My translation from the law French.

[4] Anthony Fitzherbert, *La Novel Natura Brevium* (London, 1534), fo. 89v.

[5] 31 Henry VIII, c. 8, repealed by 1 Edward VI, c. 12.

[6] Heinze documents the gradual triumph before this century of the interpretation that the act was a *lex regia* which equated proclamations with statutes and thus afforded the King the opportunity to abrogate Parliament and substitute an absolute rule.

government's intention in proposing it. In spite of widely varying interpretations of the motive,[7] all seem agreed that the original bill stated that proclamations and statutes had a co-equal force at law and that the wording must have approximated the opinion which Cromwell had received eight years earlier. It is also generally agreed that the House of Lords amended the bill to restrict the co-equality to the enforcement process alone,[8] and that the House of Commons added a proviso that proclamations could not violate the statutes, common law or customs of England, and that the penalties in them could not include death, or the loss of one's lands, goods, privileges, and offices.

Except for the proviso added by the Commons, every section of the act dealt with enforcement. There seems to have been a question as to whether proclamations were enforceable in common law courts before this time, but the statement of co-equality in enforcement resolved the matter. But the principal place of enforcement was to be a special tribunal to consist mainly of royal councillors; when it proved difficult in practice to gather enough of them to make a quorum, the act was amended in 1542 to reduce the requirement, but the reduction was to be effective only during Henry's lifetime.[9]

Professor Heinze's thorough and convincing interpretation of the provisions and motives for the acts of 1531, 1542, and 1547 is the more valuable because it sets the parliamentary debates squarely in the context of the actual way in which Henry VIII and Edward VI's Protectors used royal proclamations. He argues that Henry VIII

---

[7] The pioneer work in this century was E. R. Adair, 'The Statute of Proclamations', *EHR*, xxx (1915), 698–704. The principal protagonists on the government's motives are Professors Elton and Hurstfield. The former argues that Cromwell intended to ground the authority of proclamations on statute, so that rather than establish an independent and co-equal legislative authority the act 'subjected the prerogative to the sovereignty of king in parliament': G. R. Elton, 'Henry VIII's Act of Proclamations', *EHR*, lxxv (1960), 211. The latter argues that the intent was to create a despotism, that Cromwell preferred to base it on statute because 'it gave the illusion of popular consent...But is a thing less tyrannical because it is lawful?': Joel Hurstfield, 'Was There a Tudor Despotism After All?', *TRHS*, 5th series, xvii (1967), 98. Elton's response is in 'The Rule of Law in Sixteenth-Century England'.

[8] 'Be it therefore enacted...the King for the time being with the advice of his honorable Council...or with the advice of the more part of them, may set forth at all times by authority of this Act his proclamations, under such penalties and pains and of such sort as to his Highness and his said Council or the more part of them shall see necessary and requisite; And that those same shall be observed and kept as though they were made by Act of Parliament for the time in them limited, unless the King's Highness dispense with them or any of them under his great seal.' Interpretations before Adair read 'those shall be observed...Parliament' to refer to 'proclamations' rather than to 'observed and kept'. I have modernized the spelling.

[9] Heinze, pp. 50, 175–6.

accepted the amendments with their limitations because they did not restrict him since his use of proclamations had been within that scope, and that the express limitation was deemed acceptable in exchange for securing a general parliamentary authority for all proclamations and an improved machinery for enforcing them.[10]

We are now in a position to summarize the theoretical place of proclamations as of 1553. First, their validity and power was un-challenged. The Statute of Proclamations recognized the power and did not confer it, so that the repeal in 1547 took nothing away from their power at common law. Second, even though the explicit state-ment of limitations was lost with the act in 1547, a precedent had been set to which later Tudors returned. The focal point for the Commons had been the question of penalties, and would continue to be so in the later periods. Third, the repeal meant that the proclama-tions would no longer be grounded on a statutory basis, and so the variant interpretations which we have already seen resurfaced. Fourth, the primary use of proclamations, to deal with an emergency situation, had been stressed in the timing of its introduction into Parliament, and in the amendments added by the House of Lords.[11] Fifth, the difficult question of the enforcement of proclamations had been faced, and perhaps the special tribunal with a conciliar nucleus was simply a statement of what was traditional practice, but the repeal in 1547 left the matter open again, and particularly so in regard to their enforceability in common law courts. Most important of all, Heinze's study of the use of proclamations in the early Tudor period – before, during, and after the Statute of Proclamations – has shown that Mary and Elizabeth inherited a tradition of a limited but vigorous use of proclamations.

Several theoretical opinions are recorded in the years before 1603. The most limited in scope was penned by Sir Thomas Smith, a Principal Secretary to both Edward and Elizabeth. He asserted in his *De Republica Anglorum* that the monarch had independent authority in dealing with a number of matters, among which were included topics which were the subject matter of actual proclamations, but he explicitly mentioned proclamations only when discussing the royal controls over the coinage and weights.[12]

[10] *Ibid.* p. 174.

[11] The Lords added the words 'by the authority of this act' and 'for the time being' to the act (p. 29, n. 8 above).

[12] Sir Thomas Smith, *De Republica Anglorum. A Discourse on the Commonwealth of England, By Sir Thomas Smith* (ed. L. Alston; Cambridge, 1906), pp. 58 ff., especially p. 60. His term of office under Elizabeth was 1572-6, but the book may have been written earlier.

A more sweeping but nevertheless private opinion was expressed by Thomas Egerton in the first decade of Elizabeth's reign, seemingly framed while he was studying the law. His opinion is of interest because of his penetrating legal mind and eventual high positions. 'All that law which is positive consists in proclamations or in acts of parliament. In proclamations as if the prince by his council have thought good and expedient to publish any thing as a law. But therein hath been doubted of what effect such proclamations have been, and what pain he that breaketh them should have.'[13] Again the independent authority of proclamations and the penalties they imposed are of primary concern. We shall be returning to an opinion by Egerton, expressed in James I's reign, shortly.[14]

James Morrice presented a more public and more authoritative opinion in a reading at the Middle Temple in May 1578. 'Three manner of ways I find the king is said to make and give laws unto his subjects', Morrice began, 'that is in and by his high and great court of parliament, by his letters patent under the great seal of England, and by his princely and royal commandment.' Proclamations fell into the third category, and Morrice mentioned their use for declaring war and peace, calling on the full assistance of his subjects to defend the realm, forbidding them to leave the realm during wars and ordering them to return home, altering the coinage, and making regulations for his own pleasure and pastime. He argued that offenses against proclamations were contempts and thus punishable by fine and imprisonment. His concluding statement was certainly broader than the examples which he had cited: 'But to conclude concerning the king's commandments either by written word or proclamation, they are all so far forth binding laws unto the people as the same are agreeable to the word of God, not repugnant to the laws of the realm, impossible to be performed, or not injurious to the subject.'[15]

Limitations: time and place

The opinions which we have seen stressed the need to meet an urgent problem and thus imply that their duration was limited. It was

[13] [Sir Thomas Egerton], *A Discourse upon the Exposicion & Understanding of Statutes with Sir Thomas Egerton's Additions* (ed. Samuel E. Thorne; San Marino, 1942), pp. 103–4. A clarification of the date and authorship is in T. F. T. Plucknett, 'Ellesmere on Statutes', *Law Quarterly Review*, LX (1944), 242–9.

[14] Below, p. 57, n. 6.

[15] BL, Add. MS 36081, cited by Heinze, p. 38.

generally held that a monarch's proclamations died with him,[16] the only exception being the common sense situation where rates for coins had been set and were considered to be in force and vigor until altered. Thus Sir Edward Coke as Elizabeth's Attorney General brought an information in the Exchequer which spoke of an Edwardian proclamation on coins as 'in suo pleno robore & effectu'.[17] Even within a reign proclamations had a limited duration, explicitly recognized either when a set time was expressed, or implicitly acknowledged in words which spoke of 'reviving' a former proclamation.

A variety of circumstances effectively terminated the other proclamations. The declaratory proclamations merely announced some fact, and so cannot be spoken of as having a duration. A few were to be in force until Parliament considered the matter, and in due course legislation followed.[18] The duration of many was implicit, as in those which adjourned the law terms, or commanded the political lent, or ordered soldiers who had received press money to report for duty. Some proclamations terminated earlier proclamations, as happened when new rates of wages were announced, or new prices for wine set, or when a proclamation was reissued verbatim. Because many were issued to meet an emergency situation, a return to normal would effectively remove the need for the special provisions – as when a rebellion was put down, or a war concluded.

Not all proclamations were dispersed throughout the entire realm. The proclamations which rated wages went only to one locality, the orders concerned with piracy were sent to the counties along the seacoast, and a good number were intended just for the immediate area around London. It is not possible to determine the extent for each proclamation because the main information comes from the payments made by local chamberlains to the messengers, and the records were not kept with uniformity in many places.

Although it has nothing to do with a limitation, it can be seen that many of the proclamations which enforced statutes were issued within a few days before or after the conclusion of a law term at West-

[16] So said Elizabeth when citing a proclamation by Mary on shipping: 'which proclamations are, by reason of the said Queen's highness' death, determined and of no force' (proc. 450/497). A decision in Star Chamber in James I's reign for violations of both the Elizabethan and Jacobean proclamations on building in London probably contributed to making his use of proclamations suspect: John Hawarde, *Les Reportes del Cases in Camera Stellata* (ed. William Paley Baildon; London, 1894), pp. 318–19.

[17] PRO, E 159/409, mm. 258, 259, 260–269 r and v, Mich. 37 & 38 Eliz. Coke's information is at m. 259, and the rest are by informers.

[18] Below, e.g., pp. 107, 134.

minster. The last day of term was the traditional time when all justices assembled in the Star Chamber to listen to a charge from the Lord Chancellor on the Queen's behalf. He would stress matters which greatly concerned her and the Council and then exhort the justices to be diligent on their returns home. About a quarter of the proclamations were issued during the law terms, and another quarter within a few days after their ends – a written reminder of the charge they had just heard. In Elizabeth's reign, for example, all except one of the apparel proclamations were so issued, as were two of the three which announced coming musters of horses, two of the three on buying and selling wool, both for uniformity in religion, four of the seven which enforced the statutes on vagabonds, and one of the proclamations on guns.

Preparation: the Queens and their Councils

Surprisingly few proclamations seem to have arisen from some personal interest of the monarch. We have already noted their use in connection with Mary's coronation and marriage with Philip, with protecting the Court from the plague, with a few revenue matters – and the three Marian and one Elizabethan proclamations on hunting were the only examples of 'pleasure and pastime' in proclamations, a category which Morrice had mentioned specifically.

The purpose of several proclamations was to protect the Queen's honor, as when Mary denounced the seditious writings which libelled her and Philip, or when Elizabeth was provoked by a lecture on her religious duties in a book by Thomas Cartwright.[19] Elizabeth issued a proclamation on guns soon after shots had been fired near her barge when she was on the river.[20] Never can we find personal corrections on a draft as there are in Henry VIII's reign.[21] It would seem that the Tudor Queens restricted their use of proclamations to public policy matters.

Mary's reign was not long enough, nor were there enough proclamations during it, for us to detect the interests and influences of individual councillors. When the total for her reign is considered, less the proclamations on rebellions and wars, just over six a year were issued. Elizabeth's accession meant a return to a smaller Council and to the system of Principal Secretaries, and there was

[19] Below, pp. 204–7.
[20] Below, pp. 71–2.
[21] Heinze, p. 11.

once again the opportunity for a single person to have a large part in the preparation of proclamations.

The Principal Secretary was the ideal person to suggest the use of proclamations and to prepare the drafts, not only because of his close contact with the Queen, but also because the office entailed a special obligation to ensure the keeping of the peace.[22] Certainly he called on others to assist in preparing the drafts, and the texts would be considered and altered in meetings of the Council with the final decision by the Queen, but he guided the matter at all stages. The most thorough description of his role is in a treatise on the office written in Elizabeth's reign by Robert Beale:[23]

If it shall be needful to publish any proclamation, consider well of the matter and look unto former precedents, and therefore it shall be needful for you to have the book of proclamations printed in the time of King Edward VI and all the rest, as many as you can get, dividing them according to their matters into several bundles, to avoid confusion and long search. If the matter be according to the law then urge it, and for this purpose you shall do well to have always at hand the abridgments of Rastell and Poulton. If it be of any matter of law that is not contained in the said books, then let the draft be made by the Queen's Learned Counsel and perused by the Judges and so pass accordingly.

As new evils require new remedies, so if no provision hath been heretofore made that may be enforced by law, then her Majesty by her prerogative may take order in many things by proclamation. And herein it is good to see what hath been done in like cases in other countries. And to this purpose the books of the Edicts and Ordinances in France and of the Pragmatics in Spain may stand you in some stead. But be circumspect in applying of those precedents to this State to avoid any opinion of being new fangled and a bringer in of new Customs. Show the necessities and cause and likewise the common benefit, that it may not be thought to tend to any private respects, and let the threatening of the penalties be such as may not seem strange or excessive, against the law and liberty of the land.

This practical statement, emanating from the heart of the Queen's government, expresses a commitment to the uses and limitations of proclamations which is a complement to the theoretical expressions we have already seen. In practice the Secretary was to have a broader

---

[22] Florence M. G. Evans, *The Principal Secretary of State* (University of Manchester Historical Series, XLIII; Manchester, 1923), pp. 7–8.

[23] Printed from a manuscript which is now BL, Add. MS 48149 by Conyers Read, *Mr. Secretary Walsingham and the Policy of Queen Elizabeth* (3 vols.; Oxford, 1925), I, 439 (spelling modernized); extracts in G. R. Elton, *The Tudor Constitution, Documents and Commentary* (2nd. ed.; Cambridge, 1962), p. 126. There are no references to proclamations in other contemporary treatises on the office.

scope of operation than the treatise suggested, for instances of borrowing a text from the first half of the century were rare.[24]

Many of the drafts are in Sir William Cecil's hand, and his corrections appear on others. It is possible that he may have been amending the texts at the Council's direction, but the sheer number of drafts which reflect his involvement argues strongly that his personal preferences lay behind many. His promotion to the peerage and the cooling of his relationship with Sir Francis Walsingham, as factions developed in the Council, lessened his immediate involvement in their preparation.[25] Corrections made by Sir Robert Cecil are to be found on only three proclamations, and Sir Thomas Smith and Thomas Wilson seem to have dealt with only one apiece.[26]

An indication of the elder Cecil's preference for proclamations can be gained in part from Table 6 which plots the separately devised proclamations above the time line and the reissues and routine ones below.[27] We shall see a number of influences which reduced or ended the use of proclamations in certain matters in the pages which follow, yet even allowing for those it is noteworthy that an average of nine separately devised proclamations a year were issued during his Secretaryship, and just under four for the more secretive years of Walsingham and just over four for the younger Cecil. Sir William's penchant for explanation and rationalization was even more marked, and in the years after his assumption of the post of Lord Treasurer the number of declaratory proclamations fell markedly.[28]

Many fundamental attitudes which were held by the Queens and their advisers influenced the use of proclamations. Elizabeth's desire to maintain the differences between social ranks meant an insistence on apparel and its gradations. Sir William Cecil's efforts to keep English money from flowing abroad made him favor proclamations on apparel since many items were imported, and led to a proclamation on the exchange. The many proclamations for the political lent were but an extension of his support for the fishing industry, a concern which led him to promote legislation in 1563.[29] The attitude

[24] The 'book of proclamations' was *All such Proclamacions, as haue been sette furthe by the Kynges Maiestie*... (London, 1550).
[25] 'Most of the important royal proclamations came from his pen', said Read, *Burghley*, p. 69. On the factions, Conyers Read, 'Walsingham and Burghley in Queen Elizabeth's Privy Council', *EHR*, xxviii (1913), 34–58.
[26] Steele's list for the reign, *passim*.
[27] 'Separately devised proclamations' are defined above, p. 16.
[28] Conyers Read, 'William Cecil and Elizabethan Public Relations', in *Elizabethan Government and Society* (ed. S. T. Bindoff, J. Hurstfield, and C. H. Williams; London, 1961), pp. 21ff.   [29] Read, *Cecil*, pp. 271–5.

Table 6. *Proclamations issued per year* (*e.g.62 = 1562*)
(Separately devised proclamations above time line)

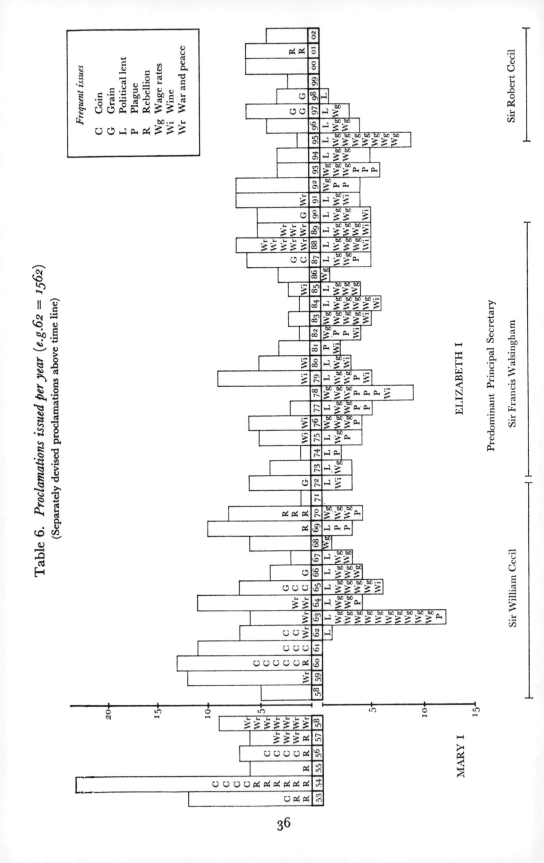

that middlemen were economic villains was widely held and influenced many of the proclamations on grain and wool. And above
all else, a fear of disorder and unrest permeated every Tudor statesman to the bone and animated many of the proclamations for
keeping the peace.

PURPOSES AND PROVISIONS

A good number of general causes occasioned many Marian and
Elizabethan proclamations. The primary reason for a proclamation
was that there was a need to inform subjects or to regulate matters
which went beyond a single local jurisdiction. The proclamations
against new buildings in London, or against vagabonds, or those
which tried to keep the peace there, were issued because the problem
spilled over into Middlesex, Surrey and Essex. Had the problem
been localized, an order to the officials of the town or county could
have sufficed. At least ten percent of the over 135 proclamations
made by the Lord Mayor of London were issued because of a royal
command to clear up a localized disorder.[30]

Only a few proclamations were the result of a long deliberative
process. The deliberations over the reform of the coinage early in
Elizabeth's reign and over the framing of measures to prevent the
export of coin in her last years involved studies for over a year,[31] but
long disagreements over the proper standards for weights and
measures delayed the proclamation which announced the new
norms substantially longer.[32] A consideration of the best means to
meet a problem could be referred to interested economic groups for
their opinions, or to the law officers to devise the proper procedures,
or to an individual councillor to draft remedies.[33] But more normally
it was a report from some local officer, or from a trading company,
or a request from a foreign ambassador which prompted the Council

[30] Corp. London RO, Journal XIX, fo. 346; XX, part 1, fos. 168v, 183v; part 2, fos.
369, 433, 433v; XXI, 41v, 237, 351v, 470; XXII, fo. 177; XXIV, fos. 79v, 135v, 149v. Fifteen
percent of his other proclamations set prices for victuals, and another ten percent
ordered the practice of archery.

[31] The earlier, Read, *Cecil*, pp. 194ff.; the charge in 1600 to begin a study, BL, Harl.
MS 38, fos. 230–3, 234–236v; deliberations, *APC*, XXXII, xix–xxi; the proc. 812/922.

[32] Study ordered in 1578, *APC*, x, 437; request in 1583 for some reformation, BL,
Lansd. MS 38/13; disagreement on standards, *ibid.* 52/13; proc. 695/797 finally issued in
1587.

[33] Economic group: *APC*, x, 322 (Merchant Staplers, leading to proc. 639/736). Law
officers: *ibid.* pp. 386–7 (term adjournment, 632/729); xx, 89–90 (Devon kersies, 744/847);
XXIV, 294–5 (winding of wool, 780/883). Councillors: *ibid.* IX, 56 (Lord Treasurer and
Lord Keeper, guns, 611/701).

to act, if it did not already have an appreciation of a problem which required a remedy.[34]

Some of the problems which elicited royal proclamations were endemic. Rumors abounded as did local disturbances which could fan into more widespread unrest. Both Queens experienced a sustained problem from the dissident religious books which challenged their religious policies. The question of piracy and of land-based abettors provoked many Elizabethan proclamations over a long span of years.

Yet the great majority of the proclamations were issued because of some immediate problem. Natural causes accounted for some of those, as when excessive rains meant bad harvests and shortages of grain, or when the plague was particularly severe. Other short-lived situations called for immediate remedies: war and rebellion, demobilizations after military campaigns, the interim settlement of religion between the Queen's accession and the meeting of her first Parliament, the closing of trade with the Low Countries when Anglo-Spanish relations temporarily broke down in Elizabeth's reign. It is particularly notable that Elizabeth's policy of granting monopolies led to many disorders which she had to disavow publicly in proclamations – a damaging bit of negative publicity.[35] Many of the proclamations in the years after the Armada tried to deal with soldiers who would not return home, but might they not have done so if the Queen had paid the arrears in their pay?

To meet those general problems which we have seen, Mary and Elizabeth issued proclamations, the three purposes of which were information, legislation, and administration.

Information

Royal proclamations offered the most effective means of oral propaganda for the vast realm.[36] Proclaimed at market crosses and

---

[34] Local officers: PRO, SP 12/36/49 (coins similar to those of greater worth, leading to proc. 533/610); SP 12/37/70 (coins, 538/614); SP 12/88/52 (London's request to stop export of grain, 541/617); Corp. London RO, Remembrancia, 1, fos. 18v–19 (buildings, 649/749); BL, Lansd. MS 20/1 (Ipswich's complaint of Englishmen serving foreign princes, 609/698). Companies: PRO, SP 12/77/69 (Merchant Adventurers, 457/507); Company of Cappers, below, pp. 148ff. Unsuccessful petitions: BL, Lansd. MS 5/46 (exchange); PRO, SP 12/106/2 (grain); SP 12/195/114, 12/177/59 (Jesuits); BL, Lansd. MS 7/62 (forbidding plays and interludes); *ibid.* 10/45 (Archbishop Grindal's request for a reissue of the proclamation on church monuments).   [35] Below, pp. 136ff.

[36] Gladys Jenkins, 'Ways and Means in Elizabethan Propaganda', *History*, new series, XXVI (1941), 105–14; Read, 'William Cecil and Elizabethan Public Relations', pp. 21–55, especially py. 22–3.

other central places, at the times when men congregated for instance on market days, they reached the widest possible audience, literate and illiterate alike.[37] They were not as effective as written propaganda, since the text was limited to several broadside sheets. The important debates in both reigns were conducted within the narrow circle of the literate and politically conscious minority in the realm.

No one would deny the potential in the proclamations for stirring men's patriotism or motivating them to act. The infrequency of their issue must have made the act of proclamation of great public interest. Yet it is impossible to escape the realization that informing the masses was generally not important to the Tudor Queens. Few of the important policy decisions were explained in the proclamations, for why should the secrets of statecraft be shared with the 'mean and lesser sort'? An argument can be made that an extensive justification in a proclamation showed a royal weakness in many cases. Mary's publication of the articles of her coming marriage with Philip was such an admission, for the dislike of the match was well known. A thorough reading of the proclamations also helps one to realize how much of their texts was given up to orders to local officials, for it was upon the latters' diligence that the real hope of reforming some problem rested.

Legislation

Regardless of the opinion held by some jurists which would have restricted proclamations to a subordinate role and denied the right to make law in them, both Mary and Elizabeth used royal proclamations to frame temporary legislation. A summary consideration of the practice is in order here, leaving specific details to subsequent chapters.

Many of their proclamations took the law in effect and extended its scope. It was already a felony to clip coins, but an Elizabethan proclamation added to the strict words the offenses of blanching and breaking, and the felonies so created were given a statutory authority when Parliament next met. The kinds of apparel which each class could wear were already expressed in statutes, and successive proclamations kept up with the newer fashions by prohibiting those which violated the spirit of the law. Similarly the newer guns which

---

[37] Sermons offered a theoretical possibility of reaching more persons, but it was illusory because of the clerics' mixed preaching abilities and political unawareness. The book of homilies in 1559 was hardly a corrective; the only addition came in 1570 when a sermon on disobedience was added in the wake of the rebellion in the north.

were made in the second half of the century were prohibited, to update the older statutory provisions. An Edwardian law forbade eating flesh during lent, and was supplemented by the Elizabethan proclamations which created new offenses for butchers, innkeepers, and other victualers who made the meat available. There were laws against forestallers and regraters of grain, and to these the proclamations added an offense for grain masters who did not supply the markets in times of dearth. As we shall see, bills which would have made the temporary offenses in the proclamations into permanent law were introduced into Parliament, usually soon after the first innovative proclamation, but rarely passed.

A few proclamations defined situations as falling within the scope of existing legislation. Elizabeth described certain dissidents who were in rebellion against their lawful princes in other countries as rebels and thus denied them access to English trade, while providing penalties for those who would assist them. Mary declared that any of the Greymes family in the western marches who did not reform and accept her pardon for their outrages should be 'deemed, reputed, and taken as enemies to us...and as manifest traitors and rebels'. In the 1590s Elizabeth used a proclamation to define trading with Spain as abetting the enemy.

Some proclamations created new offenses by taking the penalties proper to principal offenders and applying them to their accessories. This was a particularly useful technique since offenses by abettors lay in a relatively undeveloped area of the criminal law. Mary announced that those who spread seditious rumors were to be punished as their first authors, and Elizabeth similarly sought to punish those who spread dissident religious books with the punishments due to their authors and publishers. Several Elizabethan proclamations defined as piracy the actions of certain land-based abettors.

In a small but significant number of cases, proclamations created new offenses directly. They created the offense of treason for those who received or harbored the Jesuits who had entered England, and the definition lasted for several years until it was enacted in a later statute. Another Elizabethan proclamation legislated when it forbade building new structures or subdividing existing ones in and around London. The legislation which was intended for the next Parliament was not enacted but a statute was secured a few years later; when its term of years expired, a later proclamation reiterated the offenses.

The second legislative technique was to order the use of legal procedures which exceeded the existing law. These were used less frequently, and in rather circumscribed situations.

Martial law was commanded in several proclamations. It was invoked most often during the times of actual hostilities, and the only unusual extensions occurred when both Mary and Elizabeth threatened its use against anyone who received books which were the advance wave of an intended invasion. The order to execute under martial law men who had received press money but did not report for military service was in the proclamations of both Queens, but it was more notable in Elizabeth's because the Crown had already received an opinion that the offense was a felony. Martial law was invoked against demobilized soldiers and mariners who did not leave the ports and London to return home, against the same men who attempted to sell the weapons which had been issued to them for their military service, and increasingly often in the 1590s against vagabonds who often attempted to cloak their activities by pretending to be veterans. Other occasions on which martial law was threatened against civilians were in 1572 when an attempt was made to force the Prince of Orange's fleet to leave English ports, and in 1601 against trouble makers soon after the Earl of Essex's uprising had been crushed.

The death penalty was threatened outright in three cases which did not involve martial law. Mary invoked it against anyone who would attempt to avoid military service against the French by pretending to be a waterman, whose services she had declared to be so necessary as to warrant an exemption from service. Elizabeth threatened it to anyone who would affront the French who in 1572 were arriving to carry on the marriage negotiations between her and the Duke of Alençon. It was also invoked in a proclamation against piracy in 1602, but this could be a mere declaration since the offense was already capital.

Several proclamations, while not creating new offenses, did raise the penalties for existing offenses beyond those assessed in the statutes. These matters will be considered in the third part of this chapter.

Administration

Not only were the major parts of many texts of proclamations comprised of orders for local officials, but many proclamations were totally administrative with no provisions for judicial enforcement at all. Many were preventative, such as the proclamations which sought to protect the Court from the plague. Others were lengthy instructions as to the manner in which local officers were to collect the debased coins and receive back the finer reminted coins when Elizabeth reformed them, or how the Justices were to survey stocks of grain as a preliminary to ordering the markets served.

Nearly a hundred Elizabethan proclamations played a role which was specified in statute. The practice of stipulating how a monarch could use proclamations had begun in Henry VIII's reign, but the main purpose there had been to allow him to adjust prices of victual and other matters, whereas those in Elizabeth's reign tended to be more formal administrative matters.[38] Seventy-eight of Elizabeth's proclamations were merely publications of wage rates set locally, and sixteen set prices for wines. There were single instances of her exercise of the power to authorize the export of grain, to prohibit it in time of dearth, and to command that hemp and flax seed be sown. The most spectacular was the proclamation which published the sentence after the trial of Mary Queen of Scots in 1586.[39]

The need for administrative orders existed whether the proclamation was related to existing law or not. In the former case, the proclamation was a prod to local officials who often neglected the statutory charge, as is clear from the words of a proclamation on apparel: 'And because her majesty perceiveth that although the laws be very penal in both these cases, yet without some special direction given for the execution thereof reformation will not ensue.'[40] *A fortiori* administrative orders were needed for proclamations not based on statute.

The administrative procedures which were provided to assist the local officials fell within five headings: ordering searches; authorizing the seizures of items and the imprisonment of offenders; requiring safeguards such as licenses, bonds, and sureties; allowing local officers to republish a proclamation on their initiative; and holding special inquiries and receiving presentments.

Searches were regularly authorized when proclamations legislated against specific things such as new fashions in apparel or illegal

[38] On the statutes in the reign of Henry VIII, see Heinze, pp. 45–8. Statutes authorized, but Elizabeth did not use, the right to declare foreign gold coins current (5 Eliz. I, c. 1), to declare persons who seized and did not return fortresses traitors (14 Eliz. I, c. 1), and to declare pretenders to the throne traitors (13 Eliz. I, c. 1).

[39] Wages, 5 Eliz. I, c. 4. Wines, 5 Eliz. I, c. 5. Grain, export allowed, 5 Eliz. I, c. 5, and prohibited, 13 Eliz. I, c. 13. Hemp and flax, 5 Eliz. I, c. 5. Mary Queen of Scots, 27 Eliz. I, c. 1.

[40] Proc. 494/565.

weapons. The proclamations on the political lent had set offenses for victualers and others, and authorized local officers to search their shops fortnightly. Unauthorized lodgers near the verges of the Court were to be discovered by searches, as were catholic priests and the books of catholics and puritans alike. The proclamations for serving the markets with grain authorized Justices of the Peace to search grain masters' barns. And the searches could be preventative, as in the case of the authorization in the often reissued proclamation on vagabonds which commanded the Justices to search out the 'base and idle sort' and order them to leave the area.

Many of the authorizations for searches were extensions to other jurisdictions of provisions which had originally been framed for London. The earliest orders on the political lent were for Westminster and London only, but when fully developed in 1561 an addition was made: 'This manner, or the like order, her majesty commandeth to be observed as nigh as the same may be, in all places through her realm.'[41]

The commandment to seize some prohibited items such as a handgun or a forbidden piece of apparel was a logical extension to an officer's authority, but as we shall see the right to seize items and the usual assessment of forfeitures if the person was found guilty occasioned some of the greatest protests against proclamations.[42] The proclamations which enforced statutes often ordered a man held until his trial, but imprisonment was authorized in other cases as well. The distinction was made clearly in a proclamation on apparel which both enforced existing laws and legislated in newer areas:

'that is to say, [punishment] against the offenders of any of the aforesaid articles extracted out of any of the said statutes aforementioned according to the purport thereof; and for such as shall contemn any of the orders before mentioned being devised by her majesty's commandment, to attach and commit the same to prison, and to be there continued and punished as apperταineth to such as shall willfully break her majesty's commandment.'[43]

The potential for a conflict between the statutory provisions and those in the proclamations can be shown in several examples. Two nearly identical proclamations on apparel exceeded the statutes when they authorized the imprisonment of offenders for a month unless they posted a bond to answer at the next sessions for their offenses. The statute allowed only fines and forfeitures, and did not

---

[41] Proc. 477/538, the text which was reproclaimed in later years.
[42] Below, pp. 168–9, 171–4.   [43] Proc. 542/618.

authorize imprisonment. A similar excess can be found in the proclamations on weapons.

The requirements for licenses, bonds, and sureties offered the greatest potential for successful enforcement of any proclamation. Licenses were required as a means to prevent men from diverting cargoes laden for another English port to foreign destinations during a trade embargo, and to curtail the sending of English catholic youths to the schools abroad. They were used to protect the Court by controlling the access to the towns in the verge, to ensure that men of substance did not dally in London when their presence was needed in the coastal counties where their residences lay, and to limit the plays and books which could spread seditious and unsafe ideas.

Bonds and sureties offered an alternate form of control at the ports. Either one was licensed to take an armed vessel out of port, or he could be required to post a bond with sufficient sureties to insure that he would not engage in piracy.[44] Early in Elizabeth's reign the proclamations issued to prevent disorders at sea did not require bonds, but in later years they were invariably demanded. The earlier practice is an indication that many of the proclamations which had been issued to satisfy the demands of foreign ambassadors resident in London were half-hearted responses at best.[45]

Because bonds made the successful recovering of fines from offenders so much easier, the requirement to take them was used in other cases as well. Thus the tailors were to be bound not to make 'monstrous hosen' contrary to proclamations on apparel, alehousekeepers not to allow flesh to be sold on forbidden days, and retailers of wine not to sell new wine early in the season.

The right of a local officer to republish a royal proclamation was expressed in the proclamation of 1561 on the political lent, in another which enforced the statutes on vagabonds, and in an identification of foreign coins which were similar in appearance to a coin of greater value. The exercise of the first two doubtless accounted for some of the reissues which were excluded from the canon of separately devised proclamations.

The orders to make special inquiries and receive presentments showed a serious determination to secure enforcement of a proclamation. Usually the inquiries were to be conducted by one set of officials, to serve as the grist for a judicial enforcement by others. The proclamations which enforced the statutes requiring the lower

---

[44] The 'either/or' is clearly expressed in proc. 562/639.
[45] Below, pp. 84ff.

orders to wear caps on Sundays authorized 'constables, third-boroughs, tithingmen, churchwardens' to make searches and certify the names of offenders to those with judicial competence. The Aldermen who made the fortnightly searches in lent were to serve the same purpose, as were the weavers in Devon who were commanded to report to the Justices those who did not make kersies properly. A charge to couple the inquiries with judicial punishment by the same officer was more rare, as when the order was directed to the Lords Lieutenant. Occasionally inquiries were to determine if the condition of a bond had been fulfilled, so that forfeitures might be collected from one who had not kept it.

The procedures which we have just surveyed all commanded local officers to do something, but less frequently the proclamations offered some inducement to the average subject to involve him in the enforcement process. Mary offered rewards twice, once to anyone who would deliver up Wyatt during his rebellion; on another occasion she promised the statutory forfeitures to anyone who would identify those trafficking in coin. Seven of the Elizabethan proclamtions which offered rewards were issued in 1560-70, perhaps an indication that Sir William Cecil thought them worthwhile, and of the other eight most were issued between 1581 and 1588. Many of these were related to discovering the books and libels of dissident religious groups, and to dealing with officers in the ports who were negligent in enforcing the regulations on piracy. Rewards were never offered in proclamations which ordered the enforcement of existing statutes, and so there was no added incentive for an informer to be active.

Another incentive for subjects in general was the offer in some proclamations of a pardon for past offenses, provided the offender reformed himself before a date in the near future when a rigorous enforcement of the laws was to begin. This offer was made in the proclamations on apparel, on the musters of horses, on retaining, on tardy payments of debts due to the Queen, and in the proclamations enforcing the statutes on vagabonds.

ENFORCEMENT

The Council's management

It was the Council's job to ensure that the proclamations were enforced, and its management fell under the three tasks of providing supplementary orders, of explaining their meaning and dispensing from them when necessary, and of directing their judicial enforcement. Only rarely had the Council anything to do with dispersing the proclamations, since that was the Chancery's responsibility.

The most straightforward supplementary orders were the Council's letters to local officers which formed an added charge to be diligent. The uninformative entry in the acts of the Council, 'Letters to all the shires within the realm concerning the observance of the late proclamation for the reforming of the excessiveness of apparel', often masks the length and thoroughness of the effort, because when the actual text of the letter is found copied elsewhere it is often as long again as the proclamation itself.[46] Had the proclamation promised a commission, the Council would draw up the instructions to guide the commissioners, citing the proclamation and giving a new charge.[47] On other occasions the Council pointed out to local officials complaining of some problem that 'by her Majesty's proclamation there is already order taken therein'.[48]

The Council did not hesitate to add additional orders which were not in the proclamation. After the issue of a proclamation setting prices for wine in 1576, the Council ordered the Lord Treasurer to superintend the customs officials and order them to take bonds from the merchants importing the wine.[49] A proclamation in 1580 threatened the sectaries of the Family of Love with the punishments for heresy and was very severe in its tone, but the letters from the Council to the Bishops of Ely and Norwich ordered them 'to deal with them by friendly and Christian admonitions to renounce the [heretical] doctrine' and to act severely only as a last resort.[50] The proclamation of 1591 which ordered that woad be sown made no mention of the patentees on whose behalf the order had been issued, yet the Council ordered the Justices of the Peace in Dorset to enforce it on the basis of the information which the patentees would provide.[51]

Supplementary orders were often prepared for the coastal areas which had received proclamations aimed at preventing disorders on the sea, and for officers such as the knight harbinger who were charged with protecting the Court from persons infected with

[46] E.g., Flenley, pp. 101, 158–9.
[47] PRO, SP 12/36/88; *APC*, IX, 45; XIX, 292–3; XXII, 138–40, 203–4.
[48] *APC*, VII, 325–6; XVIII, 332–3; XXVI, 116–17, 328.
[49] *Ibid.* IX, 240.
[50] *APC*, XII, 232–3.
[51] *Ibid.* XXII, 81.

THE ROLES OF PROCLAMATIONS

plague.[52] The Council ordered conferences to be held locally so that the officers on the spot might devise the additional procedures which would make the proclamation effective.[53] And on occasion the Council appointed the Justices of the Assize to superintend the actions of the local officers as a means for securing compliance.[54]

The Council's explanations were of great practical importance. Thus it dealt with questions such as what should be done about the ships which had already been loaded with cargoes before the announcement of a trade embargo, whether the complaints of the hose makers in London against a proclamation on apparel were justified, and how to deal with officers who were not willing to allow patentees to exercise their grants which specifically exempted them from restrictions in royal proclamations.[55] The Council was quick to rebuke anyone who tried to twist the meaning of a proclamation for his own gain, as did the commissioners for grain in Sussex who used a restraint on transporting grain as a pretext to disallow the customary sales for the London market, or the merchant who attempted to use a trade embargo as an excuse for breaking a contract, or the country gentry who sought to remain in London in spite of a proclamation to return home, alleging that it bound only those whose estates were in the coastal counties.[56]

The dispensations from the requirements of royal proclamations show the Council's importance, because it could act in that manner only with the Queen's express allowance. It dispensed from the restrictions against exporting grain in a time of dearth, from the order that no new buildings be erected in London, and from the stipulation that officers who were not at their posts on the borders should lose their pay during their absence.[57]

To insure that the proclamations and supplementary orders were being observed, certificates were often required. Local officials would have to report on their activities to the Council, although the certificates could be due at other central offices as well.[58] Thus the

[52] Sea: *APC*, vii, 157–8; viii, 49; ix, 70, 382–3; PRO, SP 12/33/21. Court: *APC*, xxv, 513.　　　[53] *Ibid.* vii, 65–6; ix, 366.
[54] PRO, SP 12/47/13.
[55] Embargo: PRO, SP 12/33/41, 45, 47. Hose: BL, Lansd. MS 8/64. Patentee: *APC*, xiii, 48–9; xviii, 191; xxii, 77–8.
[56] *APC*, xiv, 338–9; xxi, 274–5; xxvi, 292–5.
[57] Grain: *APC*, xxviii, 28, 42–4, 69, 89–90, 230–1. Buildings: PRO, SP 12/156/41. Officers: *APC*, vii, 46.
[58] Into Chancery, wage rates and observance of the political lent; into the Star Chamber, procs. 469/526 on repairing destroyed monuments in churches, and 766/871 on guns. The only certificate on lent which I have found is PRO, E 178/142, so badly mutilated that ultra-violet is required to read it; no others seem to have survived.

Council required information about items taken as prize goods, about arrears in payments due to the Queen, about the authors of libels, and about the losses of English subjects when Anglo-Spanish relations broke down in 1569 and each nation seized the goods of the other's merchants.[59]

The third role of the Council was to superintend the judicial enforcement of the proclamations. We will see in a moment the options open to it when it was determined that they would be enforced in the central courts; here the concern is with its direction of local enforcement.

The Council could order examinations of offenders to be made locally as a prelude to later judicial proceedings, as when officers in Lancaster were ordered to examine those who had harbored Edmund Campion 'lately sent from Rome contrary to her Majesty's proclamation', and when the Master of the Rolls, the Recorder of London, and others were commanded to investigate an outrage committed outside Lincoln's Inn, and report what 'they the suspected men did after the proclamation made'.[60] When the reports showed so great an outrage that the decision was made to transfer the case to the central courts, local officers were instructed that the offenders be bound to appear there.[61] Otherwise it could direct the local officers to proceed with the punishments stated in the proclamations.[62]

Penalties and places for enforcement

Just under twenty percent of the Elizabethan and forty percent of the Marian proclamations required no judicial enforcement. Most of these were declaratory in nature, such as the repeated adjournments of law terms because of the plague. The number is particularly high in Mary's reign because many were issued during rebellions. The really operative command to the adherents of a rebel to stop assisting him or be liable to severe punishments was made in the field by a herald or a military officer of the Queen, and not by royal proclamations.[63] Another four percent of the Elizabethan proclamations announced forthcoming commissions, so that technically the enforce-

[59] Procs. 517/586, 625/720, 810/920; 742/843, 743/846, 749/853, 764/869; 581/661; 576/655 respectively.
[60] APC, XIII, 148–9, and XX, 63–5 respectively.
[61] Ibid. XIII, 72; XIV, 91; XVII, 393–4; XXI, 103; XXIV, 198; XXVII, 8–9; XXVIII, 136–7.
[62] Order the sale of goods seized in an embargo, ibid. VII, 166; order men punished who had used cancelled licenses to buy and sell wool, ibid. X, 24–5; order for strictness in enforcing the orders on grain, including not only imprisonment but rolling back the prices, ibid. XXVI, 81–3.   [63] Below, pp. 63, 66–7.

ment which followed was by the commission and not under the proclamation – but the offender probably did not appreciate the nicety.

In a relatively small number of proclamations the penalties which were stipulated went beyond the theoretical limits which we surveyed at the beginning of this chapter. We have already seen the instances in which the death penalty was explicitly threatened and the times when martial law was ordered.[64] Mary authorized the use of the pillory in a proclamation against improper winding of wool when she reissued the earlier proclamation of Edward VI nearly verbatim, and once again against men who spread rumors and against vagabonds.[65] Elizabeth deleted the requirement for the pillory when reissuing the proclamation on winding wool, but imposed it against spreaders of rumors, against men of low social rank who sold meat during lent, and against men who used commissions for making starch from grain after those had been cancelled because of a dearth.[66] She also ordered unspecified corporal punishment for men who exported grain to Spain in 1588.[67] This type of punishment seems to have been threatened only against men of the lowest social orders, as is explicitly stated in one of the Elizabethan proclamations restricting access to the Court. It ordered that offenders be whipped and punished like common vagabonds 'if the quality of the party shall so require'.[68]

Other proclamations touched property by requiring forfeitures from offenders.[69] It will be recalled that in the cases of apparel and guns some proclamations extended the scope of the statutory prohibitions to include new fashions and developments. The law ordered the forfeiture of offending items, and so the proclamations which created the new offenses called for forfeitures as well.[70] Forfeitures were demanded in a number of sea-related matters. Mary and Elizabeth demanded them from unlicensed shippers during the French wars, Mary forbade importing wines from France in the

[64] Above, p. 41. The penalty of death would, of course, have been applicable when the proclamations defined treasons (harboring Jesuits, not disclosing the Babington conspirators), felonies (abusing coin), heresies (books of the Family of Love), and piracies (land-based abettors).

[65] Proc. 423/463, a reissue of 359/380 on wool winding; 389/425 on rumors; 416/445 on vagabonds.

[66] Proc. 497/570 and 780/883 on wool winding; 492/560 on rumors; 466/521, 477/538 and nearly annual reissues of the latter on lent; 795/898 on starch.

[67] Proc. 706/807.   [68] Proc. 565/643.

[69] Forfeitures were ordered in several of the statutes which proclamations ordered enforced, e.g. 722/825 on casting filth into streams, 720/823 on standards for making cloth.

[70] Above, pp. 39–40.

same situation, and Elizabeth coupled the requirement with the use of martial law when trying to force the fleet of the Prince of Orange out of the southern ports in 1572.[71] Elizabeth called for 'forfeitures of as much as by the parties may be forfeited' from anyone shipping arms to Russia, and invoked the threat in proclamations on prize ships and piracy late in the reign.[72] When dearths threatened, Elizabeth called for forfeitures from those who exported beer, and for other offenders in grain matters.[73]

The other requirements for forfeitures were made in a variety of diverse situations: of building materials, from men who carried on construction in London when it was forbidden; of the goods and chattels of anyone caught with one of the catholic books which were intended to precede the arrival of the Armada in 1588; of the weapons and nets used in hunting in royal game parks; from men of substance who did not leave London to return to their residences along the coasts; and from Anabaptists who did not leave England as ordered by Elizabeth.[74] Negligent officials who did not enforce the regulations against piracy and other sea-related disorders were threatened with the loss of their office on several occasions,[75] and twice the threat of the loss of a corporation's franchise was made should its officers continue negligent.[76]

But in most cases there were no exact and severe penalties set forth. Instead there were threats of the Queen's 'indignation', or her 'displeasure', or of 'further punishment' or 'exemplary punishment'. Almost invariably no place of punishment was specified when those penalties were mentioned, nor were exact courts cited when there was a promise of 'further order and punishment according to the quality of the offence'.

Such vagueness in defining penalties was probably all that was needed, since the traditional punishment for contempts was fine and/or imprisonment. There was also some advantage in not specifying the exact place of enforcement because it left the Queen and her Council with a number of options. Usually punishment was desired on the spot in the locality where the offense had been committed. We have seen the Council's role in directing that enforcement, and most of the instances of punishment in the following pages will be in local courts. But if the crime was notable, or the offender

[71] Procs. 442/487, 450/497, 585/668.   [72] Procs. 481/546, 730/830, 813/925.
[73] Procs. 726/827, 781/884, 784/888.
[74] Procs. 649/749, 815/927; 699/802; 816/929; 470/529 respectively.
[75] Procs. 483/549, 562/639, 612/702, 706/807, 732/832; 735/845, 769/873 on unlawful assemblies; 784/888 on grain.   [76] Procs. 573/653, 609/698.

in a high position, then some more special punishment at the center of government was required.

Although the Council was not a court of law, it could inflict punishments of a quasi-judicial nature.[77] It could commit the offender to prison, or require him to travel up to London to 'await the Lords' pleasure' – and then delay matters so that the costs of maintenance mounted, not to mention the journey up. An even more effective punishment would be to recommend that the offender be struck from the commission of the peace or removed from some prestigious post. These methods, local or central, were available to the Council at any time of the year.

If a judicial determination was required, the offender could be required to appear before the Star Chamber in term time. Mary and Elizabeth both used that court to enforce proclamations, but it is interesting to note that it was explicitly cited as the place of enforcement in only eleven Elizabethan proclamations, and that no record of actual use in those small numbers of cases is to be found. The Star Chamber could not inflict the penalties for felonies, but it could handle the contempt separately and leave the substance of the charge to the common law.[78]

The question of whether royal proclamations were enforced in the Star Chamber, by the Council, in any other central courts, or in the counties and boroughs of England demands a search in a wide range of records. Given the quantity of so many of these records, it was necessary to choose a sample; this – regarded as a minimum – was one regnal year of Mary's reign (1 Mary), and ten of Elizabeth's, comprised of five pairs of two successive regnal years (2 and 3, 11 and 12, 21 and 22, 30 and 31, and 38 and 39 Elizabeth). Just which records were used will be specified as we now survey the courts which had a role in enforcing royal proclamations.

The decrees of the Court of Star Chamber do not survive, but there are reports of cases and other records which help in knowing the disposition of trials there. There was an active enforcement of proclamations, and when Sir Thomas Egerton began to preside over the Court as Lord Keeper he drew up a book of precedents in which cases on proclamations were used.[79] The calendar of all cases for

[77] Elton, *The Tudor Constitution*, pp. 101–2.
[78] Example below, pp. 238–40.
[79] Reports, BL, Harl. MS 2143; Hawarde, *Les Reportes del Cases in Camera Stellata.* Descriptions of the Court, including comments on the use of proclamations: William Hudson, 'A Treatise on the Court of Star-Chamber', in *Collectanea Juridica* (ed. Francis

Mary's reign was checked, as were the cases in the test years in over a quarter of the nearly one thousand boxes of Elizabethan Star Chamber papers.[80]

One of the intentions of the Statute of Proclamations seems to have been to clear up uncertainties as to whether proclamations were enforceable in common law courts, and its repeal in 1547 reopened the question. No Marian or Elizabethan proclamation assigned a common law court as the place of enforcement for any provision which rested solely on the prerogative, but since many enforced statutes one could expect to find cases based on proclamations and statutes jointly.[81] All the indictments in King's Bench and all the cases on the memoranda rolls of the Exchequer[82] have been searched for the test years.

The Justices on the circuits were already authorized to enforce many of the statutes with which the proclamations dealt, and on rare occasions a proclamation assigned a charge to punish certain other offenders. The only Assize records for Elizabeth's reign are those for the home counties, and these have been searched,[83] as have the indictments in the High Court of Admiralty for the whole of Elizabeth's reign.[84]

The Justices of the Peace in the counties, and the head officers in the boroughs, were given the most extensive commands to enforce the proclamations, whether they were based on statute or on the

Hargrave; London, 1792), pp. 1–240; Elfreda Skelton, 'The Court of Star Chamber in the Reign of Queen Elizabeth' (unpublished M.A. thesis, University of London, 1930). Egerton's book: Huntington Libr., Ellesmere MS 2768, and precedents noted in other MSS: 2652, 479, 2654.

[80] *List of Proceedings in the Court of Star Chamber, Preserved in the Public Record Office*, Vol. 1: *A.D. 1485–1558* (Lists and Indexes, xiii; London, reprinted 1963). PRO, Star Chamber 5, arranged alphabetically in Elizabeth's reign by first letter of the plaintiff's surname. I have seen all the cases in boxes 'A' (1–59) since those of the Attorney General would appear there, and for the test years, the following: B/1–66; C/1–7; D/1–10; E/1–10, 17; F/1–9; G/1–6; H/1–19; J/1–9; K/1–9; L/1–9; M/1–8; N/1–10; O/1–9; P/1–7; Q/1; R/1–11; S/1–7. The sample is more significant than it would appear, since full cases are tied together in the early boxes in a letter, and later boxes have loose bits of cases. No cases on proclamations are cited in Ifan ab Owen (ed.), *Catalogue of Star Chamber Proceedings Relating to Wales* (University of Wales Board of Celtic Studies, History and Law Series, 1; Cardiff, 1929).

[81] Any court of record could hear cases on apparel, exchange, the export of coins and grain, guns, peace in churchyards, prices of wine, tillage, and timber. King's Bench had authority for retainers and treason, and in Elizabeth's reign gained it for Jesuits and seditious words.

[82] King's Bench: PRO, KB 9/584–6, 597–603, 623–6, 647–52, 670–4, 689–94, supplemented occasionally from controlment roll, KB 29. Exchequer: memoranda rolls, PRO, E 159/330–2, 340–3, 357–60, 375–9, 393–7, 409–13; commissions, E 178.

[83] PRO, Assizes 35.

[84] PRO, HCA 1, indictments; 2/37–40, examinations.

THE RULES OF PROCLAMATIONS

prerogative. The county sessions records are complete in the second half of the sixteenth century only for Essex, Middlesex and Norfolk; these have been used. The partial records for other counties are in print in some cases, but do not yield examples of enforcement of proclamations; it should be noted, however, that printed editions rarely go beyond a recital of the criminal offense to note the authority on which the case was brought, and that there are cases in the manuscript rolls (in Middlesex, for example) which do not appear in a printed edition.[85] A sample was chosen of several towns which were counties of themselves or otherwise of great importance, and which represented a geographic diversity within England: London, Chester for the northwest, York for the northeast, Exeter and Bristol for the southwest, Southampton in the south, Norwich for the east, and the Cinque Ports of Rye and Sandwich. The printed records in the various county record series and the reports of the Historical Manuscripts Commission were used to supplement the works in manuscripts.

As will be seen in the following pages, the records of the various jurisdictions reveal a great number of examples of the enforcement of royal proclamations. It will become clear that they were enforced consistently whether in the royal central courts or in the boroughs and counties, whether administrative or judicial procedures were required, and whether the provisions were innovative or more traditional in scope. While there was no hesitation in accepting the new definitions of offenses as the basis for judicial action, it is also clear that the enforcement in a central common law court such as the Exchequer was almost invariably brought on the joint authority of a statute and a proclamation, and not on the latter alone. All this evidence indicates the government's firm purpose to use proclamations to direct the affairs of the realm in certain areas, and provides the material for evaluating their impact in the fields of security, economic and social matters, and religion.

[85] Printed sources, all for part of Elizabeth's reign only, with no cases on proclamations: Somerset, Staffs., Wilts., Worcs., West Riding, Yorks. Since the proclamations were temporary measures only, their procedures did not become part of the manuals for the Justices of the Peace, and this may account in part for any continued uncertainties about exact procedures.

REFLECTIONS: THE PROCLAMATIONS
AND THE CONSTITUTION

The fundamental constitutional question is whether the Tudor Queens used royal proclamations within the law. Both the survey of their provisions and the practical suggestions for the Secretary's role in drafting them imply that the proclamations were intended to exercise the Crown's rights in accordance with the more liberal opinion which Cromwell received in 1531, yet within the limits laid down in the Statute of Proclamations of 1539. It is also evident that the potential for exceeding those limits was greatest not when the proclamations were used to inform or to administer, but when they set forth temporary legislation and in the infrequent cases when their penalties touched life and property or authorized the more summary procedures of martial law.

The numerous cases in which the courts accepted the new definitions at law and enforced them make it certain that proclamations legislated, but it is just as clear that this legislation had three characteristics: it was temporary, it was limited, and it was inferior to and not in conflict with Parliament's legislation. Often the legislation proclaimed was expressly limited in duration; in addition, the government usually sought to make innovative measures permanent by soon after proposing a bill in Parliament and limited the prosecution of offenders to the period immediately following the proclamation's issue. The longest lapse between the appearance of a proclamation and its enforcement was six years, and normally cases were over in a few months and not repeated thereafter.

The legislation in the proclamations generally respected the limitations which had been enacted in the Statute of Proclamations. It has been seen that the penalty of death was threatened outright on several occasions, that it would have been the judicial consequence of some of the definitions of offenses such as abetting traitors, and that it could be inflicted under the extraordinary process of martial law. But in the pages to follow it will be found that the evidence to date reveals not a single instance of an execution consequent upon a proclamation, whether at martial law or under more normal processes.[1] On the contrary, we shall find several instances where local authorities will be seen to have followed the usual course of the law even though martial law had been authorized, and many more where the fines which were assessed were substantially below what had been threatened. These facts suggest strongly that many of the penalties had been intended *in terrorem populi*. Even when martial law was invoked, the offenses were already felonies, so that the practical effect was to intensify a process rather than to assign an unheard-of penalty. It must also be remembered that in practice there were different strata of penalties to correspond with the different social ranks, so that what was threatened against the lower groups in society was rarely to be used against the rest.

The cases which carried penalties of forfeitures or of the loss of offices were rare, and the Crown usually had a bill on the matter introduced into Parliament soon after. This will be investigated at some length when the proclamations on apparel and against new buildings in and around London are considered. It should be noted that the principled opposition within the House of Commons in the former matter was possible precisely because Queen Elizabeth followed the convention that permanent sanctions should be provided in Parliament and not continued indefinitely in proclamations. It will also appear that while she would not back down from seeking provisions which she saw as clearly necessary for reform, she respected the spirit of the opposition. The proclamations on apparel issued after the Commons' objections and the failures of the government bills offered a suspect the right to enter into a bond to answer the statutes at the next sessions if he was not willing to be punished immediately under the provisions of the proclamation which were based on the prerogative.[2] The most serious threat to property was the prohibition against new buildings which authorized the tearing down of structures lately erected; it will be seen that the justification for such orders depends on the insoluble question of determining whether the penalty was commensurate with the seriousness of the problem.

The inferiority of legislation by proclamation to the laws of Parlia-

---

[1] Stow noted that a man was put to death for speaking against the Queen's proclamation after the rising of the Earl of Essex in 1601, but his comment was brief and did not mention the legal authority for the execution; see below, p. 67.

[2] Below, p. 169.

ment can also be demonstrated. The former dealt only with matters of criminal law and not with the rules of property. They did not contravene the existing law, even though on occasion they offered a temporary suspension for a short duration to encourage men to reform themselves before the law was to be enforced in earnest. It will be seen that only once was there a suggestion that a proclamation violated a law, when the government was preparing to mitigate the statutes on the making of cloth on behalf of some clothiers in East Anglia, and that as a consequence the proclamation as finally drafted asserted that the privileges were to last only until Parliament acted.[3] So rather than conflict with the laws, proclamations supplemented them and/or created offenses where none already existed. Had they not created the offenses, how could the courts have taken cognizance and punished offenders?

In all those actions, the government followed a course of action which agreed with the arguments for a vigorous use of proclamations – arguments like those offered to Cromwell in 1531, listed in the first decade of Elizabeth's reign by Egerton the young law student, elaborated in 1578 in Morrice's reading at the Middle Temple, or contained in the practical treatise on the office of the Secretary by Robert Beale. But we have seen that there was also a tradition of an opposite, much more restrictive, viewpoint which was mentioned in 1531 and later asserted strongly at the judges' informal meeting in 1556. It does not seem that the argument was repeated again in the sixteenth century in theoretical form, but it was asserted with great force in the seventeenth century when apprehension grew over the use of proclamations by the Stuarts. In trying to write against the latter, several law reporters occasionally resorted to denouncing the use and intent of Elizabethan proclamations.

Thus John Hawarde attacked the proclamations which required grain masters to serve the markets in times of dearth and those against new buildings in London when cases on both were brought in the 1590s. More importantly, Sir Edward Coke reported a case on the Marian proclamation of 30 March 1558 which forbade importing wine from France because of the Anglo-French war. In August 1558 Mary decided to call for an imposition on the wine brought in by royal license, and the matters of the proclamation and the imposition coalesced in a case brought in the Exchequer against Germance Cioll. Coke drew three conclusions from the case: the proclamation 'was made of purpose to set an imposition'; it was illegal because

[3] Below, pp. 133-4.

there was no war with France; and the exact manner and time of the case had not been stated clearly. Yet he was clearly wrong in his facts, since war had been declared and the proclamation did not mention impositions which seem to have been assessed only later.[4] Coke and Hawarde seem to have been doing the same thing, namely reading back into Tudor times the grievances against proclamations which were current in the early Stuart period.

The climax of that process was Coke's opinion in 1610 on the role of proclamations. It was obtained in consequence of the debates in Parliament which had centered on James's use of proclamations. Coke argued:

'Note, the King by his proclamation, or other ways, cannot change any part of the common law, or statute law, or the customs of the realm... also the King cannot create any offence by his prohibition or proclamation, which was not an offence before, for that was to change the law, and to make an offence which was not; for *ubi non est lex, ibi non est transgressio*: *ergo*, that which cannot be punished without proclamation, cannot be punished with it...'[5]

His statement was not only squarely in the tradition of 'divers opinions' of the restrictive sort, but was almost a literal borrowing from the report of the discussion in 1556. Although Coke's opinion did not at once become authoritative, it became from the mid-seventeenth century onward the accepted interpretation of the role of proclamations.[6]

Yet of all these definitions, Coke's are the most suspect. The precedents which he cited in 1610 to buttress his arguments were either to cases which cannot be found, or which had no direct bearing on royal proclamations as such.[7] It must be remembered that Coke the-champion-of-the-common-law was a later phenomenon than Coke the Queen's-man-and-vigorous-Attorney-General. It was Coke who brought the cases in the Star Chamber on grain and

---

[4] Sir Edward Coke, *The Second Part of the Institutes of the Laws of England* (London, 1797), pp. 62–3; for Hawarde's comments, below, pp. 118–20.

[5] Sir Edward Coke, *The Reports of Sir Edward Coke, Knt.* (rev. ed. George Wilson; London, 1777), XII, 75. The opinion was eventually transferred to Part VI.

[6] See Esther S. Cope, 'Sir Edward Coke and Proclamations, 1610', *American Journal of Legal History*, XV (1971), 216, 218–19, 221. A more cautious statement very early in the Stuart period had been made by Egerton: 'Of the strength of Proclamations, being made by the King, by the advise of his Council and Judges, I will not discourse, yet I will admonish those that be learned and studious in the Laws, and by their profession are to give counsel, and to direct themselves, and others, to take heed that they do not contemn or lightly regard such Proclamations'; cited in [Egerton], *A Discourse upon the Exposicion & Understanding of Statutes* (ed. Thorne), p. 107 note 9.

[7] Heinze, p. 36.

buildings about which Hawarde complained; it was Coke who enforced proclamations in common law courts by citing them as a part
of a dual authority with statutes. Furthermore, when the debates of
1610 and other years which centered on proclamations are studied,
it emerges that all the objectionable features are Stuart in origin, not
a single Elizabethan practice being cited among them.[8]

We are therefore better advised to consider the proclamations of
the Tudor Queens on the basis of how they were actually used rather
than upon allegations made later. To be sure there were objectionable
features – instances where the limits expressed earlier were exceeded,
a too quick readiness to adopt summary procedures, examples of
misleading and deceitful arguments, and the like – but it will become
clear that the normal practice was to move within the traditional
limits with vigor. The proclamations were only one expression of the
policies and practices of the Tudor Queens, and it will not do to
dismiss them lightly or to make too much of them.[9] Their use and
impact in the different aspects of later Tudor society will show how,
why and with what effect royal proclamations were used within the
constitutional limits. It will become clear that in Mary's reign use
and impact seem to have been minimal, while Elizabeth used them
more actively than had been done in earlier reigns, and often with
significant effect.

[8] Esther S. Cope, 'Parliament and Proclamations, 1604–1629', (unpublished Ph.D.
Dissertation, Bryn Mawr College, 1969).
[9] A case in point is the logical consequence of statements about legislation in general
which are not accurate when the legislation in proclamations is to be considered. Professor Elton's argument that 'there is no prerogative power of making new laws or abroga-
ting old; legislation is the function of the king in Parliament, the united action of the
whole realm...' leaves no place for the temporary legislation of proclamations, nor does
Professor Hurstfield's statement that 'the crown in its person as legislator is a despotism'.
Elton, 'The Rule of Law in Sixteenth-Century England', pp. 278–9; Hurstfield, 'Was
There a Tudor Despotism After All?', p. 97.

PART TWO

THE PRACTICE: THE
PROCLAMATIONS AND SECURITY

3

<hr>

DOMESTIC SECURITY

To maintain the peace and security of the realm was of the utmost importance. Mary and Elizabeth faced severe challenges when men rose up in rebellion or hatched plots against them, and so the proclamations which they used to help repress the uprisings are discussed first. Both Queens constantly strove to maintain the peace in smaller matters as well, and when a particular problem vexed officials in various localities, proclamations offered the means of assisting in the reforms.

REBELLIONS AND PLOTS

Because there were no greater threats to the security of a kingdom than rebellions and plots, the law already provided more than adequate remedies to protect the monarch and the realm. There was thus little need for innovative supplementary measures in royal proclamations, but these did offer a convenient instrument for announcing danger and for reassuring all subjects that the disloyalties of a few had been overcome. Although the number and frequency of such proclamations were necessarily limited, more were used when the rebellion was directed at London and therefore posed a more immediate threat to the Queen.

Mary's reign

Mary's initial problem was to put down the rebellion which the Duke of Northumberland had moved to divert the succession to Lady Jane Grey. Jane had been proclaimed Queen in London on 10 July, but Mary's forces rallied, proclaimed her Queen, and capitalized on the popular repugnance at Northumberland's transparent scheme.[1]

<hr>

[1] Jane's proclamation and its aftermath may be followed in Machyn, p. 35; in Wriothesley, pp. 4–5; and in John Gough Nichols (ed.), *The Chronicle of Queen Jane, and of Two Years of Queen Mary...* (Camden Society, xlviii; London, 1850), pp. 1–3. The ballad with the stanza 'for my father's proclamation now must I lose my head' is quoted in *HMC 58: Bath II*, p. 15.

Mary's triumph led to her proclamation as Queen in London on 19 July 1553.[2] It was only the first of a series of rebellions that were to mark her troubled reign, rebellions which were continuing manifestations of the 'permanent crisis'[3] brought about by her pro-Spanish policies.

The Queen's determination to marry Philip of Spain awakened a fear of Spanish domination of England. In an attempt to quiet her subjects' anxieties, Mary had the terms of the proposed marriage agreement proclaimed so that men could know of the safeguards in it.[4] But the plans for a rebellion had already been made, and even though it was detected and prevented in two of the planned areas, the midlands and Devon, Sir Thomas Wyatt carried out his part when his proclamation was published in Kent on 25 January 1554.[5] The royal proclamation of 27 January offered a pardon to all who would leave Wyatt, but he prevented its publication lest his recruits be tempted.[6] When his forces clashed for the first time with the Queen's on the 28th, a proclamation the following day denounced him and his associates as traitors.[7]

Any gratification which the government felt at its initial victory was quickly dispelled when many of the royal troops deserted to Wyatt at Rochester, leaving the path to Southwark and eventually London open. The Queen's concern over a suspected number of secret sympathizers to the rebel surfaced in a royal proclamation on 31 January which allowed them free passage through Southwark to join him. Better to augment his forces, than to suffer a fifth column within.[8]

Two proclamations the following day show the extreme fluctuations of hope and anxiety. In the morning a proclamation explained how Wyatt had refused to treat with the royal commissioners sent to him – would not her subjects wonder at the strength of their Queen's forces when she revealed that she was willing to negotiate with a

[2] Proc. 388/424. The headnote in Hughes & Larkin, II, 3, summarizes the evidence for the proclamation of Mary's title and accession. Later related proclamations, *Add. Procs.*, nos. 6, 7.

[3] The phrase is that of D. M. Loades whose *Two Tudor Conspiracies* (Cambridge, 1965), is an excellent guide to the events.

[4] Proc. 398/—. General orders for its publication, PRO, SP 11/2/5; for its publication in the area of the Council of the North, copied in York CA Dept, YC/A 21, fos. 28v–30; for the Council in Wales, *HMC 31: 13th Rpt, App. IV (Corp. of Hereford MSS)*, p. 318.

[5] Loades, *Two Tudor Conspiracies*, chapters 1–3.

[6] *Ibid.* pp. 58–9. Proc. 399/440.

[7] Proc. 400/—.

[8] *Add. Procs.*, no. 9; Loades, *Two Tudor Conspiracies*, pp. 66, 70.

rebel?[9] By the afternoon her resolve had stiffened, and so she and many lords rode in harness into London where she gained much popular support when she promised to submit the marriage to Parliament's consideration. The proclamation issued that afternoon did not repeat the conciliatory offer, but its report that the rising in the midlands had been prevented reveals the source of her newly found confidence.[10] News of the detection of the conspiracy in Devon arrived a few days later, and so a proclamation which conveyed that news was published on 3 February, adding an offer of a reward for Wyatt's arrest.[11]

Wyatt launched his assault on London on 7 February, but by late afternoon he was a prisoner. Royal proclamations had no role that day; the military commanders used heralds to order him to surrender. The proclamation on 18 February was part of the process for rounding up any other supporters of his who had not already been apprehended.[12] Philip could now arrive unimpeded, and so a proclamation was issued on 1 March which ordered that his retinue be received with courtesy.[13]

Proclamations had a much different part to play in the other rebellions in Mary's reign. The plans for Dudley's rebellion had been hatched in November 1555, and by the following spring the government had learned some of the details. A series of carefully planned arrests was begun on 18 March 1556, and the interrogations which followed revealed the details of the invasion which Dudley and other exiles in France had planned to launch. So complete was the collapse on the part of the conspirators in England that the emigrés' plans never came to fruition. Nevertheless a proclamation of 1 April condemned them as traitors, and ordered watches along the seacoasts.[14] Thomas Stafford's plot was more personal, and when he actually invaded England and captured Scarborough Castle he had himself proclaimed protector of the realm. The proclamation on 30 April 1557 seems to have been issued as soon as the news of his capture by the Earl of Westmorland reached London.[15]

In both of these rebellions, the proclamations were issued only when the threat was over and the plans crushed. Whereas it was

[9] Proc. 401/442.
[10] Proc. 402/443; Loades, *Two Tudor Conspiracies*, pp. 64–8.
[11] Proc. 403/444.
[12] *Add. Procs.*, no. 10. A proclamation on aliens about this time, 404/445, might be related.   [13] Proc. 405/446.
[14] Proc. 426/466; Loades, *Two Tudor Conspiracies*, pp. 171ff.
[15] Proc. 433/473; Loades, *Two Tudor Conspiracies*, pp. 173–4.

acting under pressure during Wyatt's rebellion, the government played from strength in the declarations against Dudley and Stafford, and thus its announcements were positive rather than negative propaganda. The only other proclamation in these matters concerned the localized problems in the marches against Scotland. It offered a pardon to any of the Greymes family who within a specified period of time would enter into sureties before the Warden of the Western Marches to keep the peace there, and a similar offer was made again a few months later, not in a royal proclamation but in a local proclamation at the Queen's command.[16]

Elizabeth's reign

Behind the rebellion of the northern Earls of Northumberland and Westmorland in 1569 lay a varied complex of social, religious, and economic grievances. Suspicions about their activities had arisen early in the autumn, but the Queen was also suspicious of the loyalties of her President in the North, the Earl of Sussex, so that no one was sure of the exact state of matters there. When Sussex became convinced of the Earls' rebellious intent he issued a proclamation on his own authority which denounced them as rebels, and then he proclaimed them traitors again on the delegated authority of the Queen.[17] His proclamations were a part of the process by which the rebellion was crushed.

A royal proclamation which denounced the Earls as traitors was published first in the Queen's presence on 24 November at Windsor and then throughout the realm. The role of the proclamation – issued when the rebellion was actually being crushed in the north – was to warn of the Earls' treasons and to exhort all subjects to remain in due obedience.[18] Once it had been totally crushed, a proclamation was issued which offered the lesser participants in the uprising a royal pardon if they submitted.[19]

[16] Proc. 421/460, transmitted with a letter to the Warden, *APC*, v, 138–9. Delegation for the later proclamation, *ibid.* pp. 165–6.

[17] A good summary which used the earlier accounts is in Read, *Cecil*, chapter 23. Sussex's earlier proclamation is copied in records with dates of both 13 and 15 November, e.g., BL, Cotton MS Caligula C 1, fo. 350; York CA Dept, YC/A 24, fos. 167v–168, printed in Raine, vi, 170–1. His later proclamation is —/646, with authorization in *HMC 9: Salisbury (Cecil) I*, no. 1426.

[18] Proc. 567/645. Another proclamation on the scene in the north about the same time had a more direct bearing on the military actions: by the Deputy at Berwick, BL, Cotton MS Caligula B v, fo. 89v.

[19] Proc. 568/647. The series of printed articles to guide officers in taking the oath is proc. 569/648, not truly a royal proclamation as is clear from the instructions copied in

The rebellion of Leonard Dacres a few months later was a last gasp, and the Wardens in the Western Marches quickly put it down. No royal proclamation was issued during the uprising, but several local officers made proclamations denouncing the traitors.[20] Afterwards a royal proclamation of pardon was issued, just as had been done in the principal rising by the Earls.[21]

The only plot in which proclamations had a part in Elizabeth's reign was that of Anthony Babington, whose offer to assassinate Queen Elizabeth seemingly received Mary Stuart's consent in July 1586.[22] The government's intelligence was accurate, and when in August Babington suspected their knowledge and fled, a proclamation was prepared which ordered his arrest.[23] His arrest and examination led to a quick trial and execution, but Mary's complicity made her liable to trial according to the statute of 1585 'for the surety of the Queen's Majesty's most royal person'. That law ordered that there should be a trial by a commission composed of privy councillors and others, and that the sentence was to be published in a royal proclamation under the Great Seal.[24]

Mary's trial at Fotheringay lasted from 12 to 15 October, and was then adjourned to the Star Chamber where the final deliberations and sentence were pronounced on 25 and 31 October. Parliament began to sit on 29 October and spent nearly all its time in urging the Queen to publish the sentence.[25] It was a newly elected Parliament, since the one before had been prorogued to a date which the government felt was too late for the urgency of the process. A royal proclamation had been used to announce that the former Parliament was dissolved and to call elections for the new.[26] But the Queen

Raine, VII, 7–8. Proceedings of the commissioners, including an additional proclamation by Sussex, are in York CA Dept, YC/A 24, fo. 195v, printed in Raine, VII, 6–7. An unsuccessful attempt to plead the Queen's pardon in the proclamation to stay his prosecution for the catholic manifestations in the rebellion is noted in a case in *Depositions and other Ecclesiastical Proceedings from the Courts of Durham, Extending from 1311 to the Reign of Elizabeth* (Surtees Society, XII; London, 1845), pp. 133–5.

[20] BL, Cotton MS Caligula C I, fos. 233, 235; PRO, SP 15/15/39.
[21] Proc. 570/651.
[22] The question of her consent will always be a debated point, but seems clear to most writers. A detailed guide to the events of 1586–7 in regard to Mary is in Read, *Burghley*, chapter 18.
[23] Proc. 683/788, extant in manuscript only (BL, Lansd. MS 49/24).
[24] 27 Eliz. I, c. 1.
[25] Read, *Burghley*, pp. 351ff.; J. E. Neale, *Elizabeth I and her Parliaments, 1584–1603* (London, 1957), 103–44. Copious reprints of the documents urging the publication of the proclamation are in Camden, pp. 363–9, and in Ralph Holinshed, *Holinshed's Chronicles of England, Scotland, and Ireland* (ed. Henry Ellis; 6 vols.; London, 1808), IV, 930–40.
[26] Proc. 684/789, the only time a royal proclamation was used for this purpose.

resisted the pressure from the new Parliament to publish the sentence. Work was far advanced on the text of the proclamation, however, and on 30 November Secretary Davison sent to Lord Burghley both the Queen's suggested alterations and the previously engrossed text 'which will require some time for the alteration thereof'. Burghley was at Court at eight the next morning with the amended text, and the Queen approved the alterations after she rose at ten. The text was ready at three and was dispatched to be engrossed on parchment, but when it was ready she decided not to sign it.[27]

Elizabeth had decided to delay the publication of the sentence and not to publish it when Parliament was sitting. Soon after its adjournment on 2 December, a special form of writ was prepared so that the greatest solemnity would accompany its proclamation.[28] The chronicler Stow reported that the Lord Mayor of London

'was assisted with diverse earls, barons, the aldermen of London in their scarlet, the principal officers of the city, the greatest number of the gentlemen of the best account in and about the city, with the number of 80 of the most gravest and worshipfulest citizens in coats of velvet, and chains of gold, all on horseback in most solemn and stately manner...'

He reported that bells were rung, bonfires lighted, and psalms sung in the streets,[29] and one can note celebrations elsewhere as well.[30] This was one of the two proclamations which was sealed directly with the Great Seal, and the writ ordered that it be returned to the Chancery with an endorsement that it had been proclaimed locally.[31] While Mary Stuart awaited her execution, a rumor that she had escaped spread, and a proclamation on 6 February warned all officers to stop rumors (without mentioning any specific rumor) or else be punished themselves 'as the first author and inventor thereof'.[32] The story was not true, and on 8 February 1587 the execution was carried out.

Royal proclamations were also used in the aftermath of the rebellion of the Earl of Essex and his followers in February 1601. On Sunday 8 February, the actual day of the rising, the proclamation of rebellion was made in London by Garter King-of-Arms, the Knight

[27] PRO, SP 12/195/28, 12/195/40.
[28] Copied in Corp. London RO, Journal xxii, fos. 67v–68v: 'precipimus quod crastino die ante meridiem visis presentibus...publice proclamari faciatis...quam vobis una cum presentibus mittimus magno sigillo nostro Anglie sigillata.'
[29] Stow, p. 1240.
[30] John Latimer, *Sixteenth-Century Bristol* (Bristol, 1908), p. 84, where on its proclamation on 26 December bonfires were lighted.
[31] Notation of payment of 4d for a box in which to return it, and of 2s filing fee, in Exeter CRO, Rcvrs Accts 28–9 Eliz.   [32] Proc. 688/792.

Marshall, Thomas Lord Burghley, and the Earl of Cumberland. Arrests followed, and the incident was controlled quickly, so that the royal proclamation on the following day announced the arrests and commanded a special vigilance for capturing spreaders of rumors.[33] Essex's popularity meant that it would be difficult to deal with the general unrest,[34] and so on 15 February a proclamation was issued to command 'loose people' with no business in London to leave the city 'upon pain of death by martial law to be executed upon them' by provost marshals.[35] A flood of writing on the rising, much of it favorable to Essex, had also to be dealt with, and a proclamation on 5 April offered a reward to anyone who would give information leading to the arrest of those who spread the libels.[36]

The examination of the men who supported Essex always asked whether they had heard the proclamation, but the question meant the proclamation on the day of the rising and not the royal proclamation a day later.[37] On 28 February a man named Woodhouse was hanged 'for speaking and libelling against the Queen's proclamation and apprehending of the Earl of Essex', but there was no indication of the authority upon which his case was based.[38]

Rebellions of a less general nature were the subjects of two other Elizabethan proclamations. In 1560 she offered a pardon to men in the Tynedale and Redesdale area in the Middle Marches who had risen up.[39] There were many proclamations for Ireland, but they were published there only, the exception being a royal proclamation on 31 March 1599 which announced the reasons why a force had been prepared to go into Ireland and subdue the rebels. The Earl of Essex was to lead the expedition, yet he was not named and was referred to as 'the minister both of our justice and mercy, whose valor, wisdom, and success in other public actions' made him the man to strike terror into the rebels.[40]

---

[33] Proc. 808/913.
[34] The corresponding unpopularity of the government's actions can be seen in the often cited verse (e.g., PRO, SP 12/278/23):

> Little Cecil trips up & down,
> He rules between court & crown,
> With his brother Burghley clown,
> In his great fox-furred gown;
> With the long proclamation
> He swore he sav'd the town,
> Is it not likely?

[35] Proc. 809/916.　　　　　　　　　　　　　[36] Proc. 810/920.
[37] E.g., PRO, SP 12/278/45; 12/279/4, 75; 12/283A/9.
[38] Stow, p. 1408; Hughes & Larkin, III, 233 note 1.
[39] Proc. 474/534.　　　　　　　　　　　　　[40] Proc. 798/Irish 141.

PEACE AND ORDER

Just as there were sufficient provisions in the laws to deal with rebellions and plots, so most of the problems which threatened the maintenance of peace and order had been identified and foreseen in early legislation. In such cases proclamations were a useful public means for calling the existing laws to everybody's attention, and for demanding their enforcement. These general peace-keeping proclamations will be considered first in this section.[41] But in other instances there were new problems which called for new remedies. There had been many technological advances in the development of guns and weapons, and the general threats to peace which they offered were compounded when the government provided such arms for its military forces. The severity of the disorders consequent upon the demobilization of a large number of soldiers and mariners during the hostilities with Spain similarly had not been foreseen. In both cases royal proclamations were used to define new offenses and to provide more rigorous administrative procedures for remedying the problems, and when on occasion the danger was perceived as particularly great, the normal legal processes were suspended and martial law invoked.

Of the more general peace-keeping regulations, only one constituted a general command to enforce a large number of statutes. Mary's proclamation in 1555 dealt with nine topics including vagabonds and prompted some local officers to action.[42] The only time when Elizabeth followed the precedent was in 1561, but the breviate of thirteen statutes was not issued as a proclamation, even though a proclamation in the following year ordered the list to be enforced.[43]

Several of the proclamations for keeping the peace generally were occasioned by troubles in London. A proclamation in 1559 was prompted by quarrels between Englishmen and the servants of the French Ambassador, and another in 1590 by a riot in which apprentices broke into Lincoln's Inn – both issued presumably because more than one jurisdiction was involved.[44] Elizabeth forbade robbing

---

[41] Other proclamations concerned with keeping the peace are considered elsewhere because of fuller contexts: abettors of pirates, in Chapter 4; informers, in Chapter 6; peace in churchyards, in Chapter 8.

[42] Proc. 420/459. Notations of watches and of general enforcement throughout Middlesex, in GLC (Middx) RO, Acc. 759/1; of inquiries in South Mimms, *ibid*. Acc. 802; of supplementary orders, Norf. & Norw. RO, Norwich Mayor's Ct Bk 7, fos. 121–2.

[43] See Appendix 2 for the breviate. Mentioned in proc. 494/565, but incorrectly identified in Hughes & Larkin, II, 193 note 1.

[44] Procs. 462/513 and 725/826 respectively.

68

before her coronation, as some were inclined to do in the hope that the offense would be forgiven in the customary pardon, and enlisted help in arresting a knight who had escaped from a debtors' prison in London.[45] Another proclamation cited 'evil disposed persons in and near the city of London' who armed themselves to resist the servers of processes from the law courts, drawing on a precedent in a proclamation of Henry VIII to order their arrest. Outside London the enforcement was entrusted to the Justices of Assize or Oyer and Terminer, and to the Presidents of the Councils in the North and in Wales.[46]

Elizabeth and her Council were enraged over the actions of certain men who posed as royal messengers, carrying forged letters which ordered an unsuspecting victim to make an appearance before the Council. The messenger would then demand a fee for delivering the letters, or offer to excuse the victim from an appearance if he would make some cash arrangement with the messenger. The right to punish such offenders already existed at law,[47] but when it was found that four messengers had extorted over £3,000 in six years in the 1570s, it was decided that exemplary punishment in the Star Chamber was appropriate, and the offenders were pilloried and lost their ears.[48] When the matter became acute again in the 1590s, the Council asked the Attorney General and Solicitor General how exemplary punishment might be imposed.[49] When punishment in the regular courts and Star Chamber, and the issue of a placard to all counties in 1591, did not seem to be bringing about a reform, the Council redoubled its efforts to arrest the offenders in the winter of 1596–7.[50] One of the men arrested offered to reveal the details of the practices to the Council, and soon a proclamation was being drafted.[51]

The proclamation of 3 May 1596 offered a practical remedy when

---

[45] *Add. Procs.*, no. 13, and proc. 724/— respectively.

[46] Proc. 531/609.

[47] Sir Edward Coke, *The Third Part of the Institutes Of the Laws of England: Concerning High Treason, and other Pleas of the Crown, and Criminall causes* (London, 1644), p. 133, citing 33 Henry VIII, c. 1.

[48] Reported in *Annals Ref.*, II, ii, 205–6. Orders to apprehend men counterfeiting licenses to beg, *APC*, IX, 304–5, 311, 314, 321, 341. A precedent from 1488 for punishment in the Star Chamber, Huntington Libr., Ellesmere MS 2768, fo. 3.

[49] *APC*, xx, 80–1.

[50] Placard, *APC*, xx, 242. Order to Attorney General to proceed in Star Chamber *ore tenus* against two confessed offenders, *ibid.* xxi, 473. Order to the Treasurer of the Navy to put two of the men convicted in Star Chamber in the galleys, *ibid.* xxiv, 486–7. Arrests ordered, *ibid.* xxv, 130, 195, 270.

[51] Walter Pepper, who had been sent to the galleys in 1593, offered to inform; PRO, SP 12/256/87. Proclamation drafted by late March noted in *APC*, xxv, 312–13.

SECURITY

it informed all subjects of the practices, and told them not to make a composition with a messenger, nor to pay any fees until the messenger accompanied them to the Council where the fees would be allowed. It also warned against counterfeit licenses for begging and authorized local officers to void suspected licenses.[52] Not only were further cases brought in Star Chamber on the basis of the proclamation, but there is evidence that local officers were diligent in examining the licenses to beg.[53]

There were proclamations to suppress seditious rumors in both reigns, and although suppressing rumors was always a paramount concern it is difficult to discover what in those particular rumors called forth proclamations. Mary issued proclamations on rumors in 1553 and 1558, and evidence remains of their enforcement at Norwich and Bicester.[54] The Elizabethan proclamation on rumors which was issued shortly before the execution of Mary Queen of Scots has already been noted.[55]

A concern for maintaining order was probably a partial motive for the proclamations of both Queens which enforced the statutes on hunting and forbade killing game near the royal parks, but no evidence on their enforcement has been found.[56]

Weapons

The possession of a gun multiplied many times over the potential which a dissolute subject had for disrupting the peace, particularly if it was one of the small guns increasingly produced in the last half of the century, since they were easy to conceal. The military advantages of the weapons of the new technology were increasingly obvious, and gradually guns replaced long bows as the weapons of the army.[57] The more widespread the distribution of guns, the greater chance there was for illegal uses in robbery, poaching and other crimes.

[52] Proc. 779/882. The Council had become aware of incidents of forged licenses by late March, *APC*, xxv, 320.
[53] Cases before the proclamation noted in *ibid.* xxvii, 54, and Stow, p. 1281; afterwards, PRO, Star Chamber 5/A/47/27, B/33/21 (in which the defendant argued that his offense was before the proclamation). In normal courts after the proclamation, noted in *APC*, xxvii, 137–8; on begging licenses, Kent AO, Sandwich MS Sa/AC 6, fos. 235v, 239v.
[54] Norf. & Norw. RO, Norwich Mayor's Ct Bk 6, fo. 294; noted for Bicester in *APC*, v, 30.　　　[55] Above, p. 66.
[56] Mary, procs. 411/451a, 425/465; Elizabeth, 816/929. A proclamation preserving game issued on the authority of the Council in Wales, *HMC 31: 13th Rpt, App. IV (Corp. of Hereford MSS)*, pp. 336–7.
[57] C. G. Cruickshank, *Elizabeth's Army* (2nd ed.; Oxford, 1966), pp. 102–3.

Both Mary and Elizabeth issued proclamations early in their reigns to curb the disorderly use of swords in churchyards, and Elizabeth's proclamations on apparel regulated the length of swords in the spirit of sumptuary legislation rather than for maintaining the peace.[58] But both those uses were for special purposes and represent the only proclamations on weapons which were not concerned with the new guns. Gun powder was triumphing over blade and bow.[59]

The statutes on fire arms which antedated both reigns were generally adequate for preventing most disorders. Only men worth £100 were entitled to bear arms, and the minimum lengths of a yard for handguns and three-quarters of a yard for hackbuts or demihags were intended to prevent the concealment of weapons.[60] The single Marian proclamation on guns seems to have been issued after a shot nearly wounded the preacher at Paul's Cross, and it and the earliest Elizabethan proclamation on guns merely ordered that the existing legislation be enforced.[61]

A proclamation in 1575 ordered the enforcement of the laws, but added a new procedure to help detect the illegal possession of dags and pistols. It ordered victualers and innkeepers to forbid lodgers to bring weapons into their establishments, and to seize the offenders and the guns and deliver them over to the nearest Justice of the Peace.[62] Because the statute already authorized any subject to do those things, the proclamation only imposed a special obligation on the keepers of lodgings, and a special penalty of being disabled from their occupation for a year for non-compliance. Another provision of the proclamation allowed men of quality to carry weapons if they were displayed openly, and so partially dispensed from the law which had given that right only to men worth £100 per annum.

Another proclamation on 26 July 1579 added more innovative procedures on guns. Shots had been fired near Elizabeth's barge which was carrying her and the French Ambassador on the river.[63] However much that incident provoked the proclamation, the

---

[58] Mary, proc. 432/472; Elizabeth, 486/553, in which swords were only one among many topics.

[59] The government continued to stress the obligation of all subjects to practice on the long bow, but the enforcement was left to patentees.

[60] 33 Henry VIII, c. 6, the primary statute.

[61] *Add. Procs.*, no. 11, and proc. 459/511 respectively. A possible occasion for the former was noted in Stow, p. 1056; for the latter, in Bucks. as noted in Hughes & Larkin, II, 116, and in London, noted in a roll of memorable events there in Kent AO, Sandwich MS Sa/ZB 6.

[62] Proc. 611/701, drafted by Secretary Smith as noted in Hughes & Larkin, II, 398 headnote.   [63] *Annals Ref.*, II, ii, 297; Holinshed, *Chronicles*, IV, 425.

thoroughness of the provisions suggests that the government was well aware of the extent of the problem and had been giving some thought to the matter. Not only did the proclamation order that no guns be fired within two miles of a royal residence, but it also commanded searches for the small dags and that the larger pieces be fired only at authorized places and on proper military occasions such as the common musters. It also prohibited the wearing of privy coats of defense which some wore to intimidate unarmed subjects. The proclamation commanded that inquiries be held, and that any weapon used improperly was to be seized and sent to a royal officer of ordnance.[64]

The activities which were demanded of the local officials were entirely consistent with their desire to maintain order in their localities, and not surprisingly a good bit of evidence about their compliance is to be found. A jury convened at Norwich presented four men for illegal possession of pocket dags, and the officers there both assigned a place for authorized practice with the larger guns and convened a second jury.[65] The officials in Rye prepared a multipart charge for the constables to guide them in enforcing the proclamation, not unlike the local proclamation issued by the Lord Mayor of London for the same purpose, or the precepts issued in York.[66] The officers in Southampton went beyond the orders in the proclamation, taking recognizances in the sum of £5 from two men, with the condition that they neither make, mend, nor import pocket dags.[67] A man who wore a privy coat was arrested in Coventry, and the Council referred to the Attorney General the case of one Richard Lawles of Kent who had spoken against the proclamation.[68] Only in London was there some difficulty in enforcement, when a gentleman who served the Marquis of Northampton was stopped by the searchers appointed by the City to detect offenders, and questioned their authority.[69]

The last proclamations on handguns were issued in 1594 and 1600. The earlier of these cited the proclamations which had already been issued and ordered that they be put in 'speedy execution'. It ordered that the Justices convene juries at their next sessions, and that the

[64] Proc. 641/739.
[65] Norf. & Norw. RO, Norwich Mayor's Ct Bk 10, fos. 430, 432, 450, 451, 466, 468, 484, 485, 487.
[66] E. Sussex RO, Rye MS 1/4, fos. 305–305v; Corp. London RO, Journal xxi, fo. 41v; York CA Dept, YC/A 27, fo. 177v, printed partly in Raine, viii, 15.
[67] Southampton CRO, SC 9/3/4, unfoliated but between entries for 17 August and 16 September 1579.   [68] APC, xi, 394, 295–6 respectively.
[69] BL, Lansd. MS 32/6, with further orders for London in APC, xi, 403.

custodes rotulorum and recorders certify their compliance into the Star Chamber.[70] The proclamation in 1600 merely recited the relevant statutes on guns and ordered inquiries at the next sessions.[71]

Not only were the last two proclamations less specific than the earlier ones, but there seems to have been no local enforcement which cited them as the authority. The lack of evidence can be explained by several considerations. First, the statutes in force already denied the privilege of shooting to the lower ranks of society. A case in King's Bench in 1592 held that dags fell within the scope of the Henrician law on guns even though they were not mentioned in it, because they derived from the earlier forbidden weapons, and because they had been so explained by sundry proclamations.[72] Second, the new provisions in the proclamations seem to have been swallowed up into routine procedures, so that a reiterated charge was not needed. The obligation to make searches, as in the proclamation of 1579, was included by William Lambarde in his book for constables, and charges for inquiries on guns in leets can also be found.[73] The actual enforcement of the proclamations could then take place merely by citing the statutes as the authority, as in an indictment. But a third argument suggests to the contrary why little reformation might have followed. The proclamation in 1594 had ordered the enforcement of the earlier proclamations, but how many jurisdictions had a copy of the fifteen-year-old edict? If the proclamation had been posted as ordered, there was little chance of its survival, and since the later proclamation did not repeat the orders it was probably ignored.

Vagabonds

The royal proclamations against vagabonds fall into two distinct categories.[74] One series enforced the statute of 1572, allowing a few days grace period for rogues and masterless men to leave London before the full rigor of the law would be invoked. The others, issued in the years 1589–98, were of primary importance in the govern-

[70] Proc. 766/871.　　　　[71] Proc. 804/910.

[72] Coke, *Reports* v, 72 (St John's Case, Trin. 34 Eliz.). A case not based on a proclamation, but which states that the offenders wore the weapons *in terrorem populi*, is in Hawarde, *Les Reportes del Cases in Camera Stellata*, pp. 41–2.

[73] Constables, cited by Hughes & Larkin, II, 144 note 3; for leets, Huntington Libr., Ellesmere MS 481, fo. 243v.

[74] For orders for vagabonds to avoid the Court in time of plague, see Chapter 7. A Marian proclamation which ordered the statutes enforced and announced a commission for that purpose, 445/490.

ment's attempts to meet the problems which followed on the demobilization of returning soldiers and mariners. They are of special
interest because they invoked martial law.

In 1576 the first of the series of proclamations which ordered the
enforcement of the statute on vagabonds was published, occasioned
by troubles in London, Westminster, Southwark, and surrounding
areas. Having commanded them to leave the area, it provided for a
method of testing for compliance when it authorized special searches
in inns, tippling houses, and other places of play and gaming in and
around London. The Mayor of London was specifically authorized
to reproclaim 'this present proclamation in all places within the said
city and suburbs so often as to him shall seem needful and con-
vienent'.[75] It was reproclaimed at least four times – in 1579, 1587,
1591 and 1596 – and in those later years as in the first, precepts by
the Lord Mayor were issued, usually containing an indication that
the Queen was personally interested in seeing the problem resolved.[76]
Because the proclamations primarily enforced the law, any prosecutions would not indicate the special charge.

The demobilization of men who had served in a military capacity
outside the realm was a serious problem in 1589 and later years. The
government's intent was to move the men quickly through the ports,
preventing disorders and unlawful assemblies, and to direct them
back to their native districts and to see that they were reintegrated as
working members of their communities. But many of the men were
reluctant to return home before the arrears in their pay had been
made good, and others were tempted by the pleasures of London.
Their numbers were swollen by vagabonds who sought to give their
begging a cloak of respectability by posing as wounded or maimed
soldiers. Royal proclamations had an important part to play in the
years until 1598, at which time a statute was passed against 'lewd
and wandering persons' who posed as soldiers.[77]

The fleet which had sailed toward Spain and Portugal under the
command of Sir John Norris and Sir Francis Drake returned in 1589,
carrying many men who had the plague. The Lords of the Council
issued one of their own proclamations to protect the Court, and a
royal proclamation was issued which set out the procedures to be

[75] Proc. 622/714; Mayor's precept and supplementary orders, Corp. London RO,
Journal xx, part 2, fos. 278v, 326–326v.
[76] In 1579, proc. 637/735. In 1587, 692/—, with precept in Corp. London RO,
Journal xxii, fo. 134v, and royal charge in PRO, SP 12/202/5. In 1591, 736/—, with
precept in Corp. London RO, Journal xxiii, fo. 3. In 1596, 777/716.
[77] 39 Eliz. I, c. 17.

followed by the men for presenting their claims for back pay.[78] The men were unwilling to leave for home without their pay, and as the number of unlawful assemblies grew, about a dozen of them were hanged, presumably on the towns' and justices' authority to punish unlawful assemblies.[79]

The problem was intensified because the return of the expedition to France which had been led by Lord Willoughby was expected.[80] A royal proclamation on 13 November 1589 ordered the men to go to a Justice and receive a passport within two days, and then to return home at no slower a rate than twelve miles a day unless they were maimed. A statute enacted in 1572 had established the requirement for passports, but the imposition of a fixed rate of travel was novel, as was the requirement that the former masters should receive the soldiers back into employment. But the most unusual provision was the announcement that Provost Marshals were to be appointed to punish any disobedient soldiers by martial law.[81]

The first use of martial law on civilians had been ordered in Ireland in 1556, and in England during Mary's French wars. Provost Marshals had been used in London in 1570, and from 1585 onward they were inseparably associated with the Lords Lieutenant, serving the latter in the more menial role of hangmen. Elizabeth's uneasiness over invoking the extraordinary procedures of martial law was revealed in her instructions to the commissioners which set a three months' limit on their activities.[82]

The Queen's reluctance seems to have been in inverse proportion to the enthusiasm with which the extra authority was received by the local officers. The procedures adopted locally after the proclamation and commission, and the desire of the local officers to have the work continued, reflect their appreciation for means which they must have seen as appropriate to the problem. Yet the only examples of punishment which I have seen were in accordance with normal procedures at law,[83] and I have found no report of summary executions by

[78] Conciliar proclamation, 712/815; royal, 715/817. There was a good deal of consultation with the officials in London before the latter, *APC*, xvii, 453–4; xviii, 14, 54–6.
[79] Stow, cited in Lindsay Boynton, 'The Tudor Provost Marshal', *EHR*, lvii (1962), 444. Punishments in London, Kingston upon Thames, and Middlesex.
[80] Conciliar preparation, *APC*, xviii, 210–12, 214.
[81] 14 Eliz. I, c. 5; proc. 716/818; commissions and letters of instruction cited from *APC* in Boynton, 'The Tudor Provost Marshal', p. 445; also PRO, SP 12/228/9, 17; SP 38/1, fos. 37–8; instructions in *HMC 71: Finch I*, p. 29 (for Kent). Commissions for Essex, Herts., Kent, Middx, Surrey, Sussex, Hants. Negligent officers were threatened with punishment in the Star Chamber.
[82] Boynton, 'The Tudor Provost Marshal', pp. 440–3, 445.
[83] *Ibid.* pp. 445–50.

martial law. I suspect that such executions did occur, and that the silence of the record only shows that no comment seemed necessary. The measures did seem to cleanse the area of vagabonds temporarily.

Later proclamations on vagabonds show a shift in emphasis and an awareness of the complexity of the problem. A proclamation in June 1591 was occasioned by disorders in and around London, and the Queen announced in it the appointment of Provost Marshals to apprehend and punish all 'such as shall not be readily reformed and corrected by ordinary officers of justice'.[84] The proclamation in November 1591 distinguished between soldiers with passports who were to be given charitable relief, ordinary vagabonds who were to be punished according to the statutes, and vagabonds who claimed to have served abroad but had no passports, who were to be indicted as felons and deserters. The effect of these threats would have been to make the punishments for vagabonds which had been set in law for second offenses applicable on the first offense. It announced that Provost Marshals were to be appointed, but only to apprehend suspects who were to be punished by ordinary justice.[85] In February 1594 another proclamation was occasioned by the large number of Irishmen in London and near the Court. All natives of Ireland except those in certain exempt occupations were commanded to leave England or be punished as vagabonds. An increased vigilance at the ports resulted.[86]

Martial law was invoked again after a tumult broke out at Tower Hill on 29 June 1595. The Queen was already concerned about unlawful assemblies in London, and so on 4 July 1595 the proclamation which had been issued in June 1591 was reissued, with its command for punishment by the Provosts by martial law.[87] Sir Thomas Wilford was appointed Provost Marshal for London, and quickly apprehended five unruly youths who were indicted, arraigned, and convicted of high treason on 22 July and executed on the 24th.[88] Two conflicting dates survive for the commission to execute martial law, one before the executions (18 July) and one after (28 July), but in any

---

[84] Proc. 735/845.   [85] Proc. 740/840.

[86] Proc. 762/867. PRO, SP 12/247/66, 12/248/34. Chester CRO, ML 1/59–62, 64–6, 70, 84; ML 5/123, 222–4, 235–41.

[87] Proc. 769/873, a reissue of 735/845.

[88] Tumult and reference to treason, Stow, pp. 1280–1, used by Boynton, 'The Tudor Provost Marshal', pp. 451–2. The examination in PRO, SP 12/252/94 reveals that the men threatened to use the gallows on the Lord Mayor. Indictment, PRO, SP 12/253/48, for raising an insurrection. In the city's records, the offenses are variously described as tumults, riots, unlawful assemblies, sedition, and rebellion; Corp. London RO, Journal XXIV, fos. 25v, 37.

case martial law was not used on the five youths. A letter which was to supplement the commission was dispatched to the Justices in London, Middlesex, Surrey and Essex, ordering them to erect gallows which the Provost Marshals were to use for executing those 'vagrant and seditious persons as otherwise fear not to offend for other punishment but are found incorrigible'.[89] There appear to be no reports of further executions, nor of any which followed the publication in September 1598 of another royal proclamation, occasioned by disorders in London, which similarly threatened the appointment of Provost Marshals to punish by martial law those who would be corrected by no other.[90]

A final proclamation on vagabonds was issued in 1600, ordering the enforcement of the statute in 1598 which made it felony to pretend to having been a soldier or mariner.[91] It ordered the constables to certify their enforcement of the laws to the Justices of the Peace. Meanwhile London continued to use the Provost Marshals, but neither the office nor martial law was mentioned again in a proclamation.[92]

[89] Date of 18th, Huntington Libr., Ellesmere MS 5033, and PRO, Index, 4208, fo. 2; of 28th, Corp. London RO, Journal xxiv, fo. 38.

[90] Proc. 796/899. Precept, Corp. London RO, Journal xxiv, fo. 327.

[91] Proc. 800/905, treating other matters than vagabonds as well.

[92] E.g., Corp. London RO, Journal xxv, fo. 82 which antedates the proclamation by a few days; Boynton, 'The Tudor Provost Marshal', pp. 453ff.

4

FOREIGN AFFAIRS

The proclamations on foreign affairs concentrated on different locales than those on domestic security – away from London's central importance in the latter – on coastal counties and nearby seas where English attacks on the ships of other nations caused so many problems, and on the Court where the Queens and the foreign ambassadors discussed such problems and the more serious matters of war and peace. Rather than consider foreign affairs nation by nation, they will here be treated in the contexts of war, foreign relations other than naval matters, and sea-related problems.

WAR

England was at war with France in 1557–9 and again in 1562–4, and with Spain from the mid-1580s onward. The thirty royal proclamations which were used in the wars played varying roles and were dictated by the course of events, yet considered as a whole they fell into three categories.[1]

A small number were used in the preparatory stages of the wars. Although heralds made the actual proclamations of war, royal proclamations could be used to explain the nation's involvement, and this was as near as they came to being propaganda. They were also used to command the men who had been pressed into service to report for duty, and to order that deserters be punished.

Royal proclamations had no direct part in the hostilities since all the wars were conducted abroad. When there was a threat that England might be invaded, royal proclamations ordered men to resist. They also denied Englishmen the right to trade with nations with which England was at war, because there were not wanting those who would profit from the war; the corresponding right of

[1] Elizabeth did not use a proclamation when she sent forces into the Low Countries in 1585, but did issue an explanation. See *STC*, items 9188ff.

attacking and profiting from the shipping of the enemy was similarly granted in proclamations.

The conclusion of the war and the immediate post-war adjustments were invariably announced in the proclamation which published the peace. We have already seen the problems which arose from demobilizing the soldiers and mariners, and will deal here with the resumption of trade. A consideration of the proclamations issued in particular wars will make these and other roles clearer.

The wars with France

Only those subjects with an appalling unawareness of political realities would not have realized that England's war with France in 1557–9 was the fruit of Mary's marriage with Philip and the subordination of England's foreign policy to Spain's. A proclamation on 7 June 1557 which explained the war said nothing of this, however; it merely recited how the French King had assisted the rebellions and plots which had risen so frequently in the reign.[2] England's lack of success was to lead to the loss of Calais and also raised the spectre of an invasion of England. To neutralize the might of a French fleet about which the government learned in June 1557, a proclamation authorized Englishmen to go to the seas and attack French shipping, and this was reissued almost verbatim the following month with an added authorization to attack Scottish ships.[3] The proclamations allowed those who took spoils to keep the entire proceeds, and because that disallowed the customary shares for officers in the Admiralty and other special jurisdictions the Council had to insist that the towns along the coast allow the men to depart unimpeded.[4]

The fear of invasion was particularly acute from January 1558 onward. The Queen issued letters patent to the Marquis of Winchester making him Lieutenant for many counties with authority to punish by martial law.[5] She commanded country gentlemen to return home from London to help prepare their counties, under penalties of fine and imprisonment, forbade the importing of French wines during the hostilities, and authorized the seizure of the goods

[2] Proc. 434/474. See R. B. Wernham, *Before the Armada. The Emergence of the English Nation 1485–1588* (London, 1966), pp. 228ff. The formalities in declaring the war are in Hughes & Larkin, II, 77 headnote.
[3] Procs. 435/475, 436/476.   [4] PRO, SP 11/11/25.
[5] His patent was printed and then proclaimed in London, but although included in Steele and Hughes & Larkin as 441/486 it was not a royal proclamation.

and chattels of Frenchmen who had not left the realm as the proclamation of 7 June had commanded.[6] Martial law was threatened
in three proclamations: in March 1558 for men who had been
pressed for service but did not report; in June for anyone who kept
any heretical or seditious books which were intended to precede the
expected invasion; and in July against men who attempted to avoid
service in the forces by pretending to be watermen whom the Queen
had exempted from duty because of their importance at home.[7]
Because it was discovered that some men were using the authorization to go to the seas as a pretext for evading military service, a proclamation in May 1558 required a license for all ships leaving the
ports, with penalties of imprisonment and the forfeiture of their ships
and goods for offenders.[8] The case which was brought on the basis of
the proclamation forbidding the importing of wines was the basis for
Sir Edward Coke's denunciation of the proclamation, as has already
been seen.[9]

Elizabeth renewed the commission for concluding peace soon after
her accession, and on 12 March 1559 the peace was made and then
published solemnly in a proclamation on 7 April 1559.[10] When the
peace with Scotland was concluded soon after, the commissioners
jointly proclaimed it after their deliberations and a royal proclamation was not used.[11] Elizabeth had issued a proclamation in December 1558 which renewed Mary's requirement that ships have a
license to go to the seas, and the end of the war occasioned another
proclamation in April 1559 which freely permitted any ships under
a burden of 80 tons to go to sea for trading purposes.[12]

The peace of 1559 was only an interlude in the continuing tension
between the nations. On 20 September 1562 Elizabeth concluded a
secret treaty with the leaders of the Huguenots in which she promised
to supply men and money for their cause in return for their allowing
her troops to occupy Le Havre as a pledge for the eventual return of
Calais. The Queen disguised her actions in a proclamation on 24

[6] Procs. 440/485, 439/484, 437/481.
[7] Procs. 438/483 (but see the delegated authority to the Lord Warden of the Cinque Ports to put to death men who did not report for duty, commanded two months before: APC, VI, 230–1), 443/488, 444/489.
[8] Proc. 442/487.   [9] Above, pp. 56–7.
[10] Proc. 455/504; see headnotes and note 1 in Hughes & Larkin, II, 111, for details of the commissions, treaty and publication of the proclamation.
[11] Inaccurately called a royal proclamation in Hughes & Larkin (459.5/—), it began 'The lord commissioners...in the Queen our sovereign highness's name charge and command...', Camden, pp. 68–70.
[12] Procs. 450/497, 456/506.

September when she explained that although the Earl of Warwick was leading English troops into Normandy 'her intent is not to make war or use any hostility against the French King... (with whom she chargeth all subjects to keep good peace)....'.[13] Only in the following July did she reveal England's commitment to hostilities, when a proclamation authorized men along the sea coasts to spoil French shipping in retaliation for the similar grant by the French King.[14]

The enterprise was singularly ineffective. Warwick had to surrender after plague decimated his troops, and Elizabeth issued a proclamation on 1 August 1563 which extolled their bravery and ordered that the survivors be treated charitably.[15] The economic sanctions forbidding Englishmen to import French wines or be punished 'as aiding and comforting to her majesty's enemies' were as ineffective as the troops,[16] and her defeat was sealed when a proclamation published the peace in the presence of herself and the French Ambassador at Windsor, and then throughout the realm.[17]

The war with Spain

Elizabeth's commitment of troops to the Low Countries in 1585 signaled the beginning of outright hostilities with Spain, even though the troubles had been brewing for many years. Seven of the eleven royal proclamations related to the war were clustered between July 1588 and January 1589 in direct relation to the Armada. An earlier proclamation in November 1587 had ordered men of wealth to return to their counties to assist in the defenses, and those in the 1590s were concerned with denying Spain the benefits of English and neutral shipping.[18]

Only the proclamation of 1 July 1588 preceded the victories at sea over the Armada. It threatened anyone who possessed one of the tracts which Cardinal Allen had penned to alert English catholics to the intended invasion with execution by martial law.[19] Two other

---

[13] Proc. 497.5/—. See J. B. Black, *The Reign of Elizabeth 1558–1603* (2nd ed.; Oxford, 1959), pp. 57ff. Local proclamations made by military commanders abroad are in Holinshed, *Chronicles*, IV, 207–18.

[14] Proc. 508/777; the French actions are detailed in Hughes & Larkin, II, 227 note 1, and 228 note 2. When certain Londoners began to seize French goods and claim that the proclamation allowed this even though it had been published only along the coasts, Elizabeth commanded the Lord Mayor to stop them. He had her letter printed, and it has been included erroneously as proc. 511/579 by Steele and Hughes & Larkin.

[15] Proc. 510/578.   [16] Proc. 517/586.   [17] Proc. 522/595.

[18] Proc. 694/795 on coastal dwellers is considered below, p. 160.

[19] Proc. 699/802; see below, pp. 226–7.

proclamations invoked martial law, one against men who had been pressed for duty if they did not report, the other against soldiers who attempted to sell the weapons which had been issued to them.[20] The threat of martial law in the latter case was an escalation of the milder penalties for the same offense which had been proclaimed five months earlier.[21] Other proclamations set prices for victuals in the areas near the soldiers' camps, announced that the Parliament which had been set to meet in November would be prorogued until February, and forbade shipping grain out of the country under corporal punishment as 'aiders, helpers, assisters and abettors of the enemies' of England.[22]

Each of the measures in 1588–9 was justified by citing the danger from the Armada, a threat that lasted until the last ship had circumnavigated the British Isles and turned toward Spain. Yet several of the matters included are of special interest because of the judicial processes involved, or because a legal consensus had not yet been reached on the proper procedures.

One problem concerned the status of men who had been pressed into service. Some felt that the earlier laws on musters made the receipt of press money and refusal to report afterwards a felony, and in the Parliament of 1589 the government tried unsuccessfully to have that interpretation enacted into law.[23] The matter was referred to the Crown's legal officers in 1591, who held it to be felony if certain conditions were met.[24] Yet both Mary and Elizabeth invoked martial law regularly, during the wars and even as late as 1592 in Elizabeth's case.[25] There was no reluctance, either because of the danger, or because the offense was already capital, or perhaps because only the lower classes would be touched – or because of some combination of these reasons and of others of which we are unaware.

[20] Proc. 704/805 (4 October 1588), and proc. 708/809 (23 January 1589).

[21] Proc. 703/804 (25 August 1588), promising a 'general order' for punishment of the sellers, and a fine by the Council on the buyers, half to the informant and half for the public benefit of the county where the sale took place.

[22] Procs. 701/803, 705/806, 706/807.

[23] Coke's opinion that the matter was a felony under earlier laws was stated later in *The Third Part of the Institutes*, pp. 86–7; it is probably what he would have held earlier. On the musters, Cruickshank, *Elizabeth's Army*, pp. 17–18. The bill of 1589 is in HLRO, Supplementary Papers, Box 8, under date of 8 February 1589. On its progress in Parliament, Simon D'Ewes, *The Journals of All the Parliaments During the Reign of Queen Elizabeth, Both of the House of Lords and House of Commons* (London, 1682), pp. 422–3, 439, 441, 448, 452. It seems to have died in the conference between the Houses.

[24] The opinion and conditions are in Huntington Libr., Ellesmere MSS 2617–19, cited by the Council in its instructions in 1592, *APC*, xxii, 338–9. An order to the Vice-Admirals, Deputy Lieutenants, and Justices of the Peace to view mariners and put offenders to death is in *ibid*. xviii, 429–30.   [25] Proc. 746/850.

Another legal problem touched the sale of soldiers' weapons. The proclamation on 25 August 1588 had promised 'some general order', and that of January 1589 had imposed martial law on those who sold the weapons as well as loss of the weapon or its purchase price on the buyer. The Parliament of 1589 made the offense a felony for the seller.[26]

The question of export was more difficult because a way had to be found to deny English goods to the Spanish and yet not to inhibit legitimate trade with other countries. The proclamation issued on 9 November 1588 had forbidden exports to Spain and left the enforcement to the commissioners for grain in the various counties. Another proclamation in 1591 ordered that anyone who exported to Spain be punished as a traitor and required licenses to ship goods elsewhere. Unlicensed export was to be punished by the shipper's imprisonment, and by fines at quadruple the value of the goods on the shipper and master of the ship.[27] A proclamation the following year partially modified the regulations by allowing the unlicensed manufacture of small pieces of ordnance and by promising further rules to control its export.[28]

The final action against the Spanish which involved proclamations occurred in 1596–7 when the danger of another attempted invasion was keenly felt. In 1596 a proclamation which was primarily concerned with grain also ordered men of substance to return from London to their homes 'for the necessary defense of her realm', without an explanation of the nature of the danger.[29] The following year a proclamation authorized Englishmen to intercept ships bound from the Low Countries to the Iberian peninsula and enjoy the spoils. It established safeguards for the ships of nations allied with England, but as will be seen it was difficult to insist upon these.[30]

There were also proclamations on several matters related to war. They were not used for the ordinary musters, but three times in Elizabeth's reign they announced that commissions would soon be issued to conduct special musters of horses fit for war. The proclamations were a warning to prepare for the musters, but the latter were conducted on the authority of the commission under the great seal. Proclamations were not used for this purpose after 1580.[31] In 1588

[26] 31 Eliz. I, c. 4.   [27] Proc. 737/836.
[28] Proc. 747/851, requiring bonds to control port-to-port shipping generally (and commanded previously in the 1590s before this proclamation, APC, xix, 461–2).
[29] Proc. 784/888; below, pp. 116–17.   [30] Proc. 790/894.
[31] Proc. 534/611 in 1565, with commission in PRO, SP 12/36/88, 90 and instructions in 12/93/18. The Lord President in the North ordered additional notification to be pub-

Elizabeth had issued a proclamation which required officers to remain at their posts along the borders with Scotland or lose their pay.[32] Thereafter such orders were made in less public letters and ordinances.[33]

FOREIGN RELATIONS

The majority of the proclamations on foreign relations were issued because of problems on the seas between Englishmen and the mariners of other nations; these will be considered shortly. A number were issued in other contexts, however, and with these we can deal nation by nation.

We have already seen three of the seven proclamations which were part of Anglo-Scottish relations, in Mary's proclamation about a border rebellion, in the announcement of peace in the Anglo-French wars in which Scotland had been a participant, and in the formal publication of the sentence on Mary Queen of Scots.[34] Elizabeth issued two proclamations for keeping the peace along the borders at a time when relations were strained not only because of incidents along the border but also because of James VI's maneuvering to assert his eventual claim on the English Crown.[35] A proclamation in the summer of 1596 announced that a commission had been appointed to settle the disputes for both nations, and another was issued the following summer to announce that a treaty had been concluded, but it allowed Englishmen 'their liberty of just revenge' if the Scots did not live up to it.[36]

The most interesting proclamations on Scottish affairs were issued

lished in all parish churches, York CA Dept, YC/A 24, fos. 16–16v. Proc. 559/635 in 1569, with copies of the commission in PRO, PRO 30/26/116, fos. 191v–192, BL, Cotton MS Otho E/XI/15, and *HMC 47: 15th Rpt, App. X (Corp. of Coventry MSS)*, pp. 125–7. Commission in the North, York CA Dept, YC/A 24, fos. 135–135v, 148. See Read, *Cecil*, pp. 423–4. Proc. 647/746 in 1580, commission in PRO, SP 12/136/78; Earl of Sussex helped draft it, SP 12/168/48. Many returns are in SP 12, and many have been printed in the records series of various counties.

[32] Proc. 449/496; enforcement ordered, *APC*, vii, 10, 15, 24, 36–7, 88; officer dispensed by Council, *ibid.* p. 46.

[33] Made part of the new orders for Berwick, in *HMC 55: Var. Coll. I (Corp. of Berwick-upon-Tweed MSS)*, pp. 10–11.

[34] Above, pp. 64, 80, 65–6 respectively. Many local proclamations on the borders were made, e.g., BL, Cotton MS Caligula C ix, no. 197; Harl. MS 353, fos. 185–185v.

[35] Black, *The Reign of Elizabeth*, pp. 442ff.

[36] Proc. 782/886 in 1596; details of disorders, *APC*, xxv, 470–5; names of commissioners, Huntington Libr., Ellesmere MS 1883; articles and proceedings, BL, Cotton MS Caligula ix, no. 212, and Bain (ed.), *Calendar of Letters and Papers... Scotland*, ii, 180. Proc. 788/892 in 1597; treaty noted in Hughes & Larkin, iii, 167 note 3; proclamation noted as 'continuing the treaty' in BL, Cotton MS Caligula B v, no. 15; additional orders, Huntington Libr., Ellesmere MS 1886.

in 1569–70. Soon after Mary Stuart's flight to England in 1568, a hearing was conducted on the charges that she had been involved in the murder of her husband and in other violence which had marked the last years in Scotland. Although Mary refused to participate directly in the hearings, which lasted from October to mid-December, she did have her side of the case published in Scotland, alleging that Elizabeth had designs on Scotland and especially on James. Elizabeth had a proclamation published on 22 January 1569 to deny the charges vigorously and to assert her innocence.[37] Considering the degree of maneuvering by the Council to benefit from the situation, the proclamation with its blanket denial of all activities does not ring entirely true. The other proclamation was issued on 10 April 1570, after the Earl of Westmorland had fled into Scotland to avoid being captured for his role in the rebellion in the north. It announced that the Earl of Sussex had been authorized to take an army northward, and implied that he would enter on Scottish territory when it stated that he was commanded to treat all Scots favorably except those who had harbored the fugitives.[38] What it did not say was that his expedition was to be punitive.

Anglo-French relations involved several proclamations. We have already seen those during the wars of 1557–8 and 1562–4, and will see later those issued during her marriage negotiations with the Duke of Alençon and those which arose from sea-related matters.[39] The only other proclamation was issued in 1591, forbidding Englishmen to trade with rebels against the French King Henry IV. England had poured money and men into France in support of that first Bourbon and first Protestant King, and when Spain intervened on behalf of the Catholic League which sought to remove him from the throne, England readied an expedition to keep Brittany from Spanish control. The proclamation at this time threatened any Englishman who would trade with the League with punishment 'as traitors and relievers and succorers of her majesty's enemies', required customs officials to take bonds and sureties from anyone suspected of violating the restraint, and threatened to punish any negligent officials with the loss of their office, a year's imprisonment, and fines.[40] The Council directed the restraint with vigor,[41] and in spite of the con-

[37] Proc. 558/634; see Read, *Cecil*, pp. 397–415, and Camden, pp. 125–6.
[38] Proc. 571/652; see Black, *The Reign of Elizabeth*, p. 144.
[39] Above, pp. 79–81; below, pp. 207–10, 86ff.
[40] Proc. 732/832; see Edward P. Cheyney, *A History of England From the Defeat of the Armada to the Death of Elizabeth* (2 vols.; London, 1914–26), I, 219ff.
[41] *APC*, xxi, 72, 79–81, 103, 216, 219, 274–5, 369–70.

4-2

version of Henry France continued to be of the utmost importance in English foreign policy, but no further proclamations had a part to play.

There were a few proclamations which dealt with other nations. In 1559 Elizabeth forbade the sale of ships to foreigners, seeking to conserve them for England's use.[42] In 1561 she forbade the export of arms to Russia 'upon pains of forfeiture of as much as by the parties may be forfeited', and ordered punishment for those who spread rumors that she had made such sales.[43] The complaints of the Portuguese and Venetians arose in sea-related matters, and will be considered in that context, as will all the proclamations on Anglo-Spanish relations which were not related to the wars.

PEACE ON THE SEAS

Although there was a continuing problem of piracy on the seas, the manner of the government's dealing with it varied over the years. In the early decade of Elizabeth's reign, proclamations were issued because of the complaints of foreign ambassadors of disorders by Englishmen against their nationals. The proclamations were primarily informational and tailored for a foreign audience rather than for the English, because the will to insist on reform seems to have been absent. When in the 1570s an effort was made to come to grips with the problem, it was realized that it spilled over into the coastal areas and that measures would have to be taken to deal with the pirates' land-based abettors. Here the law was unclear, and so the proclamations provided new legal remedies, and in time were themselves challenged indirectly in the courts. From 1585 there was a system of privateering which provided a sanction for activities on the seas, and while this obviated the need for continuing remedies against piracy, proclamations were used to remedy some of the difficulties arising under the new system.

The early years: peace and trade

In the first decade of Elizabeth's reign, the number of proclamations occasioned by ambassadors' complaints was substantial.[44] They were

[42] Proc. 463/514a, which also enforced the statutes on timber because of the shortage in England.
[43] Proc. 481/546; an order to inquire into its enforcement is in Kent AO, Sandwich MS ZB 3/68, fos. 155–155v.
[44] The requests from the Ambassadors for England to take some action are to be found in the calendars of foreign state papers and in the collections of letters on diplomatic

characterized by fulsome denials that the Queen condoned the actions complained of, by orders to all subjects to stop such activities, by requirements for bonds from those going to sea that they would not harm friendly shipping, and by a nearly total lack of evidence from the jurisdictions along the coast to show whether they carried out the requirements.

French complaints in 1560 led to a proclamation which forbade the seizure of Frenchmen and ships, because some Englishmen had read into the Queen's order for surveying French ships an intimation that orders for seizure would follow quickly.[45] The end of the wars in 1564 occasioned another proclamation, ordering ships which had been preying on the French to treat them as friendly thereafter.[46] When the French attacked the Isle of Madeira and captured some ships from the Portuguese, a proclamation forbade receiving the ships in England and commanded that they be seized.[47] And when the civil wars resumed in France, a proclamation was issued in 1568 which specified how English trade was to be carried on with that nation.[48]

The most frequent proclamations were those issued because of complaints from the Spanish Ambassador. He had complained in 1568 that Englishmen were receiving rebels from the Low Countries and asked for a proclamation to stop this hospitality. He was allowed to see the draft of the proclamation and must have been pleased with its threat to punish English receivers as men who violated treaties between nations.[49]

All of the other proclamations which were issued at his request had to do with English attacks on Spanish shipping. One contemporary estimate was that 400 adventurers were so involved.[50] A proclamation in 1561 threatened 'extreme' exemplary punishment against any English mariners who attacked the Spanish under the pretext of letters of marque issued by the Scots.[51] Two proclamations were

affairs which have been used extensively by Hughes & Larkin and appear in their head-notes and footnotes to the proclamations. I have not repeated those citations in the pages which follow.

[45] Proc. 465/520.　　　　　　　　　　[46] Proc. 526/598.

[47] Proc. 548/623. Steele and Hughes & Larkin have included as proc. 479/543 another document on Portuguese affairs which was in reality a signet letter to the Lord Admiral which he had published. The Admiral's letter of transmittal is in R. G. Marsden (ed.), *Select Pleas in the Court of Admiralty* (2 vols.; Selden Society, VI, XI; London, 1892, 1897) II, 29.　　　　　　　　　[48] Proc. 555/—.

[49] Proc. 553/629; see especially Hughes & Larkin, II, 296 note 2.

[50] Read, *Cecil*, p. 289.

[51] Proc. 482/547, which promised articles for the Vice-Admirals which are to be found in PRO, SP 12/18/23.

issued in 1563 when England was at war with France. One was occasioned by abuses of the letters of marque which the English commander at Newhaven issued to attack French shipping, and the other because some English mariners were using French letters of marque in spite of the war to attack Spanish ships. In both cases the Spanish Ambassador complained that the proclamations were insufficient to stop the abuses.[52] In the following year there came a specific order to arrest a notorious pirate who preyed on Spanish shipping,[53] and the most comprehensive general order to date which was aimed at curbing attacks on Spanish and Scottish shipping. It required that offenders be apprehended, that sureties be given for English ships, and that negligent officers 'be punished as abettors to the offenders'.[54] There is evidence that bonds were taken at Rye,[55] but one has only to look down the list of watchers appointed for the coast of Wales to note the name of Sir James Crofts, one of the most active protectors of pirates, to wonder at the degree of sincerity which lay behind the orders.[56]

At this point the Spanish officials took the initiative. Margaret of Parma, Regent in the Netherlands for her half-brother Philip, closed the ports in the Low Countries to English shipping, ostensibly because of the plague but in reality because of the attacks of the English on Spanish shipping. The English were in no hurry to respond because the Merchant Adventurers had negotiated an agreement to use Emden and other northern ports, but in March 1564 a royal proclamation closed the English ports to imports from the Low Countries. Its text was longer than usual because of the lengthy recital of Margaret's actions and of the arguments (dear to Cecil) that imports diminished English treasure. It commanded that any shipping in violation of the embargo be punished by forfeitures.[57]

The Council directed a rigorous enforcement of the proclamation in London and along the coasts, ensuring that the cargoes seized for violations were sold and that the proceeds were distributed as

[52] Procs. 499/573 and 513/581. Details of the latter's publication on the Isle of Wight are in PRO, SP 12/27/54.

[53] Proc. 525/597, for Thomas Cobham; see Hughes & Larkin, II, 252 note 3; bonds from several of his men, APC, VII, 154.

[54] Proc. 519/589.

[55] E. Sussex RO, Rye MS 1/3, fos. 66–66v, 71–2, 74v.

[56] APC, VII, 151. Crofts, in all probability Elizabeth's half-brother, the son of Henry VIII and Mary Berkeley, was a protector of Robert Hickes, a notorious pirate. Neville Williams, *Captains Outrageous: Seven Centuries of Piracy* (London, 1961), pp. 57–88. Orders enforcing the proclamation, APC, VII, 154; PRO, SP 12/33/20, 21.

[57] Proc. 521/594; on the embargo and negotiations, Read, *Cecil*, pp. 288–300.

ordered.[58] In May 1564 Elizabeth published an explanatory proclamation which exempted any ships from the Low Countries which were accidently blown into English ports.[59] By November the commissioners had agreed to reopen the trade while negotiations for a treaty continued, and when Margaret accepted those terms Elizabeth did likewise and then announced the end of the embargo in a proclamation.[60] The protracted negotiations for the treaty were punctuated by two other royal proclamations which announced the continuation of trade in the interim.[61]

In late 1568 Elizabeth seized several ships which had been bound for the Low Countries and which had been blown into her western ports. The ships contained chests of money which the Spanish intended to use to pay the troops in the Low Countries now under the command of the Duke of Alva. When Elizabeth claimed that the money still belonged to those lending it and borrowed it herself, Spain's new Ambassador in England, Don Gureau de Spes, urged Alva to confiscate English property in the Low Countries in retaliation. When Alva did so, Elizabeth issued a proclamation which authorized the seizure of all Spanish property in England.[62]

The mutual seizures escalated the problem considerably. The English gradually realized that the Spanish goods which they had seized were more valuable than those arrested in the Low Countries, that the effects of the closed trade were not as severe as had been feared, and that Alva's lines of communication with Spain were effectively cut. Accordingly the negotiations were delayed, and meanwhile Elizabeth issued two proclamations in the summer of 1570 to get a valuation of the goods seized in England and arrested abroad.[63] When she learned that Alva had sold the English goods, she issued a proclamation which set out the conditions for the sale of the Spanish property.[64] The English had profited rather tidily, and when in 1573 the trade was reopened, a proclamation announced it.[65]

[58] *APC*, VII, 150, 157–60, 165–6, 243. PRO, SP 12/33/41, 55; 12/35/1. Dispensation from the embargo, *ibid.* 12/33/66.

[59] Proc. 523/596.

[60] Proc. 530/606.

[61] Procs. 537/612, 546/619.

[62] Proc. 556/632. The episode is treated fully in Conyers Read, 'Queen Elizabeth's Seizure of the Duke of Alva's Pay-Ships', *Journal of Modern History*, V (1933), 443–64. Arrests, PRO, SP 12/49/5, 8, 25 and 12/48/60. Local action, Kent AO, Sandwich MS Sa/AC 5, fos. 19–24.

[63] Procs. 576/655, 578/657. Commission to survey Spanish goods seized in England, PRO, SP 12/71/51.

[64] Proc. 538/665; commission and instructions, PRO, SP 12/85, *passim*, and 12/86/61.

[65] Proc. 595/686.

The middle years: piracy

By mid-1569 it had become clear that England must make some act of good faith about offenses on the sea if its relations with Spain and France were not to be strained to breaking point. The mutual seizures made both England and Spain realize that it was time to step back from the brink.[66] There could be no better sign of Elizabeth's good faith than firm measures against the pirates whose activities exacerbated the normal tensions.

Sufficient means for dealing with the problem existed in theory. The Lord Admiral had a network of Vice-Admirals who were charged with apprehending offenders on the coasts and then sending them to the Judge of the Admiralty, who would cause justice to be done and secure the forfeitures to which the Admiral was entitled. The Lord Warden of the Cinque Ports had similar authority along the coasts of Kent and east Sussex, areas of great importance because they lay along the main shipping lanes.[67]

The effectiveness of those officers had been impeded for a number of reasons. The Queen often allowed covert support to the Huguenots and Dutch Sea Beggars whose piracies against their catholic countrymen kept their sovereigns off balance and thus served England's foreign policy. Many officers were unsure of the degree of her support and uncertain of what was expected of them.[68] Some officers were simply unwilling to act, either because of the lawlessness which was rampant from many years of official connivance with pirates, or because the trade with pirates was so lucrative and thus popular among the coastal residents.[69]

It was gradually realized that to use persons not in the normal network of enforcement offered a way to overcome the inaction. In

[66] Wernham, *Before the Armada*, pp. 297ff.

[67] A good recent summary of the Admiral's jurisdiction is in Robert W. Kenny, *Elizabeth's Admiral. The Political Career of Charles Howard, Earl of Nottingham 1536-1624* (Baltimore, 1970), pp. 63–87; for Vice-Admirals, R. G. Marsden, 'The Vice-Admirals of the Coast', *EHR*, XXII (1907), 736–57, and samples of instructions in R. G. Marsden (ed.), *Documents Relating to Law and Custom of the Sea*, Vol. 1: *A.D. 1205–1648* (Publications of the Navy Records Society, XLIX; London, 1915), 173. For the Council's supervision, Michael Barraclough Pulman, *The Elizabethan Privy Council in the Fifteen-seventies* (Berkeley, 1971) pp. 188–95.

[68] B. Dietz, 'Privateering in north-west European Waters, 1568–1572' (unpublished Ph.D. dissertation, University of London, 1959), and James A. Williamson, *The English Channel. A History* (Cleveland, 1959), pp. 190–6.

[69] Williams, *Captains Outrageous*, pp. 57–88; David Mathew, 'The Cornish and Welsh Pirates in the Reign of Elizabeth', *EHR*, XXXIX (1924), 337–48; A. L. Rowse, *Sir Richard Grenville of the Revenge, An Elizabethan Hero* (London, 1937), pp. 157–68.

1565 a series of special commissions were issued for the coastal counties, but since they could only investigate matters and refer their findings to the Admiralty, their effectiveness was limited.[70] It was also becoming clear that to repress piracy meant not only to deal with the men who plundered on the seas, but also with those land-based abettors who victualed and prepared the ships for the voyages, and then later bought and sold the pirates' booty.

In 1569–70 Elizabeth tried to demonstrate her good faith in a series of proclamations. She had taken some steps previously, as in 1564 when she stated that anyone who assisted the pirates was to be taken as an abettor,[71] and in 1565 when she issued two proclamations which forbade Englishmen to serve foreign princes on the seas.[72] Now she sharpened and elaborated on the penalties through a series of legal definitions which created offenses: she declared that pirates were outside her protection, so that anyone could proceed against them by force; she stated that those who aided or dealt with the pirates on land were 'to be adjudged and executed as pirates'; and she threatened officials who did not enforce the proclamations with the loss of their offices, and the corporations which they served with the loss of their liberties.[73]

The particular concern with the negligent officers was the result of the Queen's discontent at the lack of reformation. The Council began to insist on action in 1570, turning its attention particularly to the Cinque Ports.[74] The member ports began to follow orders, notably the requirement in the proclamations to take recognizances from the masters of ships leaving the ports.[75] Twelve pirates were hanged in 1570, but there is nothing to identify any of them as land-based abettors.[76] It looks as though the crescendo of provisions was intended both to satisfy the ambassadors and to strike terror into the coastal inhabitants by demonstrating the government's firm purpose to come to grips with the entire problem.

[70] Warrant, PRO, SP 12/37/48 (copied in BL, Lansd. MS 8/15); instructions, 12/37/49; lists of ports and havens, 12/37/51; covering letter, *APC*, VII, 278–90; reports, 12/38/8, 9, 14, 23; 12/39/1, 6, 17; articles of inquiry, *HMC 27: 12th Rpt, App. IX (Gurney MSS)*, pp. 125–7.

[71] Proc. 526/598; above, p. 88.

[72] Procs. 609/698, 610/700.

[73] Procs. 562/639, 563/640, 573/653.

[74] *APC*, VII, 362–3, 369–72.

[75] Kent AO, Sandwich MS Sa/AC 5, fos. 19–21*v*, 24, 30*v*, 52, 89*v*–90*v*, 96*v*; E. Sussex RO, Rye MSS 1/4, fos. 48*v*–49, 52, 59; 47/2/4, some but not all of which is calendared in *HMC 31: 13th Rpt, App. IV (Corp. of Rye MSS)*, pp. 2–17. See also BL, Add. MS 32323, fos. 37–40, and Harl. MS 4943, fos. 219*v*–220.

[76] List in BL, Lansd. MS 142, fos. 80*v*–81; eight others in the same year were pardoned.

A proclamation of 1 March 1572 was even more severe. Designed to force a squadron of Dutch Sea Beggars to leave English waters, it threatened the Dutch with the forfeiture of their ships and goods, and anyone who assisted them with death by 'martial law as a manifest breaker of the common peace betwixt this realm and other realms and countries'.[77] It seems to have been the end result of a series of consultations which began on 11 February when the Council referred to the Judge of the Admiralty an inquiry from the Captain of Portsmouth and others on the question of how they were to inquire about and apprehend pirates and their abettors.[78] There is a comprehensive plan titled 'To prevent piracies' which, to judge from its continual reference to the Admiralty's jurisdiction, can only have been prepared by one of its officers. It suggested that a proclamation be drawn for the criminal matters, including the use of martial law.[97]

The actual proclamation and the commission followed the plan closely, but ignored the arguments for the Admiralty's pre-eminent role. In the instructions for the commission, Burghley had penned an addition which stated that martial law was invoked because the cause was too great 'to abide any such long delay, as the common law requires'.[80] But after some reluctance the leaders of the Dutch commanded their ships to leave, and there seems to have been no need to use martial law, even though some preliminary processes were begun which suggest that more ordinary procedures were intended.[81]

Up to this time the proclamations had been an important part of the efforts to handle piracy. But it was to be many years before they would be used to deal with piracy again. The reason lies in a legal opinion which was rendered during the effort to deal with land-based abettors in 1577, and which indirectly disallowed the definitions which had been set out in the proclamations.

It was as a result of a growing concern over the actions of the prince of Elizabethan pirates, John Callice, that the activities of

[77] Proc. 585/668; Camden, p. 214.
[78] BL, Harl. MS 4943, fo. 45.
[79] BL, Lansd. MS 28/17.
[80] *Ibid.* 13/45. See also PRO, SP 12/85/59.
[81] The fleet's leader decided to attack Brill in the Netherlands after leaving, and its capture was a momentous event in the winning of Dutch independence. That Elizabeth had not intended the sequel is argued in J. B. Black, 'Queen Elizabeth, the Sea Beggars and the Capture of Brill', *EHR*, XLVI (1931), 30–47. A report to the Lord Warden from Sandwich of a jury's presentment of offenders is in Kent AO, Sandwich MS Sa/AC 5, fo. 98. Recognizances with conditions which required certain men of Rye who had been aboard the Dutch ships after the proclamation to be ready to answer what might be alleged against them are in E. Sussex RO, Rye MS 1/4, fos. 112–113v.

1576–7 began.[82] When initial inquiries revealed that his main support came from the coastal areas in Wales, and from Cardiff in particular, the Council appointed a commission in March 1577 to investigate complicity in his piracies. The commissioners were carefully chosen 'outsiders' because of the intermingled Welsh blood lines which made an independent inquiry so hard to conduct, but no sooner had they begun than they found many obstacles from Nicholas Herbert, Sheriff of Glamorgan and Vice-Admiral. Other evidence suggested that he was a favorer and even a lodger of Callice. In April the pirate was captured, and he and Herbert were sent up to answer before the Council.[83]

We need not be concerned with Callice's indictment, conviction, and eventual release,[84] because the greatest importance lay in how Herbert's case would be handled as this would be a precedent for dealing with abetting. He was not ready to give in easily – on the very first day of Trinity term, the Council wrote to the Attorney General, the Solicitor General, and the Judge of the Admiralty to state that

'in the matter of spoils done on the sea and what concerns persons accessory by land there seems to be a difference in law...therefore it is thought meet to have the opinion of some skillful in either law for their several punishments, they are required to assemble themselves together and set down their opinions what the law is in this case, or what they think convenient to be done for the redress of so great a disorder.'[85]

The snag in the case arose from an ambiguity in the words of the statute of 1536 on piracy which gave the power 'to hear and determine such offenses after the common course of the laws of this land'. If the phrase 'after the common course' modified 'hear and determine', the substance of the offense would be left as at civil law and only the procedures of the common law used, but if it modified

---

[82] C. L'Estrange Ewen, *The Golden Chalice. A Documented Narrative of an Elizabethan Pirate* (Paignton, 1939); Edgar L. Chappell, *History of the Port of Cardiff* (Cardiff, 1939), pp. 31–5.

[83] The details of the investigation are presented, without a reference to Herbert's case in the Star Chamber and the legal opinion, in Derrick G. E. Hurd, 'Some Aspects of the Attempts of the Government to Suppress Piracy during the Reign of Elizabeth I' (unpublished M.A. thesis, University of London, 1961), pp. 176ff., and in Carys Eryl Hughes, 'Wales and Piracy, A Study in Tudor Administration. 1500–1640' (unpublished M.A. thesis, University of Wales, University College of Swansea, 1937); and in Chappell, *History of the Port of Cardiff*, pp. 32–4, and John Hobson Matthews (ed.), *Cardiff Records* (Cardiff, 1898), pp. 349–59.

[84] His confession named accomplices and was probably made when Secretary Walsingham accepted his offer (PRO, SP 15/25) to reveal all details, in a hope to win his freedom.   [85] *APC*, IX, 359, with a further request in PRO, SP 12/114/23.

'offense', it created an offense at common law. Sir Edward Coke reported the case in a different context, but he noted the corollary: one cannot indict an accessory at common law if that law does not recognize the principal offense.[86] Need we doubt that Nicholas Herbert was making a spirited defense, challenging the legality of what the government intended?

The common lawyers concluded that to help to prepare a ship for the seas made one 'accessory to the piracy, when the piracy is committed, although he receive no part of the spoils'; that it was not a felony to buy and receive pirates' goods, but that the offenders were 'to be punished by imprisonment and fine' for the contempt; that 'if any do lodge or entertain a pirate, knowing that he has committed piracy, then he is accessory to the felony' even if he had no share of the spoils. They felt that accessories on land might be tried by commissions sent into the shires on the authority of the act of 1536.[87]

The civilians argued that those who provisioned or armed the pirates in order that they might commit spoils 'are to be punished as the pirates themselves'; that aiders and relievers of pirates after the piracy is committed cannot be punished as pirates, but may be punished arbitrarily by mulct or fine; that those who bought pirates' goods knowingly were bound to restitution and 'may otherwise be punished as evil doers', and that unwitting purchasers need only make restitution.[88]

The opinions of the common lawyers offered the better potential for reform, but soon after rendering it they reversed themselves, concluding that the statute of 1536 applied only to offenses on the seas, not to offenses committed partly on the seas (the piracy) and partly on land (the abetting).[89] The practical effect was to leave the matter to be governed by the civilians' opinion, and thus in September 1577 commissions were issued, authorizing the coastal counties to try all offenses of piracy and the *misdemeanors* of aiding pirates.[90]

[86] Coke reported the case in the context of the extent of the accession pardon of James I, *The Third Part of the Institutes*, p. 112. The statute, 28 Henry VIII, c. 15, intended in part to remove the civil law's demand for witnesses which few pirates left behind.

[87] Full opinion in PRO, HCA 30/3, epitomized by Coke, *The Third Part of the Institutes*, pp. 112–13.

[88] Copy of the report in BL, Harl. MS 168/35, and in Trinity Hall (Cambridge) MS II (Admiralty No. VI), fo. 46. I owe the latter reference to Mr Michael Prichard.

[89] Coke, *The Third Part of the Institutes*, p. 112. As can be expected, Coke did not report the civilians' opinion or any of the later proceedings.

[90] Emphasis mine. Warrants for the commission (covering all offenses in the last five years), the commission, and instructions, BL, Lansd. MS 146, fos. 18v–20, and in PRO, SP 12/115/32. Reports are found spread throughout SP 12/112, 113, 115, 117–20, 122–4,

Fines were rigorously assessed, and the Council watched over the proceedings closely – by November 1578 the fines had reached a total of £1,287 3s 4d and a number of highly placed persons such as Vice-Admirals had been fined along with other abettors.[91] No trace has been found of Herbert's case; presumably he was among the men of his county fined, but in the following January he was back home and was still Sheriff.[92] Many pirates were executed in those years, but the indictments in the Court of the Admiralty show that no land-based abettors were included in those that remain.[93]

The whole episode is a striking commentary on the place of law in Tudor England. The government neither shrank from framing new legal definitions when a remedy was needed, nor tried to subvert the law when a contrary legal opinion had been rendered. Because the penalties of fines and imprisonment were clearly inadequate as a deterrent,[94] little real reformation could be expected. A bill on piracy was introduced in the Parliament of 1584–5 but does not survive, and no legislation was forthcoming.[95]

The later years: privateering and piracy

When a system of privateering against Spanish shipping was introduced in 1585, the purchase of a license legalized the actions which Englishmen eager for plunder wished to take, and thus the government channeled their avidity into a militarily useful pursuit.[96] Although the system was not promulgated in a proclamation, the complaints of the Venetian and Tuscan merchants in 1591 prompted Elizabeth to issue a proclamation which denounced the Englishmen who preyed on the ships of nations at peace with England. The form of the condition for the recognizance for privateering was part of the proclamation, and thus the whole system was in fact published.[97]

In the 1590s there was a series of proclamations on sea-related

126, 127, 129, 130, 135, and in *APC*, x, *passim*. Local examples of the commissioners' work, E. Sussex RO, Rye MSS 47/20/2; 1/4, fo. 310*v*; 47/24/3a; and in Southampton CRO, SC 9/3/3, fos. 22–4.

[91] PRO, SP 12/126/59.   [92] *Ibid.* 12/122/2.

[93] List of executions, BL, Lansd. MS 142, fos. 80*v*–81, noted in Holinshed, *Chronicles*, IV, 345. I have checked the indictments in PRO, HCA 1/2 and 1/3. Men were questioned about their awareness of the proclamation (examinations in HCA 1/39, fos. 19*v*–24, 32–5, 83, 87*v* and 1/40, fos. 30–3) but I have found no procedure based on it.

[94] Commissioners' complaint in PRO, SP 12/129/3.

[95] Information from Mrs Bette Marland.

[96] See K. R. Andrews, *Elizabethan Privateering: English Privateering During the Spanish War, 1585–1603* (Cambridge, 1964).

[97] Proc. 730/830.

matters which dealt with the proper means of accounting for the prizes brought into English ports, when the Queen had a share in the voyages. Elizabeth wanted to ensure her rights, and in practice she gained far more than that to which she was entitled.[98] The proclamations in 1591, 1592, and 1594 are a testimony to the ingenuity of the English subjects who showed the same greed as their monarch.

In December 1591 Elizabeth denounced receivers of goods from ships, when the cargoes had not been inventoried by the commissioners.[99] She must have learned more of the problem, because in the next month another proclamation was issued, this time condemning men who spoiled the prizes before customs had been paid.[100] When the greatest prize of the era, the *Madre de Dios*, was brought into English harbors in late 1592, a proclamation was issued to enlist the assistance of innkeepers and householders as well as port officials who were to reveal men who spoiled the ship before the accounting.[101] Several years later another proclamation sought to prevent all these difficulties, by forbidding anyone to go aboard a prize before it had been inventoried.[102]

Neither those efforts to stop the plundering of prizes in English ports, nor the measures to prevent indiscriminate attacks on the ships of nations friendly with England, seem to have been effective. A proclamation was issued in 1599 against the attacks on allied shipping. It was nearly identical with the proclamation of 1591 against harming Italian shipping, except that where the earlier had threatened offenders with the penalties for piracy, the later proclamation ordered 'death with confiscation of lands and goods' for taking cargoes from their ships, and the confiscation of English ships whose masters had not entered into bonds promising to respect friendly ships.[103] In March 1602 a comprehensive set of regulations for privateering was published in a proclamation, aimed primarily at the officials who were charged to license owners of ships and take recognizances.[104] There was little time left in the reign to test the effectiveness of the proposals.

[98] Her share from the *Madre de Dios* should have been £8,000 but she got from ten to twenty times that, depending on the estimates, e.g., M. Oppenheim, *A History of the Administration of the Royal Navy and of Merchant Shipping in Relation to the Navy* (London, 1896), pp. 165–6.

[99] Proc. 742/843.   [100] Proc. 743/846.

[101] Proc. 749/853; see Cheyney, *A History of England*, I, 538–42, and the instructions for the commissioners in PRO, SP 12/243/14.

[102] Proc. 764/869, in August 1594.

[103] Proc. 797/900, with draft in PRO, SP 12/270/21–2 corrected by Sir Robert Cecil and Lord Admiral Nottingham.   [104] Proc. 813/925.

REFLECTIONS: THE
PROCLAMATIONS AND SECURITY

Few instances could show better how royal proclamations were usually occasioned by crisis situations than those which concerned security-related matters. The danger to peace and order could be of such a magnitude, real or imagined, that there was no hesitation in legislating temporarily, or in providing administrative procedures which tightened up controls or helped remedy the problems.

Proclamations which legislated show clearly the need for new definitions, the manner in which the proclamations supplemented rather than supplanted the statutes, and the limits which were respected in their use. The legislation on weapons was needed because the guns offered a potential for disorders in all localities. The difficulties with demobilizing the soldiers and mariners had a special urgency not only in the short term but also because the growing numbers of vagabonds, always a source of concern late in the century, used the pitiable condition of the wounded veterans as a pretext for extending their activities. And the most obvious way to control the pirates was to deny them access to the land-based abettors who were needed to victual them for the voyages and buy the booty afterward.

The legislation on guns and abettors of piracy supplemented the existing law, by including the new weapons within the scope of the letter of the law which had known only earlier guns, and by defining accessories of pirates as guilty of the offenses committed by principals. Neither extension conflicted with or attempted to supplant the existing law. It is noteworthy that the government sought statutes on vagabonds at the various parliamentary sessions after 1588, and that when an opinion was received in 1577 which indirectly allowed what had been attempted in earlier proclamations, the government respected the lawyers' arguments. Although the proclamations on vagabonds showed a greater degree of improvisation, in reality they merely extended to a seven-county area in southern England the practices which had been used for years in London. The local officers were enthusiastic about the new powers – central and local government were at one in their efforts to deal with the problems which threatened the security and the peace.

The most vexing problem in interpretation arises from trying to fathom the motivation for using martial law against civilians. Was it to strike fear into the soldiers and mariners and to force them to move out of London quickly? The dread of martial law might have been strong enough to accomplish that, so that the need to use it might have been avoided. Was it to show that the government was determined to stop new practices which made it difficult to deal with vagabonds? The threat of martial law might drive them into hiding and obviate the need for summary executions by alleviating the problem temporarily. Did the government feel so threatened that extraordinary measures were deemed necessary, or was there a wanton disregard for the liberties of men in the lower ranks of society? Without any evidence of the actual use of martial law, we are powerless to evaluate the possibilities.

The administrative procedures in the security-related proclamations were less striking, but of great impact in several cases. Of special note are the frequent requirements for licenses and bonds as a means for controlling the ports, because in theory they promised the most thorough possible control. The searches which were authorized for guns afford an excellent illustration of how the existing law could be supplemented by administrative devices. Since no one worth less than £100 was authorized to use firearms, the searches were intended to make sure that the letter of the law would be obeyed. The searches for vagabonds which were commanded in the frequently republished proclamation for the London area, on the other hand, were preventative in nature. Several of the proclamations on guns and on items taken from privateering ships before an inventory authorized the seizure of property, but in these cases the offenders can be expected to have come from the lower social ranks.

When the proclamations are evaluated as propaganda, several varying motives can be seen. Proclamations on foreign affairs form the largest single category intended to influence opinion. Except for Mary's proclamations against Wyatt, which unintentionally revealed some governmental weaknesses, the proclamations on rebellions were cautiously triumphant and showed the Crown's control of affairs. The proclamations issued at the requests of ambassadors were almost entirely declaratory, and the lack of other measures perhaps indicates an unwillingness to take concrete actions needed for reform. Most of the denials of the Queen's awareness or complicity in the offenses on the seas were true, and her protests of innocence in the public forum thus entirely proper. But we have encountered examples of outright deception, as when Le Havre was occupied or when a punitive force was sent into Scotland, and in some other proclamations which followed foreign protests the explanations do not ring true.

From these proclamations one can also detect some attitudes and limits in the use of proclamations. A concern for London lay at the heart of many of them. Mary's 'tactical' use of them during Wyatt's rebellion is in clear contrast to her cooler, after the fact, use as propaganda in other rebellions. The proclamations which enforced the statutes on vagabonds were occasioned by disorders in London, and doubtless many of the orders concerned with demobilization were intended to safeguard the city. The most innovative proclamation on guns was occasioned by shots fired near the Queen when she was in her barge on the Thames. Other proclamations were also intended for a particular locality primarily, such as those ordering men pressed for service to report or those dealing with land-based abettors of piracy. Few seem to have been intended for many localities, though that which revealed the abuses of men posing as messengers from the Council was.

The differences in attitudes toward the different strata in society show up clearly as well. Martial law could be threatened against those of no social importance in the government's eyes, but a man of standing like Herbert could defend himself with great vigor against the government and even carry the day. But whereas most of the security-related proclamations did not infringe the liberty of action of the politically articulate, those on economic and social matters did, so that the difference in attitude will be of great importance in the matters to which we now turn.

PART THREE

THE PRACTICE: THE PROCLAMATIONS AND ECONOMIC AND SOCIAL MANAGEMENT

5

ECONOMIC MANAGEMENT FOR
THE PUBLIC INTEREST

The number of royal proclamations on economic matters was so large that they deserve very special consideration. The task is difficult not merely because of the range of interests which were concerned, but also because of the sheer numbers – nearly 225 Marian and Elizabethan proclamations.

The proclamations are also important because they illustrate such a wide range of uses: some dealt with traditional concerns such as the coinage; others implemented the statutory provisions which called for the use of proclamations, such as the rating of wages; a number of them set forth new procedures for preventing disorders by regulating the sale of meat in lent and by attempting to prevent famine by ordering grain masters to serve the markets. These new procedures demanded either the creation of new legal offenses or the provision of administrative devices such as searches and licenses. These in turn often impinged on the freedom of action of powerful persons and especially on a number of special interests such as chartered companies and governmental corporations.

Many of the proclamations regulated a part of the economy uniformly throughout the realm, others affected specific areas with unique economic interests, and still others dealt with one trade no matter where it was practiced. This chapter and the following are organized primarily according to the intention behind the proclamations, whether they were issued to serve the general good irrespective of the economic interests affected, or to serve some special group's private benefit. The latter are considered in the following chapter.

COINAGE, THE EXCHANGE, AND WEIGHTS

The regulation of the coinage was an unquestioned use of the royal prerogative,[1] and royal proclamations had traditional roles in it. The nine Marian and fifteen Elizabethan proclamations on coins fall into three categories. The most frequently issued were the publications of the rates at which domestic and foreign coins were to be valued, while others enforced the legislation which forbade exporting, melting or abusing the coins, or warned English subjects of coins which were counterfeit or which were similar in appearance to coins of a greater value.

Mary acceded to a considerable problem with the coinage, not only because it had been debased by both Henry VIII and Edward VI for their immediate profit, but also because their actions had left a legacy of discontent and distrust. Her remedy was to provide new issues of pure coins to circulate alongside the debased, and this she promised in one of the first proclamations after Northumberland's rebellion had been crushed.[2] Sixteen months later another proclamation announced that the new coins were ready.[3] The idea of a wholesale reformation had been discussed in the Council and never came to fruit,[4] but the very possibility was enough to evoke a good deal of apprehension since any such plan would of necessity involve a demonetization and losses for all. The fears became acute when prices for grain began to rise, and Mary issued a proclamation to deny the rumors that a full-scale reform was imminent.[5]

There were a number of other Marian proclamations on the coinage. Three were issued within a span of two months in 1554 to value foreign coins, first of France, then of Spain, and finally of Portugal.[6] The arrival of many foreigners for Mary's marriage to Philip occasioned the first, and the rates for the second followed almost exactly the recommendations of a group of merchants on whom the Council had presumably called for advice.[7] A proclamation was issued in 1556 to keep the coinage for Ireland and England separate, by declaring that the rose pence struck for Ireland were to have no value in England.[8] It had been thought that its publication

---

[1] Coke, *Reports*, v, 114–15; Smith, *De Republica Anglorum*, p. 60.
[2] Proc. 391/428. [3] Proc. 419/458.
[4] Study group, *APC*, v, 284.
[5] Proc. 431/471; an earlier order allowing the Lord Mayor of London to punish at his discretion those who did not accept the base coins at their fiat value is in *APC*, v, 358.
[6] Procs. 406/447, 408/448, 412/452.
[7] PRO, SP 11/4/17; *APC*, iv, 410.
[8] Proc. 429/469; Bishop of Durham's publication of it noted in *APC*, iv, 242.

in London would suffice as 'sufficient warning to the rest of the realm', but when they continued to circulate in the north a general proclamation was issued.[9] Two other proclamations dealt with the abuse of coins, the first occasioned by the discovery in Yorkshire of counterfeit coins and the Council's being notified of them, while the second aimed at enforcing the laws against exporting and melting coins.[10] There was a flurry of activity against offenders, but it seems to have been based entirely on the statutes.[11]

Elizabeth's remedy was to meet the problem squarely, to call in the old coins and to replace them with a reformed issue. This was of great benefit to the realm, but of particular advantage to the Queen herself when a way was found to carry it off at a profit. The royal proclamation of 27 September 1560 which announced the recoinage 'decried' the base coins in circulation by twenty-five percent.[12] Although the plan had long since been formed, the announcement was kept a secret, and when the news leaked out the issue date was advanced.[13] Since the fiat values of the old coins were set below the actual worth of their precious metal, the government could pay for the reminting and still make a gain. Because the striking of the new coins would take some time, two other proclamations were issued in 1561 to call in certain of the base coins when enough of the new had been struck.[14]

Those three proclamations marked the main stages of the re-coinage, but a number of subsidiary issues had to be handled as well. New values for foreign gold coins were published in October 1560 to bring them into line with the new values on English coins.[15] In November 1560 and again in November 1561 foreign gold pieces similar to English coins were valued, and the means provided to distinguish between them.[16] A more vexing problem arose over identifying certain pieces of the base money. Three types had been called in: testons, originally shilling pieces but lately current at 6d; two-penny pieces; and pennies. But since the testons were of varying

---

[9] *Eccl. Mem.*, III, i, 500–2.
[10] Proc. 427/467; see *APC*, v, 241. Proc. 428/468.
[11] *APC*, v, 250, 258–9, 356; VI, 12, 19, 21, 43, 80.
[12] Proc. 471/530. Earlier calculations were corrected by Conyers Read, 'Profits on the Recoinage of 1560–1', *EcHR*, VI (1936), 186ff., who in turn is corrected by J. D. Gould, *The Great Debasement* (Oxford, 1970), *qv* for technical aspects.
[13] Read, *Cecil*, p. 196; above, p. 21.
[14] Proc. 478/541 (19 February 1561), 480/545 (12 June 1561). Examples of local punishment of men refusing to accept testons in the interim: York CA Dept, YC/A 22, fo. 29v; Norf. & Norw. RO, Norwich Mayor's Ct Bk 7, fos. 55v, 569.
[15] Proc. 472/531.
[16] Procs. 473/532, 487/556.

degrees of baseness, and because the new fiat value of 4½d would still be excessive for a small number of the 'most base' sort, they were called down to 2¼d. The initial proclamation in September 1560 asserted that they could be identified because the copper alloy showed through or because of their special mint marks.[17] When problems arose over identification, the device of marking the coins with stamping irons was adopted.

The scheme had been mentioned in a letter to the Lord Mayor of London, but the first public notice was in the proclamation of 9 October 1560.[18] It ordered the baser testons worth 2¼d to be struck with the mark of a greyhound behind the monarch's image, and those at 4½d with a portcullis in front of the image.[19] The Mint and the Lord Treasurer opposed the plan, since it infringed in a limited way the Mint's exclusive privilege of striking coin.[20] The irons were not distributed with the proclamation, partly because their preparation took longer than anticipated, partly because the proclamation touched on matters of more urgency.[21] Some 955 irons were sent out in sealed canvas bags directed to forty-two towns or jurisdictions, accompanied by a letter of instructions for the local officials in which were commands as to where the stamping was to be done, how the stampers were to proceed, and what security measures should be taken.[22] The Lord Mayor of London issued his own proclamation and two precepts on the matter, and used the halls of eleven companies for the stamping, while in Bristol the Mayor issued a proclamation and enlisted the help of the goldsmiths.[23] The delivery of the

[17] Proc. 471/530.

[18] The letter, PRO, SP 12/14/5; the proc., 472/531. It had been conceived after 29 September, for a proclamation for London on that date (*Add. Procs.*, no. 1) did not mention it.

[19] An earlier plan called for striking the figure of a dragon; PRO, SP 12/13/40.

[20] PRO, SP 12/14/7, 12/14/14; also printed in Albert Feaveayear, *The Pound Sterling* (2nd ed., rev. by E. Victor Morgan; Oxford, 1963), pp. 81–2.

[21] The original intention, as in PRO, SP 12/14/1, was to prohibit melting and exporting the coin; the stamping of coins and a valuation of foreign coins were added later, the latter at the suggestion of Lord Treasurer Winchester, *ibid.* 12/14/15. The additions came so late that a special writ was needed for their inclusion, as in Hughes & Larkin, II, 155 headnote. The Exchequer was charged with seeing the proclamation through the printer, and this unusual process occasioned some difficulty; PRO, SP 12/14/11, 15.

[22] Number of the irons, see Sir John Craig, *The Mint* (Cambridge, 1953), p. 119; a list of jurisdictions receiving them is in W. Cunningham, *The Growth of English Industry and Commerce in Modern Times* (2 vols., rev. ed.; Cambridge, 1912), II, 132–3, but a fuller list is in PRO, SP 12/14/8; Council's letter, HMC 4: 5th Rpt (*Condover MSS*), p. 343, with extracts in Cunningham, *The Growth of English Industry*, II, 132–3; draft in PRO, SP 12/14/17.

[23] Corp. London RO, Letter Bk T, fo. 5v, and Journal XVII, fos. 270v, 274; Bristol, cited in Cunningham, *The Growth of English Industry*, II, 133.

irons to Exeter was delayed, and the townspeople refused to accept the unstamped testons. The officials were unwilling to press the matter for fear that the market would not be served.[24] Presumably the procedure was handled with dispatch in most places, since a memorandum of Cecil's a month later gives that impression.[25]

Several special problems arose during the recoinage. Some men sought to profit by melting down the testons and exporting the precious metal to gain the excess value. A proclamation of 9 October 1560 broadened the scope of the existing laws which made melting and exporting the coins a felony. It stated that related offenses such as blanching, breaking and battering the coins were to be punished by 'the most severe pain that may well be devised', and the new definitions were enacted as felonies in the next Parliament.[26] A second problem resulted from the natural tendency to raise prices during the recoinage. Some proclamations threatened to punish negligent officials who did not regulate the assize of victuals to ease the problem, and the Council reserved the right to supplement locally assessed penalties.[27]

A third problem, the spread of rumors about further falls in the values of coins, caused no end of consternation. In December 1560 a rumor circulated that the teston worth $4\frac{1}{2}$d would be withdrawn from circulation as had just happened for those worth $2\frac{1}{4}$d. In fact the rumor was well founded since less than two months later the order was published in a proclamation, but in the interim another was issued to threaten speedy and severe punishment for anyone who spread such a rumor.[28] A proclamation in January 1562 was similarly concerned with rumors but set no specific penalties, but in March 1562 another which was issued because of rumors threatened three months' imprisonment and the pillory for anyone spreading the rumors, and one month for those who did not make the authors of the rumors known.[29] Since most of the proclamations on the recoinage were administrative orders, stipulating how the base coins were to be collected and sent up or some other process, penalties were rare. In

[24] PRO, SP 12/14/31.

[25] *Ibid.* 12/14/52. For other details, see Norf. & Norw. RO, Norwich Mayor's Ct Bk 7, fo. 423; Cooper, *Annals of Cambridge*, II, 171.

[26] Proc. 472/531.

[27] Procs. 472/531, 492/560.

[28] Proc. 475/536 in December; 478/541 actually withdrawing them.

[29] Procs. 487/556 and 492/560, the latter prompted by a spurious proclamation (in Steele and Hughes & Larkin as 491/559); see Charles Oman, 'On an Alleged Proclamation of Queen Elizabeth; Dated March 4, 1562, Regarding the Coinage', *The Numismatic Chronicle and Journal of the Royal Numismatic Society*, 5th series, XII (1932), 1–12.

addition to those for abusing the coins and spreading the rumors, they were invoked only one other time, when men who did not turn in certain forbidden foreign coins were to be punished for action 'tending to the derogation of the dignity of this crown and to the manifest deceit and colorable robbery of her highness' people'.[30]

The procedures which we have just surveyed illustrate an exercise of the royal prerogative, but it is interesting to note one plan which would have involved Parliament in the process. The effect of this undated and unsigned proposal would have been to invite Parliament to legislate in order to remedy the consequences of the re-coinage – for farmers and tenants living on rents, for those in debts, for merchants who would lose in transactions of exchange – while reaffirming the monarch's right to regulate the coinage.[31] Nothing came of the plan, if indeed it was even proposed.

The recoinage was complete by 1562, but a few other proclamations on coins were issued. Two were published in 1565 to warn of foreign coins which were similar to but less valuable than more valuable coins, both prompted by reports from local officials.[32] Proclamations in 1600 and 1601 were both concerned with enforcing the statutes against exporting gold and silver. The former cited eleven specific laws, and the latter was based on a statute of Henry VII which forbade the export of coin to Ireland. Neither invoked penalties beyond those in the law, since they were adequate if only enforced.[33] A patentee had gained the privilege of enjoying the penalties for the enforcement of the statutes against exporting gold and silver in 1575, but I am unable to estimate what effect this might have had on the problem.[34]

All of the proclamations on the coinage were concerned with the domestic economy, but of course England's trading position was affected abroad as well. There was a widespread, but not unanimous, belief that the English suffered at the hands of foreigners who overvalued their own coins and undervalued the English, and it was in this context that the rates of exchange needed to be adjusted.[35] In addition, Lord Burghley had received a patent which authorized him to license and control brokers for a period of twenty-three years. A

[30] Proc. 538/614 (in 1565).
[31] PRO, SP 12/11/6.
[32] Proc. 533/610; report in PRO, SP 12/36/49; 538/614, report in 12/37/70.
[33] Procs. 801/907, 811/921.
[34] Docquet of the grant on 15 June 1576 to Ralph Lane for seven years in PRO, SP 38/1; noted in the list of grants in Huntington Libr., Ellesmere MS 2203.
[35] Read, *Burghley*, pp. 145–6; see also BL, Harl. MS 251, fos. 62–3.

proclamation on the exchange was issued six months later in September 1576, and while it did not mention Burghley or the patent, it was certainly an indication that he wished to press the patent vigorously. It ordered the enforcement of all the laws on the exchange and promised that further orders would specify the fees which the licensees could enjoy. The Council issued the order a week later, and even though it was not a royal proclamation, it did provide the operative norms which had been promised.[36] There was such an outcry against all the measures that the Council had to delegate a study of the situation to a commission. None of the complaints from the foreign merchants challenged the right of the monarch to regulate the exchange by proclamation, but they stressed how counterproductive the regulations were.[37] Although there is an account of the money exchanged over a nine month period from the date of the proclamation, it has been suggested that the system 'certainly did not last long'.[38]

Nevertheless the proclamations on the coinage and the exchange had an important role to play in enforcing the statutes, because a law of 1552 had forbidden any exchange at rates higher than those set by royal proclamations. There are many cases in the Exchequer which enforced the law, all of them citing the authority of the proclamations which published the rates.[39]

The proclamations which promulgated new standards for weights and measures also had an important impact on the market place. We have already seen how long a time the various studies took.[40] A proclamation in October 1587 announced the preparation of new balances for weighing gold coins, and two months later another proclamation commanded the local jurisdictions to purchase reformed sets of troy and avoirdupois weights.[41] A proclamation in 1602 announced new brass measures for bulk items such as bushels of grain, perhaps because separate bills introduced into Parliament in 1601 to reform the measures had not been enacted.[42] All the proclamations required local jurisdictions to send representatives into the Exchequer to purchase the weights and measures, and payments for that purpose are recorded at Exeter, Leicester, Norwich, Southampton, and York after the proclamations of 1587, and at Leicester,

---

[36] Proc. 616/706; Council's order, not a royal proclamation, in Steele and Hughes & Larkin as 618/707.
[37] Read, *Burghley*, p. 146; BL, Add. MS 48019, fos. 65–97v.
[38] Read, *Burghley*, p. 146. [39] Above, p. 32.
[40] Above, pp. 37–8. [41] Procs. 693/794, 695/797.
[42] Proc. 814/926.

Southampton, and York after 1602.[43] The primary penalties for refusing to use the new weights and measures were statutory, but additional measures were often needed, as in 1587 when the Lord Mayor of London issued supplementary precepts, in 1601 when he ordered improper weights to be defaced, and in 1602 when he ordered the officers in the wards to confiscate defective weights.[44]

Before leaving proclamations on matters related to money and weights and measures, it should be noted that Queen Elizabeth associated herself with a rather unsuccessful attempt to use a lottery, in which proclamations were issued. The original plan called for 400,000 lots to be sold at 10s each, with the proceeds earmarked for the repair of havens and other worthwhile projects. The scheme was introduced by a chart of prizes and probably by a proclamation, three others were used to defer the date set for drawing the prizes because the subscriptions ran far below the estimates, and another announced that the prizes had been scaled down to one-twelfth of the original worth.[45] One sidenote to the proceedings was the attempt made by a John Aldaye to win his release from the debtors' prison by calling to the attention of Sir William Cecil his subscription for a lot. He had felt that the prize would help him pay his debts, and hoped to use the safe-conduct which had provided for men going to pur- chase the lots as a means to stay out of prison. The judge had merely laughed at the argument, and Cecil probably did so as well.[46]

GRAIN

Royal proclamations on grain were issued only during crises, when bad harvests produced scarcities. The severity of the danger depen- ded on local conditions, yet the best measure which we have today for discovering the extent of the crises are the national averages of prices. From the most comprehensive index of prices of all grains, it can be determined that the average yearly index for Mary's reign is 387; for Elizabeth's to 1580, 339; and for the years 1580–1602, 532.

[43] In 1587: Exeter CRO, Rcvrs Accts 29–30 Eliz.; AB 4, fos. 569, 578; AB 5 fos. 55–6, 70; Book 55, fo. 196; Bateson (ed.), *Records of the Borough of Leicester*, III, liv-lv, 245; Norf. & Norw. RO, Chamb. Accts 1580–9, fos. 270–270v (Mich. 1587–8); Southampton CRO, SC 5/20/2; York CA Dept, YC/A 30, fos. 38v–39v, 46v. In 1602: Bateson (ed.), *Records of the Borough of Leicester*, III, lv, 404–5, 412–13; Southampton CRO, SC 5/20/2; York CA Dept, YC/A 32, fo. 196.

[44] Corp. London RO, Journal XXII, fo. 204; XXV, fo. 156; XXVI, fo. 25. Guildhall Libr. Wardmote Inquest Book, St Dunstan's Parish (1558–1823), fo. 72 (Ward of Farringdon Without).

[45] *Add. Procs.*, no. 25; procs. 549/625, 552/628, 554/630, 557/633.

[46] PRO, SP 12/49/80.

It is then possible to isolate those years or series of years when prices jumped markedly: 1555–6, 1562, 1573, 1579, 1585–6, 1590, 1594–7, and 1600.[47] Almost without exception the royal proclamations on grain were issued in those years alone.

They were issued either to conserve the supply of grain by forbidding its export, or to order that grain masters and other suppliers serve the market so that all could purchase necessary foodstuffs. The former case was already provided for in existing legislation, but the latter required using the prerogative to create new offenses and establish effective administrative procedures.

Regulating exports

The law allowed any English subject to export grain when its price was below 6s 8d per quarter of wheat or a proportionate figure for the other grains; in 1563 the maximum price was raised to 10s per quarter, and again in 1593 to 20s.[48] Two Elizabethan statutes 'authorized' the Queen to issue royal proclamations through which the legal export was to be conducted. When the Justices of the East Riding of Yorkshire certified in 1565 that prices there were below the limits, Elizabeth issued a proclamation specifying Kingston upon Hull as the port of export.[49]

Because actual prices rarely fell below the statutory maximums,[50] the government needed a flexible means for allowing export when specific local conditions warranted it. The Council weighed the reports from local officers and then had the Lord Treasurer manage the export through his network of customs officials, but from 1565 onward it also appointed local commissions 'for the restraint of transportation of corn and grain'.[51] A comprehensive set of grain

[47] Figures for harvest years, from Table I in Peter Bowden, 'Statistical Appendix', *Agrarian History*, IV, 814ff., qv for all sources. The index of 100 is based on the years 1450–99. The pioneering work by James E. Thorold Rogers, *A History of Agriculture and Prices in England* (7 vols.; Oxford, 1866–1900) gives a yearly price in shillings and pence, which allows a quick check against the statutory maximum prices.

[48] 1 & 2 Philip & Mary, c. 5; 1 Eliz. I, c. 13; 35 Eliz. I, c. 7. A statute sought in 1597–8 was not passed; noted in Maurice F. Bond (ed.), *House of Lords. Addenda 1514–1714* (*HMC* new series, XI; London, 1969), p. 10. On the 'authorization', above, p. 42.

[49] Proc. 532/609a.

[50] Bowden's index of 100 is equivalent to 6s 4d per quarter of wheat, but local variations would allow for export. The Council used the statutory authority to allow export on a number of occasions, but did so by letter and not by the royal proclamation which statute required. *APC*, x, 334–5; xi, 208, 222.

[51] Treasurer, e.g., PRO, SP 12/37/36, 12/83/42, 12/217/6; BL, Lansd. MS 29/21; Harl. MS 4943, fo. 511*v*; Burghley's formulary for this is in PRO, SP 12/206/69. Joint commission to the Treasurer and the Chancellor of the Exchequer late in the reign, SP 12/238/58,

regulations, discussed in a moment, was drawn up in the mid-1580s and issued regularly after 1595; it contained provisions to govern the export of grain.

Given such a variety of administrative controls, there would seem to have been little need for proclamations. But Elizabeth did issue several because her own system of licenses to export grain occasioned many abuses. The licenses were both a means of control and a source of financial gain for the Queen, but they posed a cruel threat in the time of famine when their continuance seemed to allow the profiteering adventurer to steal the bread away from needy mouths. The complaints about such activities prompted an increasingly more sophisticated series of safeguards against the abuses, but the proclamations were needed to calm the fears and to redirect the odium away from the Queen who was at the source of the problem.

A proclamation in January 1566 denounced anyone who spread rumors that the Queen was about to license the export of grain. In terms of self-justification rarely found in royal proclamations, Elizabeth explained the Council's careful supervision of the local needs and that it had determined that no harm would come to anyone if the King of Spain's request for grain for the Low Countries was allowed. But to ease public concern, she cancelled the permit to supply his request, ordered that rumors be stopped, and promised that special commissions would be issued to seek out forestallers and others who were responsible for the rise in prices.[52] The Queen was less than honest in denying that licenses had been issued generally, because the Council had earlier delegated six of its members to issue the licenses.[53] And just a fortnight after the proclamation, Cecil drafted for the Queen a license for the shipment to the Low Countries, because the scarcity had abated and thus 'the intention of our proclamation' was preserved.[54]

Another proclamation to stop the export of grain was issued in September 1572, again following after a series of licenses and pro-

12/287/11; Huntington Libr., Ellesmere MS 3484. Admiral's authority to control export noted in *Stiffkey Papers*, pp. 141–2. Copies of the commission, PRO, SP 12/92/41, Huntington Libr., Ellesmere MS 5190; see Norman Scott Brian Gras, *The Evolution of the English Corn Market From the Twelfth to the Eighteenth Century* (Harvard Economic Series, XIII; Cambridge, Mass., 1915), pp. 234–6, and Vincent Ponko, Jr, 'N. S. B. Gras and Elizabethan Corn Policy: a Re-examination of the Problem', *EcHR*, 2nd series, XVII (1964), 26ff.

[52] Proc. 541/617, which thus terminated the license to export through Kingston upon Hull.
[53] *APC*, VII, 261–4, 309.
[54] PRO, SP 12/39/28.

tests from officials in London and on the eastern coast.[55] Although the restraint was only for six weeks, much of which would have been taken up with delivering the proclamations, there were additional features such as threats that negligent officials would lose their offices, a requirement for bonds and sureties for coastal trade lest it be diverted abroad, and a charge to the Justice of Assize to supervise the local justices' compliance. Fines for illegal export were levied in the wake of the proclamation, but on the authority of the statute.[56]

There were two other proclamations to restrain export, both issued late in the reign when the system of licenses had grown and the complaints had multiplied apace.[57] A proclamation of 1590 reflected the severity of the shortages when it threatened anyone who exported grain with 'imprisonment during their lives and such fines as shall be assessed by her majesty's council upon their lands or goods', and the owners and masters of the ships who carried the grain with imprisonment or a year and the stay of their ship in port for a like time. The proclamation also suspended the licenses for exporting beer.[58] The only evidence of enforcement is a request for a dispensation and the actual issue of the commissions which had been promised,[59] so that one cannot tell if the proclamation's harsh penalties were intended *in terrorem* or seriously. In 1600 a proclamation was issued to defend the Lord Treasurer's reputation since rumors had it that he was issuing licenses in spite of a severe shortage which a late snow and lengthy rains had caused. Buckhurst had applied for the proclamation, but the chronicler Camden gauged its failure: 'But they (such is the querulous malice of the vulgar) complained the more, taxing him in secret as if he did acknowledge it, [and] railed the more against him.'[60] A rapid fall in prices eased the tense situation.

All the proclamations which were occasioned by the licenses were in reality exercises in defensive public relations; they probably did little to satisfy anyone since the first two had durations of under six

[55] Proc. 589/677; London's request, PRO, SP 12/88/53; request from eastern counties noted in Hughes & Larkin, II, 363 note 1.
[56] PRO, SP 12/88/51 1, 52; 12/89/46. The fines reached nearly £300 in Norfolk alone. Bonds required: *APC*, VIII, 85–6.
[57] E.g., to individuals, PRO, SP 12/105/92, 12/185/103; *APC*, XIII, 312–13. To corporation of Dover, *ibid.* VII, 267. Grant to a patentee on the statutes, PRO, SP 12/118/63. Protests against the licenses: Corp. London RO, Letter Bk Y, fo. 97; Z, fo. 9.
[58] Proc. 726/827; licenses to export beer had been allowed on the authority of six of the Council, *APC*, XIII, 324, then according to a commission to the Treasurer and Chancellor of the Exchequer, PRO, Index 4208, fo. 289; license to authorize the export of beer, Huntington Libr., Ellesmere MS 2290; see also PRO, Index 6800 (1585).
[59] PRO, SP 12/233/95; *APC*, XX, 31–3.
[60] Proc. 803/909; see Camden, p. 597, and Stow, pp. 1401–2.

weeks each. The effective measures touching grain are to be found when the Queen sought to control its distribution in times of shortages.

Serving the market

The distribution of grain was the responsibility of various types of middlemen, and thus they were the target of much distrust and a good bit of regulation. A statute enacted in 1551 imposed penalties of imprisonment and the forfeiture of the value of the grain for middlemen who attempted to reap profits by reselling the grain which they had purchased, either while it was still unharvested in the fields (engrossing), or on the way to the market (forestalling), or on sale in or near the markets (regrating).[61] The law allowed for punishment – what was needed was a series of preventative measures to ease the shortages.

Proclamations in earlier reigns tried to price victuals to keep prices within a range which the poor could afford, but only once was there a non-military pricing proclamation in the second half of the century, when Mary used a proclamation of Edward VI's as a precedent.[62] Another technique which had been used earlier was to order grain to the markets and to authorize searches in order to determine compliance. Elizabeth issued such a general order in 1562, ordering local officers to meet and confer how the markets might best be served, and promising further assistance. Soon afterwards she directed commissions into the counties 'to enquire of regrators of corn and to see the markets furnished', but it is fair to say that without more specific guidelines the early order could hardly be considered as more than an expression of concern.[63]

Prices began a sustained rise in the mid-1580s, and when in 1586 they reached levels double those of preceding years the Council at first renewed the commissions to restrain exports.[64] In May 1586 it prepared a more detailed set of instructions for sixteen counties which authorized the Justices to survey stores of grain, to order it to the market and set reasonable prices, and to bind obstinate grain

---

[61] 5 & 6 Edward VI, c. 14.

[62] Proc. 430/470. In *APC*, v, 352–3 there are indications that Edward Baeshe was having difficulty in providing victual for the government; he was central in the orders of 1586 – could his troubles have occasioned this earlier proclamation as well? On the earlier ones, see Heinze, pp. 109 ff.

[63] Proc. 490/558; commission, PRO, SP 12/22/29–44; PRO 30/26/116, fos. 95v–97v; BL, Add. MS 5756, fo. 39.

[64] *APC*, xiv, 79, 93, 98–9, 110–11; PRO, SP 12/178/82, 12/188/13, 12/189/86; *HMC 27: 12th Rpt, App. IX (Corp. of Gloucester MSS)*, pp. 458–60.

masters to appear before the Council to answer for their lack of cooperation.[65] The printed orders which soon embodied most of the regulations were considered the 'apogee of paternalism' by N. S. B. Gras, but a study by Brian Pearce showed how great a role royal pragmatism played.[66] A re-examination of the evidence they used show that several roles for proclamations were suggested.

The occasion for the orders seems to have been the difficulty which Edward Baeshe, victualer for the Navy, was having because his contract price for provisioning several ships was only £2,100 and yet his calculation of the costs ran to over £2,600. By threatening to exercise his option to terminate his services at six months' notice, Baeshe placed the Council in a quandary. It first considered issuing a proclamation which would order the markets to be served with grain, but the fact that the draft has no corrections suggests that it was discarded at an early date.[67] Next the Council asked Baeshe for suggestions, and he recommended that a proclamation be published each year to set prices for the ensuing year, and that anyone selling above the rates suffer a month's imprisonment and forfeit the victual.[68] A draft preamble for a proclamation which would follow his suggestions is extant, which stated that the Queen was pricing victuals on the authority of her prerogative and an 'old' statute.[69] Under either of the two alternatives, the royal proclamation would have been the principal regulatory device.

Instead the Council adopted a third suggestion, seemingly made by Sir Walter Mildmay as Chancellor of the Exchequer, and by two Justices.[70] Accordingly a printed set of orders was prepared and a royal proclamation which was to be issued at the same time to lend its sanction. The printed regulations have been called the Book of Orders, and about them Pearce wrote that it 'may not be fantastic to see in these measures a typical stroke of Elizabethan statecraft, aiming to safeguard the financial and political position of the monarchy at a moment of great difficulty and danger, and making a virtue of necessity'.[71] It is important to note that the royal proclama-

[65] Copy, York CA Dept, YC/A 29, fos. 115v–117v; memo, *APC*, xiv, 119–20.
[66] Gras, *Evolution of the English Corn Market*, p. 236; Brian Pearce, 'Elizabethan Food Policy and the Armed Forces', *EcHR*, xii (1942), 39–46.
[67] BL, Lansd. MS 48/51.   [68] *Ibid.* 48/56.
[69] *Ibid.* 48/53.   [70] *Ibid.* 48/52.
[71] Pearce, 'Elizabethan Food Policy and the Armed Forces', p. 43. *Orders deuised by the especiall commandement of the Queenes Maiestie, for the reliefe and stay of the present dearth of Graine Within the Realme* (London, 1587 [new style]). Draft printed almost entirely in E. M. Leonard, *The Early History of English Poor Relief* (Cambridge, 1900), pp. 318–26. Proc. 686/791; draft with Burghley's corrections, BL, Lansd. MS 48/51.

tion had come to have a distinctly secondary role, attacking the corn masters and making them the villains, and that this represented a conscious decision to discard a previous regulatory action to price victuals. The Council doubtless realized that the Book of Orders was too long to fit on the usual few broadside sheets of a proclamation, but by issuing them with a sanctioning proclamation they combined a great deal of administrative detail with the full prestige and legal authority of the prerogative. Many of the reports which the pro-clamation had required were indeed sent to the Council, but the next harvest was seen as clearly sufficient, and there must have been no inclination to use the information when the situation was soon to be righted.[72]

It does not even seem that the Book of Orders was intended as a guiding precedent, because when the years of scarcity began in the 1590s, the suggestion to reissue it came from outside the Council.[73] Some seemingly shorter orders were printed in 1594,[74] and in 1595 an amended Book of Orders was printed, now ordering monthly searches for grain and authorizing the Justices to take more stringent measures to command that it be brought to the market.[75] The Orders had been accompanied by letters from the Council, but soon it was felt that a public order was needed.

In July and again in November 1596 royal proclamations were published not only to order the enforcement of the Book of Orders, but also to require monthly certificates of compliance from the local officers. They also cancelled the licenses for making starch and pro-hibited the export of grain, allowing any subject to request that a Justice of the Peace investigate any suspected port officials, so that if the suspicion that he connived at export was correct the informant would gain half the fines and half the grain, while the officer would lose his office and the shipper his vessel.[76] In London the Lord Mayor issued precepts to order the Aldermen to search the taverns. In Southampton the proclamation was invoked as the authorization

---

[72] PRO, SP 12/197/42 (Cornwall), 12/198/33 (Berks.), 12/198/74 (Suffolk), 12/199/43 (Bucks.), 12/200/16 (Norfolk). *APC*, xiv, *passim*.

[73] BL, Lansd. MSS 76/39, 76/58.

[74] *Ibid.* 76/40, covering letter copied in York CA Dept, YC/A 31, fo. 90v.

[75] *A New Charge giuen by the Queenes commandement, to all Iustices of Peace...for execution of sundry orders...for staie of Graine, With certaine additions nowe this present yeere to be well obserued and executed* (London, 1595). Conciliar enforcement before the proclamations in *APC*, xxv, 8, 20–1, 25–7, 67–8, 132–3, 221, 439–41; PRO, SP 12/244/16; Devon RO, Quarter Sessions Order Bk 1592–1600, fo. 133; *HMC 2: 3rd Rpt (Duke of Northumberland MSS)*, p. 50. See also P. M. Handover, *The Second Cecil* (London, 1959), pp. 127–8.

[76] Procs. 781/884, 784/888.

for special orders for the brewers so that they would conserve grain. Searches were held and special juries formed in Sandwich to take recognizances and bind suspected offenders over to answer before the sessions.[77] The evidence from York is the fullest. Its officers took special orders with the brewers, tipplers, alehouse keepers, and inn-keepers, and issued a local proclamation to regulate the maltsters and bakers.[78] It carried on correspondence with the Justices in the East Riding, Nottinghamshire, Lincolnshire and Leicestershire so that the city's officers would be allowed to buy grain in those places.[79] The petty constables in York were charged to present those who disobeyed the royal proclamation and the city's own supplementary orders, and to take recognizances and make presentments for the sessions.[80] Certificates of actions in the various wards, lists of persons fined by the sessions, and copies of the letters sent to the Council testify to the diligence of the officers.[81]

The Council was particularly concerned with the enforcement of the proclamations in the counties by the Justices of the Peace, and issued orders for them.[82] Eventually it assigned special roles to other officers better able to supervise the local enforcement. The Justices of the Assizes were to supervise the Justices of the Peace, the Lords Lieutenant were given special charges to enforce the provisions which required the gentry to keep to their residences and provide hospitality, and the officials of the Church were commanded to preach on the observation of the orders.[83]

The Council began to feel that something more than local enforcement was required, and that exemplary punishment of several important grain masters in the Star Chamber would be proper. So in October 1597 Attorney General Sir Edward Coke proceeded against a group of Norfolk men *ore tenus* in that Court, both for their having converted houses into cottages and tenements, and for en-

[77] *APC*, xxvi, 96–8, and Corp. London RO. Journal xxii, fos. 174–174*v*; Southampton CRO, Book of Remembrance iv, fos. 187*v*, 188*v*, 198*v*; Kent AO, Sandwich MS Sa/AC 6, fos. 224*v*, 232*v*, 233–233*v*.

[78] York CA Dept, YC/A 31, fos. 218, 224, 259, 261*v*.

[79] *Ibid.* fos. 220*v*, 226v, 235*v*–236*v*, 240.

[80] *Ibid.* fos. 208*v*, 222, 223–223*v*, 225*v*, 229–229*v*, 232, 272*v*–273. Sessions of the Peace F 6, fos. 245*v*, 261*v*–262, 331.

[81] Innkeepers barred from office, *ibid.* YC/A 31, fos. 231, 233*v*; alehouse keepers fined, *ibid.* 234; brewers and tipplers fined, *ibid.* 347*v*, 349–349*v*, 356–356*v*; see also fos. 242, 272–272*v* and later discharges in Sessions of the Peace F 6, *passim.*

[82] E.g., *APC*, xxvi, 99 (Norfolk), 226–7 (Gloucs.); *HMC 24: Rutland I, 1440–1641*, p. 333 (Derbyshire); *HMC 6: 7th Rpt (George Alan Lowndes MSS)*, p. 541 (Essex).

[83] *APC*, xxvi, 94–6, 151–2, 282, 284–7; xxviii, 42–4; *HMC 43: 15th Rpt, App. VII (Duke of Somerset MSS)*, pp. 20–1.

grossing corn and buying and selling it out of the market, 'contrary to the proclamations made in the years 1586 and 1594, and to a printed book made by the Queen in the 37th year of her reign and continued now, and also contrary to the letters of the Council delivered in charge to the Justices of Assize and of the Peace'.[84] Edward Framingham was fined £500, ordered to confess his offense in Cheapside and back in Norfolk, commanded to distribute £40 to the poor and to restore the houses and lands to husbandry again, and was removed from his office as High Constable. Two maltsters and two gentlemen were fined £20 each for engrossing and ordered to confess their faults, and five others including a parson of a church were fined £40 and ordered to restore the lands to husbandry.[85] That same term Francis Parker of Kent was shown to have been an engrosser for sixteen years and to have carried corn to London in a boat each year without a license. He was fined £500, ordered to give £20 to the poor and to confess his fault while wearing papers at Westminster Hall. Nicholas Osborne 'and others' were fined £40 each and imprisoned for identical offenses.[86]

The cases just cited were reported by Hawarde, but among the records of the Star Chamber there is a bill in the same term against forty-six defendants who may be the 'others' of whom Hawarde spoke. Seventeen of the men were from Suffolk, especially Bury St Edmunds, seven others were from Norfolk, and eleven were from the town of Nottingham. The bill was drawn up first in rough form, then copied more neatly – it charged the men with offenses *contrary to* the laws and statutes, and *in contempt of* the proclamations.[87] Six of the defendants had been charged in the Exchequer by informers with violating the Edwardian statute on forestalling, but the quantities of grain which were alleged in the two courts were never the same.[88] Yet in spite of the large number of defendants and their numerous answers, replications, interrogatories, and depositions, there was remarkably little comment on the role of the proclamations, except

[84] Hawarde, *Les Reportes del Cases in Camera Stellata*, p. 76.
[85] *Ibid.* The fines are reported in a memorandum on PRO, E 159/414, m. 94, and in a special class of fines from Star Chamber, E 137/143/2, which does not include references for the later cases.
[86] Hawarde, *Les Reportes del Cases in Camera Stellata*, pp. 78–9.
[87] Rough copy, PRO, Star Chamber 5/A/50/6; fair copy, A/5/20. Numerous answers attached to A/50/6, with other answers in A/11/31–40 and 11–15, and A/12/2, 4, 5, 6, 7, and 11. Replications in A/57/19. Interrogatories, A/19/6, 7, 23, and A/28/40. Depositions, A/16/24.
[88] PRO, E 159/412, m. 149 (Hil. 39 Eliz.); 362, m. 408v (Mich. 39 & 40 Eliz.); 414, m. 135v (Hil. 40 Eliz.).

for Sir Thomas Tresham's argument that the matter should be heard in a common law court rather than the Star Chamber. Unfortunately no replication by Coke to that assertion can be found.[89]

Hawarde used his report of some of the cases as a point of departure for an attack on the use of proclamations, asserting that the charges should have been on the statutes and not on the prerogative. It will be best to delay a consideration of his arguments and motives for a while until the context is complete, but we can note here that both Coke and Lord Keeper Egerton asserted that the offenses violated the statutes, the proclamations, and the common law. Egerton cited a precedent from Fitzherbert, mentioned a statute passed in the reign of Edward I which ordered engrossers banished from the towns, and argued the necessity of punishing negligent officials.[90]

The dearth did not quickly abate, and so in September 1597 a proclamation was issued to protect the reputation of the Lord Mayor of London who had been accused of hoarding grain.[91] A proclamation in August 1598 was much more important, commanding 'the due and straight execution of all laws, statutes, and proclamations made and now in force against forestallers, engrossers, and regraters...' as well as the Council's printed orders on grain.[92] That autumn Coke entered another bill in Star Chamber, once again charging many defendants in several counties, but especially in Suffolk and Norfolk, but the book of decrees in which we could trace its disposition is lost.[93] Some of them had also been charged in the Exchequer, and Henry Sydney of Norfolk alleged the unfairness of being cited in both courts.[94] Another case in the Court's records is without date, and a private case was brought on grain in 1602, which I have not been able to see.[95] Commissions out of the Exchequer were also used in later years.[96]

[89] PRO, Star Chamber 5/A/50/6. Another bill in October 1597 accused a Suffolk man of making a riotous assembly, and only secondarily of offenses related to grain, A/51/32.
[90] Hawarde, *Les Reportes del Cases in Camera Stellata*, p. 77. Egerton stressed Framingham's obligations because of his office.
[91] Proc. 789/893.
[92] Proc. 795/898; letters of attendance for the members of the Cinque Ports to confer with the Lord Warden on its enforcement are in Kent AO, New Romney MS NR/Z Pr 3/51.
[93] PRO, Star Chamber 5/A/55/36, with most items attached to the bill. Coke's replication is in A/10/16.
[94] PRO, E 159/413, m. 194*v* (Mich. 39 & 40 Eliz.).
[95] PRO, Star Chamber 5/A/51/32; Skelton, 'The Court of Star Chamber in the Reign of Queen Elizabeth', pt 2 (44 Eliz.).
[96] PRO, E 178/2800.

The main argument in favor of all the measures which sought to have the markets served is that the danger from famine was so great that Elizabeth would have ignored the welfare of her subjects if she had failed to take innovative action. The opposite opinion is that which Hawarde enunciated: she ignored the statutes 'and thus their [Queen's and Council's] decrees and councils, proclamations and orders, shall be a firm and forcible law, and of the like force as the common law or an Act of Parliament'.[97]

Hawarde's arguments seem at fault on several counts. First, we have already seen that proclamations on grain were issued only at times of high prices. Had they been part of a plan to ignore the statutes, there would have been no reason to forego them at other times. Second, the records of the Star Chamber make clear something which Hawarde did not, that the Attorney General in bringing his cases alleged contrariety to the statutes and contempt of the proclamations and orders. There was no question that the Star Chamber was the proper place for hearing contempts, and we shall see other matters where the contempt was punished there and the substance heard elsewhere.[98] Third, the fines which were assessed were certainly not extraordinary. The Edwardian statute included a penalty of the forfeiture of the grain, and in the cases brought in Star Chamber against the defendants there were hundreds and even thousands of quarters of grain in the bill. Even allowing for a gross distortion of the actual amounts of grain kept from the markets, the fines in the Star Chamber pale before the potential forfeitures on the statutes.

The most important charge against Hawarde is that he read into the Elizabethan practice the fears and indignations which he felt because of the manner in which the Stuart sovereigns and their councillors used royal proclamations, an unwarranted assumption, as has been noted.

The important question is the effect of the proclamations on the shortages of grain. I am now stating only a hunch when I suggest that the primary target of the Book of Orders and the proclamations were the rural areas of the shires, and not the towns. The boroughs already had special powers with which to protect their inhabitants, such as the right to assess the prices of victuals and the courts in which to punish disorders. The records of the boroughs survive because they were kept in known places by a regular succession of

[97] Hawarde, *Les Reportes del Cases in Camera Stellata*, p. 78.
[98] Below, pp. 238–40.

officials, whereas the office of *custos rotulorum* in the counties rotated, and the fate of the Justices's papers often depended on the diligence and whims of particular *custodes*.[99] If my supposition is correct, the real test of the proclamations would be the degree of zeal which they inspired in the county's officials – and unfortunately that is not now measurable.

THE WAGES OF ARTIFICERS

A fifth of the Elizabethan proclamations rated wages according to the Statute of Artificers. This required the Justices of the Peace to meet yearly at the Eastern sessions, to confer with grave men in the area, to consider the circumstances of the markets, and then to set a schedule of wages for the laborers and artificers in their jurisdiction for the coming year. The schedule was to be certified into the Chancery, and upon approval at the center the rates were to be published as a royal proclamation.[100] In 1598 the requirement for certifying the rates into the Chancery and for using royal proclamations to promulgate them was dropped.[101]

The impetus behind the proclamations in the years 1563–98 thus rested with the local officers.[102] The actual process of certification can be documented from many jurisdictions,[103] but particularly for York and London. Ten schedules of rates from York are extant, of which only two can be traced in printed copies, yet the city's records note that certificates were sent to the Chancery in twenty-seven of the thirty-six years.[104] For London one can find traces of every stage in the process – orders for officers to meet to make the assessments, copies of certificates, and copies of the proclamations and their writs – but not a single printed proclamation remains. The Chancellor brought the certificates before the Council yearly, perhaps after they had been considered by a commission delegated for that purpose.[105]

---

[99] An atypical collection of Justices' papers, the more valuable for that and with many example of the Justices' work on grain in the Stuart reigns, is *Stiffkey Papers*, pp. 130ff.

[100] 5 Eliz. I, c. 4.

[101] 39 Eliz. I, c. 12.

[102] E.g., for Norfolk, in Nork. & Norw. RO, Norfolk Quarter Sessions Minute Bk 6, fo. 184v; for Devon, Devon RO, Quarter Sessions Order Bk 1592–1600, fo. 211; for London, Corp. London RO, Repertories 15, fos. 258, 339.

[103] Bristol AO, Bk of Writs, 20 June 1564; Chester CRO, MB 25, fo. 42; Cooper, *Annals of Cambridge*, II, 234; Robert Willis Blencoive, 'Rochester Records', *Archaeologia Cantiana*, II (1897), 79.

[104] York CA Dept, YC/A 23, fo. 144; 24, fos. 13, 46, 75, 110, 140, 243; 25, fos. 14v, 78v, 133v; 26, fos. 21, 69v; 27, fos. 28, 170, 239v; 28, fos. 11v, 53, 99, 144; 29, fos. 20, 197; 30, fo. 39v; 31, fos. 13v, 117v, 185.

[105] *APC*, VII, 230; XIII, 132; XIV, 187; XVI, 168; XVII, 411; XIX, 335; XXI, 308; XXIII, 65; XXVI, 68, some in years when no copies survive.

The printer's bill for 1566 indicates that seventy-seven sets were prepared, of which only three survive today.[106]

To evaluate the impact of the proclamations on wages is perhaps more difficult than in other matters. So few had been uncovered at the turn of the century that it was felt that this requirement in the Statute had become a dead letter. The rapid increase in the discovery of texts, due in great part to the diligence of Hughes and Larkin in scouring local archives, and the number of references to the actual reception in the localities of the rates printed as proclamations,[107] suggest that it was observed with some diligence. Furthermore there are indications that the government insisted on the returns of the certificates. The Queen ordered the Attorney General to compound with the Justices who had not yet made their certificates in 1565,[108] and that might have prompted the number of seventy-seven sets the following year. The officers in York responded to the subpoena which ordered them to show why they had not made a certification by sending a representative 'for proof and discharge of the same, to take up one of the proclamations in print whereby it appears that assessment and certificate was made accordingly, and to get the subpoena discharged and to pay the clerks for their fees'.[109] There is evidence of the diligence of the Lord Warden of the Cinque Ports in requiring member ports to comply,[110] but in 1567 an offer was made to allow them to compound for 13s 4d per member port per year to avoid the responsibility. Most of them continued to make the certificates, but New Romney paid and was unburdened.[111] Norwich not only continued to make the certifications, but even paid an officer in London a retainer to protect them in the matter.[112]

There are only a few instances in which a defendant was charged with paying rates higher than those assessed in the proclamations.[113] Perhaps there were more; perhaps the rates were widely followed because the maximums benefited the men in economic power who

[106] BL, Add. MS 5756, fo. 138, printed in *Stationers' Register*, I, 576.

[107] Used in *Add. Procs*. Rates and/or proof of payment for the receipt of proclamations are extant for nine counties and eighteen towns.

[108] PRO, PRO 30/26/116, which noted that many fines had already been levied.

[109] York CA Dept, YC/A 24, fo. 36.

[110] Kent AO, New Romney MS CPw 33; Sandwich MS Sa/AC 4, fos. 286, 318, and ZB 3/69; East Sussex RO, Rye MS 1/3, fo. 77v.

[111] Kent AO, New Romney MS CPc26 (the offer) and AZ 7 (concluded).

[112] Norf. & Norw. RO, Norwich Chamb. Accts 1580–9, fo. 65v.

[113] York CA Dept, Sessions of Peace F 4, fos. 9–9v, and GLC (Middx) RO, Gaol Delivery Roll 134/12, 26 September 1565, briefly noted in John Cordy Jeaffreson (ed.), *Middlesex County Records*, Vol. 1: *Indictments, Coroners' Inquests-Post-Mortem and Recognizances From Edward VI. To The End of the Reign of Queen Elizabeth* (London, 1886), pp. 50–1.

assessed the rates. The silence from the lack of evidence is deafening.[114]

THE POLITICAL LENT

Orders to abstain from meat in lent, not because of any 'popish superstition' but for the economic benefit which would accrue to the fishing industry, were an almost annual occurrence from 1559 onward. It has already been noted that these proclamations supplemented the existing laws, since whereas the latter forbade personal consumption of meat, all of the former after 1559 were aimed solely at the butchers, victualers, poulterers, innkeepers, and other sellers on the logical reasoning that to shut off the supply would prevent individual abuses. A substantial penalty of £20 was set as well as disfranchisement for citizens and the disability from continuing in the trade, and lesser vendors were threatened with the pillory. The most effective administrative device was the authorization to hold fortnightly searches, and the Crown proposed to keep tabs on the local officers through a requirement for certificates.[115]

Since the full set of orders which were published in 1561 authorized the republishing of the proclamation on the initiative of local officers, it is difficult to know just how many were made. Occasionally there were orders from the Council to demand their publications.[116] Although only two of the proclamations after 1561 are extant in print, evidence for their issue exists for twenty-six of the thirty-seven years 1562–98.

It seems that only in the early years were the proclamations the primary instruments for enforcing the lenten regulations. For the first time in 1574, and regularly from 1577 onwards, the Council sent letters to a variety of local officers which contained a more comprehensive set of regulations than those in the proclamations alone.[117]

---

[114] It is beyond the scope of this book to evaluate the actual rates assessed and their relation to the cost of living.

[115] Above, p. 40. The proclamation in 1559 came out during the interim settlement of religion and merely ordered men to observe the 'usual fasting days', proc. 453/502. The statute was 2 & 3 Edward VI, c. 19. The requirement for abstaining from meat on Wednesdays was established in 5 Eliz. I, c. 5; it was ordered enforced once by proc. 550/627, but the examples of enforcement which I have found were always based on the statute alone.

[116] *APC*, VII, 205–6; Corp. London RO, Repertories 16, fo. 434*v*; *HMC 31: 13th Rpt, App. IV (Corp. of Hereford MSS)*, p. 337. It had become so routine in Exeter that it was mentioned among the Mayor's duties in John Hooker's common-place book: Exeter CRO, MS 51, fo. 164*v*.

[117] In 1574, noted in *APC*, VIII, 196, and copied in Flenley, p. 100. In 1577, letters to Sheriffs and Justices (*APC*, IX, 260), to the Justices of Assize (*ibid.* p. 289), and to the

Beginning in 1589 the Council's articles were printed every year; they were supplemented from time to time with charts containing the points of the regulations, and with printed forms for the recognizances which were demanded, so that the local officers had merely to fill in the blanks.[118] The effect of these more sophisticated regulations was to minimize the importance of the proclamations – I have found only six instances of local enforcement after 1580 which cited the proclamations as authority, but we shall soon see copious examples from the earlier years.[119] Even if we postulate a growing indifference to the orders and admit that some enforcement could have been based on the proclamations without citing them explicitly, we cannot help but feel that the repeated reissues and certificates had become a formality.

The certificates certainly abound, however: notes that they were made occur in the records of Abingdon, Bristol, Cambridge, Exeter, Leicester, London, Norwich, Oxford, Rochester, Rye, Sandwich, and York.[120] The penalty for not making the certificate was £100, and several jurisdictions sought to be free of the obligation.[121]

The real test was the extent to which the local officers enforced the regulations, and there is much evidence to testify to their vigilance in the early years. A first step might be to issue a local order to supplement the proclamation, such as the Lord Mayor of London sent to the Aldermen and interested companies.[122] Next a jury could be

Archbishop of Canterbury (*ibid.* p. 249), who transmitted it to the dioceses via his provincial dean; Cardwell, I, 424–7. Copied in York, CA Dept, YC/A 26, fos. 107–8, printed in Raine, VII, 141–3.

[118] Innkeepers were ordered to display a chart prepared by John Story, PRO, SP 12/185/100; the printed form of the recognizance, PRO, E 180/104–5, probably as a result of proc. 800/905.

[119] E. Sussex RO, Rye MS 1/4, fo. 322v (1580); Norf. & Norw. RO, Norfolk Quarter Sessions Minute Bk 5, fo. 178a v (1581) and Norwich Mayor's Ct Bk 12, fos. 526, 633–4 (1591); BL, Lansd. MS 41/23–5, 43/29, for the city of Westminster of which Burghley was the Lord Steward (1585); Exeter CRO, Mayor's Ct Roll 23–4 Eliz., m. 24; Essex RO, Transcript of Essex Quarter Sessions, 149/40 (I owe this reference to Mr F. G. Emmison). There are many examples in the later years of enforcement based on the authority of the Council's letters.

[120] *HMC 1: 2nd Rpt (Corp. of Abingdon MSS)*, p. 150; Bristol AO, Book of Writs, 16 Eliz., 17 Eliz.; Cooper, *Annals of Cambridge*, II, 234; Exeter CRO, Rcvrs Accts, 24–5, 29–31, 33–7, 41–2 Eliz.; Bateson (ed.), *Records of the Borough of Leicester*, III, 99, 114, 120; Corp. London RO, Journal XVIII, fo. 18; Norf. & Norw. RO, Chamb. Accts 1551–67, fos. 277v, 334v, 360; 1580–9, fos. 65v, 110v, and presumably at other times when the man retained for the purpose was paid; H. E. Salter (ed.), *Oxford Council Acts, 1583–1626* (Oxford Historical Society, LXXXVII; Oxford, 1928), pp. 359, 366, 367, 383; Blencoive, 'Rochester Records', pp. 79, 82; E. Sussex RO, Rye MS Chamb. Accts 60/7, fo. 233v; Kent AO, Sandwich MS Sa/ZB 4/11, fo. 38 (via the Lord Warden at Dover); York CA Dept, YC/A 23, fo. 140v; 25, fo. 6v; 24, fos. 9v, 109, 133v.

[121] York CA Dept, YC/A 23, fo. 140v; Corp. London RO, Remembrancia I, no. 332.

[122] *Ibid.* Journal XX, pt 2, fo. 327; XXIII, fos. 234v, 376; XXIV, fos. 191v–192v; Repertories 15, fo. 43v.

impanelled to receive presentments, of which the most common in practice stated that none had offended.[123] In some cases one can find actual judicial action on the proclamations, usually resulting in a fine substantially below the amount set in the proclamation and in imprisonment.[124] Many were exempt from the regulations because the proclamations had allowed those with licenses to be excused. Licenses were granted by officers of the central government and local jurisdictions as well as by ecclesiastics, so that the net result was to restrict the provisions in the proclamations to the 'lesser sort'.[125]

SPECIFIC COMMODITIES

Because the trades in wine, wool and cloth were highly organized and competitive, any regulation of them by means of proclamations would inevitably cause some discontent and dissatisfaction whether it was based on the statutes or on the prerogative alone. The use of patents by Elizabeth complicated the matter still further. The petitions and protests of the interested parties afford the material for understanding better the impact of proclamations in these areas.

Wine

The sixteen Elizabethan proclamations which set the maximum prices at which wine could be sold appear on the surface to be rather straightforward measures. Fourteen of them were cast in a standard format which was altered only to include the new prices to be in force in the following year.[126] The first three, issued between 1564 and 1572, set prices both at gross and at retail, on the authority of two Henrician statutes for the former and an act on 1563 for the latter.[127] The eleven other proclamations with the standard format,

[123] Bateson (ed.), *Records of the Borough of Leicester*, III, 95–6; PRO, SP 12/86/12 (recognizances in Lincs.); Corp. London RO, Repertories 15, fos. 218, 222v, 223v; Norf. & Norw. RO, Norwich Mayor's Ct Bk 7, fo. 370; 9, fo. 326; 10, fos. 82, 84; E. Sussex RO, Rye MSS 1/3, fos. 13v, 73, 115, 148, 186v; 1/4, fos. 8, 39, 111, 160, 191, 234; Kent AO, New Romney MS NR/JBf8 (13 July 1563); Sandwich MS ZB 1/15, fos. 31–2; York CA Dept, YC/A 23, fos. 9, 142; 25, fo. 3v; 27, fo. 8v.

[124] Corp. London RO, Repertories 15, fos. 45, 323; 17, fo. 249; GLC (Middx) RO, 189/6–20; 195/12–32; 196/25; Kent AO, Sandwich MS Sa/AC 4, fo. 302; AC 5, fo. 126v; York CA Dept, YC/A 27, fo. 24v; PRO, SP 12/77/69; *Annals Ref.*, I, i, 368.

[125] Central: PRO, SP 12/106/70; *APC*, IX, 300; XII, 329; Huntington Libr., Ellesmere MSS 4641, 4643, 4678, 4684, 4858; *HMC 4: 5th Rpt (E. P. Shirley MSS)*, p. 368. Local: Essex RO, Typescript of Essex Quarter Sessions citing Q/SR 41/17; *HMC 4: 5th Rpt (Corp. of St. Albans MSS)*, p. 567; *HMC 55: Var. Coll. I (Corp. of Oxford MSS)*, p. 266. Ecclesiastical: Huntington Libr., Ellesmere MS 514.

[126] Issued in late November.

[127] Gross, 28 Henry VIII, c. 14 and 34 & 35 Henry VIII, c. 14; retail, 5 Eliz. I, c. 5.

issued in 1578 and later, set prices at gross only. Thus in the years 1573–7 there was a change in the use of royal proclamations which involved giving up a clear statutory right. The two pricing proclamations in those years did not follow the standard format – they were part of a clash of economic interests in the unravelling of which we can catch a glimpse of some of the complexities which could lie behind a deceptively simple series of proclamations.[128]

Part of the problem lay in overlapping and conflicting laws. A statute in 1552 had set actual prices for sales at retail, at very low levels, and it was not repealed when the statute of 1563 authorized the Queen to set prices at retail. The earlier act left informers at liberty to initiate suits in the Exchequer against vendors who allowed their prices to follow the upward spiral of the costs of the imported wines.[129] The most effectively organized group in the trade was the Company of Vintners whose newly issued charter included an exemption from the maximum prices in the act of 1552. The blanket exemption and the Vintners' dominant position in the trade made them disliked by the other merchants in London who sold wine.[130] The situation was further complicated by the ancient right of the Lord Mayor of London to hold the assize of victuals, including wine. The final element in the complicated web of interests was the practice of the Queen to grant licenses to patentees. As early as 1570, Edward Horsey had been granted the right to license sellers of wine in fourteen towns, and his license conveyed the right to set any prices the vendors wished. When in 1575 a further grant allowed him the right to license in London, the elements for real conflict were present.[131]

It began no later than May 1574 by which time the city had begun a suit against the Vintners' new grant.[132] The action must have intimidated the Company, because in September several of its members promised at a meeting of the Court of Aldermen that they and their associates would sell at retail below a maximum price of 20d.[133] In November the Council called to a meeting at the Lord Keeper's

[128] Much of the evidence is missing, and much of what remains consists of cryptic references, so that the following reconstruction must be tentative.
[129] See Corp. London RO, Repertories 16, fos. 124–124v, 126; HMC 70: Pepys MSS, pp. 93–5.
[130] André L. Simon, The History of the Wine Trade in England, Vol. II: The Progress of the Wine Trade in England During the Fifteenth and Sixteenth Centuries (London, 1907), pp. 77–8, 80; Thomas Milbourn (ed.), The Vintners' Company (Westminster, 1888), pp. 33–5; HMC 80: Sackville (Knole) I (Cranfield Papers), pp. 77–8.
[131] Patent noted in Huntington Libr., Ellesmere MS 2311; see also PRO, E 176/1, file 1, 1–5. [132] Corp. London RO, Journal XVIII, fos. 211, 443v.
[133] Ibid. Letter Bk X, fo. 336v.

house the Vintners, the city's officers, and the other wine merchants, and during the next several months we find that the officers of London required all merchants to enter into bonds not to sell at rates higher than £20 per tun at gross.[134] Presumably the meeting in November had been to assess the price informally and thus save the government the embarrassment of admitting that it was powerless to prevent so high a price from being allowed. The previous published rate was only £8 8s 6d.

The early months of 1575 were a time of reassessment, and a measure of the Vintners' determination to maintain its charter rights may be seen in some refusals to enter into the bonds and in its argument to the Council in March that it was not subject to the Lord Mayor's authority.[135] In May the city ordered a search for precedents for the Mayor's right to assess prices, and in July 1575 a royal proclamation was issued to head off still another rise in prices by informing importers who were setting off to make their purchases abroad that they would not be allowed to bring wine back at prices higher than £10 a tun.[136]

Matters came to a boil in the winter of 1575–6 when the Council ordered the enforcement of the royal proclamation, and when the city resumed its suit against the Vintners and acted to protect its citizens from suits brought in Horsey's name in the Exchequer.[137] In April 1576 the Lord Mayor issued his own proclamation setting prices at retail, prompted by the opinion which he had received that his right was unimpeded as long as the Queen did not exercise her right.[138] The Vintners and the other wine merchants began to set on paper their own claims and the denials of the other side's assertions,[139] while the Lord Mayor used the city's courts to try those Vintners who did not obey his proclamation – even going so far as to disfranchise some of the recalcitrant.[140]

---

[134] *Ibid.* Journal xvIII, fos. 206, 315v–316, 329, 339; Repertories 18, fos. 306, 315v–316, 327, 329.

[135] *Ibid.* Repertories 18, fo. 326v; Folger Shakesp. Libr., MS V.b.9.

[136] Proc. 607/694; Corp. London RO, Journal xvIII, fo. 385.

[137] *APC*, IX, 70, 123–4; Corp. London RO, Journal xx, pt 2, fo. 282v; Repertories 19, fos. 10v, 17, 32, 63v.

[138] *Ibid.* Journal xx, pt 2, fos. 285v–286; Huntington Libr., Ellesmere MS 2293; prices of £20–1 in March are noted in *HMC 24: Rutland I, 1440–1641*, p. 103.

[139] City's arguments against the Vintners, Huntington Libr., Ellesmere MS 2292; BL, Add. MS 48109, fos. 395–395v. Vintners' arguments for their privileges, PRO, SP 12/114/65; against the city, BL, Add. MS 48019, fos. 394–394v. Other merchants' arguments for their rights, PRO, SP 12/105/47, BL, Add. MS 48019, fos. 111–13; against the Vintners, *ibid.* fo. 393 and Huntington Libr., Ellesmere MS 2291.

[140] Corp. London RO, Letter Bk Y, fos. 68v, 75v, 82v; Journal xx, pt 2, fo. 293; Repertories 19, fos. 66v, 76, 82.

The Council intervened decisively. In so far as the Mayor was enforcing the Queen's proclamation, it supported his activities and called the disobedient persons whom he had uncovered into the Star Chamber. There it punished some for their contempt and remanded the others to the Mayor, to be punished on the Court's authority.[141] But it also commanded the Lord Mayor to withdraw his own proclamation, and a royal proclamation was issued on 27 July 1576 to set prices both at gross and at retail.[142] The government had been won over to the view that the fault lay with the Vintners, as is clear from a letter from the Council which accused the Company of abusing their grant 'whereof they have without reason doubled the price of wines'.[143] It therefore shifted the responsibility for taking bonds to the Master of the Rolls, raised the sum for bonds to £100, and demanded that the condition specify that wine not be sold at rates higher than the Queen's proclamation.[144] The Council told the Master of the Rolls that the Queen's intention was that the Vintners be 'the more terrified to offend against the said proclamation'.[145] Throughout the winter the Council insisted upon vigilance in London and particularly at the ports, and allowed the Vintners no flexibility other than to lower the prices for retail sales below the rates set in the royal proclamation.[146]

This diligence came to naught because the expanded grant which the Queen had made to the patentee Horsey eventually undercut all efforts to keep the prices low. The Council had to reverse itself, as is shown by its recommendation to the officials of London that they allow the Vintners and other merchants to sell at whatever prices they chose, so that they would not be at a severe disadvantage vis-à-vis the men licensed by Horsey, and by its direction to the Master of the Rolls to void the recognizances.[147] What emerged was a compromise – never to my knowledge explicitly stated – which left the control of the prices at gross to the Queen through her pro-

---

[141] *APC*, VIII, 128–30, 132, 164.

[142] PRO, SP 12/108/58. Proc. 614/705.

[143] *APC*, VIII, 176–7.

[144] *Ibid.* IX, 176–7, 180, 192.

[145] *APC*, IX, 180.

[146] *Ibid.* 240, 261, 283; x, 51–2. Corp. London RO, Journal xx, pt 2, fo. 403*v*. Twenty-four informations against London Vintners and merchants were brought in the Exchequer in 1589 by a patentee who had received a grant in 1560 to enforce certain statutes. The informations alleged that the men sold at rates higher than those set by the statutory committee, without stating that they had been published in proc. 707/808. None of them was brought to a conclusion. PRO, E 159/396, mm. 255–67, all *r* and *v* (Hil. 31 Eliz.).

[147] *APC*, x, 126–7, 150. A draft grant of some of the forfeitures on the recognizances to a Yeoman of the Chamber, undated, is in Huntington Libr., Ellesmere MS 6206B.

clamations, and the prices at retail to the patentees. The maximum price at gross formed an indirect check, and the patentees would always have the Queen's displeasure to reckon with if the prices got out of hand.

To this point our consideration has focused exclusively on London and only on a few years. The boroughs had the right under the statute of 1552 to license sellers of wine and exercised it often before the advent of the patentees.[148] There are only a few instances in which a royal proclamation was enforced by a borough before 1573, once at Southampton and once at York.[149] Afterwards the licenses which the patentees granted were usually recorded in town records,[150] but a few towns tried to maintain control, as did York and Rye in pricing wines, and York and Norwich in attempting to enforce the royal proclamations.[151] The contradiction between the grants and the proclamations was a problem, and so the officials in Chester wrote to Burghley for advice, but it seems that in nearly all cases the patentees prevailed.[152] Even in York, where they were resisted, the city's capitulation was indicated when it received from the patentees a list of the men who would not co-operate, with the clear intent that the city was to act on their behalf.[153] There is little evidence of action in the counties other than the issue of the commission and one case on the gaol delivery rolls in Middlesex.[154]

Other proclamations dealt with different aspects of the wine trade.

[148] Chester CRO, AB/1, fo. 118; Exeter CRO, AB 2, fo. 258; 3, fos. 233, 248, 267, 290; Norf. & Norw. RO, Norwich Mayor's Ct Bk 7, fo. 532; E. Sussex RO, Rye MS 1/4, fo. 243; Kent AO, Sandwich MS Sa/AC 4, fo. 300v; A. L. Merson (ed.), *The Third Book of Remembrance of Southampton*, Vol. II: *1540–1573* (Southampton Records Series, III; Southampton, 1955), 93–4; York CA Dept, YC/A 21, fo. 18v; 24, fos. 3v, 106v–107v, 108v–109.

[149] York CA Dept, Sessions of Peace F 2, under date 30 March 1565 (but see presentments on the statute of 1552 alone in *ibid*. 3 August 1575); Elinor R. Aubrey (ed.), *Books of Examinations and Depositions, 1570–1594* (Southampton Record Society, XVI; Southampton, 1914), p. 19. Informations by the Attorney General on the basis of the statute of 1552 are in PRO, KB 9/599, pt 1/3–4; 600, pt 1/3 and pt 2/175; 603/12, 23. A note of an indictment for selling wine at rates higher than a proclamation is in *HMC 31: 13th Rpt, App. IV (Corp. of Hereford MSS)*, p. 325, but seems unclear.

[150] Norf. & Norw. RO, Norwich Mayor's Ct Bk 9, fos. 118–21; 10, fos. 682, 692; York CA Dept, YC/A 28, fo. 107; E. Sussex RO, Rye MS 1/4, fo. 345.

[151] Pricing: York CA Dept, YC/A 27, fos. 130, 139, 185v; 31, fos. 227v, 231, 232; E. Sussex RO, Rye MS 1/4, fos. 262v, 275v. Enforcement: York CA Dept, Sessions of Peace F 5, fos. 85–85v; Norf. & Norw. RO, Norwich Mayor's Ct Bk 10, fo. 715.

[152] Chester CRO, ML 5/25 (letter of 24 December 1580). An earlier enforcement of the statute (and proclamation?) is in a session of the peace, MB 20, fo. 54v. But the University of Cambridge won a decree exempting it from the patentees: Cooper, *Annals of Cambridge*, II, 414–15, and *passim*, for the dispute.

[153] York CA Dept, YC/A 28, fo. 107.

[154] Commission, above note 39; GLC (Middx) RO, 276–48, true bill at a session on 19 April 1588.

In 1561 a proclamation was issued to prevent drunkenness and dis-order which came from drinking wines 'before they can be aged and their strength naturally fined'; in reality this proclamation dealt with public order more than wine.[155] A proclamation in 1579 opened the trade of importing wine to anyone, in the hope of reducing the high prices.[156] Another proclamation in 1585 was issued because the plague was so severe in Bordeaux. It forbade the import of wine from there, but threw it open to any Englishmen who traded at other ports.[157] And we have seen how both Mary and Elizabeth issued proclamations to forbid importing wines from France during the Anglo-French wars.[158]

Wool

Mary and Elizabeth each issued a few proclamations which con-cerned the trade in wool, but they seem to have had little impact because they insisted on traditional means of regulation at just the time when the forces which shaped the markets were in flux. The fortunes of the later Tudor market in wool were initially shaped by a single event, the collapse of the foreign markets for English cloth in 1551 which in turn hurt the prices for raw wool. In 1552 the Mer-chant Staplers and the Merchant Adventurers got an act passed which gained for them as much as possible of the dwindling market at the expense of the wool middlemen.[159] The crisis of the early 1550s was intensified when the Staplers lost their mart in Calais when it fell to France in 1558, and by the prolonged interruptions of trade with the Low Countries in Elizabeth's reign.

The importance of the middlemen in the wool trade was too great to be choked off by the restrictive legislation. There was a marked trend toward regional specialization in the trade, which was spurred by the growth of the worsted trade which required coarse wool from the midlands. The large clothiers with their developed resources and capitalistic organization could move quantities of wool to the cloth-making areas, but others had to rely on the middlemen, particularly on the common 'broggers' of wool and the glovers who sold the wool which remained on the fleeces they used. The Merchant Staplers began to serve as domestic middlemen as well in order to boost their

[155] PRO, SP 12/19/49 is the draft which alone is extant; proc. 484/550; similar pro-cedures by conciliar letter, *APC*, XII, 83.

[156] Proc. 645/744.   [157] Proc. 677/781.

[158] Above, pp. 79–81.

[159] The thorough study of Peter J. Bowden is an invaluable aid for understanding the statute (5 & 6 Edward VI, c. 7) and the trade in general: *The Wool Trade in Tudor and Stuart England* (London, 1962), pp. 112ff. and especially pp. 115–16.

sagging fortunes, even though they were technically restricted to the foreign trade.[160]

By the 1570s the use of licenses for wool middlemen had become the means for circumventing the earlier legislation while at the same time keeping some control over the trade.[161] In the middle of that decade prices began to rise sharply, and a proclamation on 28 November 1576 which suspended the licenses for a year and forbade the Staplers to act in the domestic trade was the government's response to the alarm.[162] Since little reformation followed, the Council six months later sent letters into twenty counties which ordered the Justices of the Peace to take bonds at £100 from the broggers that they would not buy for resale.[163] Some returns from the counties had begun to trickle in, but further enforcement seems to have been based on some of the suggestions for reform which the Council had begun to seek.[164]

The Council had asked for opinions from the Merchant Adventurers, the Merchant Staplers, and leading clothiers in several counties. Because the responses came from highly organized interests they could hardly do anything other than confirm the conciliar anti-middleman prejudices. Every group except the Staplers blamed that Company and recommended that its domestic activities be curtailed.[165] The Staplers suggested a variety of measures, including two royal proclamations – one to restrict the number of broggers and one to keep the glovers from selling the wool left on the fleeces.[166] Although the proclamations were not issued, some of their suggestions were incorporated into a letter from the Council at the end of July which ordered the proclamation of the previous November to be enforced.[167] Seemingly nothing came of the Council's demands, and there is only one response to the nearly identical reissue of the proclamation again in 1579 when prices rose again, and this touches the questions of a patentee's rights and exemptions, not the enforcement of the proclamation as such.[168]

---

[160] Licenses to courtiers also cut into the Staplers' trade, in particular that to Secretary Walsingham: Bowden, *The Wool Trade in Tudor and Stuart England*, p. 131.

[161] *Ibid.* Chapter V.   [162] Proc. 621/712.

[163] PRO, SP 12/113/21-2; instructions for the commissioners, *HMC 19: 11th Rpt, App. IV (Townshend MSS)*, pp. 3-4, printed in *Stiffkey Papers*, pp. 160-1.

[164] PRO, SP 12/115/28, 29; *APC*, IX, 366.

[165] The answers are in PRO, SP 12/114: Adventurers, no. 26; clothiers of Newbury, 25; Wilts., 27; Gloucs., 32; Worcs., 28; Suffolk, 33, 39.

[166] *Ibid.* 29-31, 39.   [167] *APC*, IX, 386; X, 24-5.

[168] Proc. 640/738; exemption requested, PRO, SP 12/115/14, granted *APC*, IX, 281. But bonds were taken for men to appear before the Queen: Norf. & Norw. RO, Norwich Mayor's Ct Bk 10, fo. 542; *APC*, XII, 193; XIII, 48-9.

By 1581 there had been a change in the Council's attitude. They conceded the necessity for the middlemen, stopped any actions against a patentee, and ordered the Justices of the Peace to let the licenses be used freely. In 1584 the Staplers were successful in obtaining a promise that no new licenses would be issued for seven years, but new grants were made at the end of that period.[169]

Proclamations were used in a subsidiary aspect of the wool trade also. The Company of Woolmen had been one of the main service groups, preparing wool for export by winding and folding it, and checking to see that no impurities had been added to increase the weight. They were vulnerable because the work was seasonal, only semi-skilled, and a victim of the decline in exports. Both Mary and Elizabeth issued the customary proclamations which enforced the statutes to protect their rights, as had earlier Tudors. It will be recalled that Mary's reissue of an Edwardian proclamation carried the penalty of the pillory, but that the Elizabethan reissues deleted the requirement for corporal punishment.[170]

Cloth

The Parliament in 1552 had produced the basic legislation for cloth manufacture as well as for the wool trade; it set the quality control requirements for the length, width, and weight of every type of cloth which was produced.[171] Other acts were passed soon afterwards to limit the trade of weaving to experienced men, and to restrict the making of cloth to corporate areas.[172] But whereas the legislation on wool was modified by a series of royal licenses, the statutes on cloth were modified on a piecemeal basis by many later laws, until nearly every important county or cloth making area gained an exemption in some way.[173]

The exemptions for two of the areas were granted first by royal proclamations and then later confirmed by acts of Parliament. The clothiers of Norfolk, Suffolk and Essex had a new set of dimensions and allowances less stringent than in the laws published on their

[169] Bowden, *The Wool Trade in Tudor and Stuart England*, pp. 141–8.

[170] Procs. 423/463, 497/570, 780/883; penalties, above, p. 49. On the Company, Bowden, *The Wool Trade in Tudor and Stuart England*, pp. 121–5; their request for the reissue, *APC*, XXIV, 294–5.

[171] 5 & 6 Edward VI, c. 6; see G. D. Ramsay, *The Wiltshire Woollen Industry in the Sixteenth and Seventeenth Centuries* (2nd ed.; London, 1965), pp. 53–4.

[172] 5 & 6 Edward VI, c. 8, and 1 Mary I, session 1, c. 7.

[173] George Unwin, 'The Merchant Adventurers' Company in the Reign of Elizabeth', in *Collected Papers* (ed. R. H. Tawney; London, 1927), p. 189.

behalf in a proclamation in 1590. This also forbade informers to bring cases on the old standards in the courts.[174] The principal reason for the proclamation was a concern to protect the English market against foreign rivals. The cloths of East Anglia were lighter and more suitable for the southern European markets, but the Dutch had been underselling them by buying English white cloth and then stretching and dyeing it. Requests for exemptions had been made often and as early as 1571, and the increasing number of informations heightened the clothiers' sense of urgency.[175]

A more immediate occasion for its issue in 1590 seems to have been to reassert the clothiers' privileges against the merchants of London. Even though a Marian statute exempted cloths which had already been tested locally by an alnager from any remeasuring, the officials at Blackwell Hall sought to enforce their rights to control the market. An earlier suit in the Exchequer had upheld their claims, but the resentment in other areas continued to grow, particularly when they saw that it was fees that the merchants wanted, not a control over quality. The Barons decided against the city when a new case was brought in 1589, and since the proclamation the following year specifically commanded the Lord Mayor to publish it in Blackwell Hall, it seems that it was partially motivated by the clash of jurisdictions.[176]

In the course of the preparation of the proclamation, we find the single known instance of an opinion within the government that the proposed course of action was illegal. Solicitor General Egerton argued,

'The statutes being general and subjects interested therein, I take it (under reformation) that this course of toleration can hardly be warranted in point of law, howbeit her Majesty's gracious pleasure being notified in this behalf, every one that has to deal in the action, is to yield all humble and dutiful obedience thereunto, and therein will the strength of this toleration consist, which should have been procured in parliament, as in the year 27 of her Majesty's [reign], seen of the western clothiers obtained in a much like case.'[177]

The Council thought otherwise, but did include in the final text a clause which indicated that it would be temporary: 'And these

[174] Proc. 720/823, of which '721/824' in Steele and Hughes & Larkin is a part.
[175] J. E. Pilgrim, 'The Cloth Industry in Essex and Suffolk, 1558–1640' (unpublished M.A. thesis, University of London, 1939), pp. 19–21, 56–61. PRO, SP 12/77/68.
[176] Ramsay, *The Wiltshire Woollen Industry*, pp. 55–7; Coke, *Reports*, v, 63–4; undated case in the Star Chamber in Pilgrim, 'The Cloth Industry in Essex and Suffolk', pp. 137–40.   [177] Huntington Libr., Ellesmere MS 2316.

tolerations to endure during our pleasure, or until by parliament the same may be further considered and established, as the like provision hath been made for western cloths in the 27th year of our reign.' A bill for that purpose was introduced in a subsequent Parliament, but not enacted.[178] The royal proclamation was reissued with a few alterations in 1601, and the Parliament of that year finally enacted the provisions into law.[179]

The second instance of an exemption from the statutes came after the Justices of the Peace in Devon had complained of abuses in the making of Devonshire kersies and dozens. The proclamation repeated their complaints and also those of the Dutch, and announced a series of mitigations. At the very next session of Parliament, the reduced standards were enacted in a statute.[180] From the fragmentary evidence, it would seem that there had been unofficial efforts to get the mitigations, both from the merchants of Totnes and from the Merchant Adventurers of Exeter, and that the matter had also been discussed with the deputies of Sir Edward Stafford who had a grant to enforce the statutes.[181] The exact nature of their co-operation or opposition is not clear, but the Adventurers did appoint two representatives to press in Parliament for a law which would make the reduced standards permanent.[182]

A proclamation in 1587 had dealt with the cloth trade generally, and not just with the interests of special areas. Again many parties were involved – the clothiers, the Merchant Staplers, the foreign company of the Merchants of the Steelyard, and the Merchant Adventurers who controlled the export of cloths from England. The latter had sought to benefit from the recovering state of the cloth market by using its role as a financial servant to the Crown to dominate the market. The Staplers were particularly threatened, especially because the renewal of their charter in 1579 did not include the right they had had formerly to use the Adventurers' mart abroad.[183]

A domestic and foreign crisis of considerable proportions in 1586–7 was to demonstrate that even the Adventurers' privileged position

[178] HMC 3: 4th Rpt (House of Lords MSS), p. 115.
[179] Proc. 807/912; 43 Eliz. I, c. 10; Pilgrim, 'The Cloth Industry in Essex and Suffolk', pp. 20–1.
[180] APC, XXII, 89–90; proc. 744/847; 35 Eliz. I, c. 10.
[181] Wallace T. MacCaffrey, Exeter, 1540–1640 (Harvard Historical Manuscripts, XXXV; Cambridge, Mass., 1958), p. 84. William Cotton, An Elizabethan Guild of the City of Exeter (Exeter, 1873), pp. 129–32.
[182] Cotton, An Elizabethan Guild, p. 132.
[183] E. E. Rich, The Ordinance Book of the Merchants of the Staple (Cambridge, 1937), pp. 72–6.

would have to yield to the common good. The market for English cloths abroad was threatened not only by the Duke of Parma's capture of cities in the Low Countries but also by the possibility that a Spanish blockade could render ineffective the privilege of using the port of Emden which the Adventurers had negotiated for one year. It was also a time of severe dearth in England, and the collapse of the cloth trade meant that many Englishmen would not have the proceeds from the sale of cloth with which to pay the ever higher prices for grain.[184] In December 1586 the government heard all parties, then decided in favor of the clothiers' request that the Adventurers be required to continue to purchase the usual quantities of cloth. They were reluctant to build up inventories which might not be sold if the markets closed abroad, but the Council warned that their failure could result in throwing the export trade open to all merchants, English and alien alike.

The threat was carried out in May 1587, first in a royal proclamation which allowed the Merchants of the Steelyard to buy and sell cloths in England, then in a supplementary printed order three days later which further opened the trade to all Englishmen and even established a mart in Westminster if strangers could not buy at Blackwell Hall.[185] Burghley had opposed the issue of the proclamation because it would make public a course of action which he felt was bound to fail; he felt that only a resurgence of the Adventurers offered any hope.[186] A year later the experiment had come to naught, and because the Adventurers' suit to operate in Hamburg in the Hanse's territory had been denied, the privileges of the foreigners in England were withdrawn in retaliation. The Staplers had temporarily escaped from the Adventurers' dominance, but only in common with all other merchants, and the end of the privilege spelled the end for them as a major force in export.[187] From henceforth the only real competition for the Adventurers was the growing number of licenses for individuals to export commodities.

[184] Thoroughly treated by J. D. Gould, 'The Crisis in the Export Trade, 1586–1587', *EHR*, LXXI (1956), 212–22, from which I have summarized the context, citing the sources only when they yield additional material on the proclamation.

[185] *Add. Procs.*, no. 4; later orders mistakenly considered a proclamation in Steele and Hughes & Larkin, 690/793.

[186] PRO, SP 12/201/18; BL, Lansd. MS 52/34.

[187] Rich, *The Ordinance Book of the Merchants of the Staple*, pp. 76–7.

6

ECONOMIC MANAGEMENT FOR

PRIVATE INTERESTS

The government's efforts at economic management served 'exclusive privileges'[1] as well as the national interest. Since much of the economic legislation of the Tudor period was demonstrably the result of successful lobbying by interested companies and corporations, it should not be surprising that a similar influence appears in the proclamations which enforced the statutes, even though no more was said of this in the proclamations than in the laws. But the proclamations served private interests even when no statutes were involved. The system of monopoly grants influenced their use as well.

Many individuals gained a privileged legal position through patents and licenses, as we have seen to some extent already.[2] There were three types of grants. The first allowed an inventor to enjoy solely the fruits of his work, and so basic was this type that it survived the legal tests late in Elizabeth's reign and in the Stuart period, and remains the basis of the law on monopolies to this day.[3] Both the theory and practice of the other two types, the license which exempted the patentee from the law and the right to be its sole enforcer, were called into question. Often the agitation reached such a pitch that Queen Elizabeth felt constrained to use proclamations to suspend or even recall them publicly.

She became involved with the grants because they offered her an opportunity to reward favorites and others with a claim on her generosity, and also because through them she was able to involve many subjects in the enforcement of the law as informers or 'promoters'.[4] The Queen and the promoters were thus partners, even if

---

[1] The phrase was used by William Hyde Price, *The English Patents of Monopoly* (Harvard Economic Series, 1; Boston, 1906), p. 9.

[2] The best studies are Price, and Margaret Gay Davies, *The Enforcement of English Apprenticeship, 1563–1642* (Cambridge, Mass., 1956), pp. 24ff.

[3] The earliest statutory restriction was 21 James I, c. 4, which sent Coke into lyric joy.

[4] Davies, *The Enforcement of English Apprenticeship*, chapters I–III.

she found their station in life and their practices distasteful. Why should she not instead reward her faithful, well known subjects by granting them the exclusive right to enforce or dispense with certain of the penal statutes, in much the same manner as monopoly patentees gained exclusive privileges?

The public outcry against individual abuses, and on occasion against the system as a whole, was the more embarrassing to the Queen because her grants were the source of the problem. Regardless of her intentions, the grants provided the authority for their activities, and the abuses redounded to the dishonor of all. It must have been galling for Elizabeth to have had to recall any of the patents in the public forum of a proclamation. The patents were used in such a wide range of activities that the number of proclamations on them was wide indeed.[5]

Before turning to specific abuses, it will be useful to consider how some proclamations were used to protect informers or to regulate their actions. The Council had considered a plan to supplant them entirely and to substitute commissions of Justices of the Peace, but the impracticality of the idea led to a modified proposal which would retain the informers but severely limit their number. A bill for that purpose was prepared for the Parliament of 1566, and while it was sitting the first proclamation on informers was issued on 10 November 1566. It has been argued that the two proposals together were an attempt 'to regulate [informers] by proclamation and legislation'.[6] Although the bill was successful, an act was passed in 1576 which specified that presentments could be made only in the county in which the offense was alleged, and another in 1589 set a limit of one year after the alleged offense during which presentments could be made.[7]

It does not seem to me that the proclamation of 1566 should be considered a part of any grand scheme to regulate informers.[8] It set no limit on their activities, nor did it attempt to legislate by means of the prerogative either the Council's plan or any alternate form of control. The proclamation stated explicitly that the occasion for its issue was a tumult around Westminster Hall, the site of the courts, in

[5] Lists are in BL, Lansd. MS 59/39 (1589), PRO, SP 12/282/28 (1589 to the end of the reign), and Huntington Libr., Ellesmere MS 2290 (17–41 Eliz.). Printed lists are in Price, *The English Patents of Monopoly*.

[6] Davies, *The Enforcement of English Apprenticeship*, pp. 63–8, argues that the plans in 1565 and 1566 were conscious stages in the government's plan to regulate informers.

[7] 18 Eliz. I, c. 5, made perpetual by 27 Eliz. I, c. 10. 31 Eliz. I, c. 5. See Davies, *The Enforcement of English Apprenticeship*, pp. 27, 65–6. [8] Proc. 547/621.

which some 'have not only beaten and ill treated diverse of the said informers but have also made great outcries against the same persons'. Any repeated offense was to be punished by three months' imprisonment and the pillory, as the Star Chamber might judge.

The difference between the royal and parliamentary attitudes on informers became more marked between 1566 and 1571. The few monopoly grants before 1570 had been limited to specific counties, but thereafter the number grew quickly and the grants were for the entire realm.[9] A new bill against informers was introduced in the session which a member described in his diary as 'being devised by the exchequer men and seeming in effect to give more scope to them than to restrain them; the same was rejected'.[10] The increasing number of royal grants was mentioned during the debates, and Robert Bell's comments on the grants and the bill led to a message from the Queen which restricted the debates in the House of Commons to the matters before it. This in turn launched Peter Wentworth on what was seemingly his maiden effort to protect the liberties of the House. The Queen promised to take order about the licenses herself.[11] Because she did not do so, the ultimate result was thirty years of intermittent parliamentary agitation which culminated in the debate during the session of 1601 and the Queen's proclamation on monopolies, lest Parliament itself produce a bill on the matter.[12]

A few months after the session of 1571, the Queen continued her former practices, not only issuing patents to individuals as before, but even undertaking an experiment by which a set of seven penal statutes was entrusted to the enforcement of two patentees.[13] Even though the experiment was abandoned four years later, the lines were drawn. Patents would be granted, and the informers allowed to pursue their traditional role. The proclamation on informers was reissued verbatim in the 1590s.[14] The remainder of the proclamations which dealt with grants either corrected the abuses of specific patentees, or were issued on behalf of some private interests, and it is to those two general classifications that we now turn.

[9] BL, Lansd. MS 59/39.
[10] John Davidson (ed.), 'Hooker's Journal of the House ommons in 1571', *Report and Transactions of the Devonshire Association*, xi (1879), 480. See also J. E. Neale, *Elizabeth I and her Parliaments, 1559–1581* (London, 1953), pp. 218–23.
[11] *Ibid.* [12] Below, pp. 146–7.
[13] BL, Lansd. MS 59/39; cancellation noted in *APC*, viii, 370–1. See Davies, *The Enforcement of English Apprenticeship*, pp. 32–4.
[14] Proc. 767/547, of uncertain date.

CORRECTING PATENTEES' ABUSES

Proclamations were used to cancel or to regulate patents in a number of areas, including concealed lands, the sowing of hemp and flax, saltpeter, and starch. The earliest were concerned with concealments. 'Concealers' kept from the Crown the titles to lands which should have escheated or been forfeited to the monarch as feudal lord, or titles which should have properly passed to the Crown when the monasteries and chantries were dissolved. Because the fact of concealment had to be discovered, the Queen granted patentees the right to make inquiries, and if lands were discovered they were conveyed to the patentee up to the aggregate limit set in his grant. The number and varieties of harassments which the patentee could inflict on 'suspected' concealers was great, and the burden of defense fell particularly hard on the clergy because of the large amounts of land which had changed hands at the dissolutions.

Grants of patents to discover concealed lands were frequently made, and since the numbers of the concealments were unknown and the limits on the grants usually rather low, the quantity which could theoretically be made was endless.[15] A book covering the years 1558–89 includes over one hundred grants of concealments.[16] One list of grants of land made to a patentee as a result of his discoveries occupies eight membranes, each twenty to twenty-four inches long, yet the total value of the reconveyances amounted to only £15 0s 8d.[17] The grantees were often courtiers; indeed, one can imagine that such a patent was a first step up an anticipated ladder of financial improvement which a suitor hoped would parallel his office-holding – a type of financial *cursus honorum*.[18] Although we must await a specialized topical study on concealments, I suspect that a part of the rivalry between Burghley and the Earl of Leicester will be found to have been fought in this arena. The clergy counted Burghley a protector

[15] Many are among the Exchequer commissions in PRO, E 178; see the references to the patent rolls in Hughes & Larkin, II, 356 note 1.

[16] BL, Lansd. MS 59/39.

[17] Huntington Libr., Ellesmere MS 1351.

[18] In PRO, SP 12/288/1 (2 November 1589) one Middlemore claims that he was first granted concealed lands but lost 500 marks because the Queen stayed his suit against the Earl of Hertford; 'in recompense' for giving up the grant he received the forfeitures from those who did not import bowstaves, and claimed to have lost £6,000 before the Queen stayed that grant; he then got the license to transport peas and beans out of the realm when the price was below 13s a quarter, only to see a time of high prices; finally he was granted the searchership of London. He probably multiplied the true results of the grants for effect, since in his present suit he asked for a new grant.

and Leicester a spoiler, and his name appears often enough in connection with the grants to make one suspect his deep involvement.[19]

Three royal proclamations ostensibly limited the exercise of the grants of concealments, in 1572, 1579 and 1600. I have not been able to discover the occasion of the first.[20] It announced that a *supersedeas* had been issued out of the Exchequer against the grants so that all subjects could beware the patentees who were ignoring the recall. A remedy was promised in Star Chamber if the subject would make the harassment known to a Justice of Assize, or two or three Justices of the Peace, or directly to the Council and Lord Keeper. But one has only to recall that these grants were issued with a *non obstante* clause which specifically excused the patentee from any proclamation to the contrary. The people would have been put on guard and the commissions of the patentee's deputies cancelled, but the original grant would remain intact and could be used again when the furor died down. Indeed, there was such an intensification of complaints from some of the bishops to Burghley the next year that he prepared a series of articles to limit the patentees' abuses.[21] His practical power as Lord Treasurer was more potent in moderating the abuses than had been the public announcement.

The second proclamation seems to have been occasioned by a complaint from John Young, the new Bishop of Rochester, to Burghley on 20 October 1579 in which he told of the concealers who were trying to undo the title to Chatham Hospital.[22] A proclamation cancelling all outstanding commissions was issued on 15 December; Burghley was probably particularly inclined to assist Young since he was a leading campaigner against the sect of the Family of Love at that time.[23]

Little relief seems to have followed, and from 1581 onward there were a series of grants of concealments to extremely influential men such as Leicester, Sir Christopher Hatton, Sir James Crofts, Sir

[19] Leicester's patent for concealed lands in the forest of Snowden is in BL, Lansd. MS 45/80. On that grant and the proclamation of 1579, see Flenley, p. 194. Strype's suspicion that Leicester was involved in the agitation which led to the proclamation in 1572 is in *The Life and Acts of Matthew Parker* (2 vols.; Oxford, 1821), II, 226. See also *APC*, XIII, 678–9.

[20] Proc. 584/666, alleged to have been issued by the Queen 'by the Lord Treasurer's means', with no evidence cited, in Strype, *Parker*, II, 224.

[21] John Bruce and Thomas Thomason Perowne (eds.), *Correspondence of Matthew Parker, D.D.* (Parker Society, XLII; Cambridge, 1853), p. 413; Strype, *Parker*, II, 224–6. Norwich, Ely, London, and Winchester were particularly vexed. *Annals Ref.*, II, i, 314–15.

[22] Proc. 644/742. For the Family of Love, below, pp. 212–14.

[23] *Annals Ref.*, II, ii, 272–3, where Young mentioned 'his [Burghley's] accustomed goodness towards all such erections and foundations'.

Edward Stafford, Sir John Perrot, and Henry Noel.[24] In vain did the clergy protest. It must be remembered that to ask the Queen to control or revoke those grants meant asking her to reverse herself and for all practical purposes admit an error, and to go back on a grant to someone greatly in her favor. Stafford's deputies in particular upset the Bishop of Lincoln when they used the clause in their patent authorizing 'aliis viis et modis' as a justification for preparing two sets of Articles of Inquiry, one with ten items to be administered to the entire clergy, the other of twenty-four to be put to all churchwardens. The items were in reality an inquiry into their manner of life and their observance of ecclesiastical regulations. Cooper protested that such an inquiry 'was more...than episcopal jurisdiction'.[25] Within a week Burghley had a *supersedeas* issued,[26] but no further proclamation appeared until 1600. Even then there was no regulation of the abuses, but rather an offer to let those vexed by the patentees make a composition with the Queen and receive a patent to their lands to 'establish their estates for themselves and their posterity'.[27] Not knowing the occasion for the proclamation, one can imagine a set of interpretations which range from the extremely favorable (a royal desire to protect subjects' rights) to the opposite (a device for generating revenue). Significantly in the second and third proclamations a commission composed of the greater officers of state was established, with the purpose in 1579 of settling cases pending at the time when the grants were cancelled, and in 1600 of arranging the composition.

Another area in which proclamations had a part was in the sowing of hemp and flax. Although the proclamation of 1579 was related to the gain of a private individual and thus fits into the second section of this chapter, it is discussed here along with the proclamation of 1589 which restrained the abuses of patentees, because both dealt with the same commodity.

Although the sowing of hemp and flax was not universal throughout England, it has been estimated from the inventories which survive that 'the spinning and weaving of them occupied the spare

[24] Leicester, above p. 140, n. 19; Hatton, Huntington Libr., Ellesmere MSS 1297, 1298 (1581); Crofts, 1258, 1260, 1262, 1262A, 1263, 1318, 1325, 1326, 1334, 1338, 1339, 1352 (1583–5); Stafford, *Annals Ref.*, III, i, 41–4, 161–8; Perrot, PRO, SP 12/103/64; Noel, Huntington Libr., Ellesmere MSS 1328, 1349, 1351 (1584).

[25] *Annals Ref.*, III, i, 166.   [26] *Ibid.*

[27] Proc. 799/904. Instructions for the commissioners, PRO, SP 12/275/128. Among the household books for 1601 in the Hardwicke MSS is a payment for 4d for four proclamations on concealments and 1s 8d for camphor balls and a box to put them in, so that the owner could claim a defense against the patentees, *HMC 2: 3rd Rpt*, p. 44.

hours of nearly one third of the labouring population'.[28] Many peasants grew small quantities and spun and wove during the winter season. Hemp was grown in areas of rich alluvial soil such as from southern Lincolnshire near the Wash along the coast through Norfolk and especially Suffolk, as well as in Dorset, Somerset and Sussex. Flax was grown in Essex, along the Kentish rivers, in the forests of Northamptonshire, and in the western shires of Gloucester, Warwick and Worcester.[29] An Henrician statute required anyone with sixty acres of arable land or pasture to sow one rood ($\frac{1}{4}$ acre) per sixty acres with flax or hemp seed, or pay a penalty of 3s 4d.[30] The statute for the maintenance of the navy of 1563 raised the requirement to one acre per sixty acres, and the penalty to £5, but specified that the statute would be in force only when the Queen so declared in a royal proclamation.[31]

In January 1579 the Queen exercised that power in a royal proclamation which was directed into all of England except the far west and north.[32] The draft with numerous corrections by Burghley is extant.[33] Although as will be seen none of the rationalizations appeared in the final text, they are of interest since they reflect many of his pet themes.

On the surface the proclamation seemed to have been issued for the general benefit of the realm, but in reality private interests were behind it. As early as 1576 Lawrence Cockson had written to Burghley to urge the benefits from sowing hemp and flax seed and to involve himself.[34] His patience seems to have paid off, for in a letter to Burghley just before the appearance of the proclamation, Cockson sent the Lord Treasurer 'the proclamation for the sowing of land with hemp and flax seed drawn by her Majesty's Attorney General', asking that it be put in effect immediately so that all would be required to buy seed before the sowing time in April and May. His interest lay in that he and his associates were the principal sellers of the seed.[35] They not only got the proclamation issued on 15 January,

---

[28] Alan Everitt, 'Farm Labourers', *Agrarian History*, iv, 426.

[29] *Ibid.*; Joan Thirsk, 'Farming Regions', in *ibid.* pp. 13, 40, 43; Thirsk, 'Farming Techniques', in *ibid.* p. 177.

[30] 24 Henry VIII, c. 4.   [31] 5 Eliz. I, c. 5, section 19.

[32] Proc. 636/734. The warrant to disperse the proclamations in PRO, PRO 30/26/116, fos. 112–114v contains the name of only twenty-five counties whereas the proclamation spoke of thirty.

[33] BL, Lansd. MS 25/99.   [34] PRO, SP 12/107/51.

[35] BL, Lansd. MS 63/18. Could the legal officers' involvement be the reason why the proclamation was issued under the signet?

but succeeded so well that the Queen directed her printer to prepare as many of the proclamations as the Treasurer and Principal Secretary would think needed.[36]

Cockson and his associates were not to be the only ones to attempt to profit from the proclamation. The penalty of £5 made the bringing of informations on the act by promoters an attractive proposition. At least seventeen cases were brought in the Exchequer in the years following. Since only one of the cases alleged an offense in a county which today's economic historians have identified as one in which the crop was normally grown, the presentments seem to have been vexatious. Furthermore, three informers were responsible for bringing nearly all the cases. The authority for them as stated in the Exchequer's records was 'tam contra formam statuti quam tenorem & effectum cuiusdam proclamacionis domine Regine'.[37]

A second group to benefit from the proclamation was a number of Norfolk men led by Robert Kyrke who received in 1583 a grant to allow them to enforce the statute, with the proceeds to be applied toward the rebuilding of the decayed pier at Sheringham which was so important to them as fishermen.[38] Some justices appear to have disliked the manner in which they exercised their grant, but the Council supported the patentees. The Lord Chancellor and other magnates who were charged with supervising the grant did, however, accede in part to the complaints by reducing the statutory fine of £5 to 5s – an interesting exercise of power in itself.[39] Kyrke and his associates were not the only persons to have enjoyed the privilege of compounding on the statute, since there were others including William Waad, an official of the Star Chamber.[40]

The activity of the Norfolk grantees affords an interesting example of how the deputies went about their work, and of how private interests made use of a royal proclamation. There is among the records of the Exchequer a commission granted to some Norfolk men which seems to relate to the grant for Sheringham, even though it mentions no reason for the inquiries which it commanded.[41] A set of instructions for the deputies is extant, seemingly related to the com-

[36] BL, Lansd. MS 63/20.
[37] PRO, E 159/377, m. 192 (Mich. 21 & 22 Eliz.); 159/378, mm. 91, 97, 97v (Hil. 22 Eliz.); 159/379, mm. 121–5, 126, 126v, 127, 127v, 128, 129, 129v, 130, 131, 131v, 132, 133, 133v, 134, 134v, 135, 135v, 136, 136v (Easter 22 Eliz.). My sample ended soon after.
[38] BL, Lansd. MSS 59/39, 63/22. See W. A. Day, 'Sheringham Pier', *Norfolk Archaeology*, x (1886), 225–55.
[39] *APC*, xiv, 42, 77–8.
[40] *Ibid.* xvi, 420; xviii, 105.
[41] PRO, E 178/2959, 24 May 1585.

mission. It instructs the deputies to show five documents: their patent, the proclamations, the articles declaring the benefits which ensue from sowing hemp and flax, the statute, and finally the articles under which examinations were to be made, which hopefully would result in compositions.[42] Although the link between the two documents is not certain, it does reveal the interplay of authorities and actions. Furthermore, there were a rather large number of informations in the Exchequer in 1587 and 1588 which were based on the joint authority of the statute and the proclamation. Fourteen were brought by Kyrke, and the rest were for other counties.[43]

The second royal proclamation on hemp and flax was issued in 1589, to restrain 'certain lewd and evil disposed persons, pretending under color of a grant from her majesty to have power and authority to execute the penalty of the statute made for the sowing of hemp and flax seed, [who] do go about...carrying with them duplicates and exemplifications of that part of the patent only which does concern the penal statute', which actions the Queen condemned as contrary to both her intentions and those of the chief patentees.[44] Just what group of deputies occasioned the proclamation is not known, but it was probably not those in Norfolk since the Council was protecting their grant at the time. It had been reported to the Council that offenders in Norfolk were using the recently issued proclamation as their authority to refuse to make compositions with the patentees. This the Council condemned, requiring the Justices to publish the Queen's desire that the Sheringham patentees be allowed to continue to enjoy their grant and receive official assistance – a perfect example of the *non obstante* clause in a grant being respected vis-à-vis a royal proclamation.[45]

In 1591–2 matters seem to have come to a head in Norfolk. Although in April 1591 the patent to Kyrke and to William Carter on behalf of Sheringham and nearby Beeston was renewed,[46] the Council in the following year authorized the Justices in Norfolk to demand an accounting and to report on the progress in repairing the

[42] BL, Lansd. MS 63/23.

[43] Kyrke's informations are in PRO, E 159/395, mm. 99–100, *r* and *v* (Trin. 30 Eliz.). Only two ever proceeded as far as a call for a jury; did the other defendants compound to avoid a costly trial? The other informations: Kent, E 159/393, mm. 288–92, 293, 293*v*, 294, 295, 295*v*, 296, 297, 297*v*, 298, 298*v*, 299–302, 303, 303*v* (Mich. 29 & 30 Eliz.); Suffolk, *ibid.* 304–10, *r* and *v*, 452–5, *r* and *v*; 465–8, *r* and *v*; 159/394, mm. 222–4, *r* and *v*, 225 (Easter 30 Eliz.); Norfolk, *ibid.* mm. 225*v*, 226 *r* and *v*, 228 *r* and *v*; Wiltshire, *ibid.* m. 227. My sample ended with 30 Eliz.

[44] Proc. 714/816, also issued under the signet.   [45] *APC*, XVIII, 191.

[46] PRO, Index 6800, under date April 1591.

pier.[47] The Justices found the accounts to be false, and that no great progress had been made in the repairs. They had had to make their own surveys of the amounts which had been paid, and a set of certificates from each of fourteen hundreds in Norfolk exists, all made in July and August 1592. The total comes to £643 7s od, with notes of other payments for which amounts could not be ascertained.[48]

Still another area of grants to patentees and the use of royal proclamations concerned saltpeter, which has been called 'the most notorious case' of turning a good patent to evil account.[49] The Queen's intentions were obvious: she wanted to provide gunpowder for which saltpeter was necessary, since it was needed for the defense of the realm; and she wished to avoid the danger of having to rely on foreign sources for such a vital commodity. Since the process of obtaining saltpeter required digging, the patent authorized the patentees' agents to dig almost anywhere, even in private homes and buildings.

The history of the Elizabethan patents for saltpeter can be divided into three stages. The first lasted until 1588, during which several sets of commissions to dig were issued.[50] The second began with the monopoly grant to George Evelin in 1588.[51] The third began with the royal proclamation of 1601 which allowed Evelin's patent and others to be tested at the common law and thus ended the period of exclusively prerogative protection for the patentees.[52] Two Elizabethan proclamations which were primarily concerned with saltpeter were issued, both during the second stage, one in 1590 and another without a date which appeared sometime in the 1590s,[53] an identical reissue. The purpose of the proclamations was in reality to assist Evelin, because they recalled any commissions still being used which had been issued in the first stage, commissions which Evelin's exclusive grant should have superseded. A secondary purpose of the proclamations was to insure that all saltpeter which was produced would be delivered to the Tower of London, and not be bought, sold or converted to some private use. The penalty for either using an old

[47] *APC*, xxii, 87–8; *HMC 19: 11th Rpt, App. IV*, pp. 8–9.
[48] Norf. & Norw. RO, Bacon and Townshend (Stiffkey) MSS, items 98–110, 115. The papers were on loan to the RO from Raynham Hall when I saw them.
[49] E. Lipson, *The Economic History of England* (12th ed.; 3 vols.; London, 1959), iii, 358.
[50] For commissions in this period, see Norf. & Norw. RO, Norwich Mayor's Ct Bk 9, fo. 213; Merson (ed.), *The Third Book of Remembrance of Southampton*, pp. 13–15; PRO, SP 12/225/47; *APC*, xiv, 163.   [51] PRO, Index 6800, under date 25 January 1589.
[52] Proc. 812/922; below, pp. 146–7.
[53] Proc. 718/820 with the misleading title in Hughes & Larkin of 'Granting Monopoly or Saltpeter'; proc. 776/—.

grant from the pre-Evelin days or for converting saltpeter to private gain was a period of imprisonment. Thus the proclamations did nothing about the abuses of some of Evelin's own deputies, and the grievances would last well into the following century.

The exclusive right to produce starch had been granted first in 1588, seemingly because the Queen wished to provide courtiers in desperate financial straits with the means of paying off their debts to her.[54] Their jealous enforcement of the patents was resented rather generally, but it became a grievance of the greatest magnitude in the time of dearth, because grain was used in making starch. Eventually three royal proclamations were issued on the matter.

Two of them appeared during the severe shortages of 1594–8.[55] The first on 31 July 1596 was primarily an order for the observance of the Book of Orders, but it also included a mention of the patent for making starch and attempted to justify it by noting that it required using bran and not corn. It forbade the patentees to make any starch from bran during the dearth 'notwithstanding her majesty's grant by the said letters patent'.[56] The other proclamation, issued on 23 August 1598, did not mention the patent but universally forbade making starch.[57] Finally, the proclamation issued during the session of Parliament in 1601 included the starch patent among those which were entirely cancelled.[58]

References to that session have cropped up again and again in the preceding pages; in the debates over monopolies during that session there came together many threads of the stories which we have been following commodity by commodity. Unable to delay any longer the discussion of monopolies by successive Parliaments, the Queen seized the initiative in 1601 by issuing a proclamation that restrained many of the abuses. This she did while Parliament was in session, and thus she headed off any further drive to produce legislation on the matter.[59] The story of those debates has been told many times,[60] but neither they nor the exact content of specific grievances are really of great importance to our study since the proclamation of 28 November was merely a tactic, a conciliatory device.

[54] Price, *The English Patents of Monopoly*, pp. 15–16.
[55] On the dearth, above, pp. 116ff.
[56] Proc. 781/884; a local proclamation against starch making on the Queen's order is in Corp. London RO, Journal xxvi, fo. 7v.
[57] Proc. 795/898.
[58] Proc. 812/922.
[59] *Ibid.*
[60] Price, *The English Patents of Monopoly*, pp. 20–2; Neale, *Elizabeth I and her Parliaments, 1584–1603* (London, 1957), pp. 352–6.

The proclamation sought first of all to exonerate the Queen from much of the odium attached to the grants, by asserting that 'some of the said grants were not only made upon false and untrue suggestions…but have been also notoriously abused…'. Then it cancelled outright a number of the grants, including starch, prohibiting their exercise under pain of her indignation. Next it allowed any subject who felt aggrieved by 'divers other privileges and licenses' to take the matter to common law, among which grants that for saltpeter was mentioned. Finally, the proclamation relaxed the prohibition against sowing woad which had been made in an earlier proclamation of the previous year.[61]

Thus came to an end the exclusive protection which the monopolist had enjoyed, but not the end of monopoly grants nor of the patentees' abuses. The Queen's action was gratefully received, and her final 'golden' speech at the end of that session of Parliament made even more secure her place in the hearts of those who had so strongly pressed her in Parliament a short time before.

In retrospect, little was done in the twelve proclamations we have just seen beyond a temporary delay in the use of a grant, except of course for the proclamation of 1601. A good deal of dirty linen had been washed in public, however, and a good number of abuses which had arisen out of the royal grants had been aired. No one can tell if the redirection of the blame which the proclamations had attempted to assign had any great effect on public opinion. The proclamations were all instruments of propaganda, differing from others in the degree of defensiveness – and to this day men are still searching for effective means to measure public opinion.

PROCLAMATIONS FOR PRIVATE INTERESTS

The proclamations in this section share two characteristics, the appearance of merely ordering the enforcement of some existing legislation, and the proffered justification that they were serving the common good. Underneath the façade, however, lay the private gain of some person or corporation. We have already seen an instance of this in the successful suit of Lawrence Cockson and associates, sellers of hemp and flax seed. The instances to be cited below – wearing woolen caps and sowing woad – expand the list, but they were not the only occasions when someone wished to share in whatever gain a proclamation might bring. The fishmongers of

---

[61] Below, p. 153.

London urged the enforcement of the proclamations on the political lent, and the officials in Lincoln instructed their members of Parliament to strive to gain for the city 'all penalties incurred by virtue of any statutes or proclamations by inhabitants of the city'.[62]

Five or perhaps six proclamations were issued to enforce the statute of 1571 which ordered the lower classes to wear woolen caps on Sundays and holidays.[63] The private interests which had a part in this legislation begun as a petitionary bill are clearly evident in the statute's list of twenty-seven areas with concentrations of cappers whom the law intended to aid. It is not surprising that there would be a similar motive behind the proclamations enforcing the law. The statute had authorized an unusually wide range of local courts to enforce its provisions: Justices of Assize in their circuits, Justices of the Peace in sessions, Sheriffs in tourns, Stewards in leets and law-days, and Mayors and Sheriffs in the courts of local corporations. To these the proclamations (which were all identical in wording) added even more: they commanded that constables, thirdboroughs, tithingmen and churchwardens should make views and searches on the required days and send a certificate of offenders to the courts which had the authority to hear and determine the offenses. All of those devices were intended to halt the 'wanton disorder of evil-disposed and light persons more regarding private fancy than public commodity', in order that the cappers might have continued employment.

The proclamations fell into two groups. The first were issued in 1572 and 1573, and nothing is known about them except that the latter was received under a writ in London.[64] The evidence surrounding the issue of the remaining four is markedly different. In every instance, the date of a proclamation coincided with the time when a commission based on the statute was issued or reissued. In none of the cases was I able to find any evidence that the proclamations were received in any towns in which I studied records. This strongly suggests that these proclamations were not sent out under writs of proclamation as was normal, but that they were carried into an area by the commissioners to aid them in their work. Thus the proclamations on caps afford the clearest instance of the issue of royal proclamations for the exclusive benefit of patentees. And

---

[62] *HMC 37: 14th Rpt, App. VIII*, p. 65.

[63] 13 Eliz. I, c. 19.

[64] Procs. 588/675, 594/681. The only evidence that the former was issued is a penned notation on the latter with a regnal year for the earlier year.

those patentees in every case were the cappers of Lichfield or Coventry.[65]

The first cluster of activity by the commissioners occured in the years 1575–7. In October 1575 the Privy Council wrote to the Solicitor General on behalf of the Company of Cappers of Lichfield and elsewhere, notifying him that the Queen had granted that Company the forfeitures under the statute of 1571 and directing him 'to set down some device and order how the same Statute may be put in execution'.[66] The result seems to have been a royal proclamation which is noted in the records of Southampton when enforced, under the date of 19 November.[67] The terms of the cappers' commission are extant, having been copied in the registers of the Council in Wales, and suggest that the reasons behind the proclamation was that little had been accomplished even though 'sundry proclamations have since [the act] been issued'. It authorized John Baylie and Robert Blunt, cappers, to search, view and find offenders, to compound with them, and to divide the fines among the cappers of the twenty-seven towns mentioned in the statute. The commissioners' accounts were to be audited by a group to be comprised of one appointee from each of the towns of Hereford, Coventry, Lichfield, Shrewsbury and Stafford. The commissioners were then to certify the results into the Exchequer each Michaelmas.[68] That the proclamation had a role to play in all of these activities is clear from the evidence of the use of the commissions in the towns of Southampton, Manchester, and Northleach, Gloucestershire. In each of those places there were special inquiries and presentments which followed exactly the terms of the royal proclamation, proceedings which were not part of the statutory process and which would not have been developed so uniformly had there not been some outside stipulation.[69] That the process could be avoided altogether is suggested by an entry in the records of Stratford-on-Avon which authorized an

[65] See *VCH Warwick*, II, 265–6 for the Company and its importance in Coventry.

[66] *APC*, IX, 36. The grant had been recommended to Burghley by Lord Paget, *HMC 9: Salisbury (Cecil) MSS, II*, p. 323. There may have been an earlier commission, since in April 1575 a capper sought and was granted the right to enforce the statute in Rye; E. Sussex RO, Rye MS 1/4, fos. 195–6.

[67] *Add. Procs.*, no. 29.

[68] Flenley, pp. 149–50.

[69] Southampton, 1576, in Hearnshaw and Hearnshaw (eds.), *Court Leets Records* pp. 138–9; Manchester, 1577, in John Harland (ed.), *A Volume of Court Leet Records of the Manor of Manchester in the Sixteenth Century* (Chetham Society, LXIII; Manchester, 1864), pp. 140, 145; Northleach, 1577, in D. Royce (ed.), 'The Northleach Court-Book', *Transactions of the Bristol and Gloucestershire Archaeological Society*, VII (1882–3), 93, 97, where the fines are 2d even though the statutory fine was 3s 4d.

alderman to pay 10s 8d 'for the agreement with the informer having the benefit of the statute for wearing of caps', and from an entry in the records of Nottingham showing that officials there paid Baylie and Blunt 40s.[70]

The next proclamation was issued sometime in 1578, when there was a renewal of the commissioners' activity.[71] The Council was very busy in 1578–80 trying to restrain the abuses under the patent. Blunt and Baylie came under suspicion, but once their accounts were received and inspected they were allowed the right to continue their activities.[72] But the evidence against them began to mount. The Sheriff of Norfolk was ordered to apprehend Baylie, and he was committed to the Marshalsea in January 1579. In an order for Blunt's arrest in December of that year it was noted that of the £900 collected only £30 had been distributed. The Auditors of the Prest were instructed to hear their accounts in February 1580, and they were both still in prison awaiting an appearance before the Council in May 1580.[73] What happened to them is not noted, but compositions were made at Cambridge in 1582–3, at Oxford in 1585, and a bill was introduced on the subject in Parliament in 1584, but since the text does not survive we cannot know what it would have provided.[74]

There seem to be no other references to caps until 1590, the time when the proclamation on caps was reissued.[75] The Company of Cappers of Coventry wrote to the Council to petition for a renewal of the letters patent to enforce the statute. The letter noted that the patent to Baylie and Blunt had been called in because of their abuses, and that it had been the diligence of the Cappers in making those abuses known which had led to the end of their patent. The Cappers noted, however, that many of the Queen's subjects 'understanding the said letters patent [to have been] called in do thereby imagine the statute to be repealed also', and so they nominated four of their number to undertake the execution of the statute if the commissions would be regranted.[76] It must have been renewed, since there are complaints in 1593 about its misuse, an allegation in

[70] Savage (ed.), *Minutes and Accounts of the Corporation of Stratford-upon-Avon*, II, 117; Stevenson (ed.), *Records of the Borough of Nottingham*, IV, 76–7.
[71] Proc. 634/683.
[72] *APC*, X, 340–1.
[73] *APC*, X, 343; XI, 26–7, 352, 384–5; XII, 32.
[74] Cooper, *Annals of Cambridge*, II, 401; Salter (ed.), *Oxford Council Acts*, p. 82; PRO, SP 12/175/36.
[75] Proc. 729/684.
[76] PRO, SP 12/235/92.

1594 that it had been 'procured by indirect means', and thus was called in, and an order in 1596 to the Sheriff and Justices in Buckinghamshire to arrest Blunt.[77] Since Blunt was not one of the four nominated by the Cappers of Coventry, it may be that he was still trying to make compositions with the unsuspecting subject, based on a grant long since called in.

The final evidence coincides with the issue of the last proclamation related to caps, in 1597.[78] The assembly at Chester met to consider the response to be made to the patentees and decided 'to give them some reward for the quiet of the inhabitants',[79] while in Bath 10s was paid to the 'commissioners for caps'.[80] The statute was repealed in 1598, and thus this particular use of proclamations for private purposes came to an end.

Another economic matter in which private interest and proclamations were mingled was the cultivation of the dyestuff woad. Its cultivation had become much more important in the latter half of the sixteenth century because the desire to produce finished cloth and not just deal in the raw wool or white cloth had grown considerably. Woad was a superior dye and attractive to the entrepreneur, especially when some began to realize that it could be up to six times more profitable a crop than corn.[81] The attraction created new problems, since in times of dearth there was great pressure to return the acres which had been devoted to woad to the cultivation of grain. The extreme profitability of the crop was also a natural attraction for those who would seek monopoly patents for its cultivation.

The first of the proclamations on woad was issued on 14 October 1585, during the first great period of scarcity in Elizabeth's reign.[82] Although not mentioned directly in the proclamation, the scarcity's effects on the clothiers was an important reason for its issue.[83] It forbade any new sowing and also the cultivation of any woad previously sown within four miles of any market or clothing town, or within eight miles of a royal residence (woad had a disagreeable odor) 'until there may be a further consideration had how the same may be suffered with some toleration'. It required those who had

[77] BL, Lansd. MS 71/60; *APC*, xxv, 519; xxvi, 73–4.
[78] Proc. 791/685.
[79] Chester CRO, AB/1, fo. 248.
[80] F. D. Wardle (ed.), *The Accounts of the Chamberlains of the City of Bath* (Somerset Record Society, xxxviii; Taunton, 1923), p. 164.
[81] J. B. Hurry, *The Woad Plant and Its Dye* (London, 1930), is the main source, followed by Thirsk, 'Farming Techniques', pp. 174–5.
[82] Proc. 678/782.
[83] Camden, p. 325.

sown woad to report the fact to the Sheriffs, who in turn were to forward certificates to the Exchequer.

An early intimation that private interests were important in the matter of woad appeared when the Council ordered the Sheriff of Southamptonshire to arrest a man named Cooper for attempting to sow woad 'contrary to her majesty's proclamation'. The response to that letter noted that Cooper, then a prisoner in Romsey, claimed 'that he put one Mr. Tyselale of Oxfordshire his master in trust to compound for so many acres as we certified might be sown about Romsey, being 50 or 60 on the whole'.[84] The letter to the Council was in fact an apology for Cooper and an assurance that the inhabitants of the area had been appeased by Cooper's promise to stop sowing, but the proclamation of rebellion had been read just in case. The meaning of the comment about Cooper and his master is unclear; it seems to hint that Cooper was operating under some license, which in turn suggests some royal grant.

A general plan to regulate the sowing of woad was issued in 1587, a scheme that probably fulfilled the promise for 'some further consideration' in the proclamation of 1585. It restricted individual growers to 20 acres and the total within any one parish to 40 to 60 acres. A fee of 20s payable to the Queen was demanded for exercising the privilege, to offset her loss on the customs paid when woad was imported.[85] The restriction was relaxed in 1589, but that year also witnessed the first licenses about which there is a certainty when Richard Leavill, a Groom of the Chamber, was licensed to sow woad in the county of Dorset.[86] The Council's letter is interesting for two reasons. It spoke of a restraint against sowing woad as if the intervening relaxation had been allowed only in specific cases and not generally. It also asked the Justices in Dorset to 'give them the names of such as were faulty, by whom they prayed to certify to the Lords of their proceeding therein'.[87] Whereas before we have seen patentees privately compounding, here one was to provide the grist for a public judicial process. The number of patentees grew in subsequent years. In 1593 William Abere of Winchester received a patent to compound with offenders and to license persons to sow woad in his

[84] Council's letter, *APC*, xiv, 91, cited in part in Hughes & Larkin, ii, 517 note 1; response, PRO, SP 12/189/15.
[85] Hurry, *The Woad Plant and Its Dye*, pp. 63–4, mistakenly calling this a proclamation.
[86] *Ibid.* p. 64, with the same descriptive mistake.
[87] *APC*, xvii, 393–4; a similar order based on a complaint by Leavill is in *APC*, xxii, 81. A conciliar order to execute the proclamation in 1593, with no mention of the patentee, is in *ibid.* xxiv, 198.

county up to a maximum of 600 acres.[88] In 1594 Leavill and Valentine Harris received grants to sow woad up to 600 acres for twenty years in the counties of Berkshire, Wiltshire, Dorset, Warwick and Worcester.[89] Abere brought suit in the Star Chamber in 1597 in the exercise of his patent. It is the sole instance of which I know where a private party sued in that Court on the authority of a proclamation, as distinct from the official suits brought by the Attorney General on the Queen's behalf. Having cited the proclamation of 1585 which forbade the sowing of woad and his own grant for compounding, Abere then accused forty-two persons of refusing to compound with him, which amounted to a violation of the royal proclamation.[90] Unfortunately, the outcome to that suit does not survive.

Abere might have had a sympathetic hearing if only because the year of his suit coincided with the worst period of dearth in the reign. A bill was introduced in the parliamentary session of 1597–8 which attempted to turn back the clock by proposing that none sow woad where it had not been sown in the past twenty years. It promised that as a result more land would be left for pasture, and that prices for butter, cheese and hay would be reduced, but the bill did not pass.[91]

On 28 March 1600 the second royal proclamation on woad was issued. It reiterated the commandment to imprison those who continued to sow woad, blamed the Justices for a lax enforcement of the earlier proclamation, and promised 'a further consideration...how the same may be tolerated' in order to find a way to protect the commonweal.[92] It was enforced at Gloucester,[93] but the main interest lies in that the Crown decided to profit from the commodity. A warrant to the Lord Keeper ordered commissions for every shire, to commissioners nominated by a quorum of two to five magnates. The commissions so appointed were authorized to go throughout the county to inquire of lands sown with woad and to license further sowing for a period of up to five years, with rents payable to the Crown for the privilege, the 'said proclamation, or any other proclamation, restraint, commandment, or other thing to the contrary notwithstanding'. The commissioners were also commanded to

[88] Huntington Libr., Ellesmere MS 2290.
[89] *Ibid.*
[90] PRO, Star Chamber 5/A/35/21, endorsed 24 May. The responses did not deal with the proclamation as such.
[91] The draft is in HLRO, Papers 27 January 1596/7 to 1 June 1607, also noted in *HMC 2: 3rd Rpt, App.*, p. 10.
[92] Proc. 802/908.
[93] *APC*, xxxi, 277, ordering the mayor to release the offenders after taking their bonds not to repeat the offenses.

enforce the proclamation against all who would sow woad without license.[94]

There was probably no intention to issue a number of individual commissions, since one commission alone was issued for an area of fifteen counties, from Worcestershire, Gloucestershire and Dorset in the west, to Leicestershire and Northamptonshire in the northeast. Among the twenty-one commissioners were Sir Julius Caesar, a Master of Requests, William Waad, a clerk of the Star Chamber, William Fleetwood, a former Recorder of London and an M.P., and others such as Francis Bacon and even the Master of the Revels.[95]

Thus what had begun as a general prohibition against sowing woad had first become the preserve in part of a few patentees, and having been reiterated in a period of dearth had finally become a revenue raising device for the Crown itself. When in 1601 the Queen issued her proclamation cancelling many of the monopoly grants, the restriction against the sowing of woad was removed.

Several topics of a miscellaneous variety can conclude the consideration of the ties between royal proclamations and individual economic interests. First, many of the items which were rejected from the canon of royal proclamations were in reality part of the efforts made by patentees to secure more effectively the benefits of grants which they had received. Among these were the grant to Richard Candeler in 1575 to make and register all policies of assurance, the grant to Humphrey Gilbert in 1570 of half the forfeitures from offenders who did not furnish horses and armor as required by law, the exemplification in 1598 of Pakington's grant for starch, and the exemplification in 1601 of the grant for customs and subsidies on fine cloths.[96] Second, we have already seen the matters of the coinage and the exchange in an earlier chapter; here we need only be reminded that the proclamation on 20 September 1576 had promised a schedule of rates for the exchange, and that a non-royal proclamation on 27 September did just that, naming three Londoners who had the exclusive right to execute orders for the exchange and to charge a fee.[97] Finally, we saw in the previous chapters that the

[94] Huntington Libr., Ellesmere MS 2404.

[95] Huntington Libr., Ellesmere MS 2405; also noted in PRO, Index 4208, p. 175, dated 26 May.

[96] Candeler, as 'proc.' 605/—; grant noted in Huntington Libr., Ellesmere MS 2290. Gilbert, 586/669, 587/673, and reissues; grant in BL, Lansd. MS 59/39. Pakington, 794/897. Cloths, 806/911.

[97] Proc. 616/706, and orders 'proc.' 618/707. Several months later a grant was made to Ralph Lane of the penalties from anyone who would make a bill of exchange at a rate higher than had been allowed; BL, Lansd. MS 59/39 (25 February 1577).

rights of corporations could be as vigorously contested as those of individuals, when the pricing of wine was at stake. It will be recalled that a patentee's right to license men who could set prices as they willed had the effect of vitiating the more general pricing restrictions.[98]

[98] Above, pp. 126ff.

7

SOCIAL MANAGEMENT

The proclamations to be considered here illustrate three of the most important motives for using these instruments. Those which were issued to help protect Englishmen from the plague show how crises occasioned proclamations. The edicts on retaining and apparel reveal a strong conviction that differences in social ranks are to be maintained. And the proclamations against new buildings in and around London emphasize the importance which that city and its welfare had in the thinking of the Queen and her Council.

The proclamations on apparel in the earlier years of Elizabeth's reign were the most notable attempt to supplement the existing laws, and the legislation on apparel introduced into the sessions of the 1570s provides the single instance of the government seeking to 'supplant' the statutory provisions – not because of a desire to act despotically but because it realized that the proper basis for its desire to regulate apparel by royal proclamations was a statutory authorization. The temporary legislation both concerning apparel and new buildings in London was complemented by administrative procedures which authorized searches, seizures, and consequent forfeitures, so that these matters provide an exceptional opportunity to consider the limitations on the exercise of royal proclamations.

For the proclamations on apparel to be successful, Elizabeth needed to dampen the desire of the gentry and the lower orders to ape the fashions of their betters. If the construction which helped make possible the growth of London's population was to be stopped, the Queen would have to restrain the speculators who saw a golden financial opportunity. In either case the Queen's actions challenged the pretensions and wishes of articulate segments of the community, and so it is not surprising that some of the strongest objections to royal proclamations were voiced over these matters.

PROTECTION FROM THE PLAGUE

The plague was a continual threat in most of the Tudor century, and when it rose to severe proportions royal proclamations were used to help provide the feeble remedies which men then knew. Nearly half the proclamations were issued in the two periods of the greatest severity, in 1563–4 and especially 1592–3.[1]

The necessity for protecting the monarch from the contagion was, of course, paramount, and four or five proclamations were published to restrict access to the Court.[2] The earliest proclamations of this type had been issued in the late 1530s, and sought to protect the monarch by general and broad orders.[3] Mary issued a proclamation of that type,[4] but the Elizabethan proclamations differed considerably in approach, since their goal was to establish a system which would allow only those who had the most urgent business at Court to approach it. They were therefore administrative in nature, ordering a complex system of licenses, interviews, searches, and physical signs that one had come from an infected area, such as wands. Thus in 1569 when the Court was at Windsor a proclamation not only authorized officials of the Court to punish unauthorized visitors, but also ordered the officers of Windsor and Eton to control the access to their towns. This proclamation served as a precedent for the others on the same matter.[5] A similar proclamation in 1593 authorized the officers of the two towns to search out unlicensed lodgers and expel them.[6] But when the royal residence was not so close to a town, the orders were simpler, as was the case with a proclamation in 1592 when the Court was at Hampton Court, and in 1593 when it was at Nonsuch.[7]

The relatively few proclamations which protected the Court should not be taken as a lack of vigilance, since less public commands only were needed when a single jurisdiction was involved. And so the matter could be handled by the Lord Mayor of London at the Council's command, or on another occasion by the officials of Kingston upon Thames.[8]

---

[1] Three in the earlier period, ten in the later.

[2] Procs. 565/643, 750/854, 755/861, 758/864, and perhaps 483/549 which expressed no motive.

[3] Proc. 176/168 on the occasion of Prince Edward's baptism was the earliest.

[4] Proc. 396/437. [5] Proc. 565/643.

[6] Proc. 758/864, preceded by a demand for a survey of the number of persons around the Court; PRO, SP 12/245/75; and followed by orders to the Harbingers to execute it; APC, xxv, 513. [7] Procs. 750/854 (see also APC, xxiii, 231–2, 241), 755/861.

[8] Corp. London RO, Journal xx, pt 1, fo. 168v; pt 2, fos. 369, 443v; APC, xxiii, 205.

The most frequent proclamations caused by the plague adjourned the beginning date of one of the law terms at Westminster. The substance of the twenty-three[9] proclamations of this type varied little: they announced that all suits were continued until a later specified date, that the financial accountings were nevertheless to be held as if the term had not been adjourned, and that the royal officials would receive instructions to carry out the postponement. On a few occasions the danger of infection was so great that the place of the courts' meeting was changed, to Hertford on three occasions, and to St Albans on one.[10] The actual provisions varied a great deal even though the substance was the same, primarily because there were many return days to which the adjournment could be made. There were eight separate returns for Michaelmas term, for example, so that the twenty proclamations dealing with it show many combinations.[11] Only once was an entire term adjourned, but an initial postponement could be followed by a second and even a third adjournment.[12]

These Elizabethan proclamations were not novel, since the earliest had been in 1543. Before then other means had been used, but the logic of so public an announcement must have been compelling. Their language was precise because legal officers participated in the drafting.[13] The actual adjournment in the courts was made, however, on the authority of writs directed to the judges.[14] Any adjournment meant a financial loss for the merchants of London, so the Queen on occasion threatened its officers with a postponement if they did not obey the orders devised to prevent the spread of the plague.[15] But other than for a few supplementary orders in London and an occasional clarification of legal matters, the proclamations left little mark on the records. The whole procedure was so routine that little notice

[9] A proclamation by the Lord Mayor of London in 1580 mentioned an adjournment of term to Hertford, which might presuppose a royal proclamation giving the order; Corp. London RO, Journal xxi, fo. 237.

[10] To Hertford, procs. 515/583, 662/765, 751/855; to St Albans, 769/865. The last two did not occur since in both cases the rest of the term was also adjourned.

[11] The most common were the fourth return day (*mensis Michaelis*) to which eight initial adjournments were made, and the fifth (*crastino animarum*) to which two were made.

[12] Entire term adjourned, proc. 514/582; the third adjournment invariably was for the remainder of the term, as were half the second.

[13] Proc. 223/246; there were no Marian adjournments. Law officers, PRO, C 82/1548 (for proc. 752/856).

[14] Proc. 564/642 and writ copied in PRO, E 159/358, mm. 1–1v; 692/724 in E 159/375, mm. 1–1v; writ for 752/658 copied in Bodleian Libr., Tanner MS 168, fo. 53v.

[15] Corp. London RO, Remembrancia, i, no. 265, and *APC*, xxiii, 220–1.

was warranted.[16] Bills were introduced in 1581 and 1601 to shorten the Michaelmas term by dropping the early return days, but neither progressed far.[17]

There were a few other plague-evoked proclamations. We have already seen how Elizabeth explained the loss of Newhaven because the plague had swept her forces, and shall soon see its part in the proclamations against further buildings in London.[18] Several proclamations dealt with localized infections: the fair at Woodstock was cancelled by royal proclamation in 1575, another limited the duration of the Bartholomew fair at Smithfield, and the Queen's participation in distributing the royal Maundy alms at Eton was cancelled once.[19] It is notable that the royal proclamations played no part in attempts to prevent or minimize the plague.[20] The Council prepared a set of orders for that purpose, first in 1578 and then again in the 1590s,[21] but they were directed to the officers and the time limitations in the proclamations would have been a hindrance.

THE MAINTENANCE OF SOCIAL DISTINCTIONS

The upper ranks

The statutes on retaining dealt exclusively with the higher social ranks, stipulating the maximum number of men who could serve men of differing ranks. The monarch reserved the right to license men to exceed the statutory norms, and Elizabeth issued thirteen such licenses in the early years of her reign.[22] Henry VII and Henry VIII had issued proclamations on retaining, but Edward VI and Mary did not.[23] The two nearly identical Elizabethan proclamations were

[16] Supplementary orders, Corp. London RO, Journal xx, pt 1, fo. 183v; Letter Bk Z, fo. 336v.

[17] PRO, SP 12/148/25 (1581); Hayward Townshend, *Historical Collections...Four Last Parliaments of Q. Elizabeth* (London, 1680), p. 205 (1601).

[18] Above, pp. 80–1; below, pp. 170ff.

[19] Woodstock, *Add. Procs.*, no. 28; Smithfield, proc. 757/863; Maundy, proc. 520/593. Fairs cancelled on royal orders without a proclamation, *APC*, x, 36; xi, 211.

[20] A proclamation in 1590 enforced a statute of Richard II against throwing offal into the ditches of London, proc. 722/825, but it was hardly a comprehensive measure; see also *APC*, xix, 430, and Charles Creighton, *A History of Epidemics in Britain* (2nd ed. with additional material; 2 vols.; London, 1965), ii, 324–5.

[21] Charles Mullett, *The Bubonic Plague and England* (Lexington, 1956), pp. 43, 58ff., especially p. 88. Each local jurisdiction issued orders to protect its own, e.g., Corp. London RO, Repertories 15, fo. 287; York CA Dept, YC/A 31, fos. 368v–369; Norf. & Norw. RO, Mayor's Ct Bk 10, fo. 520; *HMC 47: 15th Rpt, App. X (Corp. of Shrewsbury MSS)*, p. 15.

[22] Statutes listed in Hughes & Larkin, ii, 105 note 1; licenses, BL, Lansd. MS 14/1.

[23] Mary had ordered the officials of Leicester to proclaim the statute on retaining; Bateson (ed.), *Records of the Borough of Leicester*, iii, 73.

primarily a charge to the Justices of Assize and of Gaol Delivery to make inquiries on the statutes in their circuits, but aside from its offer of a grace period of six weeks during which men might reform and be exempt from prosecution, the proclamations added nothing to the statutes.[24]

There is no direct evidence to explain why they were issued in 1572 and 1583. The few mentions of retaining about that time focus on Wales, and there is a report to Burghley from Sir Henry Sidney that the latter's nominee for the post of Sheriff of Caernarvonshire was no longer one of his retainers: 'so he was until the last proclamation of letters patent against retainers'.[25] The Lord President and his Council in Wales already had authority to enforce the statutes on retaining, so that it is hard to understand why any offenses in Wales should occasion a proclamation for all of England as well.[26] John Stype commented on the lack of evidence when he stated that he mentioned the proclamations only because historians were silent about them.[27]

The proclamations which ordered gentlemen to leave London and return to their homes in the country also dealt only with the upper ranks of society. There were military motivations for Mary's proclamation in 1558 and Elizabeth's in 1587, as we have already seen.[28] Elizabeth's proclamation was longer because it established a procedure whereby men with compelling reasons for staying in London could seek licenses from their Lord Lieutenant or his Deputy.[29] The threat in her proclamation was for imprisonment and fines 'according to the quality of the offense...for the breach of her majesty's commandment tending to the public service of the whole realm'. Such a vaguely worded penalty often meant that the offenders would be punished in the Star Chamber, and indeed several were.[30]

It is noteworthy that the same orders were given in many other forms than in royal proclamations: the Council recommended merely a royal order in 1559, or deputed the Lieutenants to make the command as in 1569 and 1587, or included it in the grain orders in the dearth of 1594–8, or required the Lord Mayor of London to

[24] Procs. 582/664 (the original of which is in BL, Add. MS 33924), 664/768.
[25] PRO, SP 12/90/2, 12/107/4; *APC*, XIII, 115–16. The proclamation was not issued as letters patent.
[26] Instructions in 1560, *HMC 77: De L'Isle I*, p. 319; in 1570, *ibid.* p. 333.
[27] *Annals Ref.*, III, i, 240.
[28] Above, pp. 80–2.
[29] Proc. 694/795.
[30] Hudson, 'Treatise on the Court of Star-Chamber', II, 55.

survey the men in London, presumably so that action could be taken.[31] It would seem that royal proclamations were used only when some pressing military situation dictated a printed order which could be distributed quickly.

Apparel

The basis for the regulation of apparel was a formidable act of 1533 which set out twelve separate clauses and a like number of provisos for laymen, and a smaller number of orders and exemptions for clerics. The fundamental principle was that the gradations in society should be reflected in men's clothes, so that each rank might wear apparel of slightly less magnificence than those in the next higher order. This the act did by first dividing all subjects into twelve ranks, and then by making further distinctions within them based on the type of garment worn, the material from which it was made, and the trim and ornamentation.[32] No wonder that the official summary published in 1562 stated that the statute 'cannot be conveniently abridged, but is to be considered by reading and perusing the whole act at large'.[33] Another act in 1542 sought to capitalize on the disobedience of wives by ordering their husbands to furnish a gelding for a light horseman, a duty which otherwise he had to undertake only if he was worth a clear yearly value of 100 marks.[34] Another statute in 1555 restricted the privilege of wearing silk to men who could spend £20 a year or who were heirs apparent of knights, and increased the penalties from 3s 4d as in the Henrician act to a minimum of £10. Previously anyone down to the yeoman class could wear silk, and the act's strictness along with the high fine made it a favorite of informers.[35]

We have seen that Mary and Elizabeth both issued breviates of statutes to be enforced early in their reigns,[36] in which the laws on apparel were included. They added nothing to the laws, and so presumably one could be punished additionally only for a contempt. There is one instance of the enforcement of Mary's proclamation in the Star Chamber, presumably on that basis.[37] The Elizabethan

[31] PRO, SP 12/7/73, 12/60/4, 12/252/42, 12/254/32; *APC*, xv, 273; *HMC 43: 15th Rpt, App. VII (Duke of Somerset MSS)*, pp. 25–7; Corp. London RO, Journal xxiv, fos. 6v. 69; xxv, fo. 282; Alexander B. Grossart (ed.), *The Dr. Farmer Chetham MS* (Chetham Society, lxxxix; Manchester, 1873), p. 30 (a precept in the Star Chamber on the last day of term).   [32] 24 Henry VIII, c. 13.

[33] Mistakenly called a proclamation by Steele and Hughes & Larkin as 495/568.

[34] 33 Henry VIII, c. 17.   [35] 1 & 2 Philip & Mary, c. 2.

[36] Above, p. 68.   [37] BL, Harl. MS 2143, fo. 4v.

proclamations were different in several respects. They dealt solely with apparel, altered at times the statutory provisions or even dispensed them, and supplemented the laws with new provisions to keep up with new developments in fashion. The prodigious length of the proclamations mirrored the complex laws: only the first and third of the nine issued were as short as three broadside sheets; six was the more normal length, and the proclamation of 1580 reached eight sheets. There were normally three sections: the text of the proclamation which was a charge to obey the regulations to follow; a list of important statutory provisions culled from the laws of 1533 and 1555; and special orders devised by the Council, consisting of the new provisions and the new means of enforcement.

Because the number of proclamations was so great, we need first to get an overview of the different ways in which they were used in Elizabeth's reign, then to place them in the context of the government's unsuccessful attempts to obtain new statutes on apparel, and finally to see how the enforcement of the proclamations was shifted from the central courts to local officials.

The nine proclamations divide into three rather distinct groups. The first three (1559, 1562, 1566) were experiments in developing a system of legal and administrative devices. The government seemingly was satisfied with the results, because the second group (1574, 1577, 1580) differs only in the number of supplementary orders which were added to a nearly identical core of provisions. The third three differed markedly because they reflected the Queen's disgust at the lack of reform, and thus they (1588, 1597, 1597) dispensed from all the statutory provisions which the proclamations did not repeat. Now regulation was to be on the basis of the proclamation alone, superseding the obsolete provisions of the statutes which had not kept up with the fashions.

In part the shift to regulation by the prerogative was the result of the government's lack of success in altering the older laws. Bills on apparel were introduced into at least five sessions of Parliament.[38] The objections to the bills had both a legal and a social dimension, and none of the eventual thirteen bills which were produced ever passed. The government's fixed purpose, and the sustained opposition which it met, are important in evaluating the role of proclamations.

The place where the first proclamation was enforced was the Star

[38] Introduced in the Commons first in 1566 and 1571, and in the safer Lords in 1575, 1589 and 1597–8.

Chamber, but from that time onward the emphasis was always on local enforcement. The evidence shows a very diligent enforcement in the early years and much less later, perhaps because the later proclamations were less detailed and more hortatory, and thus were less likely to spur the local officers to action.

Turning now to a chronological consideration of the various proclamations, we find that the first, which was issued on 21 October 1559, was in general a command to enforce the existing laws. It announced that detailed procedures had been set out for the Court, but merely commanded other officials to meet and develop effective means of enforcing the laws.[39] The conciliar orders which the proclamation had sanctioned were enforced in the Star Chamber, and it is clear that the offenses had occured at Court since the defendants were delivered up by the Knight Marshal in whose jurisdiction the Court lay.[40] There was also a good bit of enforcement on apparel in the common law courts at this time. In the King's Bench and a local session of the peace only the statutes were cited as the authority for the action,[41] but nine of the twelve cases in the Exchequer in the next two years were grounded on the dual authority of the statutes and the proclamation. Four of the cases did not proceed very far,[42] but the Attorney General appeared in the other five to second the informers' actions. Two of the cases were referred to local juries and disappear from the rolls,[43] but in the remaining cases the defendants gained the right to conclude the matter by paying small fines which in no case exceeded 10s.[44] There was administrative enforcement as well when the Council ordered the Lord Mayor of London to appoint watchers to detect offenders, and in the spring he issued a precept ordering further watches for persons wearing 'great hose and other unlawful apparel'.[45]

[39] Proc. 464/517; the Council's articles are —/515.

[40] So noted in Huntington Libr., Ellesmere MS 2768, fos. 1, 29; 2652, fo. 15; 6100. Also reported in Hudson, 'Treatise on the Court of Star-Chamber', II, 114 and from thence in Wilfrid Hooper, 'Tudor Sumptuary Laws', *EHR*, xxx (1915), 438. Egerton's precedent book also notes that regulations on apparel were prepared in the Star Chamber in 1505 and 1518: Ellesmere MS 2768, fo. 9; 2652, fo. 3v; 479 (1505 only).

[41] PRO, KB 9/597 I/6 before the proclamation; 603/23 and 623/15 afterwards; York CA Dept, Sessions of Peace F 2, at session of 12 January 1562.

[42] PRO, E 159/342, m. 122 (Somerset; Hil. 3 Eliz.); 343, m. 59 (London; Mich. 3 & 4 Eliz.); 342, m. 86 (Westminster; Easter 3 Eliz.); 343, m. 6v (Somerset; Trin. 3 Eliz.).

[43] PRO, E 159/341, m. 122 (offense in Gloucs.; Mich. 2 & 3 Eliz.); 341, m. 117, case assigned to Justices of Assize in Worcs. (same term).

[44] The defendants had originally denied the charges: PRO, E 159/341, m. 118 (Hunts.; Mich. 2 & 3 Eliz.); 342, m. 36v (Herts.; Easter 3 Eliz.); 343, m. 57 (Beds.; Mich. 3 & 4 Eliz.). Fines in unfoliated mm. of fines in Mich. 3 & 4 Eliz., and Hil. 4 Eliz.

[45] See the sources cited by Hooper, 'Tudor Sumptuary Laws', pp. 437–8.

The next proclamation, in May 1562, was intended to reform 'two great enormities', one the 'monstrous abuse of apparel almost in all estates, but principally in the meaner sort', and the other the 'decay and disfurniture of all kinds of horses for service in the realm', a reference to the lack of enforcement of the act of 1542.[46] A commission was promised to enforce the latter, and thus the commissioners' actions were not technically an enforcement of the proclamation.[47] Thus the heart of the proclamation rested in the 'certain good orders...devised and accorded by her Council' which were to serve for correcting the abuses in hose and the wearing of swords and rapiers. The proclamation singled out several places where the abuses were quite pronounced,[48] and provided a number of procedures for enforcement.

So much evidence remains that it will be convenient to list the towns which implemented the different provisions. The orders for watches and searches for illegal apparel and especially for hosiers and tailors who used excessive material in hose were conducted in London, York, Exeter and Lincoln.[49] The proclamation had required the local officials to give special commands to the various companies to execute the proclamation; Exeter gave the charge to the cutlers, and London to 'several companies'.[50] It had also required bonds from masters lest their servants offend, and of cutlers, hosiers, tailors and others; this was done in London, York, Norwich, Exeter, Middlesex, Sandwich and Rye.[51] All of the royal orders were in turn supplemented by additional regulations, as was done in London and within the jurisdiction of the Council of the North,[52] and these were

[46] Proc. 494/565.
[47] PRO, E 178/733 (county Durham); 178/570 (Cumb. and Carlisle); 178/570 (Cornw.); 178/469 (Cambs. and Cambridge); 178/1052 (Hunts.); 178/1077 (Cinque Ports); 178/2473 (Worcs.); 178/2396 (Wilts.); 178/3058 (Northumb.); 178/2004 (Hants.); commission for London mentioned in Corp. London RO, Repertories 15, fo. 117v, and for Norwich in Norf. & Norw. RO, Norwich Mayor's Ct Bk 8, fo. 65, and for Exeter in Hooker's common-place book, Exeter CRO, MS 51, fo. 354v.
[48] The Chamber, the Household, London and its liberties, the universities, the Inns of Court and of Chancery, the counties palatine of Lancaster and Chester – but note that none of these are resorts of the 'meaner sort' against whom the proclamation ranted.
[49] Corp. London RO, Repertories 15, fos. 74v–75, 77; York CA Dept, YC/A 23, fos. 54–55, 151, partly printed in Raine, vi, 36–8, 88; Exeter CRO, AB 4, fo. 179; HMC 37: 14th Rpt, App. VIII (Corp. of Lincoln MSS), p. 53.
[50] Exeter CRO, AB 4, fo. 177; Corp. London RO, Repertories 15, fos. 414v, 415v.
[51] PRO, SP 12/23/12, 13 (London); York CA Dept, YC/A 23, fos. 56, 56v (the Ainsty); Norf. & Norw. RO, Norwich Mayor's Ct Bk 7, fo. 616; 8, fo. 270; Exeter CRO, AB 4, fos. 178, 183; GLC (Middx) RO, Sessions Roll 163/4; Kent AO, Sandwich MS Sa/AC 4, fo. 208v; E. Sussex RO, Rye MS 1/3, fos. 15v–18— (a total of over 220 bonds in all).
[52] PRO, SP 12/15/76, and Corp. London RO, Repertories 15, fos. 76v, 431v; Council of the North, copied in York CA Dept, YC/A 23, fos. 148v–149, printed in Raine, vi, 86–7.

commanded by a variety of precepts and subsidiary provisions in London, aimed at securing the active involvement of the Aldermen.[53] The Council demanded certificates to insure that all the orders were carried out.[54]

These administrative means were supplemented by judicial enforcement as well. Offenders were presented in Norwich, confessions recorded in Exeter and Norwich, prohibited items confiscated in London, and offenders imprisoned in London and York.[55] The punishment was often commensurate with the offender's social rank: the Court of Aldermen in London used ridicule on a lowborn man, whose 'other said monstrous hose [were] to be treasured for a time in some open place in the nether hall where they may aptly be seen and considered of the people as an example of extreme folly', while it merely took recognizances from the higher born not to continue in their faults. The number of cases in London must have been considerable because fourteen pleaders were attached to assist the Court on a rotational basis to dispatch the cases.[56] In York two men were fined 20s each, but a gentleman visiting the city from Northumberland who had violated the proclamation in three different respects was released without penalty when he promised to reform.[57] The fines assessed at the quarter sessions in Essex on the tailors who made the hose were very small, ranging from 4d to a maximum of 1s.[58]

The new regulations were not without opposition. The officials of London lodged a complaint on behalf of the clothiers for some relaxation of the rules about the lining of hose, the main grievance being that the hosiers just outside Temple Bar were making the new linings because the regulations were not being enforced as thoroughly there as in London.[59] The royal proclamation of 12 February 1566 was probably issued in part because of their request for relief because it did contain a mitigation of the earlier rules on hose. Added to it,

[53] Hooper, 'Tudor Sumptuary Laws', pp. 440-1.
[54] Certificates from the Aldermen to the Lord Mayor, Corp. London RO, Repertories 15, fos. 79, 81, 85, 88, 91, 93v; from York to the Lord President of the North, York CA Dept, YC/A 23, fos. 58-58v, 67, partly printed in Raine, VI, 39-40.
[55] Presentments: Norf. & Norw. RO, Norwich Mayor's Ct Bk 8, fo. 33. Confessions: ibid.; Exeter CRO, AB 4, fo. 212. Confiscations: Corp. London RO, Repertories 15, fo. 78. Imprisonments: ibid. 414v; York CA Dept, YC/A 23, fo. 67.
[56] Hooper, 'Tudor Sumptuary Laws', p. 441.
[57] York CA Dept, YC/A 23, fo. 57, printed in Raine, VI, 36-7. The officers had doubted whether they could fine or whether the power was restricted to the Exchequer, and received an answer that they might.
[58] Essex RO, Transcript of Calendar of Quarter Sessions, citing Q/SR 16/57; presentments on the basis of the 'statute', ibid. 27/5-7, but the statute made no mention of hose.
[59] Hooper, 'Tudor Sumptuary Laws', pp. 442-3.

however, were orders that no fencing school could operate without a license from the town, and that officials must restrain the access to such schools by men not entitled to bear the weapons.[60] Once again, one can find that searches and watches according to the new proclamation were held in Rye, London, and York where they were held parish by parish within the wards.[61] In York special inquiries were ordered to be held at the general sessions.[62] Bonds were taken of the hosiers and tailors in Sandwich and Rye, and of the hosiers and masters of fencing schools in York.[63] The searchers in York were encouraged by the city's grant to them of half the forfeitures which would be levied.[64] In Norwich the officials confiscated the outsized hose, and once again additional pleaders were assigned to assist the Court of Aldermen in handling the many cases.[65] The Council in Wales demanded certificates from the jurisdictions within its area, and on a quite different level we find for the first time that the Queen issued licenses to some courtiers to exempt them from the general regulations.[66]

The second and third proclamations went beyond the letter of the statutes, and this was clearly admitted when they distinguished between the types of punishment to be imposed.[67] But the Queen realized that Parliament was the proper instrument for making the rules permanent, and so a bill on apparel was introduced in 1566. A new bill was substituted for it and eventually passed the Commons, but the Lords in turn produced their own bill.[68] The original bill can be supposed to have reflected the provisions in the earlier proclamations, but the 'new' bill substituted for it still survives, and says nothing about hose, swords or fencing schools. It also contained a proviso that specifically stated that no one was to be impeached or molested unless he was indicted before a Justice of the Peace or of the Assize, a stipulation which certainly shows a continuity of concern in the Commons that we have seen from earlier reigns, but which in

[60] Proc. 542/618.
[61] E. Sussex RO, Rye MS 1/3, fo. 148v; Corp. London RO, Journal xviii, fo. 383, and Repertories 16, fos. 13v, 15; York CA Dept, YC/A 24, fos. 42, 76–81v, partly printed in Raine, vi, 127.
[62] York CA Dept, YC/A 24, fo. 40v.
[63] Kent AO, Sandwich MS Sa/AC 4, fos. 310, 311v; E. Sussex RO, Rye MS 1/3, fos. 149v, 151; York CA Dept, YC/A 24, fo. 42.
[64] York CA Dept, YC/A 24, fo. 47.
[65] Norf. & Norw. RO, Mayor's Ct Bk 8, fo. 385; Corp. London RO, Repertories 16, fos. 13v–15.
[66] HMC 31: 13th Rpt, App. IV (Corp. of Hereford MSS), p. 329; PRO, SP 12/39/33, 34.
[67] Above, p. 43.
[68] CJ, i, 73–5, 77; LJ, i, 646–67, 659–61; CJ, i, 80.

effect would preclude the special searches and watches which seem to have made the earlier proclamations so effective.[69] That can hardly have pleased the Queen, but there is no indication whether the bill was killed or allowed to die because of the opposition, or because time simply ran out in the session.

Eight years passed before the next proclamation on apparel. In the interim the bonds of the hosiers which had been taken according to the proclamation had been called up into King's Bench, where a patentee named Digby sought to benefit from the grant which he had obtained for the forfeitures. The grant was very unpopular, of course, in London.[70] In the parliament of 1571 a bill 'against great hose' was introduced, but the Lords refused it and there is no indication what the bill contained.[71]

The proclamation of 1574 on apparel was long on persuasion and short on procedures, probably a reflection of Burghley's role in drafting it. Both the original text with his corrections and the text as finally published focused on the loss of precious metals to pay for the imported finery, and on the ruin to young men of gentle birth from their extravagances. Burghley toned down the vivid comments on the men of good birth and redirected the blame to the lower classes; he also deleted a long recitation in the original draft about the Queen's mercy and willingness to overlook past offenses, and added a section on the reforms already made since he was such a believer in the power of example.[72] A new feature appeared in the proclamation, a schedule for women's apparel drawn by analogy from the statutes which mentioned male apparel only. The only evidence of local action is of opposition: the Inns of Court won a delay in applying the proclamation, and the officers of London sent a request to Burghley for dispensations and complained of its 'doubtful' aspects.[73] It should be noted that the proclamation did *not* contain the usual set of additional provisions which had characterized the recent issues, and it seems clear that little could be expected unless the officers' responsibilities were spelled out in detail. At this stage we should dearly like to know if any of the opposition in the parliamentary sessions had spilled over to color the local officers' attitudes.

[69] HLRO, Box 1.
[70] PRO, SP 12/83/4; Corp. London RO, Repertories 16, fos. 431, 433.
[71] J. B. Davidson (ed.), 'Hooker's Journal of the House of Commons in 1571', *Transactions of the Devonshire Association*, XI (1879), 485, a mention with no elaboration.
[72] Proc. 601/690; draft in BL, Lansd. MS 18/41.
[73] *APC*, VIII, 248; Corp. London RO, Letter Bk x, fo. 311; Repertories 16, fos. 232, 236v.

Whatever undercurrents of opposition there were found an expression during the session in 1575–6 when a bill on apparel was introduced and passed the Lords. It would seem that the bill would have authorized the regulation of apparel by means of proclamations, and when the opposition to those provisions arose in the Commons, Sir Walter Mildmay was chosen to present the objections at a conference.[74] He stated that some disliked the entire bill, 'utterly grounding themselves specially upon the reason, that where the subjects of the land have not been heretofore bound to anything but unto such as should be certainly established by authority of parliament, this act proceeding, a proclamation from the prince should take the force of law, which might prove a dangerous precedent in time to come...'.

He then delivered the expected panegyric on the Queen's good government, and continued: 'Yet what this may work hereafter in more dangerous times, when the government shall not be so directed by Justice, and Equity, is greatly to be forseen, lest by example the authority of a proclamation may extend to greater matters than these are. A thing much to be considered both for ourselves, and our posterities, the rather for that it is seen by daily experience that of precedents great hold is taken specially in the case of princes.'

Mildmay then noted that others did not think the matter so dangerous because the proclamation was circumscribed within the bill, but that the general objections to it might be summarized under four heads. The first was the order of the proclamation since the bill provided that it need not be general, and that proclaiming it in one place might bind all. The Lords agreed that this should be amended. The second objection was the greatness of the penalty which was to be the forfeiture of the garment and a fine of £10 per day, whereas Henry VIII's statute had set the fine at 3s 4d.[75] The third objection concerned the manner of enforcement, because the bill authorized any officer 'no matter how inferior' to commit a suspect to ward and take the garment off his back. The Lords replied that the penalties were necessary for a real reformation. A final objection from the Commons was the duration of the bill, set for seven years, but the Lords were obdurate. A new bill was drawn by the Commons, but nothing came of it because the Lords did not like the small penalties

---

[74] Progress of the bills: *LJ*, 1, 729–33, 749–50; *CJ*, 1, 109–15. Mildmay's speech: BL, Sloane MS 326, fos. 15–18*v* (used above); also in Harl. MS 6265, fos. 358–60 a copy with minor changes. Extracts in Neale, *Elizabeth I and her Parliaments, 1559–1581*, pp. 354–5.

[75] A convenient lapse of memory! The penalty in the act of 1555 was £10 and up.

or the means of enforcement. The session ended two days after the bill was first read in the Lords.

The Queen considered the right of arrest to be vital to the regulations, as is clear from its inclusion in the nearly identical proclamations of 1577 and 1580. It ordered all Justices of the Peace and head officers of towns to arrest suspected offenders and examine them. Persons found culpable were liable to one month's imprisonment and the loss of the item of apparel, unless they would enter into a bond to appear at the next sessions or assize. Thus the suspect had his choice of suffering the penalty in the proclamation or being bound over to take his chances with those in the statute.[76] There was much activity in London in both 1577 and 1580 in enforcing the respective proclamations, including the establishment of watches.[77] The Lord Mayor certainly did not relish his position. He was pressured from above by the Queen who had him lectured on enforcing the proclamation in the Star Chamber, by the Lord Chief Baron whose son-in-law was contemptuously used by a watcher, and by friends of the Earl of Surrey whose brother had drawn a sword on the watchers when they stopped him for wearing ruffs which had been forbidden in the proclamation.[78] The Cutlers pressed the Lord Mayor to enter a complaint because they alleged that others in the trade just outside the city disobeyed the proclamation with impunity. Other citizens of 'worshipful position' urged him to seek for them the dispensations which would allow them to wear apparel 'appropriate' to their office, even if it meant seeking an act of Parliament in the next session.[79] But evidence of enforcement in jurisdictions other than London is rare.[80]

In 1588 a proclamation on apparel was issued just after the end of the Hilary term as a reminder to the Justices who had received a charge to enforce the regulations at the usual end of term speech in the Star Chamber. A list of dispensations for courtiers was added to the usual breviates of statutes and supplementary orders.[81] The proclamation has been called Burghley's last great effort at reforming apparel, but the elder statesman confided to his son Robert that no lasting reform would follow until there was a reform at the Court and

[76] Procs. 623/717, 646/745.
[77] After 1577, Corp. London RO, Journal xx, pt 2, fos. 343, 345v, 350, 350v, 351, 375; Letter Bk Y, fos. 151v–152v, 188, 194v. After 1580, ibid. Journal xxi, fos. 35–35v, 79v, 210v.
[78] Ibid. Remembrancia I, fos. 2, 5v–6, 12, 41–41v.
[79] PRO, SP 12/176/57.
[80] Letter to all shires noted, APC, ix, 320, and copied in Kent AO, Sandwich MS ZB 33, fol 48. Searches in York with no mention of the proclamation as the authority, York CA Dept, YC/A 27, fos. 145v–146. [81] Proc. 697/798.

in London.[82] No cases of local enforcement have been discovered, and a complaint was made the following year that the proclamation had had no effect.[83] The cases in the Exchequer at this time were based solely on the statutes, and by then a patentee had gained the right to enforce the statute of 1542 on providing horses when wives offended in apparel.[84] A bill on apparel was introduced in the Lords in the session of 1589 and a new bill drawn, but no action was taken in the Commons.[85]

Two final proclamations on apparel were issued fifteen days apart in 1597, the latter of which was a set of dispensations for courtiers which had been included within the single proclamation in 1588.[86] The Lord Mayor of London issued precepts to the Aldermen and Wardens of companies to enforce it, but neither their responses nor any from other towns are to be found.[87] Still another bill on apparel was introduced in the Lords in the session of 1597–8, but it was rejected because 'their Lordships have no good liking of the said bill for sundry imperfections in the same not answerable to her majesty's proclamation touching the degrees and qualities of persons'.[88] A new bill was drawn but the session ended soon after.[89]

THE GROWTH OF GREATER LONDON

The rate of growth of the population in and around London in the sixteenth century was truly phenomenal. Any estimate is risky in the absence of sound demographic data, but it would seem that an increase from about 50,000 in 1500 to 250,000 in 1600 occurred.[90] The vitality and glory of Renaissance London have never ceased to fascinate, but here we have to be concerned with the sober realities of the difficulties which that growth entailed.

London's leaders had become sufficiently alarmed over the influx of people in the 1570s to begin to enact local ordinances and to provide means of control.[91] They knew, however, that the growth did

[82] Read, *Burghley*, pp. 528–9. [83] Cited in Hughes & Larkin, III, 3 headnote.
[84] Patent recorded in PRO, E 159/394, mm. 177–177v.
[85] *LJ*, II, 148–57.
[86] Procs. 786/890, 787/891. See *HMC 9: Salisbury (Cecil) VII*, under date 29 June 1597.
[87] Corp. London RO, Journal xxiv, fo. 237v.
[88] D'Ewes, *Journals of Elizabethan Parliaments*, p. 594.
[89] *Ibid.* pp. 545–6, 583, 588–92.
[90] On the growth in general, see Lawrence Stone, *The Crisis of the Aristocracy, 1558–1641* (Oxford, 1965), pp. 387–98, and F. J. Fisher, 'The Development of London as a Centre of Conspicuous Consumption in the Sixteenth and Seventeenth Century', *TRHS*, 4th series, xxx (1947), 37–50.
[91] Corp. London RO, Repertories 18, fos. 239v, 330.

not respect jurisdictional boundaries, and that their efforts alone would not suffice, and so in the spring of 1580 they requested a royal proclamation to handle the problem in the entire metropolitan area.[92] The proclamation of 7 July 1580 which answered that request forbade the building of new houses in London and within three miles of the city's gates, as well as the division of existing houses to allow more dwellers or 'inmates'. It clearly stated the three principal dangers of the rapid growth: the dangers to health, especially from disease and the plague; the difficulty of providing sufficient victual; and the need to maintain order in the expanding area.[93] The effort to deal with the problem was so sustained that evidence of control can be found in twenty-one of the remaining twenty-four years of Elizabeth's reign, and well into the next century.[94] Given so much evidence, it will be useful to survey briefly the issues involved, the authorities for the actions, and the places assigned to enforcement, before considering the matter chronologically.

The earliest issue was simply to prevent the erection of new buildings and the subdivision of existing structures. The proclamation authorized the local officers 'to seize all manner of stuff (after warning given) brought to the place where such new buildings shall be intended' and to convert it to public uses. Soon another issue arose: what should be done about the buildings erected illegally – was there authority to tear them down? The problem of property became more important as time went on.

The authority of the proclamation of 1580 was augmented when a statute was enacted in 1593. Indeed, the proclamation itself had stated that additional authority would be sought, and a bill seems to have been prepared for the session of 1581, but perhaps it was not read.[95] The statute of 1593 did cite the earlier proclamation and continued in force until 1601 when it lapsed, but it did not confer authority to tear down any structure.[96] A proclamation was issued again in 1602. The other authorities which were invoked between 1580–1603 were the Privy Council, the common law, and the privileges of local jurisdictions. As to place of enforcement, the first proclamation called only for local enforcement in and around Lon-

[92] *Ibid.* Remembrancia I, no. 41, the formalization of the city's suit which had been drafted in 1579, BL, Add. MS 48019, fos. 151ff., especially 153.
[93] Proc. 649/749.
[94] Thomas G. Barnes, 'The Prerogative and Environmental Control of London Building in the Early Seventeenth Century: The Lost Opportunity', *California Law Review*, LVIII (1970), 1332–63, found no examples of enforcement before 1590, as a result of using the records of the Star Chamber and Exchequer rather exclusively.
[95] PRO, SP 12/148/11, listed as 'not yet read'.   [96] 35 Eliz. I, c. 6.

don, but as early as 1581 the responsibility was shifted to the royal government.

In 1580, 1581 and 1583, the Privy Council issued orders to the Lord Mayor of London to see that the proclamation was enforced, and he in turn issued precepts to the Aldermen and Wardens of the companies.[97] In 1581 the Council demanded that presentments be made; the Lord Mayor had them cast into indictments at the local sessions and then certified them into the Star Chamber.[98] Although I have found no record of that Court's action in 1581, it did punish several men during the Michaelmas term of 1583 and would have dealt with more except for lack of time and for certain deficiencies in the indictments. It therefore directed the officers in London to make new inquiries and to bind offenders to answer in Star Chamber.[99] In the same year a presentment was made in King's Bench against a widow for keeping a bawdy house, in which she was also charged with receiving inmates. This represents the sole instance in which I have found an indictment in that Court's records framed not on a statute but solely 'contra formam proclamacionis'.[100]

By this time a variety of concerns had surfaced. The Privy Council had gone far beyond the proclamation, to seek a thorough reformation. In June 1583 it ordered the officers in London to deal with those who had built or divided structures in London even *before* the proclamation, suggesting that they proceed on the authority of the common law on the grounds that the construction created a public nuisance.[101] At the sessions for Middlesex at Finsbury in August 1588, a cobbler of Wapping entered a recognizance at £40 with the condition that he pull down the tenements which he had erected since the proclamation.[102] The Council's diligence continued, whether in the form of orders for local officials or in the correction of high ranking offenders.[103]

[97] In 1580, Corp. London RO, Letter Bk Z, fo. 103; *APC*, xiii, 201–2. In 1581, Corp. London RO, Remembrancia i, no. 262; *APC*, xiii, 217. In 1583, Corp. London RO, Remembrancia i, fos. 495, 514. Precepts in London: in 1580, Journal xxi, fo. 135; Letter Bk Z, fo. 166; in 1583, Journal xxi, fos. 276, 299, 305v.

[98] PRO, SP 12/150/45; copy of the indictment in 12/150/45 I. Were the indictments used as a basis for drawing a bill for the Star Chamber?

[99] Corp. London RO, Remembrancia i, no. 514.

[100] PRO, KB 9/659/118, from an inquiry at the Guildhall called before the Justices at the sessions for London, then called into King's Bench. She never answered the order and was outlawed; KB 29/219, m. 49v. I owe the former reference to Mr Michael Lovelock.

[101] Corp. London RO, Remembrancia i, no. 514; also from the Egerton papers, in Barnes, 'The Prerogative and Environmental Control of London Building', p. 1358.

[102] GLC (Middx) RO, 278/9, 12 August 30 Eliz.

[103] *APC*, xii, 94, 155–6; xiv, 356. Rebukes to Sir James Crofts of the Privy Council and

The role of the Star Chamber in inflicting exemplary punishment was even more pronounced in the years 1586–91. It punished several offenders in the Trinity term of 1586.[104] In 1587 the officers in and around London received commands to forward names to the Star Chamber,[105] and even though there exists no good evidence that prosecutions followed, a fragmentary interrogatory dated 1588 includes questions on the observance of the proclamation to be put to a defendant by the Attorney General.[106] Another request for information was made in the summer of 1590, and in October a special commission to examine offenders was issued.[107] When called before the commissions, an undetermined number of men promised to reform, but eighty-one others entered into recognizances ranging from £10 to £100 with conditions with required either their reform or the payment of a fine in Star Chamber.[108] In 1591 there is a mention of the commissions again, and a mention without elaboration of a decree on buildings in the Star Chamber.[109]

The statute against new buildings and other abuses was enacted in the session of 1592–3, and as would be expected there is evidence of its enforcement in the normal courts thereafter.[110] But it did not preclude the use of enforcement based on the prerogative. In 1597 the Council received a report from the commissioners whom it had appointed to certify all construction since the proclamation of 1580. They bound over at least eight offenders who had not yet answered for their actions.[111] Perhaps their certificate was the basis for the Attorney General's case against 'Negoose and others' in the Michaelmas term that year, in which the three defendants were fined £100, £40 and £20 respectively, with the further command that the houses to be torn down and the timber used for the poor.[112] A similar judgment was given against the two offenders the following year, with smaller fines but with the same requirement to pull the structures down.[113] It should be noted that the order for tearing the

the Bishop of London, Corp. London RO, Remembrancia I, no. 132, and *APC*, xII, 213 respectively. Petitions to the Council for exemptions, PRO, SP 12/138/34.
 [104] BL, Harl. MS 2143, fo. 17v.   [105] *APC*, xIV, 356.
 [106] PRO, Star Chamber 5/A/43/36, endorsed 25 June 30 Eliz.
 [107] Council's orders, *APC*, xIX, 188–9, 278–81, 324, 348–50, 371.
 [108] Barnes, 'The Prerogative and Environmental Control of London Building', p. 1343, based on PRO, E 159/423, m. 95, and E 163/15/10.   [109] *APC*, xxI, 232, 422–3.
 [110] E.g., PRO, KB 9/690 1/42–42v, 47, 50, 61, 64, 66, 67; 692/30.
 [111] Barnes, 'The Prerogative and Environmental Control of London Building', p. 1344.
 [112] Hawarde, *Les Reportes del Cases in Camera Stellata*, pp. 79–80.
 [113] Barnes, 'The Prerogative and Environmental Control of London Building', p. 1344, from a MS in the Inner Temple; also noted in Corp. London RO, Journal xxv, fos. 62—3.

buildings down was not in the proclamation, which had merely authorized the seizure of buildings materials which had not been used, but which had been dedicated to the new construction. It would seem that the requirement to tear existing buildings down was set forth first in a Star Chamber decree of 16 June 1597.[114]

The final great drive to enforce the regulations in Elizabeth's reign came in 1601–2. There are records of recognizances in both years, and after the second proclamation was issued in 1602, a total of ninety-nine recognizances dating back to October 1590 and amounting to £5,715 were estreated.[115] The proclamation of 1602 mentioned the punishments in Star Chamber and its decree, and the nine point program which it set out did include the requirement to pull down certain buildings.[116] A full set of local orders for London was prepared, including one that the names of offenders be sent up again to the Star Chamber,[117] but there is no indication of any subsequent action. The garrulous John Chamberlain wrote to Dudley Carleton that the Council 'have begun in every parish to light on the unluckiest [to pull buildings down], here and there one, which God knows is far from removing the mischief'.[118]

[114] Corp. London RO, Journal xxiv, fo. 220v.
[115] Barnes, 'The Prerogative and Environmental Control of London Building', pp. 1344–5.
[116] Proc. 815/927.
[117] Corp. London RO, Journal xxv, fos. 354v, 357 bis v; xxvi, fos. 12–12v. A wardmote inquest for St Dunstan's Parish in the Ward of Farringdon Without presented men who divided tenements, without an explicit mention of the proclamation, Guildhall Libr. MS 3018/1, fos. 74–74v; similar inquests in 1599 (fo. 67ᵃv) and before the proclamation of 1580 (fos. 23v, 25, 26, 28v).
[118] PRO, SP 12/284/46.

REFLECTIONS: THE PROCLAMATIONS AND ECONOMIC AND SOCIAL MANAGEMENT

The proclamations on economic and social matters sprang from an extremely varied range of circumstances. Those on grain, the prices of wines, and the plague were the government's reaction to crises which were caused by natural forces. The proclamations against patentees' abuses were responses to problems caused at least partially by the Crown's own policies. But a good number of the proclamations were sought by interests outside the royal government. Local interests occasionally petitioned to have the export of grain halted to conserve supplies, or to seek royal assistance in stemming the flow of people into London. Others were sought by private and commercial interests, as when the wool winders attempted to preserve their declining economic position, or when the clothing areas desired exemptions from the statutes, or when any number of patentees strove to boost their own fortunes.

The government's reaction to these forces is very instructive. The first response was often instictively conservative, sometimes supporting the Justices who used the Statute of Artificers to keep wages down, at other times attempting to restrain the levels of prices as with wine, and again insisting on restrictions on middlemen in the wool and grain trades even though their importance was becoming increasingly obvious. Similar attitudes lay behind several other proclamations which enforced the statutes on tillage and against enclosures, or which announced the legal opinion that the statute on usury was still in force.[1]

[1] Procs. 560/637, 657/758, the latter resolving the question about the extent of the duration of 13 Eliz. I, c. 8. Other miscellaneous economic proclamations: 540/616 which allowed the Scots to sell fish in non-standard barrels; 424/464 and 457/507 in which Mary and Elizabeth continued the traditional privilege which allowed merchants to carry out of the realm £4 in expense money on their voyages; and 518/587, the only non-military pricing of victual other than wine (here, hops) by Elizabeth in proclamations.

Many conflicts within the government itself were revealed in these proclamations. The Mint resisted the use of stamping irons by local officers because in its eyes that device threatened its monopoly of coining. The factions within the Council were evident when it came to the distribution of favors to patentees, and in particular when leaders in the Church sought protection from patentees for concealed lands from Burghley and his followers. Even the government's contractors could provide trouble, as when the navy victualer's ultimatum precipitated a series of events leading to the Book of Orders and eventually to the Star Chamber cases on grain.

A good number of the proclamations were negative propaganda. This was true above all of the cancellations of grants to patentees, but was also reflected in the proclamations which protected the reputations of the Lord Treasurer and Lord Mayor of London from the rumors which branded them as hoarders of grain. The failure to issue a proclamation occasionally formed a revealing admission. Thus rather than admit publicly that prices of wines were beyond the government's control, the Council had the rates published in 1574 at a private meeting of merchants and municipal authorities.

The importance of administrative measures in the proclamations is quite apparent, especially in conducting the recoinage and in protecting the Court and others from the plague. The actions of the patentees were made easier because of the series of administrative provisions in the proclamations on caps and on sowing hemp and flax seed. Most importantly, the many proclamations on lent and grain illustrate how proclamations were the first of two steps toward a degree of administrative sophistication. The proclamations instructed and sought to associate a number of local officers in the techniques in management which the Council thought effective. But in time they were superseded by even more effective devices. The Book of Orders was clearly the operative set of regulations late in the reign, with proclamations playing a subordinate yet still important role in sanctioning them. It had become clear that there was no need to provide the detailed regulations for local officers in proclamations which were aimed at a much wider audience, and that the necessarily lengthy provisions did not fit within the small amount of space available in several broadside sheets.

A good number of forces which tended to oppose the effect of proclamations are also revealed. The typical patentee had a *non obstante* clause in his grant which in theory precluded any regulation by proclamation, but of course if his abuses were great it was always possible to call in his grant. The regulations for lent were mitigated for the upper ranks of society by the licenses to eat meat which any number of secular and ecclesiastical officers issued. The force of bad example must have been a powerful influence: Burghley was convinced that no reform in apparel would occur until the Court had been reformed, and he must have been aware that the Queen's own example was hardly likely to help. And as always enforcement could break down at the local level when an unwilling officer resisted. The complaints from London's hosiers were based in no small part on the lack of diligence by the Justices in Middlesex which allowed the hosiers just outside London's gates to pander to the desire for showy apparel and thus attract customers from the city.

The many conflicts of economic interests must have rendered the proclamations less effective. The dispute over the pricing of wine brought into conflict the rights of the monarch, the city, and a number of commercial interests. We have also seen the quarrel between London and the East Anglian clothiers over sealing cloth, as well as the struggles between the Merchant Adventurers and the Merchant Staplers and those between the Vintners and other sellers of wine. The patentees were likely to come into conflict with local corporations and economic interests wherever they sought to exercise their grants. None of these conflicts appeared explicitly in the proclamations, but they are crucial to understanding their true implications.

The use of proclamations as temporary legislation which clearly anticipated later action in Parliament is evident from the laws enacted against abusing coin, for dispensations for the clothing areas, and against new buildings in London. The principled opposition to the proclamations on apparel is indicated by the failure of every bill in Parliament, and the lack of continuation to the statute on buildings suggests opposition there as well. The Commons' complaints that proclamations on apparel should not supplant the regulation by statute shows how great a change had occurred in relations between the monarch and Parliament. In Henry VIII's reign the Parliaments often delegated the day-to-day management of specific matters to him to be exercised through his proclamations, but the Parliaments of the Tudor Queens would not do this. Of all the objections voiced to the Elizabethan requests in Parliament, the one that rings truest was the complaint that any officer 'no matter how inferior' might remove a garment from a suspect's back. That touched two of the deepest and most tender beliefs of the day – consciousness of superiority and inferiority in society, and the reverence due to property. It would be inaccurate, therefore, to view the opposition on apparel and the new buildings as entirely constitutional, since a strong element of economic and social motivation must also have been present.

The proclamations on economic and social matters provided abundant examples of enforcement in the common law court of the Exchequer, in the prerogative court of Star Chamber, and in many courts at the local level, often under the active management of the Privy Council. But one must distinguish between the cases brought on general matters, and those brought by patentees. Only if the threat of prosecution had failed to move someone to compound with a patentee's deputy, or if his town had not made some settlement to keep the deputies away, would a case be brought to court. The legal action then became a second level of intimidation and was usually more successful because it demonstrated to the defendant that the deputy was in earnest. The success of this legal intimidation is suggested by the lack of conclusions to most cases brought by informers in the Exchequer, so that perhaps it is safer to argue here than in most cases that the unfinished case represented an out of court triumph for the informer. We need only compare the number of presentments by Kyrke in the Exchequer with the certificates which related how much he had collected for the pier at Sheringham to realize that most funds came from compositions.

The number of cases where proclamations were enforced judicially for public as opposed to private interests was also great, whether brought in local courts on apparel, grain, wine, and London buildings, or in the Exchequer on joint authority with a statute, or in the Star Chamber for the sake of example on grain and new buildings. The many examples of enforcement in the case of apparel in local courts suggests that the provisions struck a receptive cord. It is also clear that evidence of enforcement in this matter is lacking late in the reign, and while we can attribute some of this to the fact that the orders were then less sharp and detailed, there must be some other reason as well. It was probably one thing to regulate apparel in areas far from London, and another to try this in the city which had become a magnet to draw men of pretension and ambition. I suspect that the very degree of success in enforcement in London made men fear that the seizure of garments was going too far, and that the high social position of some offenders evoked a sympathetic response in Parliament. There was an irreconcilable difference, because the Queen was convinced that firm measures were necessary for reform. She wanted men to do as she said, not as she dressed.

The complaints about the proclamations against new buildings were not so clearly articulated in Elizabeth's reign as thereafter. Hawarde's reports tried to read back into the earlier century the charge that proclamations were being used to supplant statutes. But it is clear that the city asked for the proclamation, that the orders to tear down the buildings were not in the original proclamation but in a decree in the Star Chamber, and that the statute of 1593 did *not* authorize the removal of property. Thus we can presume that Parliament acted once again to protect property, but we can only wonder if the officials in London approved of the new procedures or had begun to go sour at the way things were moving despite their original request. We find ourselves once again in the impossible position of having to try to measure the perceived extent of the very real and very serious threat of overcrowding against a very serious and very real conviction that royal proclamations should not touch men's property. The Crown *had* respected the tradition that its temporary measures should be presented to Parliament to be made permanent, but it had not succeeded in overcoming a principled opposition.

PART FOUR

THE PRACTICE: THE
PROCLAMATIONS AND RELIGION

8

THE INTERIM SETTLEMENTS OF
RELIGION

One of the earliest and most important concerns for both Mary and Elizabeth was the settlement of religion. Each inherited a religious settlement with which she was discontented. Each called a Parliament to meet soon after her accession, to sweep away the former legislation and to restore the true religion. Each as leader of the Church followed the precedents set by her father and half-brother, by issuing a set of injunctions to serve as the work-a-day rules under which the settlement was to operate. The statutes and injunctions constituted what both Queens intended to be the permanent settlement of religion. Only in Mary's case was something more needed, since she sought and obtained for the realm a papal absolution from its schism.

In the reign of Edward VI there had been a slow, gradual move to establish protestantism in which a good number of proclamations were involved, often resorted to with such alacrity that one could suspect a willingness to use the prerogative as the primary means for instituting the changes.[1] But eventually the settlement was worked out in the format of statutes and injunctions, and it was to that pattern that the Tudor Queens returned. In Mary's reign the initial period between her accession and the injunctions amounted to just seven months; in Elizabeth's, slightly under eight. Although the permanent settlements at which they arrived were diametrically opposed, the half-sisters experienced the identical need to preserve order and to prevent religious contention, and thus there was a great similarity between the interim settlements: they regulated preaching, controlled the press, forbade plays which touched on religion and matters of state, and provided instruction on doctrine.[2] Both Queens established the interim norms through royal proclamations. Furthermore, they used proclamations to provide additional measures which were not strictly needed as part of the interim settlements, by introducing

---

[1] Heinze, p. 204.   [2] *Ibid.* pp. 205–10.

ceremonial changes and by advancing the date on which the provisions of the new statutes would become effective.

Because of Mary's plans and single-mindedness, her religious program was more quickly and neatly accomplished. The statutory,
permanent settlement was framed in the two sessions of the first
Marian Parliament. In the first, all the existing legislation on treason
was repealed except for the fundamental law of 1352. In the second,
two statutes were passed to restore the order for divine service and
for the administration of the sacraments to the practice of the last
year of Henry VIII's reign, and to protect priests from interference
while preaching or saying mass.[3] Since the acts of the second session
were to become effective on 20 December and since the Injunctions
were issued on 4 March 1554, the English part of the permanent
settlement was soon completed. Only two royal proclamations were
used in those seven months to form the interim settlement, the first of
which governed the period between Mary's accession and the conclusion of Parliament's work, and the second the time between its
enactments and the issue of the Injunctions.

The first of those proclamations was issued on 18 August 1553.[4] It
established procedures to be followed throughout the realm to prevent religious discord. Like so many other proclamations, it was
occasioned by disorders in London. At a meeting of the Privy Council
on 12 August, just nine days after Mary had arrived in London, Mary
announced her intention to follow her own religious beliefs but not to
compel others to do the same. The Spanish Ambassador wrote to his
King to indicate that she intended to publish this throughout the
realm as a proclamation,[5] but before that could be done an incident
occurred in London which seems to have provoked the actual proclamation of 18 August and to have changed it from a mere declaration into a regulatory measure. On Sunday, 13 August, the preacher
at Paul's Cross took as his theme the unjust deprivation and imprisonment which Edward's government had inflicted on the fiercely
catholic and unpopular Bishop of London, Edmund Bonner. This
infuriated the audience, so that someone threw a dagger at the
preacher, others stormed the pulpit, and the preacher had to be

[3] 1 Mary I, session 1, c. 1, leaving 25 Edward III, st. 5, c. 2; 1 Mary I, session 2, cc. 1, 2.
[4] Proc. 390/427.
[5] Philip Hughes, *The Reformation in England* (3 vols.; London, 1950–4), II, 197.

rescued. Mary immediately called the Lord Mayor of London before the Council and instructed him to send for all the curates in London, to forbid them to preach without her license. In the next few days the Lord Mayor received additional instructions which were coupled with a threat that he might be removed from office if the royal commands were not followed, and the Council wrote to the Bishop of Norwich to command him to extend the prohibition against unlicensed preaching to his diocese.[6] Finally the proclamation on 18 August made that prohibition and some new orders generally applicable throughout the realm.

The explanatory part of the proclamation dwelled on the Queen's wish not to command any subject to follow her own religion until Parliament settled the matter, and on the contentions which had recently occurred. To suppress those disorders, the proclamation ordered that no one should preach, print any book on a contentious topic, perform any play or interlude, or teach doctrine or expound scripture without a royal license, under the threat of the Queen's indignation 'and most grevious displeasure'. All local officers were charged with enforcing the proclamation: they were ordered to commit offenders to gaol without bail or mainprize and to send a certificate to the Council which would devise some exemplary punishment.

In its requirement for a royal license to preach, the proclamation was traditional because it reverted to the system of licensing which had been used in the reign of Henry VIII and at the beginning of that of Edward VI. Mary soon delegated the authority to issue the licenses to Bishop Stephen Gardiner, in his capacity as Lord Chancellor.[7] In the months immediately following the issue of the proclamation, the Council punished several offenders in a quasi-judicial way by ordering them committed to various prisons, actions which probably were based on the authority of the proclamation even though the prohibition on preaching had also been issued verbally and in a letter from the Council.[8] It may be presumed that action against the preachers who were not resident in London was in pursuance of the proclamation, but it should be remembered that the ultimate authority was the same in all instances, a royal command.

[6] *Eccl. Mem.*, III, i, 39–40 (where the authorship is ascribed to Gardiner); Stow, p. 1038; *APC*, IV, 317–21.

[7] Walter Howard Frere and William McClure Kennedy (eds.), *Visitation Articles and Injunctions of the Period of the Reformation* (3 vols.; Alcuin Club Collections, XIV–XVI; London, 1910), II, 334. Frere edited vols. I and III alone, and II with Kennedy.

[8] *Eccl. Mem.*, III, i, 77, 92. For instances of the restrictions on preachers after the proclamation, see John Foxe, *Actes and Monuments* (ed. Stephen Reed Cattley; 8 vols.; London, 1824–9), VI, 391–3.

The second proclamation of the interim settlement was published on 15 December 1553.[9] Although the text does not survive, it is possible to recover at least part of its contents from the contemporary description in Henry Machyn's diary. In part the proclamation must have been an announcement of the statutes of religion which would become effective five days later, because Machyn described 'a proclamation through London and all England that no man should sing no English service nor communion after the xx day of December, nor no priest that has a wife shall minister nor say mass'. The other part must have re-established many old ceremonies and practices, for Machyn continued 'and that every parish to make an altar and to have a cross and staff, and all other things in all parishes all in Latin, as holy bread, holy water, as palm and ashes'. In that respect the proclamation anticipated the Injunctions three months later which ordered that processions be held in Latin and that 'the laudable and honest ceremonies which were wont to be used, frequented, and observed in the Church be hereafter frequented, used, and observed'.[10]

The provision about the married clergy has attracted a great deal of attention, although in this respect the proclamation was merely a public announcement of what had already been enacted in Parliament. No deprivations of married clergy occurred until after the appearance of the Injunctions in which there were more elaborate orders. The proclamation has been interpreted as a warning of what was to come, and therefore as a reason why many of the married clergy left the realm before the deprivations began. Since the government made no attempt to stop the departure of the 'Marian exiles', and since there is evidence that Gardiner helped rather than hindered the process, any sinister interpretation of the proclamation seems unlikely. It should be noted, however, that both the new statute and the proclamation ignored the approval given to clerical marriage by the Edwardian Convocation, which had not been repealed.

By reviving many of the traditional ceremonial practices of catholicism, the proclamation legislated in ecclesiastical matters and anticipated by several months the inclusion of similar provisions in the Injunctions. Its orders would therefore be enforceable by the Church, and one can find several articles based on that part of the proclamation in the charge for the visitation of the diocese of London

[9] *Add. Procs.*, no. 8.
[10] No. 417 in Hughes & Larkin, not a true royal proclamation.

which was conducted in 1554 by the now restored Bishop Bonner.[11] Those who were impatient for the restoration of catholicism had from time to time revived catholic practices in the first months of Mary's reign. In this sense the proclamation regularized for a short period of time those previously illegal restorations.

The Injunctions of 4 March 1554 were not issued as a royal proclamation, but were textually described as 'certain articles of such special matter as among other things be most necessary to be put in execution', addressed to the Bishop of London and his officers.[12] In scope the eighteen articles were not nearly as comprehensive as those of Elizabeth, nor did they neatly continue the licensing requirements for all matters regulated in the proclamation of 18 August. The Marian Injunctions were, in effect, a revival of the canon law as it existed in the time of Henry VIII, and they thus restored the full range of former practices and provisions. Of course there would have to be new regulations in subsequent years to meet problems which could not be foreseen; some would be framed jointly with Parliament, some independently on the authority of the prerogative. Many of these form the subject of the first part of the following chapter.

The culmination of the Marian settlement was the reconciliation with Rome, ceremoniously performed on 30 November 1554 when Cardinal Pole pronounced the absolution. No royal proclamations were involved in this stage of the settlement, but the Queen had issued letters patent on 10 November which informed the realm of Pole's mission and granted subjects the authority to make their suit 'to obtain such graces, faculties, and dispensations as they shall have need of'.[13]

THE ELIZABETHAN SETTLEMENT

The Elizabethan settlement was completed within eight months. Parliament had finished its work on 8 May 1559, and its acts became effective on 24 June. The Injunctions were issued in mid-July. But the moment one compares the Marian and Elizabethan settlements beyond the identical components – statutes, proclamations, and injunctions – the similarities cease abruptly. While Mary's program was certain and crisply executed, Elizabeth was not willing to commit herself to a complete break with the past. For many reasons which anyone can discover, and for others known to herself alone,

---

[11] Frere and Kennedy, *Visitation Articles and Injunctions*, II, 335–6.
[12] Called 'articles' in Norf. & Norw. RO, Norwich Mayor's Ct Bk 6, fo. 329.
[13] In Hughes & Larkin as no. 417; not a royal proclamation.

she did not seek a full restoration of protestantism but rather wished to temporize. So proficient was she at concealing her intentions before Parliament met that men grasped at any indication of the direction of events. Watchful eyes studied her every action during services, ambassadors tried to fathom the meaning of her words, and men of both religious persuasions alternately hoped and feared for the future. When Parliament did meet, Elizabeth sought only an act of supremacy which would restore the national Church, but during the session her hand was forced. The result was an act of uniformity which revived the Edwardian *Book of Common Prayer*; the indecision of the past months was over, and England was committed to the protestant cause.[14]

The four royal proclamations which comprised the Elizabethan interim settlement are interesting not only for the temporary regulations which they imposed, but also as indicators of the Queen's sentiments. The very fact that she used twice as many as had Mary in a similar situation demands a close study of their use and enables us to conclude that she had no planned scheme of regulation in mind, but rather responded to varying problems as they became acute. More importantly there is a crucial difference in the two Queens' use of proclamations in the interim period: Mary's system of licenses clearly implied a doctrinal test, while Elizabeth concerned herself only with civil disorder.

In her first proclamation on religion, issued on 27 December 1558, Elizabeth dealt with preaching and with ceremonies.[15] By restricting all ministers to a simple, non-interpretative reading of the Gospel or Epistle of the day or of the Ten Commandments, the proclamation at a stroke forbade the expression of any explicit or implicit sentiments about the impending settlement of religion. Only the second provision hinted that there were to be changes, because it broke with the exclusive use of Latin in the litany, the Lord's Prayer, and the Creed. All else was left until 'consultation may be had by Parliament'.

Even the Queen's contemporaries were unable to fathom exactly which side stood behind the proclamation. The opening sentence mentioned the former ministers of the Church who preached to assemblies and stirred up disputes, contention and occasions of disorder, a clause which could apply equally to Marian catholics or to the leaders of the protestant congregation which had surreptitiously

[14] J. E. Neale, 'The Elizabethan Acts of Supremacy and Uniformity', *EHR*, LXV (1950), 308–11.　　　　　　　　　　[15] Proc. 451/498.

existed in London during that reign.[16] Thus when John Jewel paused on the continent during his return journey from Zurich to write to Peter Martyr, he passed along the speculations which he had just received in a letter from England:

'Some think the reason [for the proclamation] to be, that there was at that time only one minister of the word in London, namely Bentham, whereas the number of papists was very considerable; others think that it is owing to the circumstances that, having heard only one public discourse of Bentham's, the people began to dispute among themselves about ceremonies, some declaring for Geneva, and some for Frankfort.'[17]

But other protestants returning from exile felt that it was an increase of catholic preachers which had occasioned the proclamation.[18]

Because the Queen had favored neither side in the proclamation, she was able to enforce it upon preachers of either persuasion who violated the ban. It was almost immediately invoked against one Thomas Parrys who allowed an assembly to gather at Worcester Place the following day, but thereafter the ban was deemed totally effective in London.[19] The Queen encouraged the protestants by appointing several of the returned exiles as preachers at Court for lent, but any expectation which this excited was soon dashed when from late February through April the proclamation was enforced against protestants as well as catholics. Among those punished were two protestant preachers in Colchester, Pullen and Dodman, while John Murren, chaplain to the Bishop of London, and a canon of Lichfield were certainly catholics. In directing the enforcement of the proclamation, the Council demanded that the preachers make a public admission of their fault. Thus it committed Murren to the Fleet where he remained for three weeks until he agreed to confess his fault from the pulpit, and it also commanded the Sheriffs and Justices in Essex, an area where protestantism flourished, to be present when the preachers admitted their contempts before their congregations. That the Council's concern was not limited to areas relatively close at hand can be seen from letters it directed to as far away as Cornwall and Devon.[20]

[16] See A. G. Dickens, *The English Reformation* (London, 1964), pp. 272–7.

[17] Hastings Robinson (ed.), *The Zurich Letters, or the Correspondence of Several English Bishops and Others, with some of the Helvetian Reformers, During the Reign of Queen Elizabeth* (Parker Society, VII; 2nd ed.; London, 1846), pp. 16–17.

[18] *Ibid.* pp. 20–1, 57–9; the impatience of ministers for reform is alleged in Camden, p. 16, and both sides are blamed in *Annals Ref.*, I, i, 58–9.

[19] *Annals Ref.*, I, i, 59–60.

[20] *APC*, VII, 32, 59, 63, 67, 71, 87, 88, 92; *Annals Ref.*, I, i, 60–7; Henry Gee, *The Elizabethan Clergy and the Settlement of Religion, 1558–1564* (Oxford, 1898), pp. 2–3. A charge

Meanwhile the government had sought only an act of supremacy when Parliament began to sit late in January. That limited proposal had come under fire – at times the bill was amended, substituted for, and propagandized against. Finally a bill restored to nearly the first form given it was passed on 22 March 1559.[21] That the Queen intended to approve it is clearly shown by her issue of a royal proclamation, also dated 22 March, in which her assent to the bill is expressed as if it had already been given.[22] Among the provisions of the bill had been one that revived the Edwardian statute of 1547 which allowed communion to be received under two kinds. Because of the nearness of Easter (the 26th) and of the difficulties in printing and publishing a statute of such a length in so short a time, the Queen 'by advice of sundry her nobility and commons lately assembled in Parliament' declared in the proclamation that the Edwardian statute was revived and ordered that its provisions be followed.

The most fascinating thing about the proclamation is what one can discover in retrospect. It had been intended as the first public pronouncement of part of the new permanent settlement, but the Queen changed her mind and did not consent to the bill. Instead she gave in to the pressures which sought a more protestant settlement and allowed an act of uniformity to be framed as well when Parliament reconvened after Easter. The decision for the change in strategy occurred within a day or two after the issue of the proclamation, and thus the latter became the most tangible evidence of the firmness of her original purpose before her change of heart.[23]

The proclamation is also interesting for what it reveals of the Queen's priorities in propaganda. Through it her subjects would have learned that several of the Marian statutes were being repealed, and that several which had been enacted during the reigns of Henry VIII and Edward VI revived. But beyond those revelations and the necessary orders about communion, the Queen and her government saw no need to provide more information. Instead there were pious exhortations to Christian charity during the holy season, with the specific instruction that any priest who might refuse to minister under both kinds was to be left unmolested. One cannot help but conclude that the real audience at which the proclamation was directed was the House of Commons which had been pressing the

in articles for a visitation which is based on the proclamation is in Frere, *Visitation Articles and Injunctions*, III, 7: see *ibid*. I, 148–9 for later regulations on preaching.
[21] Neale, 'The Elizabethan Acts of Supremacy and Uniformity', p. 323.
[22] Proc. 454/503, reviving 1 Edward VI, c. 1.
[23] Neale, 'The Elizabethan Acts of Supremacy and Uniformity', pp. 323–5.

Queen's spokesmen so forcefully in the recent debates. Members would have noted the gracious terms which she used, and how she attributed to them only the highest of motives when she spoke of the consciences of the 'great numbers, not only of the nobility and gentlemen but also of the common people'. Her assertion that the administration of communion under two kinds was 'according to the first institution and to the common use both of the apostles and the primitive Church' must have delighted the protestant parliamentarians. By these and other unctuous remarks, the Queen doubtless intended to reassert the bond of affection between herself and those on whose support she had to rely, a bond which must have been sorely strained during the rigors of debate.

Six weeks were to elapse between that Easter and the conclusion of the parliamentary session, a period during which continued governmental vigilance was necessary not only because of the lingering uncertainty over the final shape of the settlement, but also because the hints of an imminent protestant settlement had made its favorers the bolder. Twice during that period new measures were publicly provided through royal proclamations. In both instances they prohibited the performance of plays and interludes which touched on matters of state and especially on religion. The first was proclaimed on 8 April and seems to have been intended for London alone.[24] Although the text is not extant, one can determine from the references in chronicles that it was proclaimed by a herald at arms, and one can surmise that he used only a copy on parchment and not a printed text. The prohibitions were extended to the whole realm in another proclamation which was issued on 26 May,[25] but whereas the earlier order seems to have been an outright prohibition, the later one abandoned this in favor of a system of licensing to be controlled by Mayors in towns, and Lieutenants or Justices in the shires. Any offender was subject to imprisonment for fourteen days or until he could give an assurance of his future good behavior.

Once again we have encountered orders which were originally intended for London, then made general throughout the realm, yet in both cases it would seem that an outrage in London provided the impetus. An ambassador resident in London had reported that the first proclamation had been directed at 'comedies and other diver-

[24] *Add. Procs.*, no. 14; Hughes & Larkin cite Machyn and many secondary authorities on the issue of this earlier proclamation in II, 115 headnote to 459/509; see also Adolphus Ward, *A History of English Dramatic Literature to the Death of Queen Anne* (rev. ed.; 3 vols.; London, 1899), I, 456.
[25] Proc. 458/509.

sions by which in taverns and feast days the corrupt populace used to mock of the Catholic and true religion', and the Spanish Ambassador surmised in a letter to Philip II just two weeks before the appearance of the second proclamation that Elizabeth wished to punish those persons who represented the King in their plays.[26]

Elizabeth's Injunctions, issued in mid-July, were substantially longer than Mary's since there was not much in the way of tradition on which the new Church could draw. What there was of use in the Injunctions of Henry VIII and Edward VI was retained, and the rest supplied as deemed necessary. Although the Injunctions were not issued as a proclamation, they did have a great impact on the use of proclamations.[27] They superseded the partial provisions of the earlier proclamations which had formed the interim settlement. Whereas the proclamations had issued a blanket prohibition against preaching, the Injunctions issued orders for a system of licensing, and in similar fashion its general orders for English in the liturgy supplanted the earlier partial provision. Although the Injunctions contained no provisions on plays and interludes, the requirement for all printed matter to be licensed would serve to prevent some abuses. Thus the need for more particular proclamations was obviated by the sweeping regulations which had a permanent footing.

OTHER EARLY ELIZABETHAN ECCLESIASTICAL PROCLAMATIONS

With the establishment of the permanent settlement, the Church of England was once again in its infancy, and the length of the Queen's reign would provide the conditions for its growth to maturity. Many of the problems to be met along the way were serious indeed, and some of them are discussed in the two chapters that follow. But there were several proclamations issued in the years immediately following which reflected difficulties in adjusting to the new order of things, and a discussion of them is in order in this context of early provisions for the Church.

Item 23 of the Injunctions had authorized the destruction of 'monuments of superstition', that is to say, of the images and paraphernalia of popish worship. Less than a month after the Injunctions, the removal of altars, roods, images and the like began in London under the direction of the newly nominated Bishop Edmund Grindal

---

[26] Hughes & Larkin, II, 115 note 1.
[27] Text in Hughes & Larkin as no. 460; not a proclamation.

and of the ecclesiastical commissioners. Over a three-day period late in August, such objects were burned at Cheapside, in the churchyard at Paul's Cross, and in other places throughout London.[28] It is not surprising that these activities would at times go beyond what had been authorized. On 19 September 1560, a royal proclamation forbade the excesses, and, though it gave no intimation of the cause, a draft of the proclamation mentioned abuses 'this summer past', the phrase being excised from the final text.[29]

Through the proclamation the Queen deplored the destruction of the burial monuments of noble families, pointing out that they were not 'monuments of superstition'. She argued that their destruction not only dishonored the family, but also made it more difficult to trace their lines of inheritance. Accordingly she commanded a halt to the senseless destruction and stipulated that offenders were to be apprehended and held until the gaol was delivered, then be ordered to make restitution and be further punished by fine or imprisonment. Similar penalties were provided for those who removed and sold church bells, or removed the lead from roofs.

The principal aim of the proclamation was restitution and not punishment, and because the former was to be exacted by ecclesiastical officers during their visitations, over half the text was an administrative order on procedures. If, for example, the offender who had spoiled the fabric of a collegiate or cathedral church could not be found, the visitors should order the canons to use funds not already allocated to their support to repair the monument; if the offender was dead, it gave authority to command the heirs to make restitution under penalty of excommunication.

It is difficult to evaluate the effectiveness of the proclamation other than to say that investigations were made.[30] The Church's records are particularly terse, formal and uncommunicative; when disorders are noted, the clerk dealt with the facts, and not with the authority on which the investigation was based. One can find later orders to make inquiries into the destruction of the monuments, but in such instruments as visitation articles, not proclamations. What probably happened is something analogous to the Injunctions: the responsibility for enforcement became subsumed in the normal ecclesiastical routines, so that one loses sight of the uniqueness of the original order. That might explain why no proclamation was issued when a second

---

[28] Holinshed, *Chronicles*, IV, 185; *Annals Ref.*, I, i, 69–71.
[29] Proc. 469/526, with draft in PRO, SP 12/13/33.
[30] Supplementary order in 1561, Frere, *Visitation Articles and Injunctions*, III, 109; for other articles based on these, *ibid.* I, 160–1; III, 117, 210, 268.

wave of iconoclasm broke out in 1565. One commentator has written that 'we are driven to believe either that there was wilful neglect in obeying them, or that the fever of destruction was of an intermittent and recurring nature'.[31]

Just over a year had elapsed since the permanent settlement of religion and the proclamation of monuments, time enough in which one could also take stock of some dangerous and heretical opinions within some parts of protestantism itself. England had become a place of refuge for those foreign protestants who had to leave the continent to preserve their faith from the persecution of catholic princes. Once in England they wished to preserve their own religion without interference by the English authorities as well. In 1561 Bishop Grindal of London drew up articles of inquiry into the numbers, motives, and religious opinions of these immigrants, and the results of his inquiry, coupled with a growing realization of the need for religious uniformity, seems to have been behind the royal proclamation of 22 September 1560.[32] It ordered Anabaptists to leave the realm within twenty days, or to suffer the loss of their goods and chattels and to be further punished by the ecclesiastical or temporal laws. That the Church's machinery was already engaged against them was announced when it was noted that Elizabeth had previously ordered the visitation of parishes within London and presumably along the seacoasts, both places where the refugees tended to settle. Just how greatly their dangerous and heretical views alarmed Anglicans can be seen in Bishop Jewel's description: 'just as mushrooms spring up in the night in darkness, so these sprang up in the darkness...of the Marian times.'[33]

Another provision of great interest forbade conventicles and secret congregations and ordered attendance at the services of the established Church. It had become abundantly clear in the first year of the Church's existence that an influential and vocal body within the Church was dissatisfied with the settlement and wished to see a further reform. Probably this provision was aimed at discontented elements whose practices might have included separatism and unauthorized forms of worship. If this is true, then the proclamation

---

[31] W. P. M. Kennedy, *Elizabethan Episcopal Administration* (3 vols.; Alcuin Club Collections, xxv–xxvii; London, 1924), I, lii–liii; for a summary of the destruction and the results of visitations diocese by diocese, *ibid.* pp. lxiii–lxviii, with no explicit reference to proclamations.

[32] Proc. 470/529, with draft in Cecil's hand in PRO, SP 12/13/35. See also John Strype, *The History of the Life and Acts of the Most Reverend Father in God, Edmund Grindal* (Oxford, 1821), p. 180.   [33] Robinson (ed.), *Zurich Letters*, p. 116.

would have been the first general demand for uniformity after the parliamentary settlement, and thus would have been far more ranging in intention and scope than mere opposition to Anabaptism. Mr Brook seems to incline to this interpretation, seeing this proclamation, the other issued three days earlier against destroying monuments of antiquity, and Archbishop Matthew Parker's inquiry into the state of the clergy which he had begun in November as the opening steps against protestant extremism.[34]

The concern within the Church and government over Anabaptism was sustained and at times particularly excited. In 1568 Bishop Grindal felt the danger was growing again and sent to Cecil the articles of inquiry which he had framed in 1560 as well as a copy of the royal proclamation of that earlier year. Obviously he felt that the proclamation should be reissued, because he sought an order which would force them to leave the realm in twenty days, but no proclamation on the matter was issued then or ever again during the reign.[35] As was the case with the renewal of the orders against breaking the monuments, the Queen chose a less public forum when she ordered Parker to have a survey drawn of the strangers and commanded the Justices to proceed against the noted offenders according to the law.[36] By adopting that more private course of action, she avoided drawing attention to heresy. Only in 1580 was it ever mentioned again in a royal proclamation, when the books of the Family of Love were condemned.[37]

A third aspect of religion in the years 1559–61 in which proclamations played a part lay in establishing proper procedures for the payment of pensions to those ex-religious who had been dispensed from their vows when the monasteries were dissolved. In a proclamation of 29 September 1561 the Queen confirmed her own grants of pensions and those of her predecessors. It was primarily an administrative order which set out the procedures and formulae to be used. Although the ostensible reason given was the prevention of fraud, the chronicler Camden noted that the occasion for the proclamation was mismanagement in the Exchequer which had to be corrected.[38]

The final category of initial religious concerns was reflected in the proclamation which ordered that peace be maintained in churches

[34] Victor J. K. Brook, *A Life of Archbishop Parker* (Oxford, 1962), pp. 100ff.
[35] Strype, *Grindal*, p. 181.
[36] *Annals Ref.*, I, ii, 269–71.   [37] Below, pp. 212–14.
[38] Proc. 485/551; Camden, p. 57. Many details of the pensions are to be found in PRO, E 135, e.g., E 135/1/22–4, 9/13, 16, 17.

and churchyards, and especially that a variety of secular activities which compromised those supposedly hallowed precincts be forbidden. Four identical proclamations were issued during Elizabeth's reign, the first on 30 October 1561, the last in early 1587, and two others in the 1570s without dates.[39] Abuses in London were again central to the proclamations, especially in the disorders in and around St Paul's.

There was already a statute against disorders in churches which provided only ecclesiastical penalties for quarreling and laying violent hands on others, and which further penalized the striking of someone with a weapon with the loss of an ear, with being branded with an 'F' for fraymaker or fighter, and with *ipso facto* excommunication.[40] The proclamation made a vague reference to 'laws and ordinances' in effect without referring to the Edwardian statute, doubtless because of the fundamental shift in emphasis. The statute was limited in scope and religious in tone, but the proclamation created new offenses and was secular both in its penalties and enforcers. The new offenses which the proclamation created included shooting or merely putting one's hand to a weapon in a churchyard, disturbing religious services or making business payments, or using the churches as passage-ways through which loads of goods could be carried. Fines and imprisonment were the penalties for each.

An equally important part of the proclamations was the prevention of further abuses. Accordingly the Bishop of London or the officers of the cathedral were authorized to call upon the aid of London's secular officials and could specifically request the assistance of the Aldermen, discreet commoners, and serjeants on Sundays and holy days. The fines that would be assessed, either by the Lord Mayor or by the Star Chamber, were to be used to repair St Paul's or the church in which the offense occurred. Because this part of the proclamation was preventative, traces of its enforcement are not to be found, and the city's judicial records in criminal matters do not survive.

[39] Procs. 486/553; 687/555, dated from the copy in Corp. London RO, Journals XXII, fo. 76v; the other two, 591/553, 635/554. A general charge to inquire into the matter in 1570 is copied in *The Injunctions and Other Ecclesiastical Proceedings of Robert Barnes, Bishop of Durham, from 1575 to 1587* (Surtees Society, XXII; Durham, 1850), pp. 14–15 note 1; the authority for the charge was the Ecclesiastical Commission in the Province of York.
[40] 5 & 6 Edward VI, c. 4.

9

DISSIDENT RELIGIOUS BOOKS

Opposition to both the Marian and Elizabethan permanent settlements of religion was not long in coming, nor was it ever totally absent, even though its thrust, intensity and effectiveness could vary greatly. One of the most effective techniques of the religious oppositions was the surreptitious printing and distribution of books, since the spread of printing provided a ready means for setting forth dissident religious views. That the Church and the government had an even readier access to these same techniques made no difference since what a favorable or managed press could do to convince public opinion, a hostile press could undo and even surpass. The many dissenting books, relentlessly challenging, attacking, denouncing, lampooning and controverting the official religious position, presented a continual problem.

Written dissent was certainly no new problem for the Tudors, and our consideration of the Marian and Elizabethan efforts in meeting those challenges by means of royal proclamations begins with a time some twenty years later than the first governmental participation in what had theretofore been a primarily ecclesiastical activity.[1] When the threat came from the occasional Lollard book, the Church's scheme of licensing and controlling books had proved adequate, but the influx of Lutheran books from the continent in the 1520s posed a more severe threat. Sir Thomas More, Bishop John Fisher, and even Henry VIII himself wrote to refute those views, while the ecclesiastical authorities seized and burned any heretical books that they could find. In 1530 the first secular assistance was provided when two royal proclamations were issued against those who distributed or retained the books, rather than against the authors or printers who clearly fell within the scope of the Church's prohibitions.[2] A proclamation

[1] The entire Tudor period is surveyed, including controversies in which proclamations had no part, in Frederic A. Youngs, Jr, 'The Tudor Governments and Dissident Religious Books', in *The Dissenting Tradition*, ed. C. Robert Cole and Michael E. Moody (Athens, Ohio, 1975), pp. 167–90.

[2] *Ibid.* especially note 14 for details of early enforcement in the Star Chamber and ecclesiastical courts; procs. 122/114, 129/122.

197

issued in 1538 introduced the first comprehensive scheme of secular licensing of books, an important element of control which was to be maintained by every succeeding Tudor monarch. These efforts were partly made statutory in 1543, but because the statute was primarily concerned with repressing heresy it was repealed along with all other legislation on heresy by Edward VI's first Parliament.[3] Other than to reimpose the requirements for licensing, Edward's government did little to regulate books, and little seemed needed since there was no organized catholic counter-propaganda effort.

Thus at Mary's accession there was no legislation in force against heresy nor any provision for regulating dissident books, and it remained to be seen what if any of the earlier experiences would be called upon. Eventually Mary had the laws on heresy from pre-Tudor days restored, and the matter of books was subsumed into the larger question of religious conformity. But one of her Parliaments defined the new offense of seditious writings, and in Elizabeth's reign this more secular weapon for suppressing dissident religious books came to be used against all opponents of the settlement from the 1580s onward.

PROTESTANT BOOKS IN MARY'S REIGN

To the discontent over the Marian religious settlement were added other grievances which prompted a vigorous written protestant dissent – an offended nationalism and an awakened xenophobia over her marriage to Philip, the frustration over the unsuccessful war with France, and the growing horror at the number of burnings for heresy. The Marian proclamations against the books which protested against these events had a distinctly subordinate role to play, since it was in the areas of statutory law and ecclesiastical procedure that effective remedies were framed.

A hint of the particular problem which the dissident books posed appeared in the proclamation issued in April 1554 denouncing the circulation of writings which defamed 'noblemen and other personages of good worth, credit, and fame', and commanding that anyone who kept or distributed them was to be punished in like manner as their first author.[4] Clearly it was the libels against Philip and the forthcoming marriage that elicited the proclamation, since

[3] Proc. 186/176; 34 & 35 Henry VIII, c. 1, repealed by 1 Edward VI, c. 12.
[4] Proc. 410/451. There was a great deal of unrest at the time: the shape of the religious settlement was becoming clear, and Wyatt had been convicted on 15 March and was awaiting execution.

the Spanish Ambassador had noted their circulation and a copy had been discovered among the prisoners in the Marshalsea.[5] The immediate problem was to make any complicity in spreading the writings illegal, which the proclamation did by prohibiting their circulation in a manner similar to that defined in Henry VIII's proclamations. The prisoners were examined, racked, transferred to the Tower and later returned to the Marshalsea, but one cannot tell if these measures preceded the proclamation or, following it, were based on its authority. But the much more important problem lay in finding ways to suppress the content of the writings.

The Parliament which began to sit in November 1554 solved these problems with great thoroughness. One statute was enacted to revive the earlier legislation against Lollardy, and this provided the authority for suppressing both heresy and heretical writings.[6] Then another statute created a category of 'seditious books', defining them as containing 'any false matter, clause, or sentence of slander, reproach and dishonor' to the King or Queen, or as encouraging insurrection, if the content of the writings did not fall within the scope of the basic statute on treason of 1352.[7] Embraced within these definitions were the types of writings against which the proclamation of April 1554 had been directed. The penalty for the first offense was set at the loss of the right hand, with life imprisonment and the loss of goods for subsequent offenses.

The second royal proclamation against dissident books was issued in June 1555, specifically condemning them as heretical.[8] Citing the statutes which had just been revived, the proclamation first forbade bringing into England the books of twenty-three named reformers, Hall's *Chronicles*, or any similar books, and then prohibited the use of the Edwardian *Book of Common Prayer*. The list was in reality an *index librorum prohibitorum*, a practice which had been used earlier in the proclamations of Henry VIII.[9] The Marian proclamations added the penalties of displeasure and indignation to those in the statutes and empowered secular officials (not mentioned in the legislation) to commit suspected offenders to ward until their trial.

The martyrologist John Foxe and those who have followed him attributed the occasion of this proclamation to 'a certain English

[5] *Eccl. Mem.*, III, i, 56–7.
[6] 1 & 2 Philip & Mary, c. 6.   [7] 1 & 2 Philip & Mary, c. 3.
[8] Proc. 422/461; a recognizance touching the selling of seditious books in September 1554, but without reference to the proclamation, is in Norf. & Norw. RO, Norwich Mayor's Ct Bk 6, fo. 382.
[9] The earliest was in 1530, proc. 122/114.

book, giving warning to Englishmen of the Spaniards, and disclosing certain close practices for recovery of abbey-lands'.[10] But the book *A Warning for England* was probably written before the Queen's marriage in 1554, and although it is possible that a year did elapse before it came to the government's attention, a much more likely occasion was the capture by the Lord Mayor of London early in May 1555 of 1,000 copies of a book which was later identified as that 'Dialogue' which was full 'of seditious and scandalous things against the religion and government'.[11] The identification of the 'Dialogue' arose during the trial of Sir John Cheke whom Mrs Christina Garrett saw as the guiding force in the literary warfare against the Marian regime. She regarded Cheke's trial 'merely as a pretext for crippling the whole campaign of propaganda by removing its head', an interpretation which has been challenged by Dr D. M. Loades.[12] Regardless of the exact occasion for the proclamation, there were so few additional provisions in it beyond what Parliament had already provided that it was a testimony to the thoroughness of the enactment.

It remained only to involve the Church thoroughly in the effort to repress the protestant books. Cardinal Pole was responsible for the provision of an additional set of regulations, issuing them as the second of a dozen decrees promulgated in the Legatine Synod of December 1555–February 1556. Since the recent death of Bishop Gardiner, who had figured so large in the Marian proceedings, had doubtless encouraged an intensification of the protestant propaganda efforts, Pole anathematized anyone who would print, possess, read, spread or bring into the realm any heretical or suspect books without a special license from Rome. He further invoked a decree promulgated in 1515 during the Fifth Lateran Council which forbade the printing of any book without a license from the ordinary.[13] Inquiries on books appeared in his later visitation articles,[14] but still a further step was taken when a royal commission was issued on 8 February 1557 which authorized the impaneling of juries comprised of clergy

[10] Foxe, *Actes and Monuments*, VII, 127–9; Foxe's suggestion was repeated in Holinshed, *Chronicles*, IV, 83; in *Eccl. Mem.*, III, i, 417–18; and in Cardwell, I, 197–200.

[11] Internal evidence of its date before the marriage is in *A Warnyng for Englande*, sig. A3. For the 'Dialogue', see Christina Hallowell Garrett, *The Marian Exiles. A Study in the Origins of Elizabethan Puritanism* (Cambridge, 1938), p. 117.

[12] D. M. Loades, 'The Press under the Early Tudors. A Study in Censorship and Sedition', *Transactions of the Cambridge Bibliographical Society*, IV (1964), 44.

[13] David Wilkins (ed.), *Concilia Magnae Britanniae et Hiberniae, ab Anno MDXLVI. ad Annum MDCCXVII* (4 vols.; London, 1732–7), IV, 21–6.

[14] Canterbury, 1556 and 1557, in Frere and Kennedy, *Visitation Articles and Injunctions*, II, 388, 425.

and laity in order that they might direct searches for heretical and seditious books and present offenders to the ordinaries for trial.[15]

Given such a wide range of secular and ecclesiastical provisions, one would suppose that the suppression of books played a large part in the Marian persecution, but that is not the case. A search through the pages of Foxe's 'Book of Martyrs' reveals that the charge of keeping and distributing heretical books was made against only one martyr, Ralph Allerton, and then only as one of many charges against him.[16] Thomas Green was scourged for possessing a hidden book, and many in the protestant underground in London were charged with using the *Book of Common Prayer*, an offense which by that time had been made statutory.[17] But in general, it was for deviation in opinion rather than for dealing in books *per se* that the persecutions took place. A final proclamation against books, issued on 6 June 1558, we have already seen in the context of the wars against France.[18] It will be recalled that it invoked martial law.[19] John Strype suggested that the proclamation was occasioned by Christopher Goodman's book *How Superior Powers ought to be obeyed of their Subjects*, which advocated risings against Mary.[20] The phrase used in the proclamation 'but also an encouragement given to disobey lawful princes and governors' may in fact be a veiled reference to Goodman's book.

DISSIDENT BOOKS IN ELIZABETH'S REIGN

The Elizabethan years are much more instructive in considering governmental activity against dissident books because so many religious groups wanted something other than the official religious settlement and used books to assert their arguments. Markedly different as were the programs of the parties – catholic, puritan, and separatist – there was a great similarity in what the government did to oppose them. Prevention became of greater importance, so that exceptional vigilance was used at the ports to prevent books from entering from abroad and extraordinary efforts were made to ferret out the secret presses used within the realm. The system of licensing

[15] Foxe, *Actes and Monuments*, VIII, 300–3, where this is erroneously called a proclamation. An earlier commission is in *APC*, v, 84–5; see also *Eccl. Mem.*, III, i, 199.
[16] Foxe, *Actes and Monuments*, VIII, 405–20, especially p. 417.
[17] *Ibid.* pp. 520–5, 443ff.
[18] Proc. 443/488.   [19] Below, p. 226, for one by Elizabeth.
[20] *Eccl. Mem.*, III, ii, 130–2; Holinshed, *Chronicles*, IV, 93–4, mentions French books parading their victories before the 'perfidious' English, perhaps referring to the same or similar books.

for printing was reintroduced, first in the Injunctions of 1559, then later in more detail in conciliar ordinances promulgated in Star Chamber in 1566 and 1586.[21] Almost every challenge in a dissident book was answered, although such officially sanctioned responses were almost invariably entrusted to the clergy.[22] That ensured a learned, point-by-point reply, but also the equally effective if perhaps unwitting (one wonders) result that the later books in any controversy tended to become so obtuse and long-winded that whatever spark there might have been in the original challenge was snuffed out under the length and weight of erudition. The clergy had a part to play in suppressing the books,[23] but it was distinctly subordinate to that of the secular government; it is clear that they had lost the power of initiative in these matters and had to await approval from the Queen and her Council before acting.

Thus the most important ingredients of repression in Elizabeth's reign were that intangible but crucial element of the will to prosecute, and the choice of legal means for suppression once the decision was finally made. The reluctance of many in the government to prosecute puritans is well known and documented. The Earl of Leicester was only one of many on the Council whose protection was courted by the puritans, and family ties could add another dimension to protection as is evident in the gentleness with which the separatist Robert Browne, a kinsman of Lord Burghley, was handled. Yet the dishonor and even the threat to the Queen and her policies that some books posed could eventually be so acutely felt that even the most reluctant could agree that some retaliation was in order and could participate

[21] In Hughes & Larkin as no. 460; not a royal proclamation. A reprint of the two conciliar decrees is in *Stationers' Register*, I, 322 (1566) and II, 807–12 (1586). An earlier edition of the former is reprinted in Cyprian Blagden, 'Book Trade Control in 1566', *Library*, 5th series, XIII (1958), 287–92. Strype assigned the occasion of the former to the many books over vestments, in *Parker*, I, 441 ff.; of the latter, to the concern over the books of the sectaries, in his *The Life and Acts of John Whitgift, D.D.* (3 vols.; Oxford, 1822), I, 422–5.

[22] A. C. Southern, *Elizabethan Recusant Prose 1559–1582* (London, 1950), prints as an appendix (pp. 537–8) a compilation of three lists of popish books which had been made by the clerical controversialist William Fulke, the title of the third of which was 'A Catalogue of all such Popish Books either answered, or to be answered, which have been written...since the beginning of the Queen's Majesty's reign.'

[23] The Act of Supremacy of 1559 authorized the Queen to appoint ecclesiastical commissions; the first of them included the authority to inquire 'also of all and singular heretical opinions, seditious books, contempts, conspiracies, false rumors, tales, seditions, misbehaviors, slanderous words of shewings, published, invented, or set forth...within this our realm of England, and of all and every the coadjutors, counsellors, comforters, procurers and abettors of every such offender'; 1 Eliz. I, c. 1, section 8. The text of the commission was printed by G. W. Prothero (ed.), *Select Statutes and Other Constitutional Documents Illustrative of the Reigns of Elizabeth and James I* (3rd ed.; Oxford, 1906), p. 228,

in devising both secular and ecclesiastical procedures. The legal basis on which most who produced or distributed dissident books suffered was the Marian statute against seditious books which had been made to apply to Elizabeth by the first Parliament of her reign, and which was reshaped by the Parliament of 1581 so that the offense became a felony.[24] But even though that statute was to be applied uniformly against puritan, separatist and catholic alike after the mid-1580s, the realization of its potential was slow in coming. Thus the years before the 1580s are particularly instructive in observing many experiments. Royal proclamations had a distinct part to play in these efforts, as can be seen from the consideration of the writings of different groups, protestant first, then catholic.

Puritan books

The early years of the 1570s were of great importance in the development of Elizabethan puritanism. The previous decade had witnessed a great deal of agitation over vestments and other externals of worship, symbols of the unreformed elements in the Church, but in the 1570s these concerns were pushed to the background as accidentals. In their place a part of the puritan movement put forward a positive program of reform with a new structure and a new policy for the Church.[25] Although that presbyterian program alienated many who sought a less radical reform, its sweeping boldness captured the attention of many others and caused the government no little concern.

Royal proclamations had no part to play so long as the agitation for reform remained within the intellectual confines of the reforming parties or the private deliberations of Convocation or Parliament where the changes were urged. But in 1572 the stridency of the schemes and the official determination not to yield to them became apparent. A bill introduced in the session of 1572 spoke of the order of prayer established in 1559 as 'permitted in respect of the great weakness of the people, then blinded by superstition', openly admitted that many ministers altered the form of prayer, and authorized the substitution of parts of the Calvinistic form of worship which were used in the French and Dutch congregations in England.[26] The Queen's wrath over such an invasion of her prerogative was predictably swift, and out of the frustration over her prohibitions,

---

[24] 1 Eliz. I, c. 6; 23 Eliz. I, c. 2 (see below, p. 209–10).
[25] Patrick Collinson, *The Elizabethan Puritan Movement* (London, 1967), pp. 106ff.
[26] Neale, *Elizabeth I and her Parliaments, 1559–1581*, pp. 297–304.

only the last of many signs of royal disfavor, was born the *Admonition to the Parliament*, 'public polemic in the guise of an address to Parliament',[27] in which the presbyterian leaders took their arguments out of the private forum and aired them openly before all the subjects of the realm.

There were many things which the Queen's ministers could do to meet the challenge without yet responding in kind in the public forum. The authors, Thomas Wilcox and John Field, were quickly arrested and then convicted in a London court for offending against the Act of Uniformity; there was much episcopal vigilance in suppressing the books; and Archbishop Parker called on a rising star in the Church, John Whitgift, to answer the presbyterian arguments which had by then been restated and elaborated when Thomas Cartwright had published a *Second Admonition* in September.[28] No matter how effective Whitgift's answer was, nor how much diligence the ecclesiastical officials would show, there was no corresponding official will to repress the writings. Elizabeth was suspicious of Parker's intentions and would not allow him any freedom of action, while the more puritan among the Council were equally as deaf to his litanies of lamentations as to his conviction that no effort to secure uniformity would succeed without an open show of royal and conciliar determination.[29]

The first indication of a change in Parker's favor came in May 1573, nearly a year after the appearance of the *Admonition*. By then Cartwright's *Second Admonition* had been answered by Whitgift's *Answer*, and Cartwright had responded with a *Reply to the Answer* which unwisely went beyond religious contention to include a lecture to the Queen and her Council on their religious duty:

'And therefore if this book shall come into the hands of any that have access unto her majesty, the head of the common wealth, or unto her most honorable council, the shoulders thereof, my humble suit and hearty request in the presence of God is that according as their callings will suffer them, they will put them in remembrance of these things...'

Cartwright then proceeded to multiply scriptural lessons: Moses not only brought his people out of Egypt, but wished also to lead them into the promised land; David not only reformed the abuses of Saul,

---

[27] Collinson, *Elizabethan Puritan Movement*, p. 118; see W. H. Frere and C. E. Douglas (eds.), *Puritan Manifestoes. A Study of the Origin of the Puritan Revolt* (Church Historical Society Series, LXXII; rev. ed.; London, 1907), and Donald Joseph McGinn, *The Admonition Controversy* (New Brunswick, 1949).

[28] Brook, *A Life of Archbishop Parker*, pp. 289ff.; Strype, *Parker*, II, 191–2.

[29] Brook, *A Life of Archbishop Parker*, pp. 418–19.

but wished to build a temple to replace the tent as the home of the Ark; and so on through the Old Testament – with Cartwright clearly identifying himself in the prophetic tradition.[30]

In that very month Elizabeth resolved to deal with the writings of the puritan party; what intellectual arguments and urging had not been able to do, her royal displeasure and pique could. Burghley informed Parker of her change of mind, but the Archbishop knew the battle was not won and wrote back: 'if it be not earnestly laboured on your parties which be supreme judges, long ago called on, I fear ye shall feel Muncer's commonwealth attempted shortly'.[31]

The visible sign of the gathering strength of Parker and his ecclesiastical brethren was their aggressiveness in insisting on the conformity of four of the foremost puritan preachers who were called into the Star Chamber during Trinity term, in late May or early June 1573. Edward Dering was a friend and relative of Burghley and Lord Keeper Bacon, Robert Johnson was Bacon's own chaplain, Nathaniel Wilburn was in Leicester's favor, and John Browne was chaplain to the Duchess of Suffolk; yet Parker and Bishop Sandys of London were able to press relentlessly at the session and eventually succeeded in winning orders to silence the preachers. How could Parker and Sandys have prevailed had they not had the Queen's protection? How could Parker, so long out of favor and previously reduced to a dribble of complaint, have suddenly taken the initiative and then prosecuted it so effectively in a Court to which he was only an invited guest? Emboldened by his success, he asked Burghley before leaving the court for a proclamation to suppress the writings.[32]

The royal proclamation he sought was issued on 11 June 1573, not as a result of the second printing of Cartwright's *Reply to the Answer* as has sometimes been suggested, but because that date was the last day of Trinity term and thus the logical time for a written charge to supplement the speech of the Lord Keeper on the Queen's behalf.[33] Although the proclamation commanded that the books be turned over to the ordinary and not be retained without a license, the lack of administrative instructions which could have initiated a thorough effort to repress them was a sign of the reluctant conciliar assent.

Nothing came of it. The summer witnessed not only many manifestations of favor and even adulation for the restrained puritan

---

[30] [Thomas Cartwright], *A Replye to an Ansvvere made of M. Doctor VVhitgifte, Agaynste the Admonition to the Parliament* (n.p., [1573]), sig. [A.ii.v].

[31] Strype, *Parker*, II, 255.

[32] Inner Temple, Petyt MS 538/47, fos. 479–80; Collinson, *Elizabethan Puritan Movement*, pp. 148–9.   [33] Proc. 597/687.

preachers, but there was even a reprint of Cartwright's *Reply to the Answer* which contained the printer's extraordinary apology that

'Some perhaps will marvel at the new impression of this book, and so much the more will they wonder because they shall see that with great confidence and boldness (notwithstanding our most gracious prince's late-published proclamation, procured rather by the bishops than willingly sought for by her majesty, whose mildness is such that she were easier led to yield to the proclamation of the Highest than drawn to proclaim anything against him, were it not for the subtle persuasion and wicked dealings of this horned generation...) and by the special motion of God's spirit and his protection it hath both attempted and ended.'[34]

Had not Peter Birchet, a more fanatic member of the movement, made an attempt to kill John Hawkins that autumn, thinking him to be Sir Christopher Hatton who was a known opponent of puritanism and a favorite of the Queen, little might have come of that first expression of royal dissatisfaction in the proclamation of June 1573.[35] Birchet's action so incensed the Queen that she first thought of having him executed by martial law, but cooler heads prevailed and he was left to the normal course of the law, the Queen meanwhile issuing a proclamation on 20 October 1573 which moved beyond a concern with dissident books to insist upon a rigorous enforcement of the Act of Uniformity.[36] With a cruel twist of irony the proclamation laid the blame for all irregularities in religion on the heads of the bishops who 'dissembled and winked' at the abuses.

The evidence for the enforcement of this proclamation provides a striking commentary on Tudor attitudes to law enforcement. First, no immediate action seems to have been intended, since the earliest command to any secular officer to begin enforcing the proclamation was made at the charge on the last day of Michaelmas term at the end of November, not much later than Parker's own directions to his province on the matter.[37] Second, the orders seem not to have been intended for general execution but only for specified areas, if the extant number of seventeen conciliar letters to dioceses is complete.[38]

---

[34] For Sandys's lament that none had been turned in, Strype, *Whitgift*, III, 32–5; see also *ibid.* I, 107; Inner Temple, Petyt MS 538/47, fo. 481; Collinson, *Elizabethan Puritan Movement*, pp. 149–50. The preface by the printer John Stroud is reprinted in John Ayre (ed.), *The Works of John Whitgift, D.D.* (Parker Society, XL; 3 vols.; Cambridge, 1851), I, 13–14. Stroud acknowledged his contempt in printing the work after the proclamation when examined by ecclesiastical officers in the diocese of Rochester, for which see Albert Peel (ed.), *The Seconde Parte of a Register* (2 vols.; Cambridge, 1915), I, 108–16.

[35] Collinson, *Elizabethan Puritan Movement*, p. 150.   [36] Proc. 599/689.

[37] BL, Cotton MS Titus B II, fos. 248–51; Strype, *Parker*, II, 354–7.

[38] *APC*, VIII, 140.

Third, the enforcement of the act was eventually entrusted to the ecclesiastical commissioners which was certainly a logical decision; but they had not even been mentioned among those assigned to enforce the text of the proclamation. There are fragments of correspondence to other areas, but fuller details of enforcement exist only for three dioceses.[39] Five ministers in the puritan hotbed of Northamptonshire were deprived, and in the diocese of Peterborough a form to promise to use only the authorized services was developed.[40] The officials in the diocese of Norwich were seemingly content with promises of uniformity, and there were no deprivations.[41] But in the diocese of London, or at least in the part of it within the city, many preachers and laymen were imprisoned, eventually examined by the commissioners, and then often returned to the prisons where at least one of them died from the filthy conditions.[42] Since much of the evidence comes from puritan sources which would naturally attempt to cite as many instances of persecution as possible, we are probably correct in assuming that not much was done elsewhere. It is particularly to be noted that the actual enforcement was on the basis of the statute, and that the proclamation served merely as an announcement of the coming enforcement of the law and as an indication of the Queen's firm purpose.

The effort was not lasting. A combination of events which are extraneous to this study occurred in the following years by which the bonds of understanding between the higher ranking ecclesiastics and the puritans of the non-presbyterian persuasion were re-established. Never again was a royal proclamation involved in an effort to secure general uniformity, but there were two occasions when the royal indignation over puritan writings led to proclamations, once during the negotiations over the possibility of Elizabeth's marriage to the French prince Alençon in the years 1579–81, and again when the satiric Marprelate tracts appeared in 1588–9.

The prospects of Elizabeth's marriage to Alençon were frightening in the extreme to those sincere protestants who feared that the match would be the beginning of the end for reformed religion in England. The negotiations fell into two periods, the first lasting from 1578 until the first quarter of 1580, the second resuming after the difficul-

[39] Council's letter to the Lord President in the North and the Archbishop of York, *ibid.* pp. 170–1; order from the former insisting on uniformity, York CA Dept, YC/A 25, fos. 103*v*–104.
[40] Peel (ed.), *The Seconde Parte of a Register*, I, 121–3; Collinson, *Elizabethan Puritan Movement*, pp. 151–2.   [41] *Ibid.* p. 151; Strype, *Parker*, II, 340–4.
[42] *Ibid.* II, 347; Collinson, *Elizabethan Puritan Movement*, p. 152.

ties in France subsided, from October 1580 until February 1582. Alençon visited Elizabeth secretly in September 1579, and openly for three months beginning in late October 1581.

The general malaise over the prospects of the marriage found a specific focus in the opposition within the Council, led by the Earl of Leicester. Alençon's negotiator, Jean de Simier, attempted to neutralize that opposition when in July 1579 he revealed to the Queen Leicester's secret marriage with Lettice Knollys, countess of Essex. Leicester, according to Camden, was furious at his banishment from Court and was bent on revenge: 'And there wanted not some who accused him [Leicester], as if he had suborned one Teuder of the Queen's Guard, an Hackster, to take away Simier's life. Certainly the Queen commanded by public Proclamation, that no man should offer an affront to Simier, his attendant or servants, either by word or deed'.[43] Camden's account is the only evidence we have of the issue of this proclamation; probably it was for a limited audience.

But Alençon's ostensibly secret visit to the Queen in September 1579 occasioned John Stubbs's book *The Discoverie of a Gaping Gvlf* which in turn led to the Queen's proclamation of 27 September 1579.[44] As had been the case in 1573, it was the affront to the Queen's honor which seems to have been its motivation, since the text warned against the 'interlacing of flattering glosses of her majesty and her actions to her people'. The motive may have been similar, but the purpose of the contents was strikingly different. For the only time during her reign, Elizabeth used a royal proclamation to refute rather than merely to suppress a dissident religious book. In a proclamation of unusual length, the Queen stressed the many appeals which had been made to her by Parliament for her to marry, and pictured Alençon as a protector of the Huguenots 'who cannot but attribute all the good they have got to be by his means'. The proclamation was dispatched without a writ[45] but with covering letters which commanded additional steps to suppress and refute Stubbs's arguments. The Lord Mayor of London was ordered to be present at the publishing of the proclamation, 'accompanied with some good number of aldermen your brethren and the sheriffs more than in like cases has been accustomed'; and he was further commanded to bring together the masters of the city companies to order

[43] Camden, p. 233.
[44] Proc. 642/740.
[45] For a debate in Norwich as to whether it should be proclaimed, Norf. & Norw. RO, Norwich Mayor's Ct Bk 10, fo. 469.

them to read the proclamations to their groups in turn.[46] Within a week letters went out from the Council to the bishops of eleven dioceses, ordering them to call together the leading ecclesiastics and noted preachers in the dioceses who were to be told of the Queen's firm intention 'to maintain the state of religion without any alteration or change', of her prohibition of any preaching on matters of state, and of her command that they were instead to preach due obedience to the Queen.[47]

The fate of Stubbs and his printer and publisher is well known: they were quickly apprehended, tried on the basis of the statute against seditious writings, and punished, Stubbs and his publisher losing their right hands to the butcher's knife and mallet and being further imprisoned; the printer was pardoned.[48] An offender in Marlborough who spoke lewd words about the marriage negotiations was pilloried with papers for example's sake at the command of the Council.[49]

A third proclamation in the Alençon affair appeared nearly two years later, on 18 April 1581, two days after the arrival of the French commissioners on the seacoast. It was purely cautionary, seeking to prevent any injury or insult to the negotiators, but we have seen already that it threatened the death penalty.[50] It was primarily intended for London, as is evident from the additional orders which the Council issued to the Lord Mayor, and from the precepts which he in turn issued.[51] Presumably the threat was made *in terrorem*.

The most lasting effect of the negotiations was, however, the impression which it made on the parliamentary puritans who had learned how the statute on seditious writings could be turned against puritan writers – and the presence of Stubbs who was then signing his writings 'left handed' was a tangible reminder. Thus when a strengthening of the act was proposed during the parliamentary session of 1581, there was a heated debate; the puritans labored mightily to excise from the act every remnant of its origins in Mary's reign and to add safeguards. But although the penalties for seditious words and rumors were scaled down, those for seditious writings

---

[46] Copy of letter, Corp. London RO. Remembrancia I, no. 62, noted in *APC*, XI, 270; variant form, from a MS in the Folger Shakespeare Libr., in Lloyd E. Berry (ed.), *John Stubbs's Gaping Gulf with Letters and other Relevant Documents* (Folger Documents of Tudor and Stuart Civilization; Charlottesville, 1968), pp. xxviii–xxix; Mayor's precept, Corp. London RO, Journal xx, fo. 254.

[47] PRO, SP 12/132/26–36, printed from the copy to Grindal in Cardwell, I, 435–9.

[48] For the records of his trial in King's Bench see Berry (ed.), *John Stubbs's Gaping Gulf*, p. xxvi.   [49] *APC*, XI, 357.   [50] Proc. 656/757.

[51] Corp. London RO, Journal xxi, fo. 110; Letter Bk Z, fos. 138–138v.

were actually increased to those for felony.[52] That the puritan fears were in fact well founded seems clear in retrospect, because the statute of 1581 became the basis for proceedings against puritans, separatists and even catholics.

The years 1587–93 were the climax of the governmental activity against dissident protestant books. Three separate streams of literary activity were dammed in those years: the individualistic puritan efforts of John Penry and of the Martin Marprelate tracts; the separatist writings of Penry who moved to that position in 1592, and of Henry Barrow and John Greenwood; and the efforts made against the surreptitiously organized presbyterian movement, for which the *Book of Discipline* served as a manual of organization.[53] Only one proclamation played a part, that issued on 13 February 1589 which was occasioned by the third of the seven Marprelate attacks. Wittily lampooning the foibles and worldliness of the bishops who had of late been so effective in suppressing puritanism, 'Martin Marprelate' unwittingly showed the extent of the frustration felt over the bishops' successes. Since the reputation of the Queen and her bishops was at stake, the royal proclamation condemned the 'rash and malicious purpose also to dissolve the state of the prelacy, being one of the three ancient estates of this realm under her highness, whereof her majesty mindeth to have such a reverent regard as to their places in the Church and commonwealth appertaineth'. It ordered that the books be turned in and defaced, offered a pardon to any who had concealed the books but would now co-operate, and gave strict commands against the writing, printing, distributing, favoring or assisting those or similar books, past or future.

The first two tracts in the series, the *Epistle* and the *Epitome*, had been printed in 1588; against them had been set not only the Church's officers, but also Bishop Thomas Cooper of Lincoln as the approved responder. When Cooper sought a wider readership by disguising his work under the title *Admonition* and signing it T.C., hoping thereby to evoke memories of Cartwright's *Admonition*, 'Martin' produced the *Minerals*, a broadside which dubbed Cooper 'Profane T.C.' and renewed the attack on the bishops. On the authority of John Penry the date of the *Minerals* had previously been set at about 20 February, but Professor Leland Carlson has found evidence which clearly dates it to the last days of January 1589, and

---

[52] 23 Eliz. I, c. 2. See Neale, *Elizabeth I and her Parliaments, 1559–1581*, pp. 393–8, for an account of the debates.
[53] Youngs, 'The Tudor Governments and Dissident Religious Books', pp. 177–9.

has also demonstrated convincingly that the real Martin Marprelate was Job Throkmorton, a member of Parliament, whom Penry assisted as a literary agent.[54]

Obviously the proclamation was ineffective in discouraging further printing, since four more tracts were to be produced before the arrests of the late summer brought the operation to an end. The goal of the searches had always been to trap the author, but when he eluded their efforts the searches were directed at discovering who had harbored the secret presses. There was more success there, so that Sir Richard Knightley, at whose home the *Epitome* had been printed, was captured, John Hales was charged with concealing the press at White Friars, Coventry, whither it had been removed from Knightley's Fawsley House in nearby Northamptonshire, and Roger Wigston and his wife were charged with receiving the press at their residence at Wolston Priory, six miles from Coventry.

The government's case against the defendants was made in the Star Chamber on 13 February 1590 by Attorney General John Popham. It was based on two royal proclamations, that of 13 February 1589 which we have just noted, and another of 30 June 1583 which had been issued against the writings of the separatists Robert Browne and Richard Harrison and also against 'such like seditious books or libels'.[55] Although the former sufficed for the government's case against all the defendants except Knightley, the latter had to be included in the trial since Knightley could and did argue that his actions were done 'before the proclamation, since which time he never meddled again'. The result of the trial was a foregone conclusion, so that Knightley was fined £2,000 and committed to prison at the Queen's pleasure, and the others were fined lesser amounts according to their social rank.[56] Job Throkmorton was indicted at Warwick assizes in 1590, and though (since he submitted) the case never came to trial the fact of his indictment at an assize implies that his offense was against statute law.[57] We simply cannot tell if the trial at Star Chamber was held to make an example of such a

[54] Leland H. Carlson, 'Martin Marprelate: His Identity and His Satire', in *English Satire. Papers Read at a Clark Library Seminar January 15, 1972* (Los Angeles, 1972), which particularly disputes the interpretation in Donald J. McGinn, *John Penry and the Marprelate Controversy* (New Brunswick, 1966).   [55] Proc. 667/770.

[56] T. B. Howell (ed.), *A Complete Collection of State Trials and Proceedings for High Treason and Other Crimes and Misdemeanors From the Earliest Period to the Year 1783* (21 vols.; London, 1816), I, cols. 1263-72. The convictions and fines are noted in BL, Harl. MS 2143, fo. 48v, where the fines are said to be assessed also for violating the conciliar decree of 1586 on printing.

[57] Carlson, 'Martin Marprelate: His Identity and Satire', p. 45.

defendant as Knightley, or because the government felt more secure in not having to proceed against distributors as falling within the scope of the act of 1581 when some doubt might have arisen over such an interpretation of the statute.[58] The books certainly circulated widely, and the tale of the Earl of Essex's producing one in the presence of Elizabeth is well known.

Separatist books

The reference to the proclamation of 1583 is a reminder that we have departed from a strictly chronological presentation to group together the books of rather distinct dissenting opinions. In that year, and once earlier in 1580, books of separatist groups were proscribed by royal proclamations, and it is to these that we now turn.

The earlier of the two dealt with the writings of the Family of Love, a mystical sect which had sprung up in the Low Countries under the guidance of Heinrich Niclas who 'declared himself to be the restorer of the world and the prophet sent by God'.[59] Niclas's writings were issued under the initials 'H.N.', and several were translated into English from 1574 onward. It was the appearance of these in the east of England which made the sect known to the authorities, even though it may have been introduced as early as 1560. The discovery of several Familists at Balsham in Cambridgeshire led to their being sent by the Bishop of Ely to London where in 1575 five of them renounced their heresies at Paul's Cross. The growth of the sect can be pieced together from occasional evidence, not only in the diocese of Norwich where there was a substantial population of immigrants from the Low Countries, but as far south and westward as the dioceses of Chichester and Exeter.[60] Bishop Edmund Freke of Norwich had collected some notes from their writings, and when some of these fell into the hands of the leader of the sect in England, Christopher Vitells, he initiated a literary controversy which soon engaged the talents of three clergy, John Rogers, William Wilkinson and John Knewstubbs.[61]

It is impossible to specify any particular incident leading to the

[58] But no such reluctance was shown when Thomas Alfield was indicted; see below, pp. 224–5.
[59] C. E. Whiting, *Studies in English Puritanism from the Restoration to the Revolution, 1660–1688* (London, 1931), p. 285.
[60] Cardwell, I, 451–4; *APC*, XI, 138–9, 444–5.
[61] Julia G. Ebel, 'The Family of Love: Sources of its History in England', *Huntington Library Quarterly*, XXX (1967), 333, 339.

proclamation of June 1580 which condemned the Familist writings.[62] Certainly the government's concern had been quickened in 1578 when it discovered that five Yeomen of the Guard belonged to the sect,[63] but perhaps it was simply that Knewstubbs had accumulated enough evidence about the sect by 1580 to warrant a public condemnation. After the issue of the proclamation Knewstubbs was sent to the bishops of Lincoln, Winchester, Salisbury and Worcester to share with them his knowledge of the sect.[64] The heresies were certainly to be feared and the proclamation condemned them accordingly, but perhaps as palpably felt a danger was the government's awareness that the sect encouraged its adherents to say whatever they willed to a magistrate because they believed that truthfulness was due only to another Familist. In any case, the proclamation offers the sole instance of a book being condemned in an Elizabethan proclamation as heretical; by threatening the penalties of heresy for distributing the book, it clearly stretched the words of the act of 1559 which had defined that offense for Elizabeth's reign.[65]

One can discover a flurry of activity in the months after the issue of the proclamation, including a more generous approach by the Council in allowing the bishops to proceed by gentle persuasion before enforcing the rigors of the law, but nothing of any offenders can be found beyond an order in October 1582 for the release of the Familists still imprisoned in the castle at Cambridge.[66] Yet the government's concern, and perhaps its reluctance to handle the matter by proclamation alone, was further shown when in January 1581 it referred the matter to the Convocation, making an explicit reference to the Queen's displeasure over the puritan urgings of a fast and other practices which had taken up so much time at the beginning of the parliamentary session.[67] That Convocation did not disappoint the royal expectations is suggested by Professor Neale's description of the bill introduced later in Parliament 'as a government-inspired bill sponsored by Convocation'.[68] But both the original bill and the two others that were produced failed, special objection having been raised to the penalties in the second bill which would

---

[62] Proc. 652/752.
[63] *APC*, x, 332, 334.
[64] *Ibid.* xii, 317–18.
[65] 1 Eliz. I, c. 2.
[66] William Nicholson (ed.), *The Remains of Edmund Grindal, D.D.* (Parker Society, x; London, 1843), pp. 408–12; Camden, p. 248; *APC*, xii, 231–2; Cardwell, i, 447–8; *APC*, xii, 250, 269; Strype, *Parker*, ii, 287–9; Folger Shakespeare Libr., MSS L.b.52, X.d.30(9).
[67] *Annals Ref.*, ii, ii, 333; James Wayland Joyce, *A Constitutional History of the Convocations of the Clergy* (London, 1855), p. 584.
[68] Neale, *Elizabeth I and her Parliaments, 1559–1581*, p. 410.

have punished heresy by whipping for the first offense, branding with an 'H.N.' for the second, and felony for the third.[69] Very little is known of the sect for the remainder of the sixteenth century.

Much more is known of Robert Browne and the Brownists, whose writings elicited the royal proclamation of 30 June 1583.[70] Browne had been very active in puritan circles in Cambridge, but eventually his license to preach was revoked by Richard Bancroft, the exceptional hunter of puritans whose later activities were to be such a valuable assistance to Archbishop Whitgift. Browne's inclinations towards separatism received encouragement when in the summer of 1580 he met a kindred spirit in Richard Harrison. The group which followed them into separatism settled in Norwich in 1581, removing to Middleburgh in Zeeland the following year when hostile pressures in the diocese of Norwich threatened them.[71] The southern part of that diocese, especially the area around Bury St Edmunds, had been a hotbed of puritanism. A strong drive for uniformity was led by Bishop Freke whose activities were warmly seconded by Bishops John Aylmer of London and John Whitgift of Worcester who were then exercising all authority in the province of Canterbury because Grindal was in such disfavor with the Queen. They in turn received considerable support from Sir Edmund Anderson and Sir Christopher Wray, two judges who used the Assizes to enforce uniformity. Professor Collinson has called the separatist movement of Browne and Harrison the 'direct result of the devastation of the pulpits'.[72]

As early as August 1582 the government had become aware that Browne and Harrison were busily printing books abroad and had urged the Prince of Orange to try to suppress them. In 1583 some officials in Suffolk not only discovered the printed sheets which had been imported, but seized them before they were bound into books and arrested the distributors as well.[73] At the assize in Bury in June 1583, Elias Thacker, John Copping and Thomas Gibson were charged with denying the Queen's supremacy and with distributing the writings. Although all three were convicted, Gibson submitted and was released, while Thacker was hanged on 4 June and Copping on

[69] *Ibid.* pp. 410–11.

[70] Proc. 667/770.

[71] Champlin Burrage, *The Early English Dissenters in the Light of Recent Research* (2 vols.; Cambridge, 1912), I, 94–103; Burrage, *The True Story of Robert Browne* (London, 1906); the works are edited with a useful introduction and chronology by Albert Peel and Leland H. Carlson (eds.), *The Writings of Richard Harrison and Robert Browne* (Elizabethan Nonconformist Texts, II; London, 1953).

[72] Collinson, *Elizabethan Puritan Movement*, pp. 201–5.

[73] Dwight C. Smith, 'Robert Browne, Independent', *Church History*, VI (1937), 304–5.

6 June. A few days later William Denis was convicted of the same offenses and hanged at Thetford, the books being burned at his execution just as they had been at Bury St Edmunds.[74]

The double charge against the defendants precludes our knowing what might have happened to them had they been charged solely with spreading the books. It is clear that the allegation of 'sedition' in the writings was justified, since Browne in his *A Treatise of Reformation without Tarrying for Any* had denounced those who 'pull down the head Christ Jesus, to set up the throne of the Magistrates', and who 'lift up the throne of the Magistrates to thrust out the kingdom of Christ'. The Church also, he argued, could reform religion without the state's intervention.[75] Since the proclamation was issued on 30 June, weeks after the executions, it was probably intended as a prohibition of the books in case any had been bound and distributed before the seizures. Accordingly it was aimed primarily at distributors of the books whom it commanded to be punished 'as persons maintaining such seditious actions'. No evidence of any success or failure in detecting the books elsewhere is to be found.[76] Harrison died soon afterward, and Browne began a checkered career in Scotland and later in England. The fear of the spread of the books remained, however, probably leading to the reissue of the conciliar decrees against unlicensed printing in 1586, an action which had been intended as early as 1584.[77] We have already seen how the prohibition of 'such like seditious books or libels' formed one of the authorities for the trial of Knightley and the rest in the aftermath of the Marprelate affair.

Catholic books

When we turn our attention to the dissident books produced by the catholics in the Elizabethan era, some notable changes in emphasis can be discerned. First, the books were of much more importance to

[74] Whiting, *Studies in English Puritanism*, p. 310; Albert Peel, *The Noble Army of Congregational Martyrs* (International Congregational Council Publications, 1; London, 1948), pp. 30–2. Thacker and Copping alone were mentioned in Holinshed, *Chronicles*, IV, 505, and in Stow, p. 1174; Gibson's name is also in *Annals Ref.*, III, i, 268–9. Two others may have been hanged at Bury in July 1584, as indicated by Huntington Libr., Ellesmere MSS 2076C and 2066, printed by Albert Peel, 'Congregational Martyrs at Bury St. Edmunds. How Many?', *Transactions of the Congregational Historical Society*, XV (1946), 64–7.
[75] Peel and Carlson (eds.), *The Writings of Richard Harrison and Robert Browne*, pp. 153, 154, 170.
[76] A puritan account of the execution noted that Burghley persuaded Elizabeth that puritans were her best subjects, so that she called in the Justices and deprived them of their offices because of the executions: Huntington Libr., Ellesmere MSS 2076C and 2066; no evidence exists for this, and it is disputed in *Annals Ref.*, III, i, 270.
[77] Noted by W. W. Greg, Letter to the Editor, *Library*, 5th series, XI (1956), 53.

the catholic cause, since they alone provided information and counsel to the English catholic laity who were left virtually leaderless from the time of the submission of nearly all the clergy in 1559 until the arrival in 1574 of the first 'missionary' priests from the English seminaries abroad. Even after the trickle of priests began to form an underground movement, the role of the books scarcely diminished. The corollary was that the government had to devote a great deal of attention to prevention, trying to persuade foreign princes not to allow the books to be printed in their countries, or more often sealing up the ports through which the books passed from abroad.[78] Second, the government's concern was nearly always for those who distributed the books since the authors and presses were almost invariably abroad; only a few of the approximately 250 Elizabethan catholic books were printed secretly in England. The existing law, it will be recalled, dealt with authors and printers, and so provisions against distributors were needed. That problem and the considerably larger number of catholic books accounted for a larger number of proclamations in retaliation. Third, refutation of the books by the clergy came to be the only response in the open forum. After 1570, catholic books were condemned in proclamations only when the honor of a privy councillor was at stake, when the security of the realm was threatened by invasion, or when the books could be turned to effective counter-propaganda. Finally, proclamations were used primarily to provide extensive administrative orders which tried to improve the means of detecting the books.

There were three main schools of catholic writers in the Elizabethan period against each of which proclamations were used. The 'Louvain School of Apologetics' wrote extensively in the early years. The English universities had produced many 'Elizabethan exiles' who left for the continent and settled mainly at Louvain, including a Vice Chancellor, two Regius Professors, several Masters of colleges, and many with university posts or college fellowships. It was hardly to be expected that they would leave the role of disputation behind, and when in 1559 Bishop John Jewel preached his famous Challenge Sermon at Paul's Cross, defying anyone to prove the existence in the primitive Church of many practices such as communion in one kind only, the writers abroad leapt into the fray.[79]

The 'Allen-Persons party' controlled the activities of the catholic effort from the newly founded seminary at Douai (1568) and from

[78] Examples from later years in the reign are in Southern, *Elizabethan Recusant Prose*, pp. 32–6.　　　　[79] *Ibid.* pp. 23–6, 44–50, 66ff.

the contributions made to the cause by the entry of the Jesuits (1580). The body of writings which this group produced were distinctly more political in character and provoked several of the proclamations.[80] Their control over the cause was resented by many, including a body of English catholic gentry resident in Paris, many of whom aligned themselves with those who lent their pens to support the cause and eventual succession to the throne of Mary Queen of Scots.[81]

In the last decade of the reign, a substantial cleavage arose between the Jesuits whose leaders had become increasingly convinced that only the strength of Spanish arms could win England back, and the secular priests who professed a more 'English' approach in which loyalty to Elizabeth's anti-Spanish policy had a large part. The quarrels broke into print, and since they tended to divide the catholic forces Elizabeth encouraged them even to the point of allowing some of the seculars' books to be printed with official connivance in England.[82] A consideration of the proclamations that dealt with the writings of the first two groups follows, while those in the conflict between the seculars and Jesuits are postponed to the next chapter where proclamations concerned more with the priests than the books are discussed.

By the time late in 1568 that the government felt that something more than refutation was needed in the literary warfare over Jewel's Challenge Sermon, sixty-two catholic books had been produced in the controversy. During the Hilary term early in 1569, nine men were tried in Star Chamber

'for their contempt in receiving, buying, reading, keeping, commending, and sending abroad seditious books set forth beyond [the] seas in the name of Harding, Dorman, Staphilus, Sanders, Smith, Rastell, and others, enemies to God's truth and the quiet government of the Queen, in maintenance of the usurped jurisdiction of the Papistical See of Rome. Not receiving the Communion since the Queen's reign, and hearing of Mass contrary to the Laws,'

for which offenses they were sequestered from office and fined.[83] The names of the authors cited would form a good catalogue of the Louvain contributors to Jewel's controversy. Because these men were

---

[80] *Ibid.* pp. 26–30, 49–55.

[81] Thomas H. Clancy, *Papist Pamphleteers* (Chicago, 1964), p. 6; James Phillips, *Images of a Queen: Mary Stuart in Sixteenth-Century Literature* (Berkeley, 1964).

[82] See Chapter 10, below.

[83] Huntington Libr., Ellesmere MS 2768, fo. 23, also cited in Hughes & Larkin, II, 312–13 note 2. Result noted in BL, Harl. MS 2143, fo. 24.

distributors rather than authors, the question of the proper way to proceed against them must have prompted a recognition of the ambiguities in the law.

That concern was voiced by Sir Nicholas Bacon, Lord Keeper of the Great Seal and as such the titular head of the legal system, in a speech which he delivered to the Lords of the Privy Council in the Star Chamber in December 1568. In admitting that the existing law did not cover distributors, Bacon made one of those explicit appeals to higher 'reasons of state' which one often suspects were current but rarely finds stated explicitly. Having begun his speech by referring generally to the dangers from religious factions, he turned to the particular danger of books from abroad, saying that 'albeit [the offenders] could not be brought within the compass of the laws, yet at all hands it must be confessed that thus to breed or continue factions is a very great and universal evil and for the dangers of it, necessarily to be reformed'. He then set about expounding a statute of 1563 which defined it as treason to extol the pope's authority and asked for a constructive interpretation which would embrace the distributors of the books. That in itself was noteworthy, since to construe a penal law by making its scope wider than the explicit words was against the usual practice of the courts – an objection which Bacon anticipated by saying that 'admitting it to be penal, then this question would be whether he that expounds a penal statute to the correction of a few and saving of great numbers, or he that expounds a law to the destruction of a great number and the saving of a few, does more cruelly expound the law'.[84]

That Bacon spoke not merely rhetorically is clear from the fact that the same question was submitted to the chief justices of the principal courts who at a meeting at Serjeants's Inn on 9 February 1569 gave their reply to the question 'Whether they that conveyed those books [written overseas against the Queen or extolling the pope's authority] and they that have read them have offended against the statute Anno 5⁰ Reginæ nunc or not'. The judges divided their opinion into parts, concluding that all who conveyed the books from abroad, obtained, received, read, conferred or favored them fell within the scope of the law, except for those who received or read them with no discussion or sign of approval.[85] Clearly their decision gave the government the tool that it needed to proceed against any-

---

[84] Huntington Libr., Ellesmere MS 2573, fos. 10*v*–14; there are many collections of his speeches which include this one, e.g., Folger Shakespeare Libr., MS X.d.377; a version with the year wrongly converted is in Foxe, *Actes and Monuments*, VIII, 740–2.

[85] Bodleian Libr., Tanner MS 50, fo. 136.

one involved with catholic books, not as seditious, not as a heretic, not under some penalty in a proclamation which made it contempt to deal in the books, but as a traitor. The paradox is that the decision seems never to have been used. Bacon had stated that he spoke with warrant from the Queen, but whether he stretched his interpretation of what she had in mind, or whether she was too lenient to use the decision, or whether there were other pressing reasons, the fact remains that it was not applied.

Nowhere is this more clearly indicated than in the first royal proclamation against catholic books, issued on 1 March 1569, just over a fortnight after the close of the Hilary term in which the opinion had been expressed.[86] Although the offending books were not identified by name, lest the subjects' curiosity be piqued, the proclamation did condemn certain books in circulation as 'repugnant to the truth, derogatory to the sovereign estate of her majesty, and stirring and nourishing sedition'. Yet all that it commanded was that the books be turned in to the ordinary within twenty-eight days without being read. That provision must have been self-defeating, because any subject who complied could clearly expect a thorough grilling before receiving the testimonial which the proclamation offered. But the penalty for disobeying the proclamation was not treason, but being 'punished severely, as the quality and circumstances of the offense shall require and deserve'.

Just why the provisions should be so disproportionate to the manifest danger in the books remains a puzzle. We cannot even tell with certainty why the proclamation was issued. Was there a lingering fear that others in addition to those just punished during Hilary term might still retain forbidden books?[87] Could the discovery late in February of a cache of catholic books at the house of the annalist John Stow by officials of the Bishop of London have reawakened such a concern? Stow was also under suspicion because he was aware of the Spanish Ambassador's writings which censured Elizabeth for her seizure in December 1568 of the ships carrying loan-money to pay the troops in the Low Countries.[88] Was it a real concern over the outpourings of the Louvain School? In the records of Bristol, the payment to the pursuivant was noted as being for a proclamation 'for calling in of Harding's books', even though no such identifica-

[86] Proc. 561/638.
[87] Many articles for diocesan visitations included charges to inquire about catholic books, and especially those of the Louvain group: Frere, *Visitation Articles and Injunctions*, III, 226, 285, 312, 333; Kennedy, *Elizabethan Episcopal Administration*, II, 12, 14, 51.
[88] BL, Lansd. MSS 11/2, 3, printed in *Stationers' Register*, I, 393–4.

tion appeared in the proclamation itself.[89] Or were the tepid provisions of the proclamation a mere sham, seeming to express a concern while masking the government's clandestine campaign of propaganda against Mary Queen of Scots? Professor James F. Phillips saw the proclamation as the first indication of a policy 'occasioned by the appearance in England of a group of pamphlets, presumably published "abroad", but actually produced in England with the knowledge of England's government' as 'a kind of semipublicity to an authentic history of [Mary's] misdoings'.[90] Contemporary evidence to support Phillips's argument is provided by Camden who noted that 'Divers books also came forth against her title whereby she claimed England as next heir, written with such a saucy malpertness, that the Queen resolved to prohibit them by a strict proclamation, and by way of connivance suffered the Bishop of Ross to answer them'.[91]

The difficulty in attributing an exact occasion for that proclamation highlights the complexity of the literary warfare against the Queen. Similar difficulties arise when one considers the proclamation of 1 July 1570 which condemned the scrolls and bulls of a traitorous nature then in circulation.[92] 'Scroll' doubtless refers to William Allen's 'Scroll of Articles' and 'bull' to Pius V's *Regnans in Excelsis* excommunicating Elizabeth which had been secretly posted in London for a brief time after it arrived in May 1570.[93] But a more likely explanation can be found in a letter dated 30 May 1570 which was sent out of Scotland to the two Lords Lieutenant of Worcester, championing the cause of Mary Stuart and stating that

'the commonalty of [England] is thoroughly persuaded, that the lord keeper [Bacon], master secretary [Cecil], Mr. Mildmay, and Mr. Sadler should so misgovern the state, and abuse our sovereign, that all or the most part of these dangers should arise from them, as procurers of the same: and that by them, and the paganical pretended bishops now usurping in this realm, we should be thus still drawn and continued in a religion of their devising, much worse than Turkey.'[94]

Cecil and his faction had been actively opposing the release of Mary Stuart and insisting on the dangers from catholics,[95] but more telling

[89] Bristol AO, Audits, Book 8, 1568–9, fo. 316.
[90] Phillips, *Images of a Queen*, p. 55.
[91] Camden, p. 132; articles for an inquiry based on the proclamation are in Kent AO, Sandwich MS Sa/AC 5, fo. 17v.
[92] Proc. 577/656.
[93] The word 'scroll' was added by Cecil to the draft which is in PRO, SP 12/71/34.
[94] The letter, *Annals Ref.*, I, ii, 580–2, with comment on it at pp. 274–5.
[95] Read, *Burghley*, pp. 17–29.

clues are to be found in the proclamation to identify those writings as the occasion of the proclamation.

First, the proclamation spoke of 'some part' of the realm distant from London where the libels had been posted, which fits Worcester. Second, it is very unusual to find Lords Lieutenant assigned a role in enforcing royal proclamations, yet this proclamation was an exception. It should be noted that the authors of the letter from Scotland mentioned that they had sent letters to other Lieutenants as well. Third, if one looks beyond the obvious words 'scroll' and 'bull' to see how the writings are described, it becomes clear that the proclamation was in reality a defense of the councillors' honor, and especially of the four men attacked in the letter as the 'new men' against whom much of the aristocratic northern rebellion of the past winter had been directed. So the proclamation spoke of the 'monstrous absurdities' in the writings aimed at sowing discord 'and namely in the malicious depraving of such actions as are and have been by good counsel providently devised, necessarily attempted, and well achieved by her majesty's order', especially to prevent the 'open fury of rebels and intended invasions by outward enemies'.[96]

Aside from these arguments, the proclamation was primarily a detailed administrative order setting up numerous procedures to insure the detection of the books, including an offer of rewards and a provision that concealers of books 'be attached and committed closely to the next jail as concealers and maintainers of sedition and tumult', to be held without bail until expressly released on the Queen's order or that of the Council or of a Lieutenant. But as is the situation with so many of these proclamations, only the most fragmentary evidence of any success or even enforcement is to be found. The officials in Sandwich did write to the Lord Warden of the Cinque Ports to assert their vigilance in response to his command that they keep a watch for seditious writings and scrolls.[97]

Less is known of the occasion for the third proclamation against catholic books, issued on 14 November 1570, than of any other.[98] It mentioned no specific books but described the authors as 'certain fugitives and rebels being fled now and remaining out of the realm by their seditious messages and false reports sent into the same tending to provoke others to be partakers of their malicious treasons'. One possible candidate would be John Leslie, Bishop of Ross, the ever

[96] There was a great fear of invasion at the time.
[97] Kent AO, Sandwich MS Sa/ZB 2, fo. 19v.
[98] Proc. 580/659.

faithful champion of the cause of Mary Stuart, who in 1569 had begun to have printed in London *A Defence of the honour of... Marie Quene of Scotland... with a declaration... of her right, title & interests to the succession of the crowne of Englande.* Whatever hopes he had had of Elizabeth's approbation were dashed after a few pages had been printed, so that he was forced to have it completed outside England and smuggled back in.[99] The proclamation was essentially a prayerful reflection on the deliverance from the recent rebellion, making only a summary reference to the proclamation of 1 July 1570. Its most notable feature was an increase in penalties: 'every person, so offending after this admonition, shall be taken, reputed, and punished as abettors and maintainers of the principal traitors that were authors of the same [books]'. This is the closest that Elizabeth's government came to using the opinion rendered by the judges the previous year.

The number of writings from catholic sources declined markedly in the early 1570s, but the quantity was partly offset by the more political and controversial nature of the writings produced by the Allen-Persons party. In their earlier books they took the line of championing Mary Stuart's claim while continuing to attack Elizabeth's ministers. Meanwhile the government pressed on with its 'semi-publicity' campaign against Mary, publishing *Salutem in Christo* and *A Detection of the Doings of Mary Queen of Scots* which taken together with Sir Francis Walsingham's *Discourse* of a year or two previously formed the trilogy in which the case against Mary was stated. When the *Detection* was reissued under directions from the Council, its author George Buchanan, Mary's Scottish arch-nemesis, appended to it a form of an indictment of Mary and also all eight of the casket letters.[100] The catholic response was that Burghley and Bacon were the true traitors, keeping Mary's claims unsettled for their own reasons. The most forceful expression of this argument was made in *A Treatise of Treasons* which was anonymously delivered into official hands in late August 1573.[101] By attacking the most thin-skinned of Elizabeth's councillors, a man who was her chief propagandist[102] and the author of many of her proclamations, the author of *A Treatise of Treasons* could hardly fail to draw not only blood, but also ink.

Nowhere is the personal involvement of Cecil, newly raised to the peerage as Lord Burghley, more clearly demonstrated than in his

[99] Phillips, *Images of a Queen*, pp. 88–9.   [100] *Ibid.* pp. 61–3.
[101] *HMC 9: Salisbury (Cecil) II*, pp. 55–6.
[102] Read, 'William Cecil and Elizabethan Public Relations', pp. 25ff.

activities leading to the issue of the proclamation of 28 September 1573.[103] He wrote three letters to Bacon full of complaints over the slander he had suffered, in comparison with which Bacon's insouciance stands in marked contrast.[104] On 4 September Burghley sent the book to Archbishop Parker who responded by citing the beatitudes and recommending, as had Bacon, that the attack be ignored.[105] Seemingly little consoled by his blessedness at being calumniated for God's sake, Burghley penned the proclamation to defend his honor. Cascade after cascade of abuse swept from his pen against those 'obstinate and irrepentant traitors' who with 'rooted malice' and 'furious brains' were fallen

'into another crooked course of malicious persecuting the happy estate of this country and government...wherein their final intention appeareth to be [to] blaspheme and as it were to accuse their native country with all manner of reproachful terms against the peaceable government thereof, condemning generally the whole policy of the present estate as having no religion, nor piety, nor justice nor order, no good ministers at all, either for divine or human causes...'

Burghley and Bacon were not named but can be clearly identified in the justification of 'two, who be certainly known to have always been most studiously and faithfully careful of her majesty's prosperous estate and virtuous government, employing thereto all their cares, travails, diligence and watching, with manifest loss and hinderance of their own health'. The culmination of the proclamation was the pronouncement that the books were to be 'esteemed, judged and condemned to be the words of the despisers of God's true religion, of obstinate traitors against her majesty's person...to ruin her person, and to overthrow her estate'. Any who would import or retain any such books were 'to be punished as sowers of sedition, and abettors to the treasons uttered in the same'. We are gently guided back from that pinnacle of defensive prose to the realities of human nature by the sage comment of Camden: 'Nevertheless, these books, (such is the natural curiosity of men,) because they were prohibited, were much read, until (as many times it cometh to pass) being at last condemned they grew out of request.'[106] It can be added that no evidence of any enforcement remains.

The 1570s had seen a relative lull in the production of catholic

[103] Proc. 598/688, with an endorsement on the copy at Harvard which states that it was issued against the *Treatise of Treasons*, as noted in Hughes & Larkin, II, 376 headnote.
[104] *HMC 9: Salisbury (Cecil) II*, pp. 56, 58, 59.
[105] Bruce and Perowne (eds.), *Correspondence of Matthew Parker*, pp. 444–5.
[106] Camden, p. 192.

books, with less than a dozen appearing in those years from English controversialists. The early 1580s stood in striking contrast, since in the twenty-one months between the entry of the Jesuits in 1580 and the execution of Edmund Campion in December 1581 eleven books appeared.[107] Campion unwittingly started one stream of controversy when some friends circulated his apologia in its manuscript form, and intentionally precipitated another with his *Decem Rationes* which was distributed at Oxford prior to an academic occasion in 1581. His fellow Jesuit Robert Persons wrote to defend the reasons why catholics should not attend Anglican services, and later to refute the allegations published by a turncoat minister and former student in the English seminary at Rome, John Nichols. A new genre of literary activities arose in the martyrologies of the executed priests, written in part to encourage other catholics, in part to answer the government's allegations that the priests died cowardly deaths.[108] All that literary activity was only a complement to the reinvigorated ministry carried out secretly by the priests, to which we shall return in the next chapter. Suffice it to say here that the government's heightened vigilance was reflected in the number of executions, since whereas only four had been executed before Campion's death, twenty-three met a similar fate between then and the next appearance of a royal proclamation against catholic books in October 1584.

The striking thing is that royal proclamations were not used as a means to stem the flood of catholic writings in the early 1580s. There were legal actions against several catholics who had a part in the books, but always on some other basis. Stephen Vallenger, the printer who produced the eyewitness martyrology of Campion's death which had been written by the priest Thomas Alfield, was tried in Star Chamber in May 1582. The judges noted that he could be shown to have abetted traitors, but that they would punish him for his contempt first, which they did by fining him £100 and by ordering him to be pilloried at Westminster Palace and at the cross in Cheapside, to lose an ear at each location, and to be imprisoned at the Queen's pleasure.[109] William Carter who had printed Gregory Martin's *The Treatise of Schisms* was tried, convicted, and hanged, drawn and quartered in January 1584.[110] Alfield himself was the defendant in a

[107] Southern, *Elizabethan Recusant Prose*, pp. 149–60.
[108] 'Some Hostile "True Reports" of the Martyrs', in *Miscellanea [XV]* (Catholic Record Society, XXXII; London, 1932), pp. 390–2.
[109] A full account is in Folger Shakespeare Libr., MS X.d.338; decision noted in BL, Harl. MS 2143, fo. 24; see Anthony Petti, 'Stephen Vallenger (1541–1591)', *Recusant History*, VI (1962), 248–64.   [110] Southern, *Elizabethan Recusant Prose*, pp. 352–3.

third trial, of special interest since he and a co-defendant were indicted and convicted as distributors of William Allen's *True, Sincere and Modest Defense*, on the authority of the statute of 1581 on seditious books. Alfield and Thomas Webley were hanged on 6 July 1585.[111]

Of the three remaining Elizabethan proclamations against catholic books, the first was issued on 12 October 1584 and also had something to do with Allen's *True, Sincere and Modest Defense*.[112] The main argument of Elizabeth's government through the years had been that the priests were tried and executed, not for their religion but because they were traitors. The most active champion of that argument was Burghley whose *Execution of Justice*, published in 1583, provoked Allen's reply in 1584. In the latter year, the strongest argument to date for Mary Stuart's pretensions to the English throne was produced, coupled with a renewal of the attack on evil councillors, focused this time on the Earl of Leicester. Thus the proclamation condemned both books, and even though the practice of not giving names was continued, such phrases as 'execution of justice', 'advance such pretended titles', and 'bring in obloquy and hatred her majesty's principal noblemen, councilors, judges, and ministers of justice' make identification easy. The proclamation displayed a good deal of administrative sophistication in giving special charges to 'merchants, masters of ships, officers of ports' and others to prevent the spread of the books. It tried to encourage the co-operation of all subjects by assuring them that they would not be 'molested, impeached, or troubled' for having had the books, and by offering a reward of half of the penalties and forfeitures which would be levied against any offenders whom they detected.

Leicester's reputation seems to have been a minor aspect of the proclamation, and one has only to compare its mild tones in defense of his honor with Burghley's effusive defense of himself in the proclamation of 1573. Yet the book which came to be known as *Leicester's Commonwealth* was greatly offensive to the Queen who sent personally signed letters to the Mayor, Sheriffs and Aldermen of London to defend his innocence and command their vigilance in suppressing the writings, all of which encouraged the Lord Mayor to

[111] Alfield's indictment is printed in John Hungerford Pollen (ed.), *Unpublished Documents Relating to the English Martyrs*, Vol. 1: *1584–1603* (Catholic Record Society, v; London, 1908), 112–17, and his trial at pp. 117ff. See also J. N. Langston, 'Robert Alfield, Schoolmaster, at Gloucester; and his Sons', *Transactions of the Bristol and Gloucestershire Archaeological Society*, LVI (1935), 141–63.

[112] Proc. 672/775.

issue his own proclamation 'Against the casting abroad of false libels', dated 13 February 1585. Letters were also sent into Wales where Leicester had many estates, commanding the Council there to be diligent in suppressing the books.[113]

Another proclamation was issued on 1 July 1588, clearly as a war measure, as we have already seen.[114] William Allen, by then a Cardinal, wrote a book to precede the invasion, *Admonition to the Nobility and People of England.* The Duke of Parma received the book before 13 May, had it translated into Spanish so that he could suppress or add parts, and then acted on Allen's suggestion by having the main points of it printed as a short proclamation under the title *A Declaration to the Nobility and People of England,* since in that format it would be easier to smuggle into England.[115]

These activities had been discovered by Henry Killigrew, the English agent at Parma's Court, before 6 June, and he forwarded a copy of the writings to Burghley who in turn suggested to Secretary Walsingham that the book be forbidden 'upon pain of treason' and that it be answered 'as from a number of catholics that notwithstanding their evil contempt for religion profess their obedience and prize with their lives and power against all strange forces offering to land in this realm'.[116] By the fifteenth the Lords Lieutenant had been ordered to appoint Provost Marshals to punish the authors of rumors and tales,[117] and a few days later the matter of a proclamation to suppress the writings was on the Council's agenda. The draft was ready by 24 June, but additional suggestions were made, and on 27 June it was sent to the Solicitor General.[118]

The Solicitor's involvement arose from the unusual powers conferred in the proclamation since the Great Seal was affixed directly to it, making it a sufficient warrant for the Lords Lieutenant to execute any offenders under martial law. It would violate common sense to see anything unwarranted here or in Mary's similar use in 1558 since the security of the realm was at stake in both cases.

The last proclamation in which catholic books were concerned was issued in 1602 when the controversy between the secular priests and the Jesuits came to a head. The control of the mission was at

[113] PRO, SP 12/179/44, 45; Corp. London RO, Journal XXI, fo. 407v; Letter Bk &c [*sic*], fo. 17; *HMC 31: 13th Rpt, App. IV (Corp. of Hereford MSS),* pp. 332–3.
[114] Proc. 699/802.
[115] Identified in Hughes & Larkin, III, 15 note 3. See also *CSP Spanish,* IV, 289.
[116] *CSP Foreign,* XXI, pt 4, 461, 489; PRO, SP 12/211/15.
[117] *APC,* XVI, 126.
[118] PRO, SP 12/211/22, 56, 61; *CSP Foreign,* XXII, pt 2, 26, 33–4, 47, 74.

stake, since the pope had just assigned a single officer to control its activities; the dispute takes its name from his title and is known as the Archpriest controversy. Since the proclamation[119] is clearly concerned with banishing all priests rather than with the books as such, a discussion is best reserved for the next chapter.

[119] Proc. 817/930.

IO

ELIZABETHAN CATHOLIC PRIESTS

The catholic priests who entered Elizabeth's realm secretly to minister to their co-religionists offered a more general and a more urgent threat than did the catholic books. The books could persuade and encourage, but the priests could go beyond that, winning the hesitant mind by instruction and discussion, and winning the heart and soul by reconciliation and their sacramental ministry. From 1574, the entry of catholic priests from the continental English seminaries threatened to stem the slow decline of a leaderless English catholicism, and the entry of the Jesuits from 1580 added a psychological impetus out of all proportion to their numbers. The government was not slow in providing remedies, so that the number of executions of priests is a testimonial both to the degree of concern over the priests' activities, and to the diligence with which they were hunted down. The key to the government's activity was its elaboration of the law of treason. Legislation was already in force which made it treason to deny Elizabeth's right to the throne, to try to deprive her of it, or to assert someone else's claim.[1] It was also treason to maintain the pope's authority, or to use a papal bull to absolve or reconcile Englishmen.[2] All of these statutes had been enacted by 1571, but the entry of priests from 1574 onward demanded new definitions of treason, and in these proclamations had a striking role to play.[3]

Many who write of those years do so in a polemical vein: those who justify the government's actions stress reasons of state and support its allegations of treason against the priests, while catholic writers and others emphasize the priests' exclusively religious motivation, demonstrating that they were not engaged in plots against the Queen. Such approaches usually ignore a crucial question: what legal

---

[1] 1 Eliz. I, c. 5; 13 Eliz. I, c. 1.
[2] 5 Eliz. I, c. 1; 13 Eliz. I, c. 2.
[3] The section on the proclamations of 1580–2 and their enforcement was originally published as 'Definitions of Treason in an Elizabethan Proclamation', *Hist. J.*, XIV 1(1971), 675–91. I have modified it to make it fit the context of this fuller study.

means did the government possess to counter the increased threat? It is clear that no catholic martyr was executed except for some offense – trumped up or not – against a statute.[4] Yet how might the government deal with the increasing number of priests and their lay aiders and abettors when the existing law of treason did not fully cover their activities? The Parliament of 1581 partly dealt with the problem by making it treason to persuade English subjects to adhere to the Roman religion or to forsake their obedience to the Queen, and by establishing severe fines for recusancy (absence from the Anglican services) or for attendance at mass.[5] In this and the earlier legislation, the statutes set penalties for treasonable actions; it was only in 1585 that another criterion, the mere physical presence of a priest in the realm, was added to the law of treason.[6]

The consideration of the priests' activities and of the proclamations which were part of the government's response can be divided into two phases, before and after the legislation of 1585. Before its enactment, there was a need for legal innovation. Although the Council by its letters might enforce laws already in existence, or provide for the renewal of the ecclesiastical commissions with their broad powers, the Queen and her Council must have realized that these means were inadequate to deal satisfactorily with either the priests or their abettors, or with the English youths preparing themselves abroad in the seminaries. The proclamations of 1581 and 1582 filled that legal lacuna by making new definitions, and thus by making law enforceable in the courts. Since the statute of 1585 remedied the lacunae in a permanent and comprehensive fashion, the proclamations issued after that date against the priests and their adherents no longer played an important role in law, but served nevertheless as indications of the changing nature of the catholic ministry in England and of the degree of governmental concern.

PROCLAMATIONS BEFORE 1585

Three royal proclamations were issued, in 1580, 1581 and 1582, to meet the growing challenge from the catholic forces.[7] Until that time

---

[4] This insistence on ascertaining the legal basis for the martyrs' death is stressed in Hughes, *The Reformation in England*, III, 357–62.   [5] 23 Eliz. I, c. 1.

[6] 27 Eliz. I, c. 2; on the debates over the crimes and punishments, see Neale, *Elizabeth I and her Parliaments, 1584–1603*, pp. 37–8.

[7] There are references to other proclamations in the writings of Persons which, however, probably refer to local edicts. See Leo Hicks (ed.), *Letters and Memorials of Father Robert Persons, S.J.*, Vol. I: *To 1588* (Catholic Record Society, XXXIX; London, 1942), xv; J. H. Pollen, in *Miscellanea, II* (Catholic Record Society, II; London, 1906), p. 177.

there had been a period of relative laxness in the enforcement of the laws against catholics; this dated from early 1579 and resulted primarily from the Queen's desire to continue the marriage negotiations with Alençon. Her attitude toward the marriage was mercurial in 1580: she was cold to the idea in January; by March, the necessity of an alliance with France to counter the Spanish pretensions on Portugal and to forestall a renewal of a Franco-Scottish alliance had quickened her ardor and even secured the support of those on her Council who were more inclined to the puritan cause; in May, negotiations had been effectively broken off again.[8] During those months, however, her attitude toward her catholic subjects had hardened as a result of the republication in France of the papal bull which had excommunicated her and declared her deposed.[9] That attitude was confirmed by the government's receipt in July of a list of ten articles which purported to be plans for a papal league to invade England and execute the bull.[10]

The royal proclamation of 15 July 1580 was issued to suppress rumors of that intended invasion.[11] The original draft, entirely in Burghley's hand, is notable because its tone and alleged purpose were markedly religious, stressing the Queen's obligation to 'maintain his [God's] glory and honor, by retaining her people in the true profession of the Gospel, and to keep them free from the bondage of the Romish tyranny'.[12] But once the government began to execute the priests who were arriving that summer, its propaganda denied that religious matters were involved at all. In a second draft, Burghley wanted to include a severe penalty for spreading the rumors – further punishment as 'aiders and abettors to the foreign traitors' – but this was deleted.[13] The final text as printed was thus basically hortatory: it admonished the people to continue in their duty to the Queen or to put aside 'unnatural affections' which might provoke her to severe execution of the laws, and ordered peace officers to punish those who spread the rumors as sowers of sedition.

As a public manifestation of the concern over the catholic problem, the proclamation increased the severity of the persecution which

---

[8] Read, *Mr. Secretary Walsingham and the Policy of Queen Elizabeth*, II, 13–32; J. H. Pollen, *English Catholics in the Reign of Queen Elizabeth, 1558–1580* (London, 1920), pp. 335–61.

[9] The government learned of this in April, *CSP Foreign*, XIV, 158. That this was done as a counteraction against the proposed match with Alençon is suggested by Martin Haile [Marie Hallé], *An Elizabethan Cardinal, William Allen* (London, 1914), p. 181.

[10] The articles are reprinted in *CSP Venice*, VII, 650–1.

[11] Proc. 650/751.

[12] PRO, SP 12/140/18; rated as a failure by Read, *Burghley*, pp. 244–5.

[13] PRO, SP 12/140/19.

had already begun.[14] The two Jesuit priests who had just arrived, Robert Persons and Edmund Campion, believed the danger to be much greater and retired from London immediately.[15] During the following months, the persecution continued under directions from the Council,[16] even after it was learned in December that the threat of invasion was past.[17] Relaxation did not and could not follow, not only because there was an increased aversion to Spain because of the new developments on the continent, but also because the very nature and strength of the catholic mission in England had changed, so that new measures were needed to cope with it.

Seventy-one priests had been sent from the continental seminaries in the 1570s, three of whom had already been put to death.[18] The arrival of two Jesuit priests and a lay brother in June 1580 added little to the number, but considering the impact they had, their participation was a turning point. Personality was one reason why the Jesuits became the focus of catholic hopes and of the government's severity; contemporaries and men of all ages have found Campion one of the most attractive of Elizabethan personalities.[19] But that alone was not enough to warrant such attention. The point was that the two priests openly challenged the government's position. Soon after their arrival, and at the urging of friends, the two priests wrote personal apologias for their mission, to prevent the government from issuing false statements in their name should they be captured. Campion's message was widely circulated and provoked a sensation: its confident tone caused catholics to refer to it as his 'Challenge', and his opponents as his 'Great Bragge'.[20] While we need not follow the course of their travels throughout the realm, it must be noted that their existence caused the government no small problem.

The priests assisted their personal ministrations by publishing a great number of books.[21] The issues on which they concentrated were

[14] The beginning of the renewed severity can be dated to the Council's order of 18 June 1580, *APC*, XII, 59.

[15] Pollen, *English Catholics in the Reign of Queen Elizabeth*, p. 341.

[16] *APC*, XII, 156–7. The first man accused of harboring Campion was Sir George Peckham (*ibid.* p. 282, on 18 December); since he later conformed, one cannot know what the penalty for his action might have been: *ibid.* pp. 325–6, 346.

[17] Pollen, *English Catholics in the Reign of Queen Elizabeth*, p. 360.

[18] The names of those sent are in Henry Foley (ed.), *Records of the English Province of the Society of Jesus* (7 vols.; London, 1877–84), III, 41–3.

[19] Copious citations from Persons's life of Campion are in Hicks (ed.), *Letters and Memorials of Father Robert Persons, S.J.* Persons's own memoirs are in *Miscellanea II* (see p. 229 note 7 above) and in *Miscellanea IV* (Catholic Record Society, IV; London, 1907).

[20] The term of derision was first used by Meredith Hanmer.

[21] Above, pp. 224ff.

more important than the numbers: they offered to engage in learned disputes on religious matters; then they set out to preserve the doctrinal integrity of the laity by explaining why they should not attend the Anglican services. The Anglican clergy began to make countercharges of their own as well as to refute the Jesuits. The allegation that they were traitors was first made by the puritan William Charke who had been commissioned to answer Campion's 'Challenge'. He equated the maintenance of the protestant religion with loyalty to the commonwealth, and catholicism with treason.[22] His learned allegations received substantial help from the inflammatory claims of John Nichols who wrote of the republication of the old papal bull against Elizabeth and of the treasonable speeches of both the faculty and former seminarians at Rome.[23] From that time onward the anticatholic writings focused on the charges of treason, and eventually the later proclamations carried the allegations to a far wider audience than would ever see the books.[24]

Persons responded to Charke almost immediately, and several days after his answer the royal proclamation of 10 January 1581 appeared.[25] Persons seems to have believed that the proclamation was a reply to his own book, but it hardly seems likely since both he and Charke dealt directly with the question of treason which the proclamation did not mention. The latter's primary concern was with the English students trained 'in false and erroneous doctrine' in the seminaries. It ordered parents and guardians to give the names of their dependants abroad in the seminaries to the ordinary, and to recall them within four months. Any continued financial support was to be punished as a contempt, but anyone who received, maintained, or concealed any of the priests in England 'shall be reputed as maintainers and abettors of such rebellious and seditious persons, and receive for the same their contempt such severe punishment as by the laws of the realm and her highness' princely authority may be inflicted upon them'.[26]

[22] Helen C. White, *Tudor Books of Saints and Martyrs* (Madison, 1963), pp. 207–8; Clancy, *Papist Pamphleteers*, pp. 48–9.

[23] *A declaration of the recantation of Iohn Nicholas (for the space of almost of two yeeres the Popes Scholer in the English Seminarie or Colledge at Rome)...*, sig. K.viij – L.i.v.

[24] The charge was of treasonable activities, not words. In his *A True, Sincere and Modest Defence*, Allen conceded that disloyal words had been written against the Queen by Nicholas Sanders and Richard Bristow, but alleged mitigating circumstances; see Hughes, *The Reformation in England*, III, 297–8.

[25] Proc. 655/755.

[26] Letters dated before the proclamation from the Council to the bishops which ordered them to take bonds of the parents and friends of the seminarians are in *APC*, XII, 281–2. A letter to the Lord Mayor of London eight days after its issue, commending him

The concern over the seminarians was certainly warranted. From information available now, it can be calculated roughly that there were between 210 and 220 English youths in the seminaries and schools on the continent.[27] Although the government had a copious amount of intelligence about them,[28] it knew much less about the whereabouts of Campion or Persons, or of the places which they had visited. Indeed, from the charges made later in the year against the men who harbored the priests, it appears that the government had exact knowledge of their itineraries only after 10 January – an ironic coincidence with the date of the proclamation.[29] But just why was the proclamation issued at that time? The most intriguing possibility is suggested by the proximity of the date to that projected for the opening of Parliament six days later. It seems quite likely that the proclamation was an intimation of the policy which the government hoped to secure in statutory form. But when the session began, Thomas Norton and his associates seized the initiative on religious matters, and the bills which were produced came from the committee established at his urging. No intended government bill survives, although the speeches of the government's spokesmen leave no doubt that the government wished to have steps taken to deal with the growing crisis.[30] The explanation that the government lost the initiative would help to explain why the proclamation's first concern, the students in the seminaries, was not reflected in the final legislation. Furthermore, the statute set penalties for the aiders and abettors of the priests in a restricted sense only – they were to be punished only if they aided or abetted priests who were absolving, persuading, or withdrawing subjects from their natural obedience to the Queen, or to the Romish religion. Even the penalty was a lesser one, for misprision of treason.[31]

But regardless of the occasion for the proclamation, it was very important in that its definition that abettors should be 'reputed as maintainers and abettors of such rebellious and seditious persons' was a departure from the existing legislation on treason. What the

for putting 'one Eden out of an office that he held in that City for that he was notoriously known to have brought up his children beyond the seas in Popery' is in *ibid.* pp. 315–16.

[27] See Youngs, 'Definitions of Treason in an Elizabethan Proclamation', p. 682, note 36.

[28] PRO, SP 12/146/129, 137; 12/175/110; *CSP Foreign*, xv, 250–2; BL, Add. MSS 48029, printed in Clare Talbot (ed.), *Miscellanea. Recusant Records* (Catholic Record Society, LIII; London, 1961), pp. 193–245.

[29] Godfrey Anstruther, *Vaux of Harrowden. A Recusant Family* (Newport, 1953), p. 138.

[30] Neale, *Elizabeth I and her Parliaments, 1559–1581*, pp. 382–5.

[31] 23 Eliz. I, c. 1.

proclamation did was to define the offense of being an accessory before it was clear that the activity of the principal fell within the scope of the existing laws. The seeming vagueness could have been intended to define the offense in order that it might be brought within the jurisdiction of the Star Chamber – where, as shall be seen, it was actually enforced.

There was little vagueness in the proclamation issued some fourteen and a half months later, on 1 April 1582.[32] In effect it argued the government's case that Campion and the other priests were traitors, presenting the claims to the widest possible audience. It specifically insisted that it was for treason and not for religion that the priests had been convicted. The introductory section of the proclamation was a repetition of the first portion of the proclamation of 1581, interlined with more graphic and biting phrases for greater effect.[33] The first motive for the new proclamation was that the earlier one a year before had not had the desired effect in spite of the punishment meted out to Campion. Next followed a refutation of the charge 'that some traitorously affected have of late by letters, libels, pamphlets, and books both written and printed falsely, seditiously, and traitorously given out that the said most horrible traitors were without just cause condemned and executed'. The proclamation informed all that the priests had been sent to prepare England to rise up against the Queen when invasions would come, proving its arguments by citing the recent rebellion in Ireland and from the words in the priests' books.

To protect the realm against such threats, the proclamation spelled out a number of definitions of offenses which gave the government authority to proceed against them:

all the said Jesuits, seminary men, and priests[34] aforesaid coming into these her dominions in such secret manner be, and so of all her subjects for the respects aforesaid ought to be holden, esteemed, and taken for traitors to her majesty, her crown, and realm; and that all such as... wittingly and willingly receive, harbor, aid, comfort, relieve, and maintain any such [priest] as is aforesaid, shall be and ought to be dealt with, used, and proceeded on as willing and witting aiders, comforters, relievers, and maintainers of traitors...and that every such person as shall have any such [priest] in his or her house...and shall not forthwith...cause him

---

[32] Proc. 660/763.

[33] The draft, corrected by Burghley but with no changes in the legal definitions, is in PRO, SP 12/152/3.

[34] In good legal fashion, the phrase 'Jesuits, seminary men, and priests' is repeated each time; for brevity's sake, I have substituted the word 'priest' in brackets wherever the longer phrase was used.

to be brought before the next justice of the peace or some other public officer...shall be deemed, taken, and dealt with as a maintainer and aider of traitors as aforesaid; and that any person wittingly concealing any such [priest] or their practices aforesaid, shall be deemed and taken to be in case of misprision of treason...and that...all such of her majesty's subjects as be at this present of the said seminaries and societies erected beyond the seas as aforesaid, and shall not return within one quarter of a year after this proclamation made, as all other which after the publication hereof shall pass over the seas and be of any the seminaries or societies erected as aforesaid, shall be *ipso facto* taken, reputed, and esteemed to be traitors to her highness' person, her crown, and realm; and that all maintainers, aiders, relievers, and comforters of such persons shall be esteemed, taken, and dealt with as maintainers, aiders, relievers, and comforters of such traitors.

Of the two reasons alleged in the text – the lack of reformation and the increase in seditious writings – the second would seem to have been the most important. To the already existing genres of catholic literary writings, the controversial, instructional and devotional books, had been added a fourth, martyrologies. In many respects the government provoked them, since many works had been printed to show how the government's charge of treason had been 'proved' at Campion's trial, while others were issued to demonstrate the cowardly way he allegedly faced execution. His 'confession' was often cited, from which proofs against those who harbored him were drawn. The potential damage to the catholic cause from all these writings could be enormous. Catholics began to produce their own books immediately, at first concentrating on his resoluteness and piety at the execution, then later taking issue with the 'proofs' of treason and asserting that he was executed for religion, not treason. The most impressive account of his execution was written by a fellow priest and eye-witness at his martyrdom, Thomas Alfield.[35] His book was circulated in London during the last days of February or early in March 1582, with an appendix or 'discovery' of Anthony Munday annexed, since Munday had already published several works against Campion.[36]

But apparently it was the English translation of Person's *De Persecutione Anglicana* which was the immediate cause of the proclamation. Persons had left England in 1581 believing that the increased persecution made persuasion by the written word more effective than

[35] For Alfield, above, pp. 224–5.
[36] [Thomas Alfield], *A True Reporte of the Death and Martyrdome of M. Campion...Sherwin...Bryan...at Tiborne the First of December 1581.* The 'discovery' of Munday begins at sig. D.iiijv.

personal ministration. His writings on the persecution appeared on the continent in late 1581 and quickly became the most influential piece exciting continental catholics to contribute to the special collection for the English seminaries.[37] To the English translation, entitled *An Epistle of the Persecution of Catholickes in England*, the translator 'G.T.' added a preface in the form of a letter to the Council, charging them in no uncertain terms not only with a cruelty that surpassed anything yet seen in Europe, but also with persecuting for religion's sake.[38] Few charges were more likely to evoke a response, and the proclamation was probably just such a reply. As such it was a tool of propaganda, showing men throughout the realm that the treason of the priests had been adjudicated in a royal court, and tarring with the same brush all those who aided any priest. More importantly, by means of the legal definitions the proclamation provided the means to deal with the problem at law.

The proclamation of 1581 had not specified any place of enforcement but in fact it was enforced in the Star Chamber. There is no record of the cases in the archives of that court, but instead one finds the proceedings and/or penalties recorded among the minutes of the Council (clearly marked 'at the Star Chamber') or in unofficial reports. The cases against the harborers of Campion are under the dates of 24 November, 30 November, and 15 December 1581. Of the eight who confessed to the charges, four were pardoned upon their submission, one was later pardoned when she proved her religious conformity, another was found guilty in a lesser degree and was freed when he proved his conformity before the Lord President at York, and two were committed to the prison of the Fleet. Three persons denied the charges, of which two were dismissed when on oath they denied the allegation which had purportedly been based on Campion's confession, and one was ordered to stand further trial, but was never mentioned again in the Council's minutes. As is usual when the business of the Star Chamber is mentioned in the Council's minutes, the entries were concerned with the disposition of the defendants, that is to say, with the question of into whose safekeeping or into

[37] It was also used by the Guise family as a warning about what would happen to France if Navarre ever came to the throne: Simpson, *Edmund Campion*, p. 468.

[38] Thomas Norton wrote to Walsingham on 27 March that a book had appeared calling him 'rackmaster' and charging him with having so tortured Bryant that the priest was left one foot longer than God had made him. Both charges are in the English translation of Persons's book and allow it to be dated: PRO, SP 12/152/72. Continental editions included plates depicting the torments the priests suffered, notably the barbarity of hanging, drawing, and quartering; see Anthony Petti, 'Additions to the Richard Verstegan Canon', *Recusant History*, VIII (1966), 289–90.

which gaols they were committed, or what bonds and/or securities were required, rather than with the legal basis for the case. Thus under the three trial dates cited, there was no reference to the proclamation as the basis for the trials, although from an earlier entry it is clear that the offense was alleged as against the Queen's proclamation.[39]

The other case dealing with Campion's harborers was earlier in time than those found in the Council minutes, and was noted only in an unofficial report of the cases and fines.[40] It is clear that the proclamation of 1581 was the basis of the charge against at least one of the defendants because he pleaded that his offense had been committed before the proclamation.[41] The three most illustrious defendants were William Lord Vaux, Sir Thomas Tresham, and Sir William Catesby, who unlike the others denied the charges. One cannot be sure that the entire case was based on the proclamation, because a memorandum of Burghley's found elsewhere indicates that their offense occurred in the summer of 1580, and there is no mention in the report of the alleged date of the offense.[42] Father Anstruther, the biographer of the Vaux family, has suggested that the entire trial was part of the attempt to blacken the name of Campion, since his alleged confession was the principal proof of the charges. He has further suggested that the court was 'fishing for information' about Vaux and the two knights by 'using for bait' the specific, minute, and undeniable details of the offenses of the three lesser co-defendants; no exact offense or date could be laid against the former since the confession of Campion was a fabrication.[43] Nevertheless all six were found guilty, fined amounts ranging from 500 marks to £1,000, and committed to the Fleet until they conformed in the duty they owed the Queen.

The one major gap in the minute books of the Privy Council unfortunately coincided exactly with the period during which the

[39] *APC*, xiii, 260–1, 267–8, 289–91. The first entry against harborers of Campion is *ibid.* pp. 148–9 (2 August 1581); other entries leading up to the trials are found under the dates of 6, 7, 14, 18, and 30 August; 21 September; 29 October; 1, 7, 12, 22, and 27 November; and 4, 6, and 12 December.

[40] See Anstruther, *Vaux of Harrowden*, pp. 120–7, the main source for which are the Tresham papers, *HMC 55: Var. Coll. III*, pp. 22ff. An account is in BL, Harl. MS 859, fos. 44–51, printed in *Archaeologia*, xxx (1894), with an introduction by John Bruce who edited it. An account in the Ellesmere MSS is printed in Anthony Petti (ed.), *Recusant Documents from the Ellesmere Manuscripts* (Catholic Record Society, LX; London, 1968), pp. 5–13. Fines recorded in BL, Harl. MS 2143, fo. 12*v*.

[41] Walter Powdrell; see Anstruther, *Vaux of Harrowden*, p. 125.

[42] Anstruther, *Vaux of Harrowden*, p. 136.

[43] *Ibid.* pp. 132–40, especially pp. 138–9.

proclamation of 1 April 1582 was in force. Records exist, however, of two trials of the highest ranking catholic nobleman of that period, Philip Howard, Earl of Arundel, in which charges based on the proclamation are to be found.

Arundel was first tried in the Star Chamber on 17 May 1586.[44] Lord Chancellor Bromley in his opening statement indicated that Arundel was being tried to disprove the claims made in various catholic circles that he had been falsely imprisoned. Now the Earl was to answer such 'grievous contemps' as should be alleged against him, 'Wherein, although matter should fall out of a higher nature than was to be dealt with in this Court, yet they agreed to so much thereof as concerned his contempt, and reserved the rest to be dealt with elsewhere at her highness' good pleasure.'[45] Attorney General Popham then presented as three charges three separate contempts, the first of which was

'in contempt of two several proclamations set forth by her highness, the one in January the xxxiiii[th] year of her Majesty's reign and the other in April following straightly charging and commanding all her Majesty's subjects of this realm not to receive, succor or entertain any Jesuit or Seminary priest by any manner of means upon peril to be taken and accounted as receivers, abettors or comforters of traitors to her Majesty and the realm.'[46]

Having cited the influx of priests and their dangerous practices, Popham charged that Arundel had 'both before and about the beginning of the last parliament received and entertained in his house and company three several Jesuits or seminary priests, viz.: one Weston a Jesuit as himself confessed at the bar, and one Bridges & Hall being both seminary Priests'.[47] With no doubt a certain relish Popham noted how Arundel had himself sat in judgment in Star Chamber in 1582 and 'upon a like manner concerning the same Jesuits & seminary Priests' had 'very constanly pronounced and affirmed in open Court that in his opinion all such perverse and obstinate papists were generally to be deemed and taken as traitors to her Majesty'.[48]

When the time came for Arundel to argue against that charge and two other contempts committed in a letter charging the Queen with partiality against him and his attempted flight overseas, he tried to

[44] J. H. Pollen and William MacMahon (eds.), *The Ven. Philip Howard Earl of Arundel, 1557–1595: English Martyrs*, vol. *II* (Catholic Record Society, xxi; London, 1919), 138–44.
[45] *Ibid.* p. 140.
[46] *Ibid.* pp. 140–1.
[47] *Ibid.* p. 141.
[48] *Ibid.* p. 142.

excuse himself 'with supposed matter of conscience error and ignorance, & with earnest protestations of an innocent intent in all his proceedings'. Yet 'after proof made of the several offenses & contempts aforesaid, confessing his said offences', he submitted and begged the court to intercede for him with the Queen so that her displeasure might be lifted. No detail either of the proofs or of the usual gratuitous comments made by individual judges when they presented their opinion of the case are to be found. Instead, having again noted that the court avoided those things which might touch him in 'a higher degree', the reporter noted that he was fined £10,000 and returned to the Tower to remain a prisoner at the Queen's pleasure.[49]

It was nearly three years before Arundel was brought to trial for those 'higher' matters, this time before a specially convened court of his peers, the Court of the Lord Steward.[50] As was the case in the earlier trial, the charges against him were multiple. The actual proceedings during the trial again survive in an abbreviated summary, yet for the purposes of this study the exact words of the indictment are most telling. It first recited the conspiratorial meeting at which the catholic leaders (Allen, Campion, Persons, and others) plotted on 31 March 1580 to kill the Queen and invade the realm, then noted that the Queen's proclamation of 1 April 1582 had been issued. That part of the proclamation which set forth the concise definitions of abetting treason by receiving or maintaining the Jesuits or seminary priests was cited in Latin, but with the penalty more harshly stated than in the original proclamation.[51] Then Arundel was charged with knowingly receiving Weston and Bridges on 10 September 1584. After this first count of the indictment, Arundel was further charged with other treasons, including conspiring to depose the Queen, adhering to the plans of Cardinal Allen, and other similar things, culminating in the charge that he favored the invasion plans of the Armada.[52]

It is evident first of all that there was no hesitation whatsoever in

[49] *Ibid.* p. 144.

[50] *Ibid.* pp. 220ff., edited from PRO, KB 8/49.

[51] 'Et quod omnes post publicationem predicte proclamationis scienter & voluntarie receptarent, hospitarent, auxiliarent, confortarent, releuarent, & mantenerent aliquem talem Jesuitam, Seminarii hominem, seu Sacerdotem (ut predicitur) tractarent & super eos procederent (ut supra) scienter & voluntarie, confortatores, releuatores & manutentores proditorie, committent altam prodicionem versus personam maiestatis suae', yet Arundel knowing the priests to be seditious and traitorous men, having come into the realm for treasonable purposes 'postea & diu post proclamacionem...factam & proclamatam... receptavit & manutenuit, proditoriis propositiis & intentionibus...' in *ibid.* pp. 225–6.

[52] *Ibid.* pp. 225–31.

accepting the legal definitions set forth in the proclamation. Equally important, this charge in the context of the entire indictment was certainly not as qualitatively important as the rest.[53] It would seem that the first count was included to increase the number of allegations: the offense against the proclamation did not even appear in the pre-trial list of charges. Serjeants Puckering and Shuttleworth did, according to the report, mention the offense against the proclamation in their exposition of the charges, but no detail is given. The sentences pronounced by the different peers did not distinguish between the different counts of the indictment, except for a statement by Lord Norris – 'Upon my hand I take him to be guilty of all the Treasons contained in the Indictment' – and one would be rash to read too much into that.[54] Indeed the mass of evidence concerned with Arundel both before and after the trial mentioned the proclamation very seldom. He died while in confinement in the Tower, and the sentence was never executed.

PROCLAMATIONS AFTER 1585

After the statute of 1585 made it treason *ipso facto* to have been ordained a catholic priest since the beginning of the Queen's reign, the argument which the government continued to press in its propaganda had a solid foundation in the law. The events of 1588 gave the government a great psychological lift; it never failed to press home the continuous involvement of the catholic leaders abroad in the plans for the Spanish invasion of England. Although the catholics within the realm might point to their steadfastness and loyalty when the Armada had threatened, any appreciation which the government might have felt was modified by the renewed fear of invasion in the early 1590s and by the increasing number of seminary priests.[55]

It was in order to publicize the new measures for detecting priests that a royal proclamation was issued in October 1591.[56] In one of the longest texts ever issued, the government set forth four developments as the justification for the new procedures. It first told of Philip II's actions in committing his Spanish forces in 'a most unjust and a dangerous war for all Christendom against the French King'. Next

[53] Nor quantitatively so: eleven lines of a seventy-six line indictment.
[54] *Ibid.* p. 273.
[55] The new seminary at Valladolid was sending about ten a year from its inception; see the Appendix in Albert J. Loomie, *The Spanish Elizabethans. The English Exiles at the Court of Philip II* (New York, 1963), pp. 237–8.   [56] Proc. 738/837.

it related how Philip had secured the election of 'a Milanese, a vassal of his own' (Gregory XIV) as pope, and how the new pope had himself supplied troops to assist Philip in France. Then the new erection of seminaries for English students in Spain was condemned, since out of them, as from other continental seminaries, priests were sent into England to win the Queen's subjects from the loyalty they owed her. Finally, the proclamation spoke of the prospects of another attempt at the invasion of England, 'known to us... by sundry means... greater for this year to come than ever he [Philip] had before'. The activities of Persons and Allen abroad were roundly condemned, especially their having assured Philip that if he mounted a new invasion the next year 'many thousands' would arise to help him.

Many of the reasons alleged in the proclamation have a lack of compelling urgency. The seminary in Valladolid had been in existence since 1589;[57] the first Spanish troops in France arrived a year before the proclamation; the entry of the papal troops was more recent, but still quite a while before its issue. The real threat was of a new invasion, and from intelligence reports the agent of these warlike plans was known to be Sir William Stanley. Stanley had indeed presented a plan for employing his troops in an attack on Alderney in the Channel Islands, during the months of October and November when Elizabeth's fleet was normally never at sea. The capture of that 'Gibraltar' of the Channel Islands would not only provide a jumping-off place for sorties against England, but would be well located to intercept supplies sent to France to assist the troops which England had committed to help Henry IV. It appears that the government knew that Stanley had projected an enterprise and perhaps of its timing, but did not know of his goal or that Philip and his advisers had rejected the plan.[58]

There were other reasons for a general sense of malaise at the military prospects of England which would have further inclined Elizabeth to take a firm stand against a priestly fifth column. She had committed two bodies of troops to serve in France, to protect Brittany and Normandy from Spanish occupation so that they could not serve as staging areas for an attempted invasion. One of those contingents had been placed under the command of Sir John Norris

[57] Edwin Henson (ed.), *Registers of the English College at Valladolid 1589–1862* (Catholic Record Society, xxx; London, 1930), pp. viiff.
[58] The fullest discussion is in Loomie, *The Spanish Elizabethans*, pp. 145–50. For the government's awareness, see *HMC 9: Salisbury (Cecil) IV*, p. 131; PRO, SP 12/240/54; *APC*, xxi, 220–1, 470–1.

and sent to Dieppe; the other under the Earl of Essex had been destined for the siege of Rouen which Elizabeth suspected would be yielded up to Spain by leaders friendly to them. The forces under Essex had been committed only for two months, and the Queen was particularly annoyed by the dilatory tactics of Essex and Henry IV. Her reluctant extension of the time during which her troops might serve was an indication of her discontent over the whole enterprise.[59] A sharper reverse had been suffered on the seas. Sir Richard Grenville had engaged in a foolhardy but brilliantly heroic engagement in the Azores with a Spanish fleet, with the result that for the first (and as it happened, the last) time in Elizabeth's reign an English naval defeat had occurred. The propaganda in England soon afterwards emphasized the heroism, but the sense of loss was keenly and apprehensively felt within the government.[60]

To provide remedies to meet these threats, the royal proclamation spelled out a number of measures, the most important of which was an announcement of the establishment of new commissioners in the various counties who were empowered to inquire as to the presence of priests and to apprehend them. The Queen commanded the assistance of all subjects in two ways: first, the heads of households, landlords and governors of societies were ordered to conduct an inquiry into the church-going practices of those in their charge, questioning their activities during the past year; second, all subjects were to make known to the commissioners any persons who had come from abroad as part of the catholic cause, on pain of being themselves punished as 'abettors and maintainers of treason' if they did not provide the information. Armed with the intelligence from those two sources, the commissioners could carry out their task effectively.

At the heart of the matter were the commissions which the proclamation promised. Issued under the Great Seal, they were the authority for the commissioners to do what the proclamation commanded,[61] and a printed series of questions for the commissioners to use in the examinations was also provided.[62] The usual lengthy procedures followed: lengthy correspondence to handle the many

[59] *HMC 9: Salisbury (Cecil) IV*, pp. 133–4, 139–41, 143–6; *CSP Venice*, VIII, 555–6, 558–9, 562; Black, *The Reign of Elizabeth*, pp. 413–15.
[60] Black, *The Reign of Elizabeth*, pp. 412–13; Rowse, *Sir Richard Grenville of the Revenge*, pp. 300–29.
[61] Warrant, *HMC 9: Salisbury (Cecil) IV*, p. 148; a copy of the commission, probably a model for the others, PRO, SP 38/2 (27 November).
[62] In Hughes & Larkin as no. 739, not a royal proclamation.

questions and problems;[63] a bit of improvisation, as when the commissioners in Buckinghamshire sent out subordinate orders to require each parish to make a certificate;[64] and very thorough reports from some, and complaints from areas such as Lancashire and Cheshire that the proclamation had little effect and that little was done.[65] All the enforcement was strictly of the commission, and not of the proclamation, but the system of registers and searches which had been intermittent before was now given such a precision through the proclamation's publicity that the 'Cecilian inquisition', as one catholic called it, was feared for its thoroughness. A statute in 1593 restricted convicted recusants to within a five-mile radius of their residence.[66]

Because the proclamation was in large part a propaganda instrument, it elicited many answers from the catholic press. Robert Persons, one of the proclamation's main targets, was the first to respond; writing under the pseudonym Philopater, his reply ran into five editions in Latin and others in German and French.[67] Another Latin reply was penned by Thomas Stapleton under the name Didymus, while Richard Verstegan wrote twice in English and Robert Southwell wrote also, even though his work was not printed until 1600.[68] All the catholic responses were confident in tone. At first sight this might appear surprising, but the confidence seems to have sprung from a realization that the members of the Council most hostile to catholicism had died, and that Spain's power (for those who placed their hope there) was still formidable. In a different sense the proclamation was acclaimed as of positive benefit to the new seminaries. The earliest brief history of the new foundation at Valladolid was written to respond to the query of an English catholic in exile who wanted to know the 'true story' of the seminary, as opposed to the version in the proclamation. The first full annals written thirty years later, reflecting on the increased number who had come to study, called the proclamation in retrospect a certain instrument of divine providence.[69]

[63] E. Sussex RO, Rye MS 47/45/7, transmitted from Dover Castle; *APC*, xxii, *passim*; xxiii, 27–8.

[64] J. W. Garrett-Pegge (ed.), 'A Paper from a Family Deed-Chest', *Records of Buckinghamshire*, viii (1903), 276–84.

[65] Certificate from Warwickshire, PRO, SP 12/243/76; from Lancashire and Cheshire, 12/240/138.

[66] Quoted in A. O. Meyer, *England and the Catholic Church under Elizabeth* (London, 1916), p. 350.

[67] Clancy, *Papist Pamphleteers*, pp. 238–40.

[68] *Ibid.*; see also PRO, SP 12/242/17; *HMC 2: 3rd Rpt, App.*, p. 43; Huntington Libr., Ellesmere MS 2089.

[69] Henson (ed.), *Registers of the English College at Valladolid*, pp. ix–x, 266.

But whatever strength and unity the catholic cause mustered in reply to the challenges of 1591 was soon dissipated in the middle years of the 1590s in a squalid debate over the control of the mission. When Cardinal Allen died in 1594, the question of leadership became acute. The secular priests resented the disproportionate influence of the Jesuits, and particularly the latter's pro-Spanish policy. Persons's book in 1594 which asserted the rights of the Spanish Infanta above those of the Stuarts was but the last of many grievances which the seculars felt. In 1598 an Archpriest was appointed, but under the terms of the establishment he was required to consult with the Jesuits in all matters of importance. Even though a secular, George Blackwell, was named to the post, this was little consolation, and the seculars decided to appeal to Rome since the instruments involved were issued not by the pope directly but by Cardinal Caetani. With that appeal began a series of events which would eventually involve the issue of a proclamation on 5 November 1602.[70]

When the government learned of the conflict, it quickly decided to assist the seculars, by then known as the Appellants because of their appeal to Rome. The two priests who were allowed to go to Rome were harshly treated, and when a papal brief was issued to confirm the appointment of the Archpriest all the priests submitted. The matter should have ended there, but Blackwell decided to insist that the Appellants should acknowledge that they had been in a state of schism when the appeal was being made. His vindictive approach occasioned a new appeal to Rome, this time centering on the question of the priests' 'schismatical' state.

The Council had begun to realize that the situation could be exploited. In June 1602 one of the priests, Thomas Bluet, had an audience with Elizabeth herself in which he related the seculars' dislike of the Jesuits, the detestation in which the plots against her were held, and promises of future co-operation. She then began to allow the books which the seculars wrote to be printed secretly within the realm,[71] and collusively 'banished' four of the Appellants who were meant to argue at Rome. With the assistance of the French, the Appellants were able to have the provision for consultation with

[70] The sketch of the controversy which is given above is summarized from Thomas Graves Law, *A Historical Sketch of the Conflicts between Jesuits and Seculars in the Reign of Queen Elizabeth* (London, 1889), and his *The Archpriest Controversy. Documents Relating to the Dissensions of the Roman Catholic Clergy, 1597–1602* (2 vols.; Camden Society, new series, LVI, LVIII; London, 1896, 1898). Proc. 817/930.
[71] Gladys Jenkins, 'The Archpriest Controversy and the Printers', *Library*, 5th series, II (1947), 180–6.

the Jesuits removed and to obtain a declaration that they had not been in schism, but their request that no future anti-English literature should be allowed was defeated by the Jesuits who in making their representations were assisted by the Spanish Ambassador. The Jesuits were also able to obtain a set of severe penalties for 'any one who under whatsoever pretext should communicate with heretics to the prejudice of Catholics'.[72]

We shall never know the extent to which Elizabeth had intended to go to procure an accommodation with the priests; the prohibition against further intercourse with heretics interrupted the negotiations. That she was stung by the turn of events and felt the necessity to placate the opposition which her tentative efforts had generated at home is clear from the tone of the proclamation issued soon after word of the papal brief arrived in England. Were one unaware of her part in the controversy, the proclamation would be familiar reading, a mere rehash of the government's claim that all priests were traitors. But since we know that the priests had hoped for much from her encouragement, and that some had thus written of a new era, we can understand that Elizabeth's tones of indignation were aimed primarily at reassuring the sincere protestants who feared her willingness to be accommodating. And so the Queen rebuked the priests' audacity by which they

'almost insinuate thereby into the minds of all sorts of people, as well the good that grieve at it as the bad that thirst after it, that we have some purpose to grant toleration of two religions within our realm where God ...doth not only know our innocence from such imagination, but how far it hath been from any about us...'

To prove her point, the Queen ordered that all priests should leave England or suffer the full rigor of the laws. Such a command, it should be noted, was far more lenient than the strict letter of the law. The seculars were also offered the option of disavowing any further disloyalty and promising their submission to the Queen; even if they did not accept, they were allowed nearly two months' grace, until 1 January, before they had to be out of England. The Jesuits were told to leave at once, and that the laws would be enforced against them at the end of thirty days. By allowing a period for their compliance, the Queen was exercising her prerogative power of dispensing with the law temporarily.

Some of the seculars did decide to submit. One wrote a letter

---

[72] Law, *The Archpriest Controversy*, I, xxiii; the brief was dated 5 October 1602.

which remains unsigned, but more importantly, thirteen priests as a group prepared a protestation of allegiance which they hoped would satisfy the terms of the proclamation and delegated four of their number to negotiate on the matter. But the Queen's death was only a short time off, and in the interim no action was taken. The proclamation died with the Queen, and it and the negotiations over it[73] were the end of an era – the end of what might have been, had there been a détente, as she seems to have wished.

[73] Meyer, *England and the Catholic Church under Elizabeth*, pp. 221–3, 456–7; PRO, SP 12/287/14; Law, *The Archpriest Controversy*, II, 246–8.

REFLECTIONS: THE
PROCLAMATIONS AND RELIGION

Proclamations on religion provide a number of contrasts. There is first of all the difference between the proclamations of the interim settlement and those against books or the priests. Even though many of the former were provoked by particular disturbances, yet their provisions went beyond the immediate causes to set forth binding governmental policy, while the latter tended to deal only with the problem at hand. Both Mary and Elizabeth intended to alter the religious settlement which they inherited, and just as they knew that Parliament's action was necessary in order to make a permanent settlement, they also knew that the prerogative held the necessary powers to legislate temporarily for the interim. Neither hesitated to use these powers – indeed, who else could have handled the matter? It could hardly be entrusted to the Church which was soon to be reformed, nor could Parliament be expected to act within such a short period of time. But once the permanent settlement was enacted and the Injunctions in force, the immediate need for a temporary settlement was gone.

Most of the proclamations which were called forth arose because of attacks on the Queen's honor, or upon men closely associated with her. Mary's protection of Philip's honor, Elizabeth's reaction to Cartwright's lecture on her religious duty, the offense taken at Browne's castigation of the entire civil magistracy, Stubbs's attack on Alençon, the fury at Martin Marprelate's ridicule of the episcopacy, Burghley's indignation at the books which attacked him as a 'new man' with selfish motives, and Leicester's disgust over the 'Commonwealth' – all these are of one piece in the reactions which they produced. When one adds the threats both Queens felt at the books intended to precede an invasion of England, and Elizabeth's affront at Mary Stuart's claims, the occasion for nearly every proclamation on books has been mentioned. In other cases the dissident books met a stony royal silence, to be answered only in the rarefied and less dangerous atmosphere of academic dispute. In such a way were the common sort protected from the threats posed by the dissident writings.

Some fruitful comparisons can be made between the proclamations of the two Tudor Queens, and in most ways they mirror the well known inclinations of each. Even though Mary's interim settlement was secular in approach because she could not work through the Church which she inherited, the revival of the heresy laws soon after gave a distinct ecclesiastical character to her reign, and also obviated the need for many proclamations. The more secular approach of Elizabeth is exemplified in the new regulations on peace in churchyards which differed from the religious emphasis of the Edwardian laws, to some extent in the effort by Bacon to have the catholic books condemned as treasonable, and above all in the uniform application later in the reign of the statute against seditious books against catholics, puritans and separatists alike. The loss of the initiative by the clergy in Elizabeth's reign was strongly underscored by the delays in issuing proclamations against notable cases of puritan dissent, especially in the *Admonition* and Marprelate controversies.

The proclamations provide less well known and more telling evidence of the differences in emphasis in the two reigns when their use as propaganda is compared. Mary seems to have been under a certain personal compulsion to explain the changes in religion and to justify her plans to marry Philip. Elizabeth provided not the least shred of gratuitous information and certainly did not parade her opinions before the masses. Rather early in the reign she wooed those Parliamentarians whose opinions really mattered, and later she used proclamations effectively to tarnish the reputation of the priests and to denounce them as traitors. But the proclamation of 1602 is a reminder not to take the rationalizations in proclamations always at face value, because hidden behind what must have seemed a rather routine condemnation of the priests lay a story that showed her open to changing circumstances. Both the Queen and the priests had come a long way from the belligerency of the previous decades, even if the time for a true accommodation was not yet at hand.

Administrative procedures were much less important in proclamations on religion than in other matters, primarily because the former concentrated on the informational and legislative aspects. The detailed orders as to how dissident books were to be turned in to the authorities were certainly subordinate to the intention of protecting the honor of the monarch or a councillor. Definitions of the offenses of the catholic seminarians abroad were followed up by orders to diocesan officials in London to inquire after those who had gone abroad. At least two students were called back by their parents, and we have seen that an official in London was dismissed from his office because he had a son abroad.[1]

The use of proclamations to set forth temporary legislation was of particular interest here because the definitions touched the highest offense in the land, treason, and because the courts showed no hesitation in accepting those definitions and acting upon them. But the examples of legislation exhibit those qualities which have been seen in areas other than religion: they were temporary, the proclamation of 1582 effectively superseding the one a year earlier, and in turn being supplanted by a statute in 1585; they supplemented the law rather than supplanting it, because the offenses of accessories in these matters were not already established at law; and the enforcement of the proclamations was a matter of short duration, particularly in the case of Campion's abettors whose trial was over within a month after his execution. Only when an example was to be made of a man of high social rank, Knightley and Arundel, was the trial delayed much beyond the date of a proclamation.

The legislation in 1581 and 1582 provides a deeper insight into the complicated motivations of the time, and particularly into the difficult question of Elizabeth's religious policy. Many writers have stressed her leniency, and Professor Neale in particular has most clearly argued the political corollary that any mitigations to severe legislation proposed as a result of parliamentary debates are to be attributed to her intervention in favor of more moderate measures. Yet there had been no necessity for issuing the proclamations of 1581 and 1582 except as legal means to an end, and their scope was wider than the statutes of 1581 and earlier, and their penalties more severe than in the statutes of 1581 and 1585. It does show that her own policies could on occasion be more severe than even her Parliament would accept.[2]

---

[1] Kennedy, *Elizabethan Episcopal Administration*, II, 134, noted in *Annals Ref.*, III, i, 57, with the comment that the visitation was authorized by the proclamation of 1581. The two students called home left Rheims 2 March 1581, but there is no indication of the proclamation, but only a terse entry 'parentum literis domum revocati discesserunt', in Fathers of the Congregation of the London Oratory (eds.), *The First and Second Diaries of the English College, Douay, and an Appendix of Unpublished Documents* (London, 1878), p. 176. For the dismissed official, see pp. 232–3, note 26 above.

[2] This aspect of leniency is stressed throughout Professor Neale's *Queen Elizabeth I* (London, 1934). His case for her intervention in 1581 is made in *Elizabeth I and her*

The evidence for the enforcement of the proclamations on religion is mixed. The Privy Council enforced the proclamations of the interim settlements quasi-judicially, particularly against those who violated the ban on preaching. Yet there is little evidence that the proclamations against books were enforced widely. No doubt the activities of authors, printers and distributors were of necessity clandestine, and little of what they did was written down; the number of copies of any given book which actually reached circulation may have been so small that the threat would be limited; the dissident books may have reached only a few regions; and the orders for searches would have led to activities which were not so likely to be recorded locally as would judicial determinations. Yet when all allowances are made, one is left with the distinct impression that enforcement was not really a major aim of the proclamations against books, whereas the defense of the royal honor was.

When the proclamations were enforced judicially, as they were against Campion's abettors, against Knightley, and against the Earl of Arundel, the trials were doubtless staged for full effect. In that sense the trials were another layer of propaganda, continuing the public arguments which had been expressed in the proclamations. The trials were thus in the tradition of Tudor statecraft which sought to teach obedience to all the subjects of England by making a public example of the disobedience of men who by right and by birth should have provided the examples of loyalty.

The proclamations on religion reflect in many ways what has been learned generally of the use of these instruments by the Tudor Queens. Most were official reactions to some crisis or disorder, as for example when Mary or Elizabeth feared an invasion of men or ideas. Like all proclamations, they selected from among a variety of techniques to frame remedies which could be applied in a number of jurisdictions. The proclamations on religion represent a rather more effective use of propaganda than was usual in other proclamations, and display rather less emphasis on administrative remedies.

In particular they exemplified the different ways in which proclamations supplemented and complemented the existing laws. There were new definitions of offenses during the interim settlements

Parliaments, 1559–1581, pp. 387–8; the case for her intervention in 1584–5 is not made so directly but strongly implied. Many issues were involved in the former bill, and my argument would not preclude her exercise of some rather stable inclination in her actions, such as refusing to require catholics to refuse communion. It argues, however, that one must not attribute all instances of mitigation to one facet of her personality.

when temporary norms were needed, and in those cases where the law did not comprehend accessories, as for the aiders of the priests. None of these supplanted the existing law, and the efforts made first in the proclamations led usually to more permanent legislation by Parliament.

How one ultimately assesses the propriety of the Marian and Elizabethan proclamations must depend to a great extent on personal judgment. There are gaps in the evidence at many points, and one has to surmise motives and reasons fairly often. It is possible to interpret the threats, penalties and definitions in some matters as a sacrifice of individual rights to the Queens and their Councils. It is just as possible to view them as necessary measures which were evoked by serious situations that threatened the commonwealth. I believe that the evidence in these pages has shown a consistent pattern followed by both Queens, a pattern of vigorous employment which nevertheless respected the traditional limitations.

However that may be, it is apparent that the seeds of conflict were sown, and that Mildmay showed himself a prophet: 'Yet what this may work hereafter in more dangerous times, when the government shall not be so directed by Justice, and Equity, is greatly to be foreseen, lest by example the authority of a proclamation may extend to greater matters than these are.'

APPENDIX 1

A CANON OF ROYAL
PROCLAMATIONS, 1553–1603

The following is a chronological list of the Marian and Elizabethan proclamations accepted as the canon for the purpose of this study. When a proclamation can be dated only to a year, it follows all others with definite dates for that year. The actual title, if any, is provided within quotes. The numbers assigned by different authorities are provided: those by Steele, in the column headed 'St'; by Hughes and Larkin, 'H & L'; in my list of additional proclamations, 'Add', to which one may refer for full bibliographical citations.[1] Elizabethan proclamations which were included in one of Dyson's collections are indicated by the letter 'D'.

THE PROCLAMATIONS OF MARY I

H & L	St	Add	Date	Title
—	423		18 July 1553	Rewards for the apprehension of the Duke of Northumberland
388	424		19 July 1553	Proclaiming Mary's Accession
389	425		28 July 1553	Against seditious rumors
—	426	6	30 July 1553	Dispersing unlawful assemblies
390	427		18 Aug. 1553	Against religious contention
391	428		20 Aug. 1553	'A Proclamation set fourth by the Quenes maiestie, With the aduise of her moost honorable counsell, for sylver and Golde, and the valuation of euery of the same, newe set furth by her heighnes'
392	429		1 Sept. 1553	Remitting Edward's subsidy
393	430		1 Sept. 1553	Concerning coronation service
—	431	7	1 Sept. 1553	Against Northumberland and his confederates
394	432		24 Sept. 1553	Coronation pardon
395	433		20 Nov. 1553	Fuel for London
—	—	8	15 Dec. 1553	Religious ceremonies and practices
396	437		17 Dec. 1553	Vagabonds to leave Court
397	438		early 1554	Wool trade with Low Countries
398	—		14 Jan. 1554	Marriage Articles with Philip

[1] Add. Procs.

253

H & L	St	Add	Date	Title
399	440		27 Jan. 1554	Pardon to Wyatt's supporters who will leave him
400	—		c28 Jan. 1554	Declaring Wyatt's treason
—	—	9	31 Jan. 1554	Declaring Wyatt's treason
401	442		1 Feb. 1554	Wyatt's treasonable purposes
402	443		1 Feb. 1554	Wyatt's treasonable purposes
403	444		3 Feb. 1554	Reward for Wyatt's arrest
404	445		17 Feb. 1554	Foreigners to leave England
—	—	10	18 Feb. 1554	Rebels and aliens to Marshalsea
405	446		1 Mar. 1554	Philip to be treated courteously
406	447		4 Mar. 1554	Valuing foreign coin
408	448-9		8 Mar. 1554	Valuing foreign coin
409	450		15 Mar. 1554	Parliament to meet at Westminster and not Oxford
410	451		c10 Apr. 1554	Seditious bills to be destroyed
411	451a		2 May 1554	Conserving royal game
412	452		4 May 1554	'A Proclamation touching Coygnes'
—	452a	11	22 June 1554	Regulating handguns
413	453		21 July 1554	Nobles to attend royal marriage
414	454		25 July 1554	Regnal styles
416	455		15 Sept. 1554	Vagabonds to leave London area
418	456		13 Nov. 1554	Enlarging Rockingham Forest
419	458		26 Dec. 1554	'A Proclamation set forth by the Kyng and Quenes most excellent maiesties with thaduice of theyr most honorable counsayle of certeyne moneyes and coynes of fyne gold & fine sylver with the valuation of the same, newlye set forth by theyr highnesse'
420	459		26 May 1555	Enforcing many statutes
421	460		31 May 1555	Pardon to northern rebels
—	—	12	31 May 1555	For Blessed Sacrament and Scripture
422	461		13 June 1555	Heretical and seditious books
423	463		c12 Nov. 1555	Against false winding of wool
424	464		18 Dec. 1555	Privileges in carrying money for Merchant Adventurers
425	465		1 Feb. 1556	Preserving game at Greenwich
426	466		1 Apr. 1556	Declaring Dudley's treason
427	467		3 Apr. 1556	Against counterfeit coins
428	468		27 Apr. 1556	Against melting coin
429	469		19 Sept. 1556	Irish coin not current in England
430	470		c26 Sept. 1556	Pricing victual
431	471		22 Dec. 1556	Suppressing rumors about coins
432	472		17 Mar. 1557	Regulating swords and weapons
433	473		30 Apr. 1557	'A Proclamation set fourth by the Kynge and Quenes maiesties, agaynste Thomas Stafforde, and others traytours his adherentes'
434	474		7 June 1557	Reasons for war with France
435	475		9 June 1557	License to attack French at sea
436	476		8 July 1557	License to attack French and Scots at sea
—	479		5 Dec. 1557	Announcing repayment of Queen's debts
437	481		27 Jan. 1558	Authorizing apprehension of Frenchmen in England
438	483		29 Mar. 1558	Against sailors' desertions

H & L	St	Add	Date	Title
439	484		30 Mar. 1558	Against importing French wine
440	485		30 Mar. 1558	Gentlen to return to their homes in country
442	487		3 May 1558	Against unlicensed maritime activity
443	488		6 June 1558	Martial law for heretical and treasonable books
444	489		July 1558	For manning the Navy
445	490		1558	Vagabonds to leave London area
446	491		1558	Suppressing seditious rumors

THE PROCLAMATIONS OF ELIZABETH I

D	H & L	St	Add	Date	Title
D	448	493–4		17 Nov. 1558	Proclaiming Elizabeth's accession
	—	495	13	21 Nov. 1558	Against robbing before coronation
D	449	496		20 Dec. 1558	Ordering officers to service at border with Scotland
D	450	497		21 Dec. 1558	Licensing shipping and restraining piracy
D	451	498		27 Dec. 1558	Regulating preaching and religious ceremonies
D	453	502		7 Feb. 1559	Political lent
D	454	503		22 Feb. 1559	Reviving Edwardian statute on communion under two kinds
	—	—	14	Apr. 1559	Prohibiting religious interludes
D	455	504–5		7 Apr. 1559	Announcing peace with France and Scotland
	—	—	15	early 1559	Concerning Marian bishops
	456	506		28 Apr. 1559	Licensing merchant shipping
D	457	507–8		1 May 1559	'A Proclamation for the Marchauntes Aduenturers'
D	458	509–10		16 May 1559	Prohibiting religious interludes
D	459	511–12		17 May 1559	Enforcing statutes on handguns
D	462	513		13 Aug. 1559	'A Proclamation for keeping of the peace in London'
D	463	514–14a		23 Aug. 1559	'A Proclamation against selling of Shippes'
D	464	517–19		21 Oct. 1559	Enforcing statutes on apparel
D	465	520		6 Jan. 1560	Releasing French ships
D	466	521		25 Feb. 1560	Political lent
D	467	522–3		24 Mar. 1560	'A Proclamation for declarying the Quenes Maiesties purpose, to kepe peace with Fraunce and Scotlande, and to prouyde for the suretie of hir kyngdomes'
	—	524		1560	For maintenance of artillery
D	468	525		24 May 1560	'A Proclamation to adiourne part of Midsommer Terme'
D	469	526–8		19 Sept. 1560	'A Proclamation against breakinge or defacing of monumentes of antiquitie, being set vp in Churches or other publique places for memory, and not for superstition'
D	470	529		22 Sept. 1560	Deporting Anabaptists
D	471	530		27 Sept. 1460	Announcing recoinage

D	H & L	St	Add	Date	Title
—	—	1		29 Sept. 1560	'The Summarie of certaine Reasons, which have moved Quene Elizabeth to procede in reformation of her base and course monnies, and to reduce them to their values, in sorte as they may be turned to fine monies. Appointed to be declared by her Maiestie, by order of her Proclamation, in her Citie of London'
D	472	531		9 Oct. 1560	Valuing foreign coins
D	473	532–3		2 Nov. 1560	Identifying coin
D	474	534		4 Nov. 1560	'A Proclamation for pardon to them of Tyndale and Riddesdale'
D	475	536–7		23 Dec. 1560	Suppressing rumors about coin
D	477	538–9		17 Feb. 1561	Political lent
D	478	541–2		19 Feb. 1561	Calling in base coins
D	480	544–5		12 June 1561	Calling in base coins
D	481	546		8 July 1561	Forbidding exporting arms to Russia
D	482	547		21 July 1561	Against pirates harming Spanish
—	—		16	mid 1561	Against unlawful games
	483	549		2 Sept. 1561	Vagabonds to leave Court
	484	550		18 Sept. 1561	Forbidding early sale of new wine
D	485	551–2		29 Sept. 1561	Regulating payment of pensions to ex-religious
D	486	553		30 Oct. 1561	'A Proclamation made for the reurent vsage of Churches and Churchyardes'
D	487	556		15 Nov. 1561	Valuing foreign coin
D	488	557		30 Jan. 1562	Suppressing rumors about coin
	489	—		c31 Jan. 1562	Political lent
D	490	558		10 Mar. 1562	Ordering victual to market
	492	560–1		13 Mar. 1562	Suppressing rumors about coin
	494	565–6		7 May 1562	Regulating apparel
D	497	570–1		10 Aug. 1562	'A Proclamation against the deceiptful wynding and folding of Wooles'
	497.5	—		24 Sept. 1562	Dispatching forces to Newhaven
D	498	572		21 Dec. 1562	'A Proclamation for the speedy payment of the Queenes Rents, Tenthes, and other dueties'
D	499	573		8 Feb. 1563	Against pirates harming Spanish
—	—		17	early 1563	Political lent
D	501	574		7 June 1563	Wage rates: Rutland
	502	—		8 June 1563	Wage rates: Kent
	503	—		mid 1563	Wage rates: Exeter
D	504	—		mid 1563	Wage rates: New Windsor
D	505	575		8 June 1563	Wage rates: Lincolnshire
	506	—		9 June 1563	Wage rates: York
	507	—		12 June 1563	Wage rates: Lincoln
D	508	577		13 July 1563	Licensing seizure of French prizes
D	509	576		July 1563	Wage rates: Southampton
D	510	578		1 Aug. 1563	Explaining loss of Newhaven
	512	—		3 Aug. 1563	Wage rates: London
D	513	580–1		1 Sept. 1563	Against pirates harming Spanish
—	—		18	mid 1563	Wage rates: Cambridge
D	514	582		21 Sept. 1563	Adjourning Law term
D	515	583–4		10 Dec. 1563	Adjourning Law term
	516	585		Dec. 1563	Prohibiting portraits of Queen

D	H & L	St	Add	Date	Title
D	517	586		8 Jan. 1564	Prohibiting import of French wines
	—	—	19	Feb. 1564	Political lent
D	518	587–8		30 Jan. 1564	Lowering price of hops
D	519	589–90		18 Feb. 1564	Against pirates harming Spanish
D	520	593		23 Mar. 1564	Cancelling Maundy ceremony
D	521	594		23 Mar. 1564	Halting imports from Low Countries
D	522	595		30 Apr. 1564	Announcing peace with France
D	523	596		11 May 1564	'A Proclamation to explane the Quene's Maiesties meanyng vpon a former made in March last'
	524	—		15 June 1564	Wage rates: Exeter
D	525	597		31 July 1564	Ordering apprehension of pirate Thomas Cobham
D	526	598		31 July 1564	Ordering arrest of pirates
	527	—		12 Aug. 1564	Wage rates: London
D	528	599–600		11 Nov. 1564	For full payment of Privy Seal loans
D	529	603–4		22 Dec. 1564	Setting prices for wines
D	530	605–6		29 Dec. 1564	Renewing trade with Low Countries
	—	607	20	14 Mar. 1565	Political lent
D	531	608–9		21 Mar. 1565	Prohibiting assaults on arresting officers
	—	609a		22 Mar. 1565	Licensing export of grain from East Riding, Yorks.
D	533	610		1 June 1565	Prohibiting use of foreign debased coins
D	534	611		14 July 1565	Enforcing statutes on horse and armor
	535	—		15 Aug. 1565	Wage rates: London
	536	—		Aug. 1565	Wage rates: Lidd
	—	—	21	1565	Wage rates: Sandwich
	—	—	2	1565	Wage rates: York
D	537	612–13		16 Oct. 1565	Continuing trade with Low Countries
D	538	614		1 Dec. 1565	Prohibiting counterfeit and foreign coins
D	539	615		20 Dec. 1565	Setting prices for wines
D	540	616		22 Dec. 1565	Gauging Scottish fish barrels
D	541	617		20 Jan. 1566	Against engrossing grain
D	542	618		12 Feb. 1566	Regulating apparel
	—	—	22	early 1566	Political lent
	543	—		May 1566	Wage rates: London
	544	—		June 1566	Wage rates: Exeter
D	545	—		June 1566	Wage rates: Northamptonshire
D	546	619–20		8 July 1566	Continuing trade with Low Countries
D	547	621		10 Nov. 1566	Protecting informers
	548	623		11 Jan. 1567	Against those troubling the Portuguese
	—	—	23	15 Feb. 1567	Political lent
	—	—	24	1567	Wage rates: Southampton
	—	—	3	1567	Wage rates: Exeter
	—	—	25	Summer 1567	Proclaiming the lottery
D	549	625		3 Jan. 1568	Deferring lottery date
D	550	626–7		24 June 1568	Enforcing abstinence on Wednesdays
	551	—		6 July 1568	Wage rates: London
D	552	628		13 July 1568	Advancing date for drawing the lottery
D	553	629		15 July 1568	Ordering arrest of Low Country rebels in England
D	554	630–1		2 Nov. 1568	Postponing date for drawing lottery
	555	—		Nov. 1568	Prohibiting arrest of Frenchmen or French goods

D	H & L	St	Add	Date		Title
D	556	632		6 Jan.	1569	'A proclamation to admonishe all persons to forbeare traffique in the king of Spaynes contrays, with other aduertisementes for aunswering of a generall arrest made in the lowe countreys of the Duke of Alva'
D	557	633		9 Jan.	1569	Announcing reduced prizes in the lottery
D	558	634		22 Jan.	1569	'A Proclamation declaryng the vntruth of certaine malitious reportes deuised and publisshed in the Realme of Scotlande'
D	559	635–6		3 Feb.	1569	Enforcing statutes on horse and armor
	—	—	26		1569	Political lent
D	560	637		1 Mar.	1569	'A proclamation for maintenaunce of Tillage'
D	561	638		1 Mar.	1569	Prohibiting seditious books
D	562	639		27 Apr.	1569	'A proclamation to represse all piracies and depredations vpon the Seas'
D	563	640–1		3 Aug.	1569	'A proclamation against the maintenaunce of Pirates'
D	564	642		28 Sept.	1569	Adjourning law term
D	565	643		3 Oct.	1569	Prohibiting access to royal Court
D	566	644		23 Oct.	1569	Adjourning law term
D	567	645		24 Nov.	1569	Declaring treason of the northern Earls' rebellion
D	568	647		18 Feb.	1570	Pardon for northern rebels
D	570	650–1		4 Apr.	1570	'A proclamation of the Queenes Maiesties pardon graunted to certaine of her subiectes vppon the west borders, hauyng offended by Leonard Dacres abusyng of them, in a rebellion lately stirred by him'
D	571	652		10 Apr.	1570	'A declaration of the iust, honourable, and necessarie causes, that move the Queenes Maiestie to leuie and send an armie to the borders of Scotland, with an assuraunce of her intention, to continue the peace with the crowne, and quiet subiectes of the sayde Realme of Scotlande'
	572	—		30 Apr.	1570	Wage rates: London
D	573	653		6 June	1570	Ordering dismissals of officers negligent in repressing piracy
D	574	654		8 June	1570	Wage rates: Kingston upon Hull
	575	—		June	1570	Wage rates: Chester
D	576	655		30 June	1570	Inviting claims for goods seized by the Spanish in the Low Countries
D	577	656		1 July	1570	'A proclamation made agaynst seditious and trayterous Bookes, Billes, and Writinges'
D	578	657		20 July	1570	Requiring goods seized from the Spanish to be declared
D	579	658		24 Sept.	1570	Adjourning law term
D	580	659		14 Nov.	1570	'A Proclamation agaynst manteyners of seditious persons, and of trayterous bookes and writinges'
D	581	661		24 Nov.	1571	Announcing repayment of Queen's loans

D	H & L	St	Add	Date	Title
D	582	663–4		3 Jan. 1572	'A Proclamation for the execution of the lawes agaynst vnlawfull Reteyners &c'
D	583	665		14 Jan. 1572	Announcing sale of confiscated Spanish property
D	584	666–7		13 Feb. 1572	Revoking commissions to inquire into concealed lands
	—	667a	27	1572	Political lent
D	585	668		1 Mar. 1572	'The fourme of the Proclamation to be published in the port townes, and market townes, or other publique places, within the limittes of the Commission geuen by the Queenes Maiestie, the first of March, 1571. to sundry persons of credite, for reformation of disorders vpon the sea coastes'
	588	675		29 Apr. 1572	Enforcing statutes on hats and caps
D	589	676–7		16 Sept. 1572	'A Proclamation for restraint of transportation of grayne beyond the seas'
D	590	678–9		22 Dec. 1572	'A Proclamation for prises of wines'
D	591	553[bis]		1572	For peace in churches and churchyards
	592	—		c12 Feb. 1573	Political lent
D	594	681–2		28 Apr. 1573	Enforcing statutes on hats and caps
D	595	686		30 Apr. 1573	'A Proclamation for the restitution of thentercourse betwixt the kingdomes, countreys, and subiectes of the Queenes maiestie and the king of Spayne'
	596	—		Apr. 1573	Wage rates: London
D	597	687		11 June 1573	Enforcing use of *Book of Common Prayer*; repressing objectionable books
D	598	688		28 Sept. 1573	Against seditious books
D	599	689		20 Oct. 1573	'A Proclamation agaynst the despisers or breakers of the orders prescribed in the booke of Common prayer'
	600	—		Mar. 1573	Political lent
D	601	690		15 June 1573	Regulating apparel
D	602	691		1 Oct. 1574	Adjourning law term
	604	—		c17 Feb. 1575	Political lent
	606	—		Apr. 1575	Wage rates: Chester
D	607	693–4		15 July 1575	Setting prices for wines
	—	695	28	20 Sept. 1575	Postponing Woodstock Fair
D	608	696–7		26 Sept. 1575	Adjourning law term
	609	698		26 Oct. 1575	Prohibiting mariners' service with foreign princes at sea
D	610	699–700		28 Oct. 1575	Prohibiting going to sea without a license
	—	—	29	19 Nov. 1575	Enforcing statutes on hats and caps
	611	701		Dec. 1575	Against carrying weapons
D	612	702		26 Mar. 1576	Offering rewards to discover authors of seditious libels
	613	—		12 May 1576	Wage rates: London
D	614	704–5		27 July 1576	Setting prices of wines
D	615	703		July 1576	Wage rates: Canterbury
D	616	706		20 Sept. 1576	'A Proclamation for the ordering of the exchange of Money vsed by Merchants, according to the Lawes and Statutes of the Realme'

D	H & L	St	Add	Date	Title
	617	—		24 Sept. 1576	Wage rates: Chester
D	619	708–9		29 Sept. 1576	Adjourning law term
D	620	710–11		10 Nov. 1576	Renewing trade with Portugal
D	621	712–13		28 Nov. 1576	Against buying up wools; regulating wool fells
D	622	714		14 Dec. 1576	Enforcing statutes against vagabonds
	—	—	30	1577	Political lent
D	623	717–18		16 Feb. 1577	Regulating apparel
	—	—	31	10 Aug. 1577	Wage rates: Southampton
D	624	719		16 Sept. 1577	Adjourning law term
D	625	720–1		30 Sept. 1577	Announcing payment of the Queen's debts
	626	—		4 Oct. 1577	Wage rates: Doncaster
D	627	722		15 Oct. 1577	Adjourning law term
	—	—	32	31 June 1578	Wage rates: Bath
	628	—		28 July 1578	Wage rates: London
	—	—		Aug. 1578	Wage rates: Exeter
D	629	724		22 Sept. 1578	Adjourning law term
D	630	725		20 Oct. 1578	Adjourning law term
D	632	729		14 Nov. 1578	Adjourning law term
D	633	730–2		24 Nov. 1578	Setting prices for wines
D	634	683		1578	Enforcing statutes on hats and caps
D	635	554		1578	For peace in churches and churchyards
D	636	733–4		15 Jan. 1579	Reviving statute for sowing of hemp and flax
D	637	735		31 Jan. 1579	Enforcing statute against vagabonds
	638	—		17 Feb. 1579	Political lent
	—	—	34	17 Feb. 1579	For purveyors in London
D	639	736–7		28 Feb. 1579	Renewing trade with Low Countries; regulating wool fells
D	640	738		30 Apr. 1579	Against buying up wool
	—	—	37	9 June 1579	Wage rates: Bath
	—	—	35	Summer 1579	Commanding Courteous Treatment of French Ambassadors
D	641	739		26 July 1579	'A Proclamation against the common vse of Dagges, Handgunnes, Harquebuzes, Calliuers, and Cotes of Defence'
	—	—	36	20 Aug. 1579	Wage rates: Southampton
D	642	740		27 Sept. 1579	Denouncing 'Gaping Gulf'
D	643	741		24 Nov. 1579	Setting prices for wines
D	644	742–3		15 Dec. 1579	Cancelling commissions to enquire on concealed lands
D	645	744		20 Dec. 1579	Licensing free import of French wines
D	646	745		12 Feb. 1580	'A Proclamation vvith certayne clauses of diuers Statutes, & other necessary additions, first published in the xix. yeare of the Queenes Maiesties reigne, and now reuiued by her highnes commandment to be put in execution, vpon the penalties in the same conteined'
	—	—	38	1580	Political lent
D	647	746		14 Apr. 1580	'A Proclamation for horsemen and breed of horses for seruice'
D	649	749–50		7 July 1580	Prohibiting new buildings in London and surrounding areas

H & L	St	Add	Date	Title
650	751		15 July 1580	Against rebels and traitors dwelling abroad
651	—		5 Aug. 1580	Wage rates: London
652	752		3 Oct. 1580	'A Proclamation against the Sectaries of the Family of loue'
653	753		3 Nov. 1580	'A Proclamation for the prices of wine'
655	755–6		10 Jan. 1581	'A Proclamation for reuocation of students from beyond the seas, and against the reteining of Jesuites'
656	757		18 Apr. 1581	Commanding honor be shown to the French ambassador
657	758–9		19 May 1581	Reviving the statute against usury
658	760		21 Sept. 1581	'A Proclamation for adiournment of parte of Michaelmas Terme. 1581'
659	761–2		11 Nov. 1581	'A proclamation for the prices of wine'
660	763		1 Apr. 1582	'A Proclamation to denounce Jesuites traitours'
—	—	39	1582	Wage rates: Exeter
661	764		18 Sept. 1582	'A Proclamation for adiournment of parte of Michaelmas Terme. 1582'
662	765		8 Oct. 1582	'A Proclamation for keeping the Terme at Hertford Castell, and for adiournement of the same, from Mense Michaelis, vntill Crastino Animarum'
663	766		16 Nov. 1582	'A Proclamation for the prices of Wine'
664	768		19 Apr. 1583	'A Proclamation against Retainers'
666	—		2 June 1583	Wage rates: Colchester
667	770		30 June 1583	'A Proclamation against certaine seditious and scismatical Bookes and Libelles. &c.'
668	—		23 Aug. 1583	Wage rates: London
—	—	40	1583	Wage rates: Barnstaple
—	—	41	27 Aug. 1583	Wage rates: Exeter
669	771–2		6 Nov. 1583	'A Proclamation for the prices of wines'
670	—		27 Feb. 1584	Political lent
671	—		7 July 1584	Wage rates: London
—	—	42	1584	Wage rates: Exeter
—	—	43	1584	Wage rates: Southampton
—	—	44	1584	Wage rates: York
672	775		12 Oct. 1584	'A Proclamation for the suppressing of seditious Bookes and Libelles'
673	776		13 Nov. 1584	'A Proclamation for the prices of Wines'
674	—		18 Feb. 1585	Political lent
676	—		16 Aug. 1585	Wage rates: London
—	—	45	27 Aug. 1585	Wage rates: Exeter
—	—	46	1585	Wage rates: York
677	781		14 Oct. 1585	'A Proclamation against bringing in of Wines or other Merchandise from Bourdeaux, in respect of the Plague being there'
678	782		14 Oct. 1585	'A Proclamation against the sowing of woade'
682	—		16 June 1585	Wage rates: London
683	788		11 Aug. 1586	Ordering arrests of those in the Babington plot

D	H & L	St	Add	Date	Title
D	684	789		15 Sept. 1586	'A Proclamation notifying the dissolution of the Parliament that was prorogued vnto the xiiii day of Nouember. 1586'
D	685	790		4 Dec. 1586	'A true Copie of the Proclamation lately published by the Queenes Maiestie, vnder the great Seale of England, for the declaring of the Sentence, lately giuen against the Queene of Scottes, in fourme as followeth'
D	686	791		2 Jan. 1587	Ordering that markets be supplied with grain
D	687	555		c21 Jan. 1587	For peace in churches and churchyards
D	688	792		6 Feb. 1587	Suppressing seditious rumors
	689	—		Mar. 1587	Political lent
	—	—	4	20 May 1587	Enlarging the market for cloths
	691	—		3 Aug. 1587	Wage rates: London
	—	—	47	1587	Wage rates: York
	692	—		c8 Oct. 1587	Enforcing the statutes against vagabonds
D	693	794		12 Oct. 1587	'A Proclamation for reforming of the deceipts in diminishing the value of the coines of Gold currant within the Queenes Maiesties dominions, and for remedying the losses that might growe by receiuing thereof being diminished'
D	694	795-6		2 Nov. 1587	Ordering gentlemen to return to their country homes
D	695	797		16 Dec. 1587	'A Proclamation for Waights published by the Queenes Maiesties commaundement'
	696	—		11 Feb. 1588	Political lent
D	697	798-9		13 Feb. 1588	'A declaration of the Queenes Maiesties will and commaundement, to haue certaine Lawes and orders put in execution, against the excesse of Apparell, notified by her commandement in the Starre-Chamber the xiij. of Februarie in the xxx. yeere of her reigne'
D	699	802		1 July 1588	'A Proclamation against the bringing in, dispersing, vttering and keeping of Bulles from the Sea of Rome, and other Traiterous and sedicious Libels, Bookes and Pamphlets'
	700	—		20 July 1588	Wage rates: Exeter
D	701	803		7 Aug. 1588	Pricing victual near Tilbury Camp
	702	—		24 Aug. 1588	Wage rates: London
D	703	804		25 Aug. 1588	Forbidding soldiers to sell arms
	—	—	48	1588	Wage rates: York
D	704	805		4 Oct. 1588	Ordering pressed soldiers to report for service
D	705	806		14 Oct. 1588	'A Proclamation for the prorogation of the Parliament from the xij. of Nouember next comming, to the iiii. of Februarie following'
D	706	807		9 Nov. 1588	'A Proclamation for the restraint of transportation of Graine'
D	707	808		26 Nov. 1588	'A Proclamation for the prices of Wines'

D	H & L	St	Add	Date	Title
D	708	809–10		23 Jan. 1589	'A proclamation concerning the Souldiors appointed to serue in her Maiesties seruice beyond the Seas, vnder the charge of Sir Iohn Norris and Sir Francis Drake'
D	709	812		13 Feb. 1589	'A Proclamation against certaine seditious and Schismatical Bookes and Libels, &c.'
	710	—		14 Feb. 1589	Political lent
	711	—		24 June 1589	Wage rates: Kent
	713	—		23 July 1589	Wage rates: London
D	714	816		24 July 1589	'A Proclamation, inhibiting the execution of any exemplification of her Maiesties graunt of the penaltie of the Statute for sowing of Hemp and Flaxe seede'
D	715	817		24 Aug. 1589	Prohibiting unlawful assembly
	—	—	49	1589	Wage rates: Exeter
D	716	818		13 Nov. 1589	'A Proclamation against vagrant souldiers and others'
D	717	819		18 Dec. 1589	'A Proclamation for the prices of Wines'
D	718	820		13 Jan. 1590	'A Proclamation for the calling in and frustrating all Commissions for the making of Salt-peter granted forth before that to George Evelin and others, the 28. of Ianuary. 1587. whereby many of her Maiesties subjects were greatly abused, as also that all peter made by the said later Commissions doe bring the same into her Maiesties store, &c.'
	—	—	50	Mar. 1590	Political lent
D	720–1	823–4		13 Mar. 1590	Mitigating the statutes for wool cloth in Norfolk, Suffolk and Essex
D	722	825		6 June 1590	'A Proclamation commaunding the execution of an Acte of Parliament, prouided for auoiding of dangerous annoyances about Cities, Borroughes and Townes within the Realme'
	723	—		4 Aug. 1590	Wage rates: London
	—	—	51	1590	Wage rates: York
D	725	826		24 Sept. 1590	Setting curfew for apprentices
D	726	827		8 Oct. 1590	'A Proclamation forbidding the transportation and carriage of all manner of graine and Beere out of the Realme, to endure vntill the next Michaelmas hereafter following. The viij. of October, 1590'
D	727	828		1 Dec. 1590	'A Proclamation for the prices of Wines'
D	729	684		1590	Enforcing statute on hats and caps
D	730	830		3 Feb. 1591	'The Queenes Maiestie proclamation, declaring her Princlie intention to inhibit her subiects vpon most extreme paines, from offending on the Seas; any persons in their ships or goods, being the subiectes of any Prince, Potentate, or State, in amitie with her Maiestie'
	—	—	52	1591	Political lent

D	H & L	St	Add	Date	Title
	731	—		12 Apr. 1591	Wage rates: Hertfordshire
D	732	832		14 Apr. 1591	'A Proclamation to forbid all maner of persons to resort to any Townes held by the French Kings rebels, or to traffique with any of them, vpon paine to be punished as Traitors: with a declaration of the iust Causes of the said prohibition. Giuen vnder her Maiesties signet at Greenwich the xiij. day of April 1591, and of her Maiesties reigne the xxxiij. yeere'
	735	845		20 June 1591	Prohibiting unlawful assembly under pain of martial law
	736	—		8 Aug. 1591	Enforcing statute against vagabonds
D	737	836		16 Sept. 1591	'A Proclamation straightly commanding that no Corne nor other Victuall, nor any Ordonance, nor furniture for shipping be carried into any of the king of Spaines countries, vpon paine to be punished as in case of Treason: nor that any of the like kinds be carried out of the Realme to other Countries without speciall licence vpon great paines'
D	738	837-8		18 Oct. 1591	'A declaration of great troubles pretended against the Realm by a number of Seminarie Priests and Iesuits, sent, and very secretly dispersed in the same, to worke great Treasons vnder a false pretence of Religion, with a prouision very necessary for remedy thereof. Published by this her Maiesties Proclamation'
D	740	840		5 Nov. 1591	Placing vagrants under martial law
D	741	841-2		17 Dec. 1591	Setting prices for wines
D	742	843-4		29 Dec. 1591	'A Proclamation to be published in Cornewall, Deuonshire, Dorcetshire and Hampshire, for restitution of goods lately taken on the Seas from the Subiects of the King of Spayne by way of Reprisall'
D	743	846		8 Jan. 1592	'A Proclamation to charge all persons that have gotten any mander goods into their possession, which haue beene taken on the Seas this last yeere, and haue not bene customed, to restore the same vpon paine to bee punished as Felons and Pirates'
D	744	847		20 Jan. 1592	'A Proclamation for the reformation of sundry abuses about making of Clothes, called Deuonshire Kersies, or Dozens, whereby the Statutes made in Queene Maries time, for the weight, length, and breadth thereof, may be duely obserued hereafter'
D	746	850		2 Mar. 1592	Against deserters from the Navy
	—	—	53	July 1592	Concerning pressed mariners
	—	—	54	1592	Wage rates: Exeter

D	H & L	St	Add	Date	Title
D	747	851		11 Sept. 1592	'A Proclamation by her Maiesties commandement, forbidding the making or forging of any Iron Ordonance, aboue the quantitie of the piece commonly called the Minion, without the Queenes speciall licence: and prohibiting also the cariage out of the Realme to any forraine parts, of any maner of Ordonance of brasse or Iron, vpon the paines hereafter contained in the Proclamation'
D	748	852		18 Sept. 1592	'A Proclamation for adiournment of part of Michaelmas Terme. 1592'
D	749	853		23 Sept. 1592	Ordering declaration of goods from Spanish vessel taken as a prize
D	750	854		12 Oct. 1592	'A Proclamation to restraine accesse to the Court, of all such as are not bound to ordinarie attendance, or that shall not be otherwise licenced by her Maiestie'
D	751	855		21 Oct. 1592	'A Proclamation for keeping the Terme at Hartford Castle, and for adiournment of the same from Mense Michaelis, vntill Crastino Animarum'
D	752	856		22 Nov. 1592	'A Proclamation to adiourne the Terme ending for Michaelmas vnto Westminster, to beginne at Octabis Hillarij'
	753	—		24 Apr. 1593	Wage rates: Chester
D	754	860		28 May 1593	Adjourning law term
D	755	861		18 June 1593	'A Proclamation to restraine accesse to the Court, of all such as are not bound to ordinarie attendance, or that shall not be otherwise by her Maiestie' [sic]
	756	862		30 July 1593	Wage rates: East Riding, Yorks.
D	757	863		6 Aug. 1593	Postponing Bartholomew Fair because of plague
	—	—	55	1593	Wage rates: York
D	758	864		15 Sept. 1593	'A Proclamation to reforme the disorder in accesse of greater number of persons to the Court, than haue iust cause so to doe'
D	759	865		24 Sept. 1593	Adjourning law term
D	760	866		22 Nov. 1593	'A Proclamation to adiourne the Terme ending for Michaelmas, vnto Westminster, to begin at Octabis Hillarij'
D	761	540		c17 Feb. 1594	Political lent
D	762	867		21 Feb. 1594	'A Proclamation for suppressing of the multitude of idle Vagabonds, and auoyding of certaine mischievous dangerous persons from her Maiesties Court'
D	763	—		10 Apr. 1594	Wage rates: Devon
D	764	869		1 Aug. 1594	'A Proclamation against all persons, that disorderly enter into shippes that are brought as Prizes into any Hauen, and that doe secretly buy or conuey away the goods before they be customed, and allowed as lawfull Prize'
	765	868		30 Aug. 1594	Wage rates: Canterbury

D	H & L	St	Add	Date		Title
D	766	871		2 Dec.	1594	'A Proclamation against the carriage of Dags, and for reformation of some other great disorders'
D	767	622			1594	Protecting informers
D	—	715			1594	Enforcing statute against vagabonds
	768	—		8 Mar.	1595	Political lent
D	769	873		4 July	1595	'The Queenes Maiesties Proclamation for staying of all vnlawfull assemblies in and about the Citie of London, and for orders to punish the same'
D	—	875	5	30 Aug.	1595	Wage rates: Cardigan
	—	—	56		1595	Wage rates: York
	770	—		30 Aug.	1595	Wage rates: Exeter
	771	877		30 Aug.	1595	Wage rates: Higham Ferrers
D	772	878		30 Aug.	1595	Wage rates: New Sarum
D	773	876		30 Aug.	1595	Wage rates: Lancaster
D	774	—		30 Aug.	1595	Wage rates: Devon
	776	—			1595	Revoking commissions on saltpeter
D	777	716		11 Feb.	1596	Enforcing statute against vagabonds
	—	—	57	27 Feb.	1596	Political lent
	778	—		Apr.	1596	Wage rates: Chester
D	779	882		3 May	1596	'A Proclamation against sundry abuses practiced by diuers lewd & audacious persons falsly naming themselues Messengers of her Maiesties Chamber, trauelling from place to place with writings countefeited in forme of Warrants: As also against another sort of vagabond persons that carrie counterfeit Pasports wherewith to begge and gather almes'
D	780	883		29 May	1596	'A Proclamation concerning the true and lawfull winding of woolles'
D	781	884		31 July	1596	'A Proclamation for the dearth of Corne'
D	782	885-6		20 Aug.	1596	'A Proclamation commanding all persons vpon the Borders of England, to keepe peace towards Scotland, vpon the like Proclamation by the King of Scots towards England'
	—	—	58		1596	Wage rates: York
D	784	888		2 Nov.	1596	'The Queens Maiesties Proclamation, 1. For obseruation of former Orders against Ingrossers, & Regrators of Corne, 2. And to see the Markets furnished with Corne. 3. And also against the carying of Corne out of the Realme. 4. And a prohibition to men of hospitalitie from remouing from their habitation in the time of dearth. 5. And finally a strait commandement to all officers hauing charge of Forts to reside thereon personally, and no inhabitant to depart from the Sea coast'
	785	—		8 Apr.	1597	Wage rates: Chester
D	786	890		6 July	1597	Regulating apparel

D	H & L	St	Add	Date	Title
D	787	891		23 July 1597	'Certaine notes out of the Statutes for dispensations with sundry persons not being in any certaintie before expressed, whereof all such persons, as thereby are to be dispensed withall, may be better enformed, by perusall of the said Statutes vnto which they are to be referred'
D	788	892		13 Aug. 1597	'A Proclamation commaunding all persons upon the Borders of England, to keepe Peace towards Scotland, upon the like Proclamation by the King of Scotts towards England'
D	789	893		15 Sept. 1597	Defending Lord Mayor against rumors of hoarding grain; ordering grain to markets
D	790	894		27 Sept. 1597	'A Proclamation publishing certaine iust causes for prohibition and stay of cariage of Victual, and other prouisions of Warre by Seas into Spaine, for continuance of the King of Spaines purposes to inuade most vnjustly her Maiesties Dominions; With authoritie for the stay thereof by Sea'
D	791	685		1597	Enforcing statute on hats and caps
	793	895		26 Feb. 1598	Political lent
D	795	898		23 Aug. 1598	'A Proclamation for the restreining and punishment of Forestallers, Regraters and Ingrossers of Corne and Graine, and for the prohibition of making any maner of Starch, within her Maiesties Realme and Dominions'
D	796	899		9 Sept. 1598	'The Queenes Maiestie Proclamation for supressing of the multitudes of idle Vagabonds, and for staying of all vnlawfull assemblies, especially in and about the Citie of London, and for orders to punish the same'
	—	—	60	1598	Against seditious books
D	797	900		8 Feb. 1599	'The Queenes Maiesties Proclamation, declaring her Princely intention to inhibite her Subiects vpon most extreme paynes from offending on the Seas, any persons in their Ships or goods, being the Subiectes of any Prince, Potentate or State, in Amitie with her Maiestie'
D	798	153(Irish)		31 Mar. 1599	'The Queenes Maiesties Proclamation declaring her princely resolution in sending ouer of her Army into the Realme of Ireland'
D	799	904		14 Jan. 1600	'A Proclamation for the publication of her Maiesties most gracious commission vnder the great seale of England, for auoyding of the trouble and charges that grow by concealements, and that her

APPENDIX I

D	H & L	St	Add	Date	Title
					Highnesse louing subiects may compound for securities of their estates from her Maiestie for a perpetuall quiet to them and their posterities'
D	800	905		14 Jan. 1600	'A Proclamation for the due obseruation of Fish days, suppressing of vnnecessary number of Alehouses, and for the better execution of the late acte for punishment of Rogues, Vagabonds and Beggars'
D	801	907		18 Mar. 1600	'A Proclamation concerning Coyne, Plate, and Bullion of Gold and Silver'
D	802	908		28 Mar. 1600	'A Proclamation inhibiting the sowing of Woad'
D	803	909		2 June 1600	'A Proclamation conteyning her Maiesties pleasure, how those shalbe dealt withall, which haue falsly slandered her Maiesties proceedings and her Ministers, by spreading vile and odious Libels, and brutes to stirre discontentment among her people: containing also a sharpe commandement to all Iustices of Peace and other principall persons in the Countreys, to see Ingrossers of Corne and Graine duely punished'
D	804	910		21 Dec. 1600	'A Proclamation prohibiting the vse and cariage of Dagges, Birding pieces, and other Gunnes, contrary to the Law'
D	807	912		7 Feb. 1601	'A proclamation for the clothiers of Suffolke Norffolke and Essex'
D	808	913–15		9 Feb. 1601	Declaring Earl of Essex a traitor
D	809	916–18		15 Feb. 1601	Declaring martial law on vagabonds in and around London
D	810	920		5 Apr. 1601	Offering reward for information on libels circulating against the Queen
D	811	921		3 July 1601	'A Proclamation for prohibition of transporting moneys into Ireland'
D	812	922		28 Nov. 1601	'A Proclamation for the reformation of many abuses and misdemeanours committed by Patentees of certain Priuiledges and Licences, to the generall good of all her Maiesties louing Subiects'
D	813	925		20 Mar. 1602	'A Proclamation to represse all Piracies and Depredations vpon the Sea'
D	814	926		early 1602	'A Proclamation for Measures, published by the Queenes Commandement'
D	815	927		22 June 1602	'A Proclamation concerning new buildings and Inmates, in or about the Citie of London'
D	816	929		15 Sept. 1602	Preserving Queen's game
D	817	930		5 Nov. 1602	'A Proclamation for proceeding against Iesuites and Secular Priestes, their Recuiers, Relieuers, and Maintainers'

NON-ROYAL PROCLAMATIONS

Not royal commands: made by others

Mary (6)

Procs. 393.5/— (herald); —/439 (Wyatt); —/441 (Iseley); —/547 (Pope);
—/477 (Lieutenant General); —/478 (Lord Mayor of London).

Elizabeth (45)

a. Privy Council's lenten orders: Procs. —/811, —/822, —/831, —/848,
—/857, —/872, —/880, —/889, —/896, —/901, —/906, —/919, —/924,
—/931.

b. Other conciliar proclamations: Procs. —/515 (apparel); —/773
(posts);[2] 712/814 (returning soldiers); 728/829 (regulations for troops in
Low Countries); 745/849 (returning soldiers); —/858 (returning soldiers);
—/870 (restraining access to Court); —/881 (posts); —/928 (against
engrossing wool).

c. Others: Procs. 451.5/— (herald);[3] 459.5/— (commissioners concluding peace); —/548 (instructions for Vice-Admirals); —/591 (plague
order for Westminster);[4] —/592 (plague order for London);[5] —/601
(order regarding swans); —/646 (Lord President's proclamation during
northern rebellion); —/660 (orders for ecclesiastical commissioners);
—/662 (orders for commissioners for concealed lands); 605/— (regulating

---

[1] See the general discussion above, pp. 9–12.

[2] Request that these 'articles' be set in print, PRO, SP 12/163/77. This 'proclamation'
was featured in an advertisement by Rank Xerox in the international edition of *Newsweek*,
24 March 1969.

[3] There is no indication that Elizabeth's style was commanded to be proclaimed under
a writ; it was proclaimed three times on St George's Day in three languages (texts in
Bodleian Libr., Ashmolean MSS 763/II.4 and 1120/II), and the ordinances made by the
Earl Marshal a few years later specified that 'the proclaiming of the Queen's Majesty's
style' was the work of Garter King-at-Arms. *Ibid.* XVIII/I. Yet there was a writ of proclamation for the styles of Philip and Mary after their coronation (proc. 414/454).

[4] An order from the Queen to Sir William Cecil as Steward of Westminster and Sir
Ambrose Cave as Steward of London, ordering them to take order for the plague, is in
PRO, SP 12/48/70.   [5] *Ibid.* Printed by the city's printer, John Daye.

rates for insurance); —/723 (plague order); —/767 (orders for ecclesiastical commissioners); —/778 (order regarding swans); —/784 (orders for Vice-Admirals); —/800 (Lord Treasurer's order for balances and weights); —/813 (orders for ecclesiastical commissioners); 724/— (ordering arrest of fugitive);[6] —/834 (orders from the Admiralty); —/835 (Lord Admiral's order); —/— (personal order of Lord Burghley [in Dyson only]); —/902 (Spanish general); —/903 (military commander's order on prices for victuals).

Not royal commands: statutes

Mary (5)

Procs. 395.5/436; —/434; —/435; —/462; —/482.

Elizabeth (4)

Procs. —/499; —/500; —/501; 457.5/—.

Royal commands, not under writ of proclamation

Mary (6)

Procs. 407/— (Injunctions for religion); 415/— (pardon on occasion of coronation);[7] 417/455a (ordering obedience to Cardinal Pole [letters patent]); —/480 (relief for Calais); 441/486 (Winchester's patent of lieutenancy);[8] 447/492 (order for posts).

Elizabeth (41)

a. Church briefs and supporting letters:[9] Procs. 476/535; 500/—; 593/680; 603/692; 631/726; 648/747; —/748; 675/780; 681/787; 719/821; 734/—; 775/879; 783/887.

b. Supplementary articles framed by the Council: —/— (breviate of statutes in 1561);[10] 495/567 (apparel); —/624 (chart of prizes for the lottery); 569/648 (oath for northern rebels's pardon); 586/669 (breviate of statutes on unlawful games); 618/707 (rates for the exchange); —/774 (supplementary orders for the post); —/777 (supplementary orders for the post); 679/— (breviate of statutes on unlawful games); 739/839 (articles for the commission against Jesuits); —/874 (supplementary orders regarding unlawful assemblies).

c. Exemplifications of official grants or orders: 479/543 (regarding Portugese shipping); 511/579 (punishment for illegal seizure of the French);[11] —/783 (private statute); 690/793 (allowing many merchants to buy and sell cloth);[12] 733/833 (regarding posts).

[6] The Council's order, referring to its 'warrant', is noted in *APC*, xix, 478–9.

[7] Issued as letters patent. Yet, as was the case with the proclaiming of the royal style, the pardon in 1553 (proc. 394/433) was issued under a writ and proclaimed.

[8] Noted as proclaimed in London in Corp. London RO, Journal xvii, fo. 66, but it was common for such patents to be proclaimed on the recipient's initiative.

[9] See Wyndham Anstis Bewes, *Church Briefs or Royal Warrants for Collections for Charitable Objects* (London, 1896). [10] Above, p. 68.

[11] An order from the Privy Council commanding the Lord Mayor of London to cause the Queens 'letters...be printed and set up in diverse open places' is in Corp. London RO, Repertories 15, fo. 279v. [12] Above, p. 135.

d. Exemplifications by patentees of grants: 587/673 (unlawful games); 698/801 (playing cards); 794/897 (starch); 806/911 (customs on fine cloth).

e. Other: 452/498a (pardon on occasion of coronation); 460/— (Injunctions for religion); 461/— (ordering homilies to be used in churches); 680/785–6 (regarding the execution of two priests);[13] —/— (prayer for military forces [Dyson only; probably in 1596]); 792/— (deporting merchants of the Hanse);[14] —/— (prayer for military forces [Dyson only, 1599]); 804.5/— (regarding deportation of negroes).[15]

Not proclaimed

Elizabeth (6)

491/559 (coinage);[16] 654/754 (piracy);[17] 665/769 (reforming the calendar); 776.5/— (prohibiting the export of coal);[18] 805/932 (authorizing copper coins).

Irish proclamations in Dyson

Elizabeth (3)

—/Irish 86; —/Irish 99; —/Irish 126.

Renumbering

Elizabeth (3)

493/562 and 496/569 are really parts of 494/565; 721/824 is really part of 720/823.

OTHER NON-ROYAL PROCLAMATIONS

Legal

Proclamations were often a part of legal and statutory processes, and it is these which form the bulk of the entries under 'proclamations' in standard legal references.[19]

---

[13] Referred to as a 'declaration' to be 'publicly read and published', enclosed with the Council's letter and not under a writ in *APC*, xiv, fos. 57–8.

[14] The copy in PRO, SP 12/266/14 includes an endorsement which notes that the restraint passed by immediate warrant under the hands of four of the Council.

[15] A draft letter which began 'After our hearty commendations'.

[16] Above, p. 107 n. 29.

[17] It hardly seems likely that Elizabeth would have approved this proposal which promised that she would make restitution for the possible future piracies of men whom she had licensed to go to the seas in a peaceful manner.

[18] An opinion that it did not appear is in John U. Nef, *The Rise of the Coal Industry* (2 vols.; London, 1932), ii, 218.

[19] See for example the references as cited above, p. 3 n. 1.

Heralds and marshals

In addition to their role in publishing royal proclamations,[20] heralds proclaimed the styles of the monarchs and of nobles, and degraded the presumptuous from pretended dignities.[21] The marshals proclaimed the Queen's arrival when she was on progress.[22]

Proclamations related to parliamentary matters

The statutes of Parliament were not distributed to be proclaimed after the early years of Elizabeth's reign.[23] There were proclamations to call and adjourn Parliament, and to announce the commissions for collecting the subsidies which had been voted.[24]

Local

The most wideranging proclamation was one made when a mayor assumed his office: it usually covered the whole range of important orders to be observed in the town, and in the case of Chester this amounted to twenty-four items.[25] We have already seen how many of the local proclamations in London were supplementary to royal proclamations.[26] The number and variety of the local proclamations was great, including regulations for the conduct of the local market and especially for preventing the access of 'foreigners' until the locals had been served,[27] orders against nuisances,[28] measures designed to prevent the spread of plague,[29] announcements of fairs, plays, and mirths,[30] and orders for freemen to reside within the borough or forfeit their privileges.[31]

[20] Above, pp. 25-6.
[21] E.g., a notation of 'The order for proclaiming styles and largess' in *HMC 5: 6th Rpt (Marquis of Ripon MSS)*, p. 142; the heralds' proclamation at Windsor to degrade the Earls of Northumberland and Westmorland from the Garter after their rebellion is noted in PRO, SP 12/59/40.
[22] *HMC 18: 11th Rpt, App. III (Corp. of Southampton MSS)*, p. 18; *HMC 27: 12th Rpt, App. IX (Corp. of Gloucester MSS)*, pp. 470-1.
[23] Above, p. 11.
[24] E.g., York CA Dept, Chamb. Accts 5, fo. 70*v*; 6, fo. 59; 7, fos. 56*v*, 58*v*.
[25] *HMC 7: 8th Rpt, Pt I (Corp. of Chester MSS)*, p. 375.
[26] Above, p. 37.
[27] Norf. & Norw. RO, Mayor's Ct Bk 7, fo. 573; E. Sussex RO, Rye MS 1/4, fo. 331*v*; Kent AO, Sandwich MS Sa/AC 5, fo. 189; York CA Dept, YC/A 21, fos. 74-74*v*.
[28] Kent AO, Sandwich MS Sa/AC 4, fo. 67.
[29] Norf. & Norw. RO, Mayor's Ct Bk 10, fo. 520; Exeter CRO, AB 3, fo. 183.
[30] *HMC 37: 14th Rpt, App. VIII (Corp. of Lincoln MSS)*, p. 67; Cooper, *Annals of Cambridge*, II, 425; Chester CRO, AF/1/12.
[31] Exeter CRO, AB 2, fos. 330-1; 3, fo. 183.

INDEX